D0898174

THE LION OF FREEDOM:

FEARGUS O'CONNOR AND
THE CHARTIST MOVEMENT, 1832-1842

JAMES EPSTEIN

CROOM HELM
London & Sydney

© 1982 James Epstein
Croom Helm Ltd, Provident House, Burrell Row,
Beckenham, Kent BR3 1AT
Croom Helm Australia Pty Ltd, First Floor,
139 King Street, Sydney, NSW 2001, Australia
Reprinted 1984

British Library Cataloguing in Publication Data

Epstein, James
    The lion of freedom: Feargus O'Connor and the
    Chartist movement, 1832-1842.
    1. O'Connor, Feargus
    2. Trade-unions — Great Britain
    3. Chartism
    I. Title
    322.4'4'0924   HD8393.0/

    ISBN 0-85664-922-8

Printed and bound in Great Britain by
Biddles Ltd, Guildford and King's Lynn

CROOM HELM SOCIAL HISTORY SERIES

General Editors Professor J.F.C. Harrison and Stephen Yeo,
University of Sussex

CLASS AND RELIGION IN
THE LATE VICTORIAN CITY
Hugh McLeod

THE INDUSTRIAL MUSE
Martha Vicinus

CHRISTIAN SOCIALISM AND
CO-OPERATION IN VICTORIAN
ENGLAND
Philip N. Backstrom

CONQUEST OF MIND
David de Giustino

THE ORIGINS OF BRITISH
INDUSTRIAL RELATIONS
Keith Burgess

THE VOLUNTEER FORCE
Hugh Cunningham

RELIGION AND VOLUNTARY
ORGANISATIONS IN CRISIS
Stephen Yeo

CHOLERA 1832
R. J. Morris

WORKING-CLASS RADICALISM
IN MID-VICTORIAN ENGLAND
Trygve Tholfsen

THE COLLIERS' RANT
Robert Colls

PATERNALISM IN EARLY
VICTORIAN ENGLAND
David Roberts

THE FELLOWSHIP OF SONG
Ginette Dunn

WOMEN WORKERS IN
THE FIRST WORLD WAR
Gail Braybon

YOUTH, EMPIRE AND SOCIETY
John Springhall

THE ORIGINS OF BRITISH
BOLSHEVISM
Raymond Challinor

THE MERTHYR RISING
Gwyn A. Williams

KEIR HARDIE: THE MAKING
OF A SOCIALIST
Fred Reid

SEPARATE SPHERES: THE
OPPOSITION TO WOMEN'S
SUFFRAGE IN BRITAIN
Brian Harrison

THE RISE OF THE
VICTORIAN ACTOR
Michael Baker

AN ARTISAN ELITE IN
VICTORIAN SOCIETY
Geoffrey Crossick

THE PEOPLE'S HEALTH
1830-1910
F. B. Smith

INDUSTRIAL CONFLICT
IN MODERN BRITAIN
James E. Cronin

RICHARD BAXTER AND
THE MILLENNIUM
William M. Lamont

PROSTITUTION AND VICTORIAN
SOCIAL REFORM
Paul McHugh

THE LION OF FREEDOM

The lion of freedom comes from his den,
We'll rally around him again and again,
We'll crown him with laurels our champion to be,
O'Connor, the patriot of sweet liberty.

The pride of the nation, he's noble and brave
He's the terror of tyrants, the friend of the slave,
The bright star of freedom, the noblest of men,
We'll rally around him again and again.

Though proud daring tyrants his body confined,
They never could alter his generous mind;
We'll hail our caged lion, now free from his den,
And we'll rally around him again and again.

Who strove for the patriots? was up night and day?
And saved them from falling to tyrants a prey?
It was Feargus O'Connor was diligent then!
We'll rally around him again and again.

Anonymous: Welsh female Chartist
Popularised by the Chartists of Leicester

CONTENTS

LIST OF TABLES

LIST OF ABBREVIATIONS

In text and notes:

ACLL	Anti-Corn Law League
BPU	Birmingham Political Union
CNA	Central National Association
CSU	Complete Suffrage Union
GNCTU	Grand National Consolidated Trades' Union
GNU	Great Northern Union
LDA	London Democratic Association
LWMA	London Working Men's Association
NCA	National Charter Association
NUWC	National Union of the Working Classes
RA	Radical Association
USC	Universal Suffrage Club

In notes only:

Add. MSS	Additional Manuscripts, British Library
HO	Home Office, Public Records Office
MH	Ministry of Health Papers, Public Records Office
NS	*Northern Star*
PMG	*Poor Man's Guardian*
PRO	Public Records Office
TS	Treasury Solicitor's Papers, Public Records Office

ACKNOWLEDGEMENTS

This book is a revised version of my Birmingham University PhD thesis (1977). I am grateful to the Department of Medieval and Modern History at Birmingham and the Social Science Research Council for having supported this research for three years, and to the American Council of Learned Societies for a grant towards revising this thesis for publication. Chapter Two, 'The *Northern Star*', has appeared in slightly longer form in the *International Review of Social History*, 21 (1976), and I thank the publishers for their permission to reproduce it here.

My greatest debt is to Dorothy Thompson. Not only did she supervise my thesis research with much patience but with a critical eye and generous spirit. Her friendship and counsel have proved invaluable. Over the years she has passed on numerous references from her own research.

I hope that my debt to the work of Edward Thompson and Iorwerth Prothero will become apparent to the reader. They both offered encouragement for which I am most grateful. David Jones was ever willing to share his 'Celtic enthusiasm' for the Chartist movement. I also benefitted from the sympathetic, though not uncritical, reading of my thesis which John Saville and Richard Johnson provided as thesis examiners. Eileen Yeo read the entire thesis with great care and made valuable suggestions for its improvement. More than this, as an undergraduate at Sussex University, she inspired my interest in social history. For many years John Belchem has shared with me his ideas on nineteenth-century popular politics. I have learned much from our discussions and from John's work on Henry Hunt and O'Connor. More generally, I am thankful to the many researchers I met over the years at Colindale, the Public Records Office and any number of public houses; they made me feel that we had embarked upon a collective effort to recover the history of working people. I have tried to acknowledge more specific debts in my footnotes.

My final debt is to Ann Wharton Epstein. She knows the extent of her help and I hope the extent of my gratitude.

FOR ANN

INTRODUCTION

Feargus O'Connor was Chartism's most prominent national leader. Above all other leaders, it was O'Connor who fired the imagination and inspired the loyalty of a generation of working people. The absence of any authoritative study of his leadership represents one of the most outstanding gaps in our knowledge of the British labour movement in the nineteenth century. O'Connor's reputation went into decline with the decline of Chartism as a mass movement of working-class social protest. In the wake of Chartism's final defeat, in the 1850s and 1860s, the British labour movement assumed an essentially reformist character, concerned with securing limited social, economic and political gains for limited sections of the working class. As the consciousness, tone and direction of working-class radicalism changed, so did the style and character of radical leadership. It is hardly surprising that the 'respectable' trade union and radical leaders of the post-Chartist period rejected a discredited style of mass political leadership associated with O'Connor and the failure of Chartist protest, preferring to identify themselves with the movement's more moderate or 'rational' advocates whose style of leadership more closely anticipated their own.[1] An extremely anti-O'Connorite bias was reflected in the first history of the movement, published in 1854 by R. G. Gammage — himself an active participant in the movement, involved in the embittered leadership disputes which plagued Chartism in decline.[2]

The historians who turned to the writing of Chartist history in the early twentieth century, Mark Hovell and Julius West, reinforced this anti-O'Connorite tendency.[3] Informed by a Fabian political perspective, they accepted uncritically the judgements of Francis Place and William Lovett. In these studies O'Connor emerged in the role of the destroyer of a movement born of the idealism of a small group of enlightened London artisans amenable to the politics of class cooperation. The image of O'Connor as a vainglorious, self-seeking rabble-rouser became part of the orthodoxy of British labour history. Nor did O'Connor fare much better at the hands of the early Marxist historians of Chartism.[4] To such historians O'Connor, despite the working-class basis of his leadership, appeared as a 'backward-looking' leader, devoid of the socialist perspective necessary to lead a

1

successful working-class revolutionary movement. O'Connor had fallen uncomfortably between two traditions of working-class history, that of labour reformism and orthodox Marxism — both of which failed, to varying degrees, to deal with Chartism upon its own terms.[5]

More recently, with the publication of *Chartist Studies* (1959), there has been a serious attempt to get back to the local roots of Chartist protest. In his introductory essay to *Chartist Studies*, Asa Briggs noted that a proliferation of local Chartist histories was an essential prerequisite to any new narrative history of Chartism. Since then there has been such a proliferation, although there remains no satisfactory narrative history of the movement.[6] At its best, such local work has provided valuable insight into the character of rank-and-file Chartist activity; however, all too often, such studies have suffered from the lack of a national framework to which to relate local protest. Without losing sight of the locality as the centre of activity for most Chartists, an understanding of Chartism must take into account the attempt to transcend local diversity, to create a sense of national class consciousness and to establish a national political party of the working class. The realisation on the part of local militants that Chartist success was dependent upon an unified national movement was as crucial to the development and course of Chartism as were the local differences which so often split its ranks.

A study of O'Connor's leadership involves a reassertion of the importance of Chartism's national dimension. This does not imply a consideration of the problems of national leadership in isolation from the local Chartist experience. Throughout this study there is an attempt to relate O'Connor's leadership to local Chartist support. One of O'Connor's greatest strengths was the attention which he paid to local Chartism and his constant efforts to bring a national perspective to local working-class agitation. Furthermore, the task of revising the traditional view of O'Connor is integrally linked to the task of asserting the independence, intelligence and agency of Chartism's rank and file. The consistent failure of historians to deal with O'Connor as a serious political leader, the assertion that he lacked principles and was willing to place his individual designs above the interests of the movement are not merely unfair to O'Connor but involve an implicit judgement upon the hundreds of thousands of working people who supported him. Chartism's rank and file did not blindly follow O'Connor; their support was founded upon astute political judgement stemming from their own political experience. Nor should the emphasis here on O'Connor's leadership and his extraordinary ability to rally mass working-class support around the figure of the radical gentleman of the platform obscure one of the most distinctive features of Chartism: the movement's capacity in localities throughout the country to generate a leadership from within the ranks of the working class.

Chartism was a class movement. It was O'Connor's insistence upon the need to construct and maintain an independent working-class movement which won him the support of working-class radicals. During the Chartist period working people were exposed to an ongoing process of proletarianisation. But while the control of capital over labour was increasing over the whole spectrum of artisan trades, the uneven development of industrial capitalism meant that various sections of the working class were at different stages in the protracted transition from small producer to full proletarian: some workers still retained substantial vestiges of an artisan status; others, like the Lancashire handloom weavers or Nottinghamshire stockingers, had lost all but the memories of an artisan past; a small minority were already part of a factory proletariat. But they shared a common experience of profound significance, and from that shared experience Chartism drew its strength. Chartism marked the culmination of a tradition of artisan radicalism and culture which E. P. Thompson has so brilliantly reconstructed in his seminal study, *The Making of the English Working Class*. In a sense, it is in the period of mass Chartist agitation, 1838-1850, that Thompson's thesis — that between 1780 and 1832 'most English working people came to feel an identity of interests between themselves, and against their rulers and employers' — finds its ultimate proof, and an answer to critics who maintain that he has merely traced a minority tradition of artisan radicalism. Throughout the period under consideration in this study, it is an essentially artisan perspective which continues to inform the working-class struggle for political democracy. The Chartist movement marked no major break in terms of working-class political ideology; it was rather its unprecedented levels of sustained commitment and national organisation which distinguished the Chartist achievement, an achievement 'unparalleled anywhere else in Europe'.[7] It must also be noted, however, that on the other side of the class divide, England's ruling class had broadened its socio-political base, and regained a cohesion and self-confidence which became increasingly apparent from 1832 onwards.

This study is not intended merely as a political biography of O'Connor, but rather forms part of an attempt to move towards a general history of Chartism and to provide an interpretive framework for understanding this complex political movement. The book concentrates upon the principal institutions of national Chartist leadership and organisation: the platform and the mass demonstration, the Chartist press, the National Convention, the National Charter Association. The emphasis is very much on O'Connor's role as an organiser and agitator rather than as a political thinker or theoretician, because it was in the former role that he made his greatest contribution to the Chartist movement. O'Connor's significance derived not from the originality of his political ideas, but rather from the extent to which he came to embody the ideas of an established radical tradition and from his ceaseless efforts to give these ideas organisational and agitational form within real situations of political struggle. The book is limited in chronological scope; it covers neither the whole of O'Connor's political career nor the whole of the movement's history. This concentration does not stem from a view of the lack of importance of the movement's later history, which in many respects is more problematic than the earlier history. On the contrary, the 'general strike' of 1842, the changing currents within the working-class movement in the mid-1840s, Britain's 1848, the final assimilation of sections of the movement into the ranks of mid-Victorian popular liberalism are all subjects which demand the sort of detailed attention which is here offered for the early years. Indeed, until this work is done, we will continue to have a partial and inadequate view of Chartism.

The book covers the period from 1832 to 1842 — from O'Connor's election to the British Parliament for County Cork and his first contact with England's working-class radicals through his ascendancy over the national leadership of Chartism. The book is organised into seven chapters. The first deals with O'Connor's career as a radical Member of Parliament and his efforts as an independent agitator, in conjunction with the radicals of London and the North of England, to lay the foundations for a sustained, national movement for universal suffrage. The years from the passing of the Reform Bill to the emergence of the Chartist movement in 1838 form a crucial period for understanding the development of working-class radicalism. As E. P. Thompson has noted: 'There is a sense in which the Chartist movement commenced, not in 1838 . . . but at the moment when the Reform Bill received Royal Assent.'[8] The second chapter deals with the history of the *Northern Star*, Chartism's most important journal, established and owned by O'Connor and inextricably linked to his status as a radical leader. The establishment of the *Star* as a national journal of the working class was essential to the emergence of Chartism and to sustaining the movement's national character. The third chapter is concerned with O'Connor's central role in the coming together of Chartism in 1838, principally through the agency of the mass platform. But while O'Connor came to prominence through his command of the platform, in the familiar role of the radical gentleman orator, one of the main contentions of this study is that among O'Connor's most important contributions as a national leader was his ability to turn his appeal as a charismatic demagogue towards the creation of more permanent forms of working-class organisation and leadership. The chapter also considers the nature of the Chartist mass demonstration, the rhetoric of violence and recommendations to arm and the notions which underpinned Chartism's early revolutionary tone. The fourth chapter offers a detailed account of the Chartist National Convention of 1839 and a discussion of the problems of devising a Chartist strategy during the most important year of the movement's history. With the dissolution of the Convention and the failure of constitutional protest, groups of determined Chartists moved towards insurrection. The abortive risings of 1839/40 form the subject of chapter five. The final two chapters consider the redirection of the movement in the early 1840s. One of the most remarkable achievements of Chartism was the reorganisation of the movement and the construction of a national organisation in the wake of defeat and government repression. While there remained tension between O'Connor's style of charismatic leadership and the emergence of newer, more bureaucratic forms of leadership and organisation within this period, there was also a sense in which O'Connor's support lent an all-important legitimacy to the National Charter Association. There is an extensive discussion of the problems of national Chartist leadership: the maintenance of national Chartist unity and direction, the conflict over democratic leadership, the formulation of a social programme for Chartism. The final chapter examines a recurrent dilemma which faced Chartism's local and national leadership, that of formulating a coherent response to the cooperative overtures of middle-class reformers. It is also within this context that there is offered a reassessment of Chartist strategy at the 1841 general election. The chapter concludes with a brief consideration of the crisis of 1842, a crisis which had crucial repercussions for the subsequent history of the movement.

Throughout the writing of this study the author has been conscious of the difficulties of approaching history through the perspective of one prominent leader, of seeing problems and criticisms from a single vantage point. This difficulty has been compounded by the task of confronting long-established views at many points and offering alternative interpretations. However, as will hopefully become clear, the point has not been to propose another, 'O'Connorite', orthodoxy, much less to write a hagiographic tribute, but rather to reopen discussion and to restore to historical respectability the career of one of Britain's most remarkable radical leaders.

NOTES

1. See R. Harrison, *Before the Socialists: Studies in Labour and Politics, 1861-1881*, London 1965, ch. 1; F. M. Leventhal, *Respectable Radical: George Howell and Victorian Working Class Politics*, London 1971.

2. See J. Saville's introduction to R. G. Gammage, *History of the Chartist Movement*, Cass ed., London 1969.

3. M. Hovell, *The Chartist Movement*, Manchester 1925; J. West, *History of the Chartist Movement*, London 1920. Hovell's view of O'Connor's leadership has been incorporated in the most recent narrative history of the movement, J. T. Ward, *Chartism*, London 1973.

4. See T. Rothstein, *From Chartism to Labourism*, London 1929; R. Groves, *But We Shall Rise Again: A Narrative History of Chartism*, London 1938. Groves's work, in particular, offered an important counter-balance to the Hovell approach and remains a study of considerable merit, particularly with regard to the career of G. J. Harney. More striking than the deficiencies of the early Marxist studies has been the general failure of British Marxist historians to provide a history of the movement.

5. G. D. H. Cole in his *Chartist Portraits*, London 1941, offered a less dogmatic approach than earlier historians of the movement, stressing the variety of interests and influences which came together to form Chartism. However, Lovett was still presented as the prototype of the skilled artisan. See D. Thompson, 'Radicals and Their Historians,' *Literature and History*, no. 5, 1977, pp. 104-07.

6. A. Briggs (ed.), *Chartist Studies*, London 1959, p. 2. The best general account of the movement is D. J. V. Jones, *Chartism and the Chartists*, London 1975.

7. I. Prothero, *Artisans and Politics in Early Nineteenth-Century London: John Gast and His Times*, Folkestone 1979, p. 1.

8. E. P. Thompson, *The Making of the English Working Class*, Penguin ed., Harmondsworth 1968, p. 909.

1 THE ROOTS OF LEADERSHIP: 1832-1837

*Nothing in history happens spontaneously, nothing worthwhile
is achieved without the expense of intellect and spirit.*[1]
— *E. P. Thompson*

*The idea that a spontaneous movement of the masses will 'spon-
taneously throw up' a leadership and a policy is moonshine.
Leaders who come to the front in hours of crisis have invariably
years of preparation behind them however obscure it may be.*[2]
— *J. T. Murphy*

Historians of Chartism have generally ignored the origins of Feargus
O'Connor's radical leadership. Yet both O'Connor and working-class
radicals throughout England and Scotland constantly referred to
O'Connor's career as a radical member of Parliament and, more
especially, to his efforts to coordinate nationally the forces of working-
class radicalism between 1835 and 1837. If we are to see leadership in
terms of a relationship, an interaction between leaders and rank-and-
file support, then an account of O'Connor's early radical career is
crucial to an understanding of his Chartist leadership. When we look
for the roots of Chartism we will find many of the roots of this
leadership — in the disillusion with the 1832 Reform settlement; in
the agitation for an unstamped press and the efforts to propagate a
radical critique of early industrial capitalist society; in the opposition
to the new Poor Law and the increasing centralisation of government
authority; in the assertion of the right to collective organisation of
labour; in the opposition to the coercion of Ireland and the suppression of Canadian independence; in the alienation from the reformism
of middle-class radicals and their leaders. O'Connor did not emerge
spontaneously as a radical leader; he did not merely move in a matter
of months from the anti-Poor Law platform to the position of Chartism's most prominent leader. Nor was the flourishing of a mass
movement in 1838 for the establishment of working-class political
power a spontaneous development; throughout the country local
radicals had been struggling for years to lay the foundations for such a
movement. During these crucial pre-Chartist struggles O'Connor

7

emerged as a steady, trusted and colourful leader. Through hard work, organisational foresight and his constant efforts to bring together a national working-class movement for universal suffrage, he gained the well-earned respect of working-class radicals. More than any other leader it was O'Connor who gave expression to the growing coherence of the radical movement during this pre-Chartist period.

I Radical Member of Parliament: 1832-1835

In 1833 Feargus O'Connor, age thirty-seven, came to London as one of the representatives of County Cork at the Reform Parliament, and as a member of Daniel O'Connell's Repeal Party. One of the foremost leaders of the English working class in the nineteenth century embarked upon his political career as a spokesman for the redress of Irish grievances. O'Connor's radicalism was, however, never merely an Irish product.

O'Connor came from a family closely identified with the revolutionary struggles of the 1790s. Although members of a wealthy family of Irish Protestant landowners with considerable influence in County Cork, both his father, Roger, and uncle, Arthur, broke with the Tory ascendancy traditions of family and social class to embrace the cause of Irish national independence. Deeply influenced by the French revolution, and especially by the ideas of Voltaire and Volney, they became republicans and free-thinkers. Both men were among the most prominent leaders of the United Irishmen in the 1790s, suffering imprisonment, and in Arthur's case banishment, for their revolutionary convictions.[3] His family background and early upbringing provided O'Connor with a sound radical education. At his father's home at Dangan, County Meath, the radical press was carefully studied. Cobbett's *Political Register,* Leigh Hunt's *Examiner* and *Hansard* were part of the family's required reading.[4] Like many Irish nationalist leaders, Roger O'Connor was in close contact with prominent English radicals. Sir Francis Burdett, radical MP for Westminster, was a close family friend, as was Thomas Hardy, founder of the London Corresponding Society; and on several occasions Roger O'Connor became directly involved in the turbulent politics of radical Westminster.[5]

Feargus O'Connor's own active political career started when he moved to Fort Robert, County Cork. Although he mixed congenially within local gentry society, O'Connor gained an unusual popularity

among the local peasantry. Unlike many gentleman farmers of the
district, he did not flee the Whiteboy violence which swept southern
Ireland in early 1822; in contrast, he sympathised with the popular
resistance to the payment of tithes and rent, and may have been
active in the armed confrontations which took place between guerrilla bands and the British army.[6] In 1822, O'Connor also published
his first political tract, *A State of Ireland*, which took its title from a
well-known pamphlet of Arthur O'Connor's. The pamphlet was an
open attack on the landlords, clergy, grand jurors and magistrates of
Ireland.[7] It was dedicated, significantly, 'to the people of England'.
Along with English radicals such as Cobbett, O'Connor stressed the
importance of the suppression of Irish rights and liberties for the
English people. Under threat of arrest, O'Connor spent over a year in
London, where he almost certainly moved in radical circles. Thomas
Hardy wrote his father that Feargus, 'a young man of very fine
talents', called on him regularly, and that he was lodging at the same
house as Wolfe Tone's son.[8]

When he emerged as a popular Irish leader in 1832, O'Connor
constantly referred to his identification with the cause of popular
resistance in 1822, 'when a bare association with you was considered
as little short of treason'.[9] On his return to Ireland, however, he
appears to have taken no part in the agitation for Catholic emancipation, 1824-29. He later maintained that this was because he regarded
O'Connell's campaign as tailored merely to the designs of the Catholic middle class.[10] During these years O'Connor dedicated himself to
farming and continuing the legal studies which he had begun before
moving to County Cork at the King's Inn, Dublin. In late 1826, he
enrolled at Gray's Inn, London, and was probably called to the Irish
bar in 1830.[11] Thus O'Connor followed the career of so many of
Ireland's popular leaders.

It was in late 1831 and 1832 that O'Connor came forward as a
radical champion of Irish rights, as the reform movement and the
anti-tithe agitation gathered pace. At county meetings called to support the Reform Bill he introduced himself as an advocate of universal
suffrage, annual parliaments, vote by ballot and Irish national independence; at mass anti-tithe demonstrations he urged the total abolition of tithes, the repeal of the Union between Ireland and England
and the organisation of united mass protest of a constitutional character. As a Protestant, he attended vestry meetings in his own parish
and fought stubbornly to have the cess lowered, denouncing the
petty jobbery and corruption of the Established Church; as a lawyer,

he attended the assizes sessions in order to defend tithe resisters.[12] O'Connor was an ubiquitous and untiring agitator. William J. O'Neill Daunt, friend, neighbour and fellow campaigner in 1832, observed:

> Feargus's strongest point was his great physical energy. He was indefatigable in his agitation. In all quarters of the compass, wherever a popular muster of sufficient magnitude was announced, there was usually to be seen the popular agitator with the brawny muscular figure, the big round shoulders, the red curly tresses overhanging the collar of his coat, the cajoling smirk, the insinuating manners, and the fluent tongue.[13]

By summer 1832, the tithe war had reached threatening dimensions throughout southern Ireland. In July, anti-tithe meetings were declared illegal in County Cork, as calculated 'to excite terror and alarm'. In defiance of this ban O'Connor continued to address anti-tithe meetings and was arrested in September, along with several other speakers, although charges were eventually dropped.[14] The anti-tithe movement was characterised by a sense of communal resistance to the impositions of external authority. In this respect, it had much in common with the spirit of the anti-Poor Law movement in which O'Connor was to take an important part as a leader of English workers.

During these campaigns O'Connor's greatest asset as a popular leader came to light: his command of the platform. His sonorous voice, imposing stature, fiery red hair and gentlemanly appearance combined with an intuitive grasp of the emotional roots of collective social protest to form the basis of his appeal as an orator. O'Connor was a romantic in an age steeped in popular romanticism: 'His mind was crammed with legendary poetry, and on the whole there was in those times . . . a mystical spirit in the man that found an utterance in pouring out his feelings to an impassioned peasantry . . .'[15] He radiated self-confidence as he demanded social and political justice for Ireland. His very presence on the platform created the impression of overwhelming strength. His brand of charismatic demagoguery had to be seen and heard to be appreciated. Contemporary journalists often observed that no written report could capture the essence of his performance.

> He was remarkably ready and self-possessed. He was capable of producing extraordinary popular effect. He had a very great declamatory talent. . . . As a stimulating orator in popular assembly he was unexcelled. It is true he dealt largely in bombast, broken metaphor, and inflated language; but while you listened, those blemishes were lost in the infectious vehemence of his spirited manner; you were charmed

with the melodious voice, the musical cadences, the astonishing volu-
bility, the imposing self-confidence of the man, and the gallant air of
bold defiance with which he assailed all oppression and tyranny. The
difference between his spoken and printed harangues was surprisingly
great.[16]

Not only his command of the platform, but O'Connor's commitment
to the mass platform as the primary agency for generating fundamental socio-political reform dates from 1832.

When he realised the extent to which the reform measures were to
increase the electorate of his own constituency, O'Connor announced
his intention to 'open up' County Cork, a seat unopposed since 1812,
and oppose the influence of some of the most powerful landlords in
Ireland. He stood not merely as an uncompromising repeal candidate
and ardent opponent of the tithe, but as a radical supporting universal
suffrage, annual parliaments and vote by ballot.[17] Having gained
O'Connell's support, O'Connor undertook the arduous task of organising the voters of County Cork. A spirit of popular democracy
prevailed throughout southern Ireland at this election, with the
popular candidates usually pledged to repeal of the Union.[18] O'Connor's return for County Cork was a remarkable victory; not only did
he secure a huge majority, without bribery, but he also carried his
running partner, Garrett Standish Barry who was only a conditional
repealer.[19] Contemporaries were deeply impressed by O'Connor's
achievement. John O'Connell, the 'Liberator's' son, later wrote:

> Perhaps the queerest election that occurred in the three Kingdoms was
> that of Feargus O'Connor as a member for the important County Cork.
> Without money and without previous influence, personal or political, an
> unknown and not overwealthy squire of an obscure part of the county,
> set out to attack and overturn the influence and sway of the most
> powerful and richest landed aristocracy in Ireland; and, thanks to his
> indomitable energy and audacity, and to the ready and ardent patriot-
> ism of the people, which only required to be called into action, he
> succeeded.[20]

Thus O'Connor arrived in London not merely as a joint in O'Connell's 'tail'. He came as the representative of the largest county in
Ireland and one of the country's most popular seats. Already acclaimed
a champion of the people and a master of the platform, he came
determined to represent the interests of the 'real' Irish people — the
impoverished peasantry and the urban artisans. His family's connection with the Jacobin tradition and contact with French and English
radicalism imbued him with a political consciousness which already

went beyond the populist Catholic nationalism of O'Connell.

While it is important to emphasise O'Connor's radical background on entering English politics, it is equally important to remember the crucial prominence of Irish affairs in English radical circles. As E. P. Thompson has shown, the alliance between Irish nationalism and English radicalism dated from the 1790s.[21] Thus Thomas Cooper, the Leicester Chartist leader, noted the significance of O'Connor's family history to English radicals: 'the connection of his family with the "United Irishmen" and patriotic sufferers of the last century, rendered him a natural representative of the cause of political liberty'.[22] Motions in favour of repeal of the Act of Union were commonplace at English working-class meetings, and the radical unstamped press gave extensive coverage to Irish affairs throughout the early 1830s.[23] England already possessed a large Irish population. Irishmen were leading members of radical groups throughout the industrial North and in London. The London Irish were one of the major groups who composed London radicalism at the time of O'Connor's arrival in the Metropolis. In late 1832, in the wake of the reform agitation, it was the alliance with the Irishmen of the Anti-Union Association which revitalised the National Union of the Working Classes and ensured that the Union remained a vibrant force in 1833. This also meant that Irish affairs, particularly repeal and opposition to coercion, became even more central to the activities of the NUWC which had always been sympathetic to the Irish cause and which included Irishmen like John Cleave, James Osbourne and J.R. Mansell in leadership roles.[24] Thus rather than excluding him in any way from English radical politics, O'Connor's position as an Irish MP pledged to repeal and universal suffrage assured him of a favourable reception.

Within a month of his arrival in London, O'Connor was on the radical platform. Almost the first act of the Whig Government was to propose a bill for the coercion of Ireland, and O'Connor immediately gained the attention of the London radicals for his fierce parliamentary opposition to this measure. He was the main speaker at a meeting called by the NUWC to petition the government concerning their intention to coerce Ireland. At this meeting O'Connor dwelt on what was to become a recurrent theme, his insistence that an essential affinity of interests existed between the Irish people and the English radicals and the need for cooperation between these two groups.

They said we will coerce these Irish agitators, and then we will coerce the radicals of England (hear). He would say in the face of the world he was a radical (cheers), and it was now the interest of the Irish agitators and the radicals of England to unite for their common safety (hear). If this bill (the Irish Disturbance Bill) is allowed to become the law of Ireland it must be the law of England . . .[25]

The English radicals had not long to wait for the fulfilment of O'Connor's prediction concerning the possible coercion of English radical agitation. In May, the metropolitan police attacked a radical demonstration at Cold Bath Fields convened by the NUWC to discuss Richard Lee's proposal for a National Convention of the English and Irish.[26] For English radicals the suppression of Irish protest provided a display of the coercive powers at the state's disposal and an indication of the Whigs' readiness to employ such powers. Throughout the country indignant groups of radicals organised meetings to protest against the government measures; the *'Destructive' and Poor Man's Conservative*, one of Hetherington's unstamped papers, published the 'List of the Scoundrels who voted for the First Reading of the Bill for Polandizing Ireland'.[27]

From the first session of the Reform Parliament it became obvious that the government of Earl Grey had little to offer either the English or Irish labouring classes, as Irish coercion was followed by proposals for a new Poor Law. Bronterre O'Brien put the matter succinctly when he later commented:

What was the first act of that Reformed Parliament? The Coercion Bill for Ireland. What was the last act of the first session? The New Poor Law for England. Why did that base Parliament pass both these acts? To place the labouring classes of both countries at the feet of the rich assassins, who rob, brutalize, and enslave the population of both.[28]

The passing of the Reform Bill had severed the working class from the middle class politically and marked the beginning of a crucial phase in the development of British working-class radicalism, characterised by a growing sense of working-class disillusion with the Reform Parliament and the Whigs. Along with this increasing distrust and hatred for the Whigs, there developed a more gradual resentment towards the parliamentary radicals, and especially Daniel O'Connell. These radicals' predilection for 'practical' reform, their compromising attitude towards the Whigs, especially after 1834, and the taint of 'Malthusianism' alienated many working-class radicals. It also reinforced a growing consciousness of the need for an independent national working-class movement. O'Connor's own political experience during his years in Parliament paralleled the development of this more general discontent within English working-class radical-ism. It was this coincidence of individual experience with wider class forces which enabled O'Connor to project a collective sense of protest so successfully when he turned from Parliament to extra-parliamentary agitation in 1835.

It was on the issue of the repeal of the Union and his opposition to O'Connell that O'Connor really came to the fore. While leading a party pledged to repeal, O'Connell opposed raising the issue in Parliament, on the grounds that a repeal motion would be over-whelmingly defeated and that the debate would be unfavourably reported in the English press. He argued that more time was needed to organise popular opinion in both England and Ireland.[29] O'Connor came forward as the leading opponent within the Repeal Party of this position. At a private meeting of the party he forced a vote on the issue and despite O'Connell's narrow majority in favour of postpone-ment, O'Connor announced his resolve to move the repeal of the Union, if O'Connell refused.[30] He addressed the electors of County Cork: 'Our Great General will not lead the little band to fight — I WILL. . . . the battle must be fought. Of course we shall be beaten.' He reminded his supporters of the importance placed upon the repeal pledge at the last election, and 'the sacrifices which you made to add one to the list of the advocates of that measure'.

> We deprecated the Moderates as 'Wait-a-whiles'; we looked upon the moment as having arrived when all Ireland should cry aloud for liberty. If you put any other than the straight-forward meaning upon the pledge; — if you meant to encumber it with time, and place, and incident, and all the little dovetailed minutiae of electioneering trickery . . . if such are your views, I am not a fit and proper person to represent your senti-ments.[31]

Although the O'Connellite Dublin *Pilot* denounced O'Connor's insubordination, a significant section of the Repeal Party and influen-tial sections of the liberal Irish press, including the *Freeman's Jour-nal*, backed his stand. It was only after another meeting of the party voted by a larger majority in favour of postponement and much cajoling by O'Connell, along with the promise to organise popular support during the recess to back a repeal move at the next parlia-mentary session, that O'Connor reluctantly withdrew his motion.[32] The English radicals, concerned with the question of repeal, looked with interest upon these internal dissensions within the Irish party, but tended to remain neutral.[33] The people of County Cork were less reticent. The *Cork Mercantile Chronicle* summed up the feeling in O'Connor's constituency:

> We have had some experience of the manner in which voters were induced last election to forego bribes, and give their suffrages to 'two repealers'. It was not by telling them that the repeal question would not be brought forward this session, or that it was a question which its great advocate was unprepared to argue . . . They have thrown cold water on the ardour of the people — they have shaken confidence — they have greatly increased the difficulties which already beset their case.[34]

The eventual break between O'Connor and O'Connell was the result neither of a mere clash of like temperments nor thwarted ambition. There is little evidence to suggest that O'Connor initially set out to challenge the authority of the leader of the Repeal Party.[35] However, O'Connell's conservative handling of the party and his willingness to compromise most aspects of the party's social and political programme, together with his unshakable faith in the tenets of laissez-faire political economy and hostility towards trade unionism, gradually alienated O'Connor, many Irish supporters and the English working-class radicals. His compromising party management led to the Lichfield House Compact and the formal alliance which kept the Whigs in office until 1841. Despite his occasional talent for abusing the Whigs, O'Connell favoured support for the Whigs as the lesser of two evils and was willing to sacrifice the independence of his parliamentary party to this end.[36] Reverence for bourgeois political economy culminated in O'Connell's vote in favour of the relaxation of factory legislation and his move to establish a parliamentary committee to investigate trade union activities following the case of the Glasgow cotton spinners in late 1837. These tendencies were reflected between 1833 and 1835 in O'Connell's initial refusal to bring forward repeal, his determined opposition to a poor law for Ireland, his willingness to compromise on tithe abolition and in his opinion on the legality of the sentencing of the Dorchester labourers. On all these issues O'Connor found himself in opposition to O'Connell.[37]

The repeal issue underscored many of the differences between the two leaders. O'Connell represented primarily the interests of the Catholic middle class and the larger tenant farmers. While dependent upon the mobilisation of mass popular support in order to exact concessions from the government of the day, revolutionary social and economic change was abhorent to him. O'Connell was a parliamentary tactician, a pragmatic opportunist who regarded the demand for the repeal of the Union, as he did most Irish political and social demands, as negotiable.[38] O'Connor, in contrast, saw repeal, however ambiguously defined, as an irrevocable demand, the necessary first step towards the social and economic regeneration of Ireland.[39] The repeal pledge was not merely a pawn to be sacrificed to Lord John Russell and the Whigs over dinners at Lichfield House. At a public dinner at Cork, in November 1833, O'Connor protested vehemently when O'Connell invited the government to 'enter into a competition with me to see whether they could, by their measures, take many of the repealers from my standard'. In his own speech, O'Connor likened O'Connell and repeal to Frankenstein and his monster, and called on Irishmen to fight 'for Repeal, the whole Repeal, and nothing but Repeal'.[40] Although relations between the two leaders became increasingly strained, an absolute breach did not occur during O'Connor's parliamentary career. As an Irish MP, he continued to refer to the leader of the Repeal Party in respectful tones, while asserting his own political independence by remaining openly critical of O'Connell's conduct over issues such as tithe abolition, proposals for mitigated coercion and an Irish poor law. The eventual open breach between the two leaders, which followed O'Connell's public attack on O'Connor and the English ultra-radicals in 1836, was to have far-reaching practical consequences for the course of both English and Irish popular protest over the next decade.

While a member of the House of Commons O'Connor looked principally to the people of County Cork for approbation of his political conduct. He told the Commons in 1834: 'My pride is, that I do not represent the barren surface of the soil, but that I represent those people who cultivate the soil, and make it available and valuable to its owners.'[41] It was in County Cork that O'Connor's style of popular leadership flourished — on the platform, at election hustings and in the courtroom. He returned home at the end of each session of Parliament to take up the campaigns for Union repeal and the abolition of the tithe. He promised to resign at the end of each session and put his record to the test of popular opinion, maintaining that all candidates should be compelled to do the same. Thus he instituted the radical demand for annual parliaments in his own constituency.[42] By placing himself before a free assembly of both electors and non-electors, O'Connor also gave symbolic expression to his commitment to the right of universal suffrage. O'Connor's determined radicalism and practical expression of democratic faith not only won him enormous popularity in southern Ireland, it also impressed the English radicals.[43]

In the courtroom O'Connor also took up the struggle for popular rights. Trained as a lawyer, and an outspoken critic of the system of Irish justice, he attended the Cork assizes and offered his services to people, usually tithe offenders, from whom he could expect little or no financial remuneration.[44] He gained a reputation as a legal counsellor of the people, a role he was later to assume in English radical politics. This reputation was enhanced both in Ireland and England in late 1834, when he championed the cause of the victims of the 'Rathcormac Massacre'. At Rathcormac, County Cork, troops attempting to collect tithes in arrears fired on a crowd of peasants gathered to protect the haggard of the Widow Ryan. Twelve people were killed and many more seriously wounded in an incident which underscored the increased powers accorded to the military in the attempt to control tithe resistance. O'Connor, who was in Ireland campaigning for reelection to Parliament and agitating for the abolition of the tithe, not only denounced this latest act of tyranny from the platform, but led the prosecution at the inquest, wanting to move a charge of wilful murder against the officers and clergy who initiated the slaughter. He also brought the matter onto the floor of the Commons. The Rathcormac massacre received publicity in the English radical press and radical societies contributed for the relief of the victims and their families.[45]

On the platform, within the Repeal Party and in the courtroom O'Connor championed the most extreme demands for Irish social justice, coupled with the basic principles of British radicalism. In the Commons he boasted a similarly impressive radical record. It was not only O'Connor who was later to note his solid radical labours as MP for County Cork. When the radicals of Barnsley called upon the Scottish radicals to invite O'Connor to stand for Glasgow in 1837, they recommended them to examine his speeches and votes while in Parliament.[46] O'Connor took an active part in debates, particularly on Irish affairs, bringing the defiant tone of the anti-tithe platform onto the floor of the Commons. He constantly chastised the Whigs for having reneged upon their promise of principled reform which had brought them to office, and warned of the consequences of their betrayal. While maintaining that there was little to choose between the Tories and Whigs in their treatment of Ireland, he argued that the Whigs were more despicable: 'They have promised everything — they have performed nothing; — they have violated every pledge they made to the people of Ireland . . .'[47] His hostility towards the Whigs which developed largely out of his Irish political experience was to assume particular importance when O'Connor turned to

English radical agitation.

Most significantly, with regard to his later career in English radical politics, O'Connor, perhaps more than any other Irish MP, fought alongside the English radicals both within and outside Parliament. In the tradition of Paine and Cobbett, he supported all measures aimed at lessening the burden of taxation upon the unrepresented. He voted for the abolition of impressment and spoke against military flogging; he supported Ashley's factory bill, triennial parliaments and an address to the Crown to recognise no disposition of Poland contrary to the Treaty of Vienna. O'Connor continually took the floor to defend the freedom of the press.[48] When present, he joined the small band led by Cobbett who opposed the Poor Law Amendment Act at every stage — although O'Connor later exaggerated his part in this opposition.[49] In short, O'Connor's parliamentary record reflected most of the struggles and disappointments of both the radicals and the Irish party.

Two issues above all confirmed the English radicals favourable impression of O'Connor's radical zeal: his support for the Dorchester labourers and his defence of the editors of the radical *True Sun* newspaper. Probably no single act, besides the introduction of the new Poor Law, generated more working-class hostility towards the Whig Government than the transportation of six trade unionists from the Dorsetshire village of Tolpuddle for administering illegal oaths to members of the Agricultural Labourers Union. In the Commons O'Connor immediately denounced the government, and declared that 'Earl Grey, Lord Brougham, the noble Lord, the Paymaster of the Forces, and the right honourable Secretary for the Colonies, should be on board the hulks in place of those unfortunate men . . .'[50] The case of the Dorchester labourers assumed particular importance among London radicals and trade unionists, as an issue around which all could unite. Along with O'Connell and Hume, O'Connor was prominently associated with the early defence of the victims, speaking at meetings organised by the London radicals for their defence. However, O'Connor's unequivocal condemnation of the Whigs and declaration that the men were both morally and legally innocent contrasted with O'Connell's view that the sentence was legal and his admonition that trade unionists must proceed legally.[51]

The freedom of the press, as well as the right to collective protection of labour, was under attack. In May 1833, the government brought charges against the editors of the *True Sun*, Patrick Grant and John Bell, under the law of libel for advocating the non-payment of house and window tax in order to force its replacement by a property tax. Although a stamped daily paper, the *True Sun* was among the most influential radical papers of the day and closely linked to the struggles of the unstamped.[52] O'Connor, one of the MPs campaigning most forcefully against the law of libel as detrimental to the freedom of the press, came forward as the chief spokesman in defence of the *True Sun*. The close association which he formed with the paper and its editor, John Bell, was to prove important to his early radical agitation in England. Apparently, he also helped to edit the paper during this difficult period.[53] The prosecution of the *True Sun*, which resulted in the imprisonment of Grant and Bell for six months in 1834, was an issue which rallied radical opposition throughout London and the provinces. O'Connor chaired a series of meetings at which John Cleave, Henry Hetherington, Robert Owen, Dr Arthur Wade and O'Connell spoke. In Parliament O'Connor presented the London radicals' petition against the editors' imprisonment, and moved a motion for an Address to his Majesty to pardon Grant and Bell which was easily defeated. O'Connell while supporting the *True Sun* outside Parliament lamented O'Connor's maladroit parliamentary tactics in accusing the Whig Government of hypocrisy and called on him to withdraw his motion.[54]

Support for the principle of a free press and the right of working people to combine to defend their livelihood are transitionary themes in O'Connor's early radical career. When he helped to found the Marylebone Radical Association, in autumn 1835, the sustained agitation for the return of the Dorchester labourers and the movement for the total repeal of the newspaper stamp formed the core of their activity. We can already detect important features of O'Connor's developing radicalism in a speech he delivered at a meeting called to petition for the release of Grant and Bell. First, there was his firm declaration that 'The people were the only legitimate source of power — the only tribunal . . .'

> He did not . . . feel proud at being a member of the House of Commons; he felt disgusted at being so; he felt more pride at being a member of the Trade Union [of Dublin].

Secondly, there was his strong emphasis upon the need for unity. The people were not apathetic, but merely unorganised. Thus 'a connecting link should be established between the Radicals of every degree'. O'Connor never doubted that the people had the power to overcome their oppressors, if they were only united. This conviction led to a series of attempts to organise the London artisans into one political movement and culminated in O'Connor's enormous effort to impart national unity to Chartism. Thirdly, O'Connor's outright hostility towards the Whigs was evident. While never a tory-radical, he held the Whigs in utmost contempt as deceivers of the people.[55] An inspired radical propagandist, O'Connor's actual range of ideas was neither wide nor original, but corresponded with a traditional artisan radicalism which asserted the right to universal suffrage, freedom of thought and education, the labourer's right to the product of his own labour and to a portion of the soil.

At the general election held in early 1835, O'Connor held his County Cork seat with a large majority. He stood again as a radical and a repealer, although he played down his differences with O'Connell and maintained that tithe abolition should now be their immediate aim. As in earlier election contests, O'Connor's assistance was sought by other popular candidates, several of whom — including John O'Connell — owed their return to his exertions.[56] His own election victory, however, was short lived. The local Tories petitioned against his return and a select committee found he lacked the necessary £600 freehold qualification. Thus, in June 1835, O'Connor lost his parliamentary seat.[57] The loss of his parliamentary seat, together with his differences with O'Connell, presumably now precluded an effective career as an Irish radical leader. His departure from Parliament also coincided, significantly, with the formalisation of O'Connell's alliance with the Whigs, a move about which O'Connor initially remained uncritical, at least in public.

Previously a popular Irish MP actively sympathetic to the radical cause in England, O'Connor now embarked upon a career primarily as a leader of English working-class protest. O'Connor was not, however, simply thrown into English radical politics through his exclusion from Parliament and Irish leadership. He had already secured a footing within London radical politics, having gained the notice and respect of many English radicals. In turn, he was impressed by the radicalism of the English working class and their sympathy towards Ireland. Furthermore, it was in the columns of the unstamped press, most notably O'Brien's articles for the *Poor Man's Guardian*, that O'Connell's leadership was being most sharply attacked, along with that of the English parliamentary radicals of whom O'Connor was also becoming increasingly critical.[58] O'Connor's Irish background, while obviously important, does not provide the sole key for understanding his radicalism or his appeal as a popular leader. The facility with which O'Connor moved from Irish popular politics to English radical agitation reflects both the quality of his own radicalism and the English radicals' concern for the Irish cause. For both O'Connor and the English working-class radicals the fate of the Irish peasant and that of the English worker were closely linked. The exploitation of cheap Irish labour held down industrial wages in England and their numbers helped to provide the elasticity in the labour force so important to the development of early industrial Britain. O'Connor's appeal for social justice for Ireland — union repeal, tithe abolition, some form of poor relief, security of tenure, corn rent, etc. — also implied a cessation of Irish immigration and competition in the English and Scottish labour market. O'Connor continued to bring Irish affairs, and especially the question of repeal, to the fore in England because they were meaningful to English working-class radicals.

II The Oldham By-Election:
O'Connor's 'English Political Birthplace'

Speaking in May 1835, at a meeting of the NUWC, O'Connor announced:

> He was delighted, after the dull and plodding labours of Parliament, to find himself again on a public stage, where there was fair play for all. He thought that a man might be just as useful without as within the House.

He went on to advocate the total repeal of the newspaper stamp, the repatriation of the Dorchester labourers, the expulsion of the Bishops from the Lords and an elected second chamber, short parliaments, total freedom of religious conscience and an end to sinecures and corporate monopoly.[59] In late June, however, O'Connor travelled to Oldham to attend the by-election occasioned by the death of England's greatest radical journalist, William Cobbett.

The constituency of Oldham was of particular importance to the working-class radical movement. Through a system of extensive exclusive dealing and community pressure the Oldham radicals had been able to return two thorough-going radicals, Cobbett and the radical factory owner John Fielden, to the Reform Parliament. Throughout the country radicals looked to Cobbett and Fielden to represent the interests of the working class in Parliament. The relationship between Oldham's radical MPs and the local working-class community served as a model for the radicals' conception of real democratic representation. Pledged to an exhaustive list of radical demands, Cobbett and Fielden were held accountable to the Oldham Political Union, under the leadership of veteran radicals like John Knight and William Fitton.[60] Not surprisingly, O'Conor was attracted by the prospect of representing one of the most radical localities in England.

However, the choice of a successor to Cobbett proved problematic. Even before Cobbett's death there had been signs of disunion within the ranks of Oldham's radicals. Serious disagreement had developed between Cobbett and the radical dissenters, an important section of the local radical alliance led by the middle-class radicals James Holladay, Jessie Ainsworth and William Knott, over the issue of the separation of church and state.[61] These dissensions were exacerbated upon Cobbett's death, when Fielden and the local Cobbettites proposed bringing forward Cobbett's son, John Morgan Cobbett, whose equivocal attitude towards church disestablishment prompted the radical dissenters to bring forward an alternative candidate, John Ashton Yates. It is unclear upon what understanding O'Connor travelled to Oldham. Upon his arrival, however, he found much dissatisfaction with Cobbett's views and saw an opportunity to unite the radicals behind his own candidature. O'Connor pledged himself to a comprehensive catalogue of radical principles, including church disestablishment, and offered his record in Parliament and his conduct towards his Cork County constituents as evidence of his radical earnest. He promised to withdraw immediately, however, if Cobbett satisfied the demands of local radicals. The *Manchester and Salford Advertiser*, a paper closely associated with Fielden, commented that O'Connor 'left the most dauntless Radical in Oldham behind in his profession of political faith'. George Condy, the paper's editor, expressed his 'unqualified pleasure' upon hearing O'Connor's radical principles and advised radicals: 'You cannot accept less from any candidate'.[62]

O'Connor set out to take Oldham by storm. Edwin Butterworth, a local journalist, described him as 'a blazing Irish orator', 'a fiery furious radical if not Republican'. The radical dissenters threw their support behind O'Connor, and Yates withdrew; the Cobbettites, however, remained hostile. No doubt many radicals shared the opinion of the cotton spinner James Greaves who felt that O'Connor should have waited for Cobbett before launching his own campaign. Suspicions about Cobbett's lukewarm radicalism and evasiveness with regard to taking pledges were confirmed, however, upon his arrival in Oldham. While local radical opinion remained fairly evenly divided, O'Connor was now drawing support from working-class radicals as well as the dissenters. Greaves, who along with John Knight tried to persuade the two election committees to agree upon one candidate, came over to O'Connor's party, as did the local Huntites. Following the hustings, the tailors, shoemakers, mechanics and several other trades issued declarations in support of O'Connor, threatening exclusive dealing. From Manchester and Middleton the ultra-radicals called upon the Oldham electors to return O'Connor. O'Connor marginally won the show of hands at the hustings and Cobbett called for a poll. Knight made a final, unsuccessful attempt at mediation, proposing that the two election committees jointly canvass the voters and the party with less support resign.[63]

O'Connor went to the poll, although he withdrew at mid-morning running slightly behind Cobbett with thirty-two votes. The seat was lost to the Tory candidate by thirteen votes, with a considerable portion of the electorate abstaining. The radicals had lost a seat which had been uncontested at the last general election. Naturally recriminations followed. While many blamed the Cobbettites for inviting an unsatisfactory candidate to stand and condemned Fielden for trying to manipulate proceedings, O'Connor drew criticism for having gone to the poll with no chance of victory.[64] The radicals reasserted their dominance at Oldham, in 1837, when they united to return Fielden and General W. A. Johnson.

For O'Connor, his sortie into radical Lancashire politics was of particular significance. This was his first glimpse of the industrial North, the future centre of support for his Chartist leadership. He had spent fifteen days in a Lancashire factory town.

> I saw England for the first time with the naked eye . . . I then for the first time saw the Rattle Boxes and their victims. I was up betimes every morning, and watched the pallied face, the emaciated frame, and the twisted limbs, wending their way to the earthly hell.[65]

He had come to the constituency of William Cobbett and entered the strong-hold of the late Henry Hunt. He had made contact with some of the staunchest working-class radicals in the country, veterans of radical agitation. Especially important was his friendship with John Knight, through whom he was later to claim an almost spiritual link with Hunt. Following his defeat, O'Connor addressed a meeting of several thousand operatives at Manchester, and declared his intention to fill the leadership gap caused by Hunt's death.

> Ever since the days of Henry Hunt, until this day, the radical reformers

had been without a person to rally under. . . . he would fill up the vacancy caused by the death of Henry Hunt. (Hear.)[66]

Although O'Connor continued to look to the possibility of a return to Parliament in the role of the 'people's representative', he returned to London with the beginnings of his concept of advancing a national working-class movement from a London base. Within less than six months, he was to return to Lancashire and Yorkshire as the repre-sentative of the Great Marylebone Radical Association. Thus, in a sense, Oldham was O'Connor's 'English political birthplace'[67]; how-ever it was not among the industrial proletariat of Lancashire, but among the radical artisans of London that he began his career as a radical organiser.

III London Radicalism

(i) *Metropolitan Radical Associations*

O'Connor dated his leadership of the agitation for an independent working-class party from the founding of the Great Marylebone Radical Association. In contrast to most historians of Chartism, who have traditionally traced the organisational and programmatic origins of the movement through the endeavours of William Lovett and the London Working Men's Association, most Chartists regarded O'Con-nor as the 'founding father' of Chartism, the prime initiator of the national movement for universal suffrage. O'Connor constantly based his claim for confidence in his leadership upon his pre-Chartist record of radical agitation. He considered the principal achievement of this agitation to have been the final severance of the radical movement from all forms of Whiggery.[68] Certainly his role in the formation of Radical Associations in London, the North of England and Scotland was vital to the emergence of Chartism, and crucial to any understanding of the widespread support for his leadership by 1838.

By summer 1835, O'Connor was playing a prominent role along-side Thomas Wakley, the radical MP for Finsbury, Owen and Carlile, at meetings held at Owen's Charlotte Street Institute in support of the Dorchester labourers and the freedom of the press. These were the two issues which also preoccupied the group of Marylebone radicals who met at John Savage's rowdy Mechanics' Institute public house in Circus Street.[69] The Marylebone radicals were a group of small merchants, shopkeepers and artisans who had fought since

1827 to gain control of the local parish government in order to reduce rates. The parish radicals were great proponents of local self-government, opposed all forms of government centralisation, especially the new Poor Law and the metropolitan police. They had been extremely active in the reform agitation.[70] When O'Connor came together with these radicals to form the Great Marylebone Radical Association, in September 1835, he was building from a strong local radical base. The Association's 'Declaration of the Rights of Man', an embodiment of Painite radicalism, started from the premise that 'The end of society is the *public good*, and the institution of government is to secure to *every individual* the enjoyment of his rights.' Universal suffrage, equality before the law, security of person, the full enjoyment of the fruits of labour, freedom of thought and speech were among these rights. Particular emphasis was placed upon the need for education: 'Instruction is the want of all; society and government ought, therefore, to do all in their power to favour the progress of reason and truth; and to place instruction within the reach of all.'[71]

Over three thousand radicals attended the first public meeting called by the Marylebone Radical Association, held at Owen's National Exchange Bazaar and intended to encourage the formation of other Radical Associations. O'Connor took the chair. He declared that 'The people must now take matters into their own hands', and proposed the popular radical objective of the establishment of a National Convention of the people. John Savage, Dr Arthur Wade, Thomas Murphy, John Cleave, the veteran radical John George, Carlile and O'Connell all spoke. Support was also forthcoming from the unstamped press, especially from O'Brien in the *Poor Man's Guardian*. O'Brien congratulated the Association for demanding that all members support universal suffrage and for not having fallen for the O'Connellite humbug of mere suffrage extension; societies 'founded on the same principles' must be 'formed in every town and village in the empire'.[72] By May 1836, at least eight more RAs had been established at Surrey, Southwark, Greenwich, Chatham, Tower Hamlets, Westminster, Finsbury and Lambeth.[73] Formed generally around preexisting local radical groups, the RAs reflected the highly localised nature of London working-class politics. Weekly meetings to discuss prearranged topics of social and political interest were held at local taverns. The local Associations did come together, however, to take up common issues at all-London meetings; and the Associations' major leaders — O'Connor, Savage, Wade, Macconnell, Cleave, Thomas Murphy, S. Saunders, John Bell — imparted some measure of unity by attending meetings in most districts.

The social composition of the RAs was, like most London radical organisations before 1839, a mixed one. The parish radicals tended to be lower middle class. Savage was a linen draper turned publican; George Rogers of Bloomsbury was a prosperous tobacconist; Thomas Murphy of St Pancras was a coal merchant. But the local leadership was drawn more generally from the ranks of the skilled artisans, radicals who had been active in the NUWC, the unstamped campaign, various attempts at general unionism, cooperative production and retailing.[74] The carpenter Thomas Goldspink — ex-NUWC committee man, a leading figure in the Builders Union (1832-34), member of the Dorchester Labourers Committee — was among the founders of the Marylebone RA. The hatter Thomas J. White was secretary of the Lambeth RA; James Edwards, secretary of the Silk Skein Dyers Union, was secretary of the Tower Hamlets RA; the bricklayer James Brown was secretary of the Surrey RA. The RAs involved many radicals concerned with the production and sale of radical journals: the publishers Cleave and Hetherington; the journalists John Bell, Thomas Macconnell, William Carpenter and George Edmonds; the 'victims' of the unstamped John Sharp and Thomas Heins (secretary of the Chatham RA). Middle-class radicals such as Dr Wade, an Anglican vicar, and H. S. Chapman, a lawyer, were active in the affairs of the RAs. D. W. Harvey, radical MP for Southwark, often took the chair at meetings of the Southwark and Surrey RAs; Thomas Wakley occasionally attended meetings of the Marylebone RA, where he was a great favourite as leader of the parliamentary opposition to the newspaper stamp.

The RAs included several veteran radicals: at Southwark, John George, who had been a member of the London Corresponding Society; at Finsbury, Thomas Preston, the Spencean shoemaker who had been involved in the Cato Street conspiracy; at Marylebone, Thomas Cleary, who had been Major Cartwright's secretary. The RAs also included many future leaders of London Chartism: the Westminster radicals William Hassell and George Huggett, Henry Ross of the Lambeth RA (future member of the National Charter Association Executive), John Simpson and John Parker of the Surrey RA, Thomas Wall and Dr R. T. Webb of the Marylebone RA and Joseph Williams of the Finsbury RA (future delegate to the first Chartist Convention).[75] However if the metropolitan RAs looked forward to Chartist days, the Associations were built upon the remnants of the NUWC. Declining in support since late 1833, the NUWC finally amalgamated with the Great Marylebone RA in December 1835, at a meeting of the NUWC at the Hope coffee-house.[76] More important, however, than any formal union were the strong links in terms of personnel and in the continuity in the struggles for universal suffrage and an unstamped press. The carpenter John Russell, who had been secretary of the NUWC since 1833, became secretary of the Marylebone RA. The parish radicals were crucial in the formation of both the NUWC and the Marylebone RA, as they were to be to early London Chartism. Thomas Sherman, active in the Surrey and Finsbury RAs, held one of the last classes of the NUWC together in Spitalfields; Heins, Hassell, Goldspink, Huggett and Simpson were among the last active NUWC leaders.[77] John Cleave, perhaps the most important leader of the NUWC, became one of the principal leaders of the RAs. Finally, like the NUWC, the RAs drew support from a large number of Irish radicals: Cleave, Murphy, Macconnell, O'Brien, Cleary, James Hogan, John Grady, William Duffey, William Hoare.[78]

The first major initiative of the Marylebone RA was to memorialise the Home Secretary for the return of the Dorchester labourers. O'Connor headed a deputation to wait upon Russell. Many of the RAs' members were trade unionists, former members of the Grand National Consolidated Trades Union, and served either on the Central London Dorchester Committee or various local committees to secure their return. Together with the Dorchester Labourers Committee, the RAs were the most prominent London organisations agitating for the unionists' return.[79]

Most significantly, with the demise of the NUWC, the RAs became the leading organisation in the final stages of the struggle for an unstamped press. O'Connor's major contribution to London radicalism, 1835-36, was his effort, through the RAs and their Central Committee, to coordinate this agitation. It would be difficult to exaggerate the importance of the struggle for a free press. At a meeting of the Chatham RA called to oppose the stamp, Mr Owden, 'an uneducated man', maintained:

> The subject which we are met to discuss lies at the root of all evil. Our misrulers know that we are ignorant, and they therefore presume to tyranize over us — they, under this presumption, palmed upon us the Irish Coercion Bill, and the Poor Starvation Bill — but once political light were thrown upon the minds of the people, their enemies would never dare to propose such measures.[80]

In early 1836, O'Connor joined Macconnell, formerly a close associate of Owen's, in urging a final push for total repeal of the taxes on

knowledge. At a meeting of the Southwark RA, O'Connor proposed
that the RAs join in a concerted drive to remove the obnoxious stamp,
an issue which he believed had temporarily to take priority over the
agitation for universal suffrage. The RAs quickly endorsed this policy,
following an all-London meeting at the Institute, Theobalds's Road,
where plans to petition Parliament were discussed. Support was also
forthcoming from the Radical Associations which O'Connor had recently established in Yorkshire and Lancashire.[81] An outdoor demonstration was called for Easter Monday to coincide with this petitioning campaign. Several thousand met on Primrose Hill to demonstrate
for total repeal and against the latest sentences imposed upon Cleave
and Hetherington. A deputation from this meeting waited upon
Spring Rice, Chancellor of the Exchequer.[82] The Surrey, Southwark
and Marylebone RAs were particularly active in spring of 1836,
campaigning for total repeal and in support of John Sharp, leading
member of the Southwark RA imprisoned for his involvement in the
unstamped.

The announcement of government proposals for merely reducing
the stamp to a penny, in April, increased the bitterness of ultra-
radicals. The government measures were clearly designed to kill the
cheap working-class press. James Savage told a meeting of the Marylebone RA:

> If they pass this law, we shall feel it a declaration of war against us, the
> working class, and that we . . . shall be justified in taking arms into our
> hands against the useless ones.[83]

O'Connor put the issue clearly:

> the great object of the Whigs had been to separate the middle and the
> working classes; and that a penny stamp would go to secure this object.
> The middle classes would have much cheaper newspapers than they
> hitherto had, but the working classes would have no papers at all.[84]

In an eloquent address 'To the Radicals of England', O'Connor called
on radicals throughout the country to organise opposition to the
government measures which he maintained threatened the very
existence of an independent radical movement.[85] Throughout April
and May 1836, the RAs tried to direct and organise public opinion
and to influence radical MPs on this issue. These efforts culminated,
in late May, at a meeting in White Conduit Fields, addressed by
O'Connor, Cleave, Hetherington, O'Brien, Savage, Murphy, Goldspink, Preston, Sharp and John Hanson of Huddersfield. O'Connor
assured the meeting:

That, before the subject was given up, they would make, with the soap
which had been recommended them, a lather which would serve the
editor of the unwashed *Times* to shave himself with.[86]

However, with the reduction of the newspaper stamp and the
extinction of the unstamped, the Metropolitan Radical Association
disintegrated. By summer 1836, centralised organisation had ceased
to exist and those Associations which continued to function fell back
on local roots. Over the next year various RAs came forward to
support O'Connor's proposal for an Universal Suffrage Club, oppose
the new Poor Law and the proposals for a rural police; some militants
remained active throughout 1837 within local RA branches.[87] In
October 1837, the case of the Glasgow cotton spinners revitalised the
Great Marylebone RA, as it did the RAs at Southwark and Lambeth,
with O'Connor, Savage, Webb and Goldspink again taking the lead.[88]
As the first cause which the Marylebone RA had embraced had been
that of the Dorchester labourers, it was fitting that their last stand
should be in support of the Glasgow spinners. Besides the important
role the RAs played in the final stages of the unstamped agitation and
in support of the Dorchester labourers, they provided an important
organisational link between the NUWC and the London Chartist
movement into which their last vital groups merged in early 1838.

For O'Connor the Radical Association provided essential experience in the organisation of popular politics in England, and served to
acquaint him with some of the difficulties peculiar to radical agitation
in London. It also highlights O'Connor's early concern for working-
class education and cultural control, something overlooked in most
evaluations of his leadership. His leading role in the activities of the
RAs brought him into close cooperation with the articulate radical
artisans of London. Their strong craft pride, independence and long
radical tradition were important influences upon his development as
a radical leader. O'Connor also secured a place among the principal
leaders of London popular politics. By 1836 his presence was obliga-
tory as a guest at the major radical public dinners — those held in
honour of Hetherington and Cleave and to celebrate the pardon of
the Dorchester labourers. His association with the struggle for a free
press was celebrated in popular ballad.

> So to conclude these lines,
> I hope you are not offended,
> We hope before it's long
> The Times will be amended,
> Here's Wakley, three times three,

And every man of Honour,
Who fights for the People's Right
With Macconnell and O'Connor.
(Britons' Rights or the Unstamped Newspaper)[89]

(ii) *The Universal Suffrage Club*

During the final stages of the unstamped campaign, O'Connor had tried, unsuccessfully, to weld the RAs into a more coherent, centralised organisation. At a delegates meeting, chaired by Hetherington, he proposed the formation of a central committee for the RAs which would meet weekly to coordinate radical agitation. He also suggested that such a central committee develop close links with the trade societies throughout the country in order to establish a national trades association to defend unionists in the event of government prosecution. 'His object was to institute an immense committee — an amalgamation of the trades in which . . . all working men would be represented.' At the same meeting, O'Connor put forward his idea for establishing a working men's club. 'He anxiously desired to establish a cheap club for the working classes, where they might have refreshments and useful moral reading at a low price . . .'[90]

In June 1836, O'Connor tried to reorganise the forces of London radicalism behind his plans for an Universal Suffrage Club. He proposed establishing a radical club, managed by working men, where artisans could gather to read and debate. Few historians of Chartism have associated O'Connor with this type of educational, self-help venture. Yet the similarities, in terms of both membership and objectives, with the London Working Men's Association are unmistakable. The objectives of the Universal Suffrage Club were:

> To elevate the moral, intellectual, and political character of the Working Classes; to afford them more opportunities for friendly intercourse with each other; and for forming a more substantial compact between them and such men of learning, and political and moral integrity, as are desirous of making common cause with their less affluent brethern; for placing happiness within the reach of all;— to soften, and eventually subdue, the asperity of the aristocracy and the middle classes towards the working portion of the people;— to prove to all their enemies the fitness of the working classes to manage their own affairs, both locally and nationally . . .[91]

The three artisans who composed this prospectus — Goldspink, T. J. White and Richard Cameron (bracemaker) — were all RA members and all joined the London Working Men's Association. It was not the divisions, but rather the continuities and overlapping organisational links of such radical artisans which characterised London radicalism. While there is considerable truth to Francis Place's view of the Universal Suffrage Club as an attempt on the part of Augustus Beaumont and O'Connor to undermine the LWMA — there was discontent over the Association's gradualist tone — it is perhaps more accurate to view the two associations as parallel developments. Both evolved out of the collapse of the unstamped agitation. The USC was the offspring of the RAs, just as the LWMA grew out of the Association of Working Men to Procure a Cheap and Honest Press.[92] Both Hetherington and Cleave supported the project, as did other RA leaders — Bell, Wade, Russell, Murphy, Macconnell, Rogers, Williams, Hogan, Sherman, Edmund Stallwood (the Hammersmith radical) and D. W. Harvey. If the USC was intended to be less exclusive than the LWMA, the emphasis upon the need for working-class respectability, the relatively high subscription, the planned library, newspaper and periodical room, as well as dining room, underline the basic similarities between the two associations. Although all USC members were to be accorded voting rights, in contrast to the LWMA's policy of merely conferring 'honourary' membership upon gentleman radicals, the same objection to non-working men having a voice in the management of affairs soon surfaced.[93]

Much of the significance of the USC, as with the LWMA, was as a manifestation of radical artisan culture and consciousness, 'as part of a continuing experiment in elite politics'.[94] Yet the move to establish the USC had wider objectives, however ill-conceived and unrealised. Thus Hetherington's *Twopenny Dispatch* hailed the first public meeting held to establish the USC, on 4 July 1836, somewhat preposterously as 'The first National Convention'. And support was forthcoming not only from the Finsbury, Marylebone, Lambeth and Southwark RAs, but northern RAs, such as those at Manchester and Middleton, where the prospects for forming USC branches were discussed.[95] O'Connor and other radicals envisaged the USC as an association from which to advance a wider national movement for universal suffrage.

The efforts to form the USC were short-lived. The club house which O'Connor at one time offered to purchase was never built. Opposition from certain LWMA members, dissension over the role of non-working men and the intense localism of London radical politics all contributed to the failure. While O'Connor's attempt to reestablish a centralising political force was unsuccessful, it underscores the problem which he faced in setting out to organise nationally from a London base which he found difficult to unify behind his own leadership. Its huge size, pronounced localism and four hundred different trades meant that London lacked a distinct sense of community. As E. P. Thompson has observed: 'Popular movements in London have often lacked the coherence and stamina which results from the involvement of an entire community in common occupational and social tensions.'[96] There was also a sense of London's aloofness, its separateness and self-sufficiency. In the industrial towns of the North, usually dominated by one industry, O'Connor found a more unified communal response to his organisational initiatives. He often complained of the apathy of the London artisans, comparing them unfavourably with their provincial comrades.[97] The radical London artisans were highly independent, possessing their own culture and organisations. Their desire for direct democratic control over their institutions made them suspicious of gentlemen and leaders in general. Still, the contrast between metropolitan and northern radicalism should not be overdrawn. The weavers and factory hands of Lancashire and Yorkshire shared many of the same artisanal values as London's working-class radicals, the same striving for various forms of economic, cultural and political independence. Like the northern workers, London's artisans, particularly trades such as tailors, carpenters, shoemakers, cabinet-makers, faced the ever-increasing subordination of labour to the power of capital. However, the process of subordination was more advanced, the degree of dependency more severe and uniform in the industrial North; clearly the 'geographic shift northwards . . . gave to radicalism a more fully proletarian base'.[98] In November 1836, O'Connor became an honourary member of the LWMA, in the activities of which he took some part, but increasingly he was centring his energies on the districts of England's industrial North.

IV Northern Radicalism

The Great Marylebone Radical Association was important not only to O'Connor's emergence as a London radical leader, but also to his emergence as a national leader. From the outset O'Connor and other radicals saw the establishment of the Radical Association in London as merely the first step towards the creation of a national network of local Radical Associations. Thus, in response to the interest of several provincial radical groups, O'Connor headed north for a three week tour, in December 1835, as the representative of the Marylebone RA.[99] Wherever he spoke Radical Associations were established: Manchester, Stockport, Oldham, Rochdale, Leeds, Halifax, Huddersfield, Barnsley, Bradford, Keighley, Hull, Sheffield. Often addressing two or three meetings a day, O'Connor demonstrated the boundless enthusiasm for agitation which became the hallmark of his Chartist leadership.

From the platform O'Connor outlined the RA's five-point programme: universal suffrage, no property qualification for MPs, vote by ballot, annual parliaments, equal electoral districts. He combined historical claims to these rights with claims based on natural right, and emphasised the continuity of radical tradition and principle. Thus he told the Keighley radicals: 'But the Radicals of today are the Radicals of Major Cartwright's time; he professed those principles which we now seek to obtain.' Property should be the basis of neither the suffrage nor a man's right to sit in Parliament, as property was valueless without labour.

> What signifies twenty thousand acres of barren soil, if it was not the application of your labour. Take one of these cotton mills, and place your looms in it, let them remain until Doomsday, and they would rot without your labour before they produced anything.

O'Connor preached opposition to the new Poor Law and support for factory regulation, while making it clear that it was not machinery but rather the abuse of machinery to which he was opposed.[100]

Wherever he spoke O'Connor stressed the need for organisation: 'We are not organized; we have the force, the power but we want the organization . . .' No longer could they depend upon well-disposed Whigs, the time had arrived 'to set up business on our own account', to establish their independence from both parties. He told the Hull radicals: 'we must have no such thing as the Radical-Whig in Hull . . . the Radical-Whig is a non-descript animal . . .' O'Connor maintained that a unified radical party in the country could return thirty members to Parliament pledged to radical principles who 'would preserve the balance of power' and be in a position to demand radical concessions. He aspired to a position which O'Connell's party held but failed to exploit. However, one of O'Connor's main objectives was to canvass support for plans to convene a National Convention in London, as a rival to Parliament. He informed northern radicals, 'we mean to try the success of a bold and nervous experiment'.

> We of the Radical Association propose to divide the population into districts, and to send from each district a delegate . . . up to the House of Delegates (which is to be called the 'the Bee-Hive') . . . so we shall see how the opinions of the people agree with the opinions of the representatives in Parliament; then we shall see if they are satisfied with the franchise as it is . . .[101]

O'Connor's popularity was quickly established. He made an immediate and lasting impression on working-class audiences. The Barnsley radical, John Vallance, recalled the first time he heard O'Connor:

> On one occasion, it might be the occasion of his first visit, I stood in the crowd which had assembled to hear him; and this was my first sight of him. His figure was tall and well proportioned, and his bearing decidedly aristocratic. He wore a blue frock coat and buff waistcoat, and had rings on the fingers of each hand. In a graceful manner, and in emphatic language, he told the Radicals of Barnsley that he had sold off his horses and dogs, had greatly reduced his establishment, and come weal come woe, he would henceforth devote his whole life to promote the well-being of the working classes. . . . The language of O'Connor, to ears accustomed to little else than the Barnsley dialect, as spoken by pale faced weavers and swart cobblers, sounded like rich music.[102]

O'Connor presented himself in the familiar role of the radical gentleman of the platform. He consciously assumed the mantle of Henry Hunt, and was almost immediately accepted in this role. Thus the newly formed Keighly RA wrote to the Marylebone RA:

> while we have had to lament the death of that champion of rational liberty, Mr. Hunt, another has risen in his place equally fearless and independent, and we believe possessed of even superior ability.[103]

Particularly important was the support which O'Connor won among local radical leaders, radicals whose efforts laid the foundations for the Chartist movement in the North. This support was based upon a set of established radical principles which O'Connor advocated. Peter Bussey, chairman of the Bradford meeting and soon to become secretary of the Bradford RA, declared:

> I come forward on this occasion with greater pleasure than ever I did at any political meeting before, as the principles which Mr. O'Connor has come here to advocate, are those which I hold sincerely from my heart. (Cheers.)[104]

At Manchester O'Connor shared the platform with radicals such as George Condy, the Owenite socialist George Fleming, the ten-hours activist Matthew Fletcher (later the Bury delegate to the first Chartist Convention), and the veteran Huntite the Rev. James Scholefield.

At Oldham John Knight and James Greaves made certain that the Oldham Political Union adopted the programme of the Radical Association. O'Connor discussed the prospects of working-class radicalism with key West Riding leaders, men such as Bussey, William Rider, Lawrence Pitkeithley — all future delegates to the Chartist Convention — and Joshua Hobson, the foremost martyr of the provincial unstamped and the future publisher and editor of O'Connor's *Northern Star*. Support was forthcoming from local radicals like John Hanson, Stephen Dickenson, Thomas Vevers, Christopher Tinker and John Leech (Huddersfield); Arthur Collins, Joseph Crabtree, Aeneas Daly and Joseph Lingard (Barnsley); James Ibbetson (Bradford); John Sugden (Keighley); Henry Rawson (Halifax); and P. T. Bready (Sheffield).[105] These were some of the local leaders who kept radical agitation on the boil between O'Connor's fleeting visits.

The Radical Associations of Lancashire and Yorkshire were based upon existing local radical groups and leaders who had been agitating for universal suffrage, a free press, the release of the Dorchester labourers and a ten-hour day. O'Connor attempted to coordinate these local working-class groups within a national organisation capable of giving unified direction to their political and social demands. No such national organisation emerged in 1836; plans for a National Convention were postponed. This coming together had to wait for the economic depression of 1837, the government's attempt to abolish outdoor relief in the North and the mass platform campaign for universal suffrage which heralded the advent of Chartism. Still, many of the RAs which O'Connor established on his first missionary tour remained active, especially those of the West Riding. The RAs at Manchester, Bradford, Barnsley, Halifax, Leeds, Hull, Huddersfield and Keighley agitated through May 1836 for the repeal of the newspaper stamp, in defence of the West Riding 'victims' — Hobson, Mann and Ibbetson — and organised opposition to the new Poor Law.[106] On subsequent tours O'Connor revitalised many of the original RAs as well as helped to establish new ones. The Halifax, Barnsley and Bradford RAs remained active into 1838, eventually merging into the Chartist movement through the Great Northern Union.[107]

With the waning cohesion of the metropolitan RAs and the difficulties with the USC project, O'Connor was drawn increasingly towards radical agitation in the North, particularly by the tone and temper of the factory movement and the opposition to the new Poor Law, neither of which had broad appeal in London. With the decline of the unstamped agitation, London's radical artisans retreated into more educational modes, well exemplified by the activities of the LWMA; in the industrial North, however, the working-class movement was gaining momentum. It was in the North that the principles of bourgeois political economy were being confronted most sharply by the forces of working-class protest. Significantly, in summer 1836, O'Connor joined Richard Oastler and the Rev. J. R. Stephens, the most prominent champions of the factory movement, for the first time at a meeting in Oldham. O'Connor told the Oldham radicals: 'If Mr. Oastler was a tory as he avowed, he should be highly delighted to see many such tories.'[108] On this and subsequent tours, O'Connor became closely identified with the ten-hours movement and, more particularly, with the emergent resistance to the new Poor Law. The platform alliance which developed between O'Connor and the tory-radicals Oastler and Stephens inspired working-class agitation throughout the North. However, O'Connor's willingness to cooperate with Oastler and Stephens was indicative of neither some form of latent tory-radicalism nor political opportunism, but reflected agreement on the crucial question of political economy and highlighted the importance of the social demands implicit in the struggle for universal suffrage.

O'Connor insisted that the English radicals were 'democratic radicals', and pledged that were the Tories returned to office he would turn his energies to attacking Toryism. Yet he was at his best when denouncing the Whigs.

> The Whigs ask us if we cannot go part of the way with them. We have often invited them to accompany us, but they have deceived us, for the moment they get to Whig cross, they bid us good night. (Laughter and cheers.) We ask them to go to justice to Dorchester, and they went to Bantry Bay; we asked them to grant a loan of fifteen millions for effecting the liberation of the slaves, and they made it into a grant of twenty millions; we asked them to go to justice for Ireland, and they gave us the Coercion Bill; we asked them to go into the abuses of the Old Poor Law . . . and they took us into bastiles, and there they left us. Do they suppose that public opinion is going to stand still — do they think that a great manifestation of Radical principle like this is going to be put down by either Whig or Tory, or by both united?[109]

O'Connor came to personify working-class opposition to Whiggery in all its guises. This was well exemplified at Halifax, in autumn 1836, where O'Connor was at the centre of a bitter dispute between local working-class radicals and middle-class reformers. The radicals had proposed that O'Connor be invited to a local reform dinner in honour of Charles Wood, local Whig MP, and Edward Protheroe, the defeated Whig-radical candidate at the last election. Although the joint committee initially approved this proposal, they reversed their decision under pressure from the Whig Reform Association. As a gesture of protest, the radicals resolved to hold a rival dinner at which O'Connor was guest of honour. Protheroe attended both dinners in order to plead the dangers of disunity in the reform ranks, but his qualified opposition to universal suffrage and the ten-hours bill and his qualified approval of the new Poor Law were in stark contrast to O'Connor's brand of ultra-radicalism. 'He didn't come there to listen to the modifications of principles', declared O'Connor, 'or for any electioneering purpose, he came to instruct his political children. (Cheers, and "you're welcome".)' O'Connor's intervention at Halifax was publicised thoroughly in the radical press; locally it marked a decisive breach between middle-class and working-class radicalism.[110] In a period marked by localism in political affairs, O'Connor was able to intervene in such local contexts with remarkable success and give national prominence to local radicalism.

O'Connor found an outlet for his boundless radical zeal in the role of itinerant organiser and demagogue. His constant theme was the need for organisation and working-class unity. In an address 'To the Working Men of England', published in late 1836 — on the eve of economic recession and the Poor Law Commissioners' attempt to introduce the new Poor Law into the North — O'Connor noted his earlier endeavours to mobilise radical opinion and the improved prospects for radicalism nationally.

> some fourteen months ago, I prepared you for the coming trial. I told you, when you complained of apathy, that a money-panic or a labour-panic, would place radicalism in the ascendant, and that it would be necessary to martial [sic] public opinion during prosperity, in order that any reverse may be met by a decorous and judicious co-operation; rather than by bluster, brute-force retaliation, and destruction of property, the never-failing resources which, upon the first shock of adversity present themselves to disorganised community.
>
> . . . you have suffered from apathy; and although I cannot rejoice in the cause which arouses you from it, yet I do rejoice in the prospect which your union promises . . . The coming crisis will prove to the working classes of all crafts, that their cause is one and the same.

Thus O'Connor was acutely conscious of the need for working-class protest to be the expression of a well-organised movement, prepared for sustained agitation and with a well-defined set of rationally articulated demands, rather than a spontaneous reaction to economic distress. He also noted that although mass demonstrations were valuable for the expression of public opinion, it was within smaller, more regular groups that the real business of radical organisation had to take place.[111] O'Connor's role on the mass anti-Poor Law platform and at the mass demonstrations for universal suffrage which led to the emergence of Chartism should not obscure this emphasis upon permanent forms of radical organisation. It is a serious misconception to view O'Connor's demagoguery as antithetical to a role as organiser.

During the winter of 1836/37, O'Connor extended his organisational activities beyond his London/Yorkshire/Lancashire base. In November, he made his first appearance at Nottingham, his future constituency, in order to establish a Radical Association. As at Halifax, his visit proved an important phase in the local working-class radicals' efforts to counter the influence of middle-class reformers intent on maintaining an alliance between Whigs and radicals. At Newcastle he conferred with local radical leaders and held a public meeting. O'Connor proceeded north to Scotland at the invitation of the newly formed Scottish Radical Association and its president, Dr John Taylor. Taylor was a prominent ultra-radical with close contact with the trade union movement and editor of the radical *New Glasgow Liberator*. During this tour O'Connor, along with Taylor, helped to establish RAs at Glasgow, Paisley, Kilmarnock, Cummock, Edinburgh, Leith, Dundee and Dunfermline. The Scottish Radical Association eventually merged into the Chartist movement. From this tour emerged an important leadership alliance between O'Connor and Taylor. O'Connor also made contact with other local leaders important to the birth of Scottish Chartism, such as Hugh Craig, Abram Duncan and John Fraser.[112] Throughout the industrial North of England, Scotland and London, O'Connor was establishing all-important links between various radical groups and their leaders. His constant touring facilitated the growing sense of radical unity essential to the emergence of Chartism. On his return to Yorkshire, O'Connor was welcomed with public entries and large-scale processions, dinners and crowded meetings.[113] His presence was regarded as an occasion to demonstrate the growing strength and unity of working-class radicalism.

V O'Connor, O'Connell and the English Radicals

The autumn of 1836 saw the final breach between O'Connor and
Daniel O'Connell. At a Dublin meeting of the General Association of
Ireland, in August, O'Connell accused the English radicals of indifference towards Irish needs. He also denounced O'Connor, as the
leader of the ultra-radicals, and instructed the people of County Cork
to have nothing to do with him — 'let him stick to the radicals of
England'.[114] Here was O'Connor's official excommunication from
Irish popular politics. In response to their hostility towards his Whig
allies, O'Connell proclaimed O'Connor and the English radicals
'tory-radicals'. O'Connell regarded opposition to the Whigs as indi-
rect support for the Tories, the gravest political sin. His own attitudes
towards factory regulation, the new Poor Law and trade unionism,
together with his Irish policy, also drew increasing working-class
criticism. The London radicals immediately rallied to the defence of
their own and O'Connor's reputation. The newspapers of Cleave,
Hetherington and Bell denied that the radicals' opposition to the
Whigs implied support for the Tories or an abandonment of the cause
of Irish rights; in turn, they exposed O'Connell's growing list of
radical betrayal. Cleave, Hetherington, Murphy, Hoare and James
Watson took the lead at a meeting called to support O'Connor at
which even Lovett spoke. Several hundred O'Connellites, however,
ensured that the meeting was a chaotic affair.[115] By autumn 1836
many Anglo-Irish radicals, such as Cleave and Murphy, who had
formerly supported O'Connell came to regard him as an opponent of
the interests of both the Irish and English labouring classes; the
majority, however, remained loyal to O'Connell. This rift within the
Anglo-Irish ranks weakened the radical movement throughout the
country, but especially in London and the industrial North.[116]

The final break was dramatic, marking a pivotal point in the development of pre-Chartist working-class radicalism, but the differences
had been apparent for some time. Thus, by summer 1834, O'Brien
had assumed a position of implacable hostility towards O'Connell in
the columns of the *Poor Man's Guardian*. O'Brien carefully analysed
the perplexing twists and turns which characterised O'Connell's
leadership and charged that O'Connell — 'blessed with a conscience
that stretches like Indian rubber' — courted a radical image merely
to serve the interests of the middle classes.[117] In a tone which came
to characterise an ultra-radical critique of middle-class radical leadership and 'whig-radicalism', Bell denounced the parliamentary

radicals, and O'Connell in particular, for their mere token opposition to the Whig penny newspaper stamp.

> The Whigs have triumphed. The press is still to be taxed. The opposition of the Parliamentary Radicals promised to be of the most courtly kind. . . . Mr. O'Connell will make a sounding speech in favour of an untaxed press, *and then* — the matter will be arranged to the satisfaction of all parties in the House! The Whigs and the Parliamentary Radicals understand each other but too well!
>
> The productive classes of England have been once more betrayed by their leaders. Had Mr. O'Connell chosen, he could have forced the Whigs to repeal the whole of the taxes on political intelligence. It has suited Mr. O'Connell, however, to abandon this mighty cause. His price is the Irish Municipal Corporations Bill . . .[118]

Ultra-radicals came to regard O'Connell as the most recent in a series of popular leaders turned apostate, who having gained influence through the mass support of the people deserted the cause of popular rights for the fruits of government favour. It would be difficult to exaggerate the symbolic importance which O'Connell's apostasy was to assume for Chartists. Just as Hunt and O'Connor came to symbolise the virtues of principled, incorruptible leadership, O'Connell epitomised the popular leader who had trafficked in politics, forever damned for his unprincipled betrayal of the Irish and English people at the hands of the 'base, brutal and bloody Whigs'.[119]

Despite past differences, O'Connor had taken care not to attack O'Connell in personal terms during his first year's agitation in England. His desire to promote cooperation between the English and Irish labouring classes and his apprehension of alienating the support of the Irish radicals in England influenced this public attitude.[120] In April 1836, the Barnsley RA invited O'Connell to attend a public dinner; and he presided over a dinner given by the Hull RA at which O'Connor was toasted.[121] This compatibility, however, was becoming increasingly strained. O'Connor and the ultra-radicals were moving in direct opposition to O'Connell. While O'Connor was campaigning for the creation of an independent radical party, opposed to any Whig alliance, O'Connell was committed to support for the Whigs in return for reformist concessions for Ireland. Furthermore, as the first moves were made to introduce the new Poor Law into the industrial districts, working-class opposition to the Benthamite attitudes of O'Connell and the philosophic radicals intensified.

O'Connor replied to O'Connell in *A Series of Letters . . . to Daniel O'Connell*, published in October 1836, and which constituted a comprehensive critique of O'Connell's leadership since emancipation. Well argued and detailed, these letters represent some of O'Connor's finest political writing. He prefaced his attack on O'Connell with an open letter to the Whig Government in which he catalogued their abuses of power and commented upon the popular disaffection with the 1832 Reform: 'Perhaps one of the greatest anomalies in our history, is the fact of so generally popular a measure, so soon creating disgust — a disgust arising out of the Whig use made of it.' Only universal suffrage would now satisfy the people. Like the Whigs, O'Connell had betrayed popular trust in the interest of the middle classes of England and Ireland. According to O'Connor, O'Connell's attack on the English radicals was occasioned by the rebukes he suffered at the hands of the radicals intent on exposing the discrepencies between his radical professions outside Parliament and his parliamentary alliance with the Whig Government: 'you [O'Connell] declared yourself a Radical, but the Radicals told you that you were a Whig'. O'Connor also gave prominence to the charge, current in the radical press, that in return for a £1000 political contribution from several prominent Manchester cotton manufacturers O'Connell had changed his position on the question of the regulation of factory hours. O'Connell's support for Poulett Thomson's attempt to amend the Factory Act, so as to allow twelve-year-olds to work more than an eight-hour day, created bitter working-class resentment. Most working-class radicals came to accept Oastler's depiction of O'Connell as a 'political-economist-Malthusian Whig'.[122]

By late 1836, it was no longer possible for radicals to support both O'Connor and O'Connell's leadership. The Barnsley RA, dominated by Anglo-Irish linen weavers, held a series of meetings to discuss the differences between O'Connor and O'Connell at which the overwhelming majority sided uncompromisingly with O'Connor. From Halifax the radicals proclaimed O'Connell 'forever politically damned in the estimation of all real Radicals'. George Condy, Irishman and former admirer of O'Connell's, denounced O'Connell in the columns of the radical *Manchester and Salford Advertiser*.[123] Thus O'Connor's break with O'Connell became the focal point of a more general collapse of amicable relations between O'Connell and the English working-class radicals to which O'Connell put the final touches in late 1837 with his attack on trade unionism. The break with O'Connell came to mark the severance of working-class radicalism from any form of whig-radical or middle-class radical alliance and the rejection of the principles of political economy, defining characteristics of the emergent Chartist movement. The vehemence with which Chartists assailed O'Connell reflected the threat posed by his continual attempts to reforge such a middle-class/working-class alliance.

Despite the enmity of O'Connell and his exclusion from Irish popular politics, O'Connor continued to attempt to offer political direction to Irish workers in England and to maintain a dialogue between English working-class radicals and Irish trade unionists and radicals.[124] Always conscious of the importance of working-class unity, he insisted upon the English radicals giving prominence to Irish demands. O'Connor managed to retain the support of some sections of the Irish working-class population in England, as well as some radicals in Ireland led by anti-O'Connellites such as the Rev. Thaddeus O'Malley and Patrick O'Higgins.[125]

VI The Central National Association and the London Working Men's Association

While increasingly committed to northern agitation, O'Connor continued to take an active part in the affairs of metropolitan radicalism. He regarded the establishment of a strong radical movement in the nation's capital as crucial to the movement nationally. O'Connor upbraided the London radicals for their relative inactivity, and complained: 'You are more divided than the Radicals of other places.' He drew particular attention to the prominence of 'that portion of politicians called pocket politicians (that is now the Whig-Radicals)' in London.[126] As in other localities, O'Connor set out to to expose these politicians and to reinvigorate radical agitation. He confronted the Whig-radical 'pocket politicians' at a meeting at the Crown and Anchor called to establish a memorial monument to the Scottish radical martyrs of 1793-94. Joseph Hume was the prime mover in organising this meeting, along with other parliamentary radicals — including Grote, Bowring, Leader, Villiers, Warburton, Molesworth and O'Connell. Accompanied by John Bell, O'Connor disturbed the harmony of this meeting, denouncing the proceedings as calculated to strengthen the Whigs and moving an universal-suffrage motion. Hume, who tried to conceal the fact that the Scottish martyrs had been advocates of universal suffrage and annual parliaments, ruled that O'Connor's motion was outside the purpose of the meeting. The following day Place wrote to Grote denouncing O'Connor and Bell and lamenting their success in turning the artisans at this meeting against the Whig-radical organisers.[127] In early 1837, O'Connor, Bell and O'Brien maintained a constant attack on Whig-radicalism, as a counter to Hume's household suffrage campaign which was based on a policy of continued popular support for the Whig Government. While prepared to accept household suffrage as a significant step towards universal suffrage, they maintained that working-class radicals could support no political party pledged to anything less than universal suffrage.[128] The direction these radical leaders offered was important in sustaining the independence of working-class radicalism.

At the LWMA meetings called to support universal suffrage and Canadian independence, at the third annual dinner on behalf of the Dorchester labourers and at the radical dinner held to celebrate Paine's birthday in his own Hammersmith district, O'Connor took his place among the leaders of metropolitan radicalism. He was also involved in one more pre-Chartist organisation based on London. In March 1837, he joined with O'Brien and Bell to support James Bernard's scheme to unite agricultural labourers, small farmers and urban workers under the auspices of the Central National Association.[129] O'Connor had been associated with Bell since 1833 when he had agitated in defence of the editors of the *True Sun*. Bell had been involved in both the Metropolitan RA and the USC scheme, and both leaders were active in the affairs of the LWMA as honourary members.[130] O'Brien, the most important radical journalist of the 1830s, had also supported O'Connor's organisational initiatives. Following the failure of his own unstamped journal, *Bronterre's National Reformer*, O'Brien became joint editor of Bell's stamped *London Mercury* early in 1837. Around this time O'Connor and O'Brien formed a close friendship and a leadership alliance which was to continue through the early years of Chartism. The clarity of O'Brien's analysis of the sources of economic exploitation within capitalist society, shifting the emphasis away from 'Old Corruption' towards the middle classes and the system of production and exchange, had an important influence upon O'Connor's thinking. However, O'Connor never drew a sharp distinction between the 'old' and 'new' radical ideologies, but rather incorporated aspects from both analyses of exploitation and class power without any apparent sense of contradiction.[131]

The initiator of the Central National Association was James B. Bernard, a Cambridgeshire farmer, Fellow of King's College, Cambridge, and an interesting marginal figure in English radical politics of the 1830s. Not a democrat, he combined ultra-tory attitudes concerning the proper social order with a radical hatred for the monied middle class. The reformed House of Commons was already too democratic for Bernard, as it had allowed the commercial classes to gain political ascendancy. The major practical reform for which he persistently campaigned was a massive currency inflation which held a particular attraction for farmers suffering from high fixed rents and falling wheat prices. By 1837 he was predicting the imminent collapse of the Bank of England as a prelude to social revolution.[132] At first sight, it is difficult to understand the willingness of experienced radicals such as O'Connor, O'Brien and Bell to join forces with Bernard; no doubt his promise of financial aid for the struggling *London Mercury* provides some part of the answer. There was, however, a deeper rationale underlying this alliance. Despite fundamental disagreements, English radicals took Bernard's works — *Theory of Constitution* (1834) and *Appeal to the Conservatives* (1835) — seriously. O'Brien had devoted long series of articles in the *Poor Man's Guardian* to a discussion of Bernard's ideas. While noting 'the strange mixture of radicalism and toryism', he showed respect for Bernard's sincere desire to advance the condition of the working class and for his intellectual capabilities. O'Brien was particularly impressed by his treatment of the system of usury; and although he pointed out difficulties involved in his currency proposals, he found them preferable to Attwood's. The question of money and exchange systems was central to radical economics. The critical indulgence which O'Brien showed towards Bernard stemmed from a mutual identification of the middle class as the main enemy.[133] The willingness of these radicals to cooperate with tory-radicals was the other side to their opposition to 'sham-radicalism' and the 'Malthusian-Whigs'. Furthermore, Bernard's proposed alliance between small farmers, agricultural labourers and urban workers held great attraction for working-class radicals, particularly for London Spenceans like Allen Davenport and Charles Jennison who became CNA members. The vision of the independent toiler of the soil remained a powerful force among urban workers. The CNA also proposed a national organisation at a time when the LWMA was still content to remain an exclusive group of London artisans. Finally, Bernard had come to the realisation that universal suffrage would have to be among the objects of any urban-based radical alliance. Thus there was much that was organisationally and ideologically attractive in the CNA proposal.

The CNA programme included universal suffrage as the means to social reform, and listed the protection of native industry, shorter working hours, the abolition of the new Poor Law and currency reform among its ends.[134] Despite subsequent hostilities, the CNA was not conceived as an organisation antagonistic to the aims of the LWMA. The lack of ideological disagreement is exemplified by the number of radicals who were initially members of both groups — including Vincent, Hartwell, Rogers, Hetherington (for a short while), O'Connor, Bell, O'Brien, Murphy, White. In a letter to the *London Mercury*, O'Brien rejoiced that the CNA boasted 'the elite of the "London Working Men's Association"' among its members.[135] The CNA shared also strong links with O'Connor's earlier radical ventures, and included old allies like Wade, Stallwood and Ross. The parish radicals Murphy and Rogers became the treasurers of the CNA, and T. J. White, still active as secretary of the Lambeth RA, became secretary. It was only after the open clash between the CNA and the LWMA leadership that dual membership became incompatible for LWMA men like White, Vincent and Hartwell who left the CNA. Around June 1837, however, the CNA was reinforced by the active membership of G. J. Harney and his associates from the East London Democratic Association. Mostly former members of the NUWC, they included Thomas Ireland, Charles Neesom, Edward Harvey, Joseph Fisher and Allen Davenport. Formed in early 1837, the ELDA was under the influence of republican and Spencean ideas.[136]

At the centre of the CNA's failure was the distrust many radicals had for the Association's president, a distrust shared by O'Connor. Bernard's toryism and anti-democratic manner alienated support.[137] The hostility of Hetherington and his influential *London Dispatch* also weakened the CNA. Hetherington resigned from the CNA provisional committee over the acceptance to the committee of John Watkins, who had been dismissed as treasurer of the NUWC. The following week the *Dispatch* denounced Bernard and the CNA in an editorial entitled 'A New Attempt at Political Delusion' which dwelt upon Bernard's anti-democratic opinions.[138] With relations between Hetherington and O'Brien already severely strained, an editorial slanging match ensued between the *Dispatch* and *Mercury*. The dispute escalated to the point where the LWMA was under constant attack in the *Mercury*. The LWMA was sharply criticised upon two points: its exclusiveness and its tolerance of middle-class radicals as honourary members who supported the new Poor Law. While the LWMA had condemned the new Poor Law, the Association's policy of cooperating with radicals such as Place, Dr Black, Hume and O'Connell on the basis of broad political principles seemed to provide practical refutation of such condemnations.[139] Thus following the Dorchester labourers dinner at which Hume, Molesworth and Roebuck, as well as O'Connor, were guests of honour, Bell commented:

> It is strange, moreover, that Messrs. Lovett, Vincent, & co., who profess so much anxiety, that *working men should depend on themselves alone* . . . are, somehow or other, always found unable to take any public step, except under the express patronage of Malthusian members of Parliament. For men, indeed, who are so anxious to shake off the degrading dependence of labourers on the wealthy classes, the managers of the machinery of the W.M.A. contrive to look uncommonly comfortable, as they sit, cheek by jowl, at public meetings, with the Malthusian owners of ten thousand a year.[140]

Until the convening of the Chartist Convention in 1839 many radicals, particularly in the North, continued to regard the LWMA as under the control of middle-class 'Malthusians'. Thus if there were few formal ideological differences between the CNA and LWMA, the LWMA's identification with these representatives of middle-class radicalism provided ample scope for suspicion and bitter controversy.

O'Connor's own association with the CNA was one of qualified support and leadership. Certainly he was well disposed towards building an association in London which sought a national character and close links with the anti-Poor Law movement. But although he was obviously prepared to cooperate with tory-radicals, he had little faith in Bernard or his brand of toryism. He was also unwilling to join Bell and O'Brien in open battle against Hetherington and the LWMA. It was not until late 1837, over the Glasgow cotton spinners case, that O'Connor chose openly to shake the LWMA. He was wary of creating irreconcilable splits within the ranks of working-class radicalism; and although many LWMA members, such as Lovett, may have resented his influence, they acknowledged his status as among the most prominent leaders of popular radicalism. His relations with Hetherington remained quite amicable and, unlike Bell and O'Brien, he was treated with respect in the columns of the *Dispatch*. No doubt O'Connor felt disinclined to involve himself in the acrimonious personal dispute between O'Brien and Hetherington, although he certainly shared many of the criticisms voiced in the *Mercury* concerning the political orientation of the LWMA.[141]

Yet despite its shortcomings, the CNA played an important role in establishing national radical links, particularly between the London and northern radicals. Strongly and actively opposed to the new Poor Law, the CNA attracted the interest of northern radical leaders such as Peter Bussey, Joseph Crabtree and John Doherty; and J. R. Stephens was, at least nominally, a member of the CNA provisional committee.[142] In May, O'Connor, Bernard, Bell and O'Brien attended the great Yorkshire anti-Poor Law demonstration, as did Hetherington and Owen. This meeting represented an important coming together of radical forces; the platform at Hartshead Moor reflected a wide spectrum of radical opinion — from the tory-radicalism of Oastler to the socialism of Owen. The CNA leaders — O'Brien, Bell and Bernard — created some dissension by their insistence on the primacy of universal suffrage at an anti-Poor Law meeting. Although he spoke within the spirit of the meeting, establishing historically the working man's right to relief and condemning vigorously the Malthusian 'cant of surplus population', O'Connor also stressed the overwhelming importance of universal suffrage to the working class. He agreed with Owen that it was possible for the people to improve their social condition without the possession of the franchise, but added:

> yet it appears to me to be absolutely necessary for the people to have control over the man who has dominion over his life, his labour and his property. (cheers.) The suffrage, therefore, is the question after all, and I am determined, wherever I meet you, be the subject under consideration what it may, to bring forward the question of Universal Suffrage. (burst of applause, and cries of 'That's it'.) . . .

A large section of the meeting clearly approved of the CNA and O'Connor's efforts to raise the question of political power. The enormous popularity which O'Connor had established in the North was also in evidence. The *Dispatch* reported that his reception 'was indeed most glorious . . . Feargus appears to be the idol of the people of Yorkshire, for no man could have been more enthusiastically received'.[143]

Perhaps most significant was the CNA attempt to offer a national plan for the general election of July 1837. The CNA adopted O'Brien's proposal, whereby radicals throughout the country would propose candidates to stand at the hustings in order to win the show of hands. These candidates would then be considered the 'real' representatives of the people and would assemble in London as a rival body to Parliament. O'Brien's plan was a variation on the concept of the National Convention of the people, deeply rooted in radical ideology, and as such was an important precursor to the establishment of the Chartist National Convention.[144] At the 1837 election O'Connor stood at Preston, O'Brien at Manchester and Bell at Coventry; the CNA also endorsed Oastler at Huddersfield, Stephens at Ashton, Augustus Beaumont at Newcastle, Crabtree at Sheffield and Murphy at Marylebone. O'Brien suggested that other CNA and LWMA members be declared worthy candidates where no local radicals came forward. It was hoped that the general election might thus precipitate a general coming together of radical forces.

O'Brien's plan did not get beyond the first stage in 1837. Success depended upon local radicals throughout the country standing at the hustings and organising support in their districts rather than a few London leaders standing in the provinces. Bell went to the poll and collected a mere forty-three votes in one of the most open constituencies in England.[145] In Hunt's old constituency O'Connor overwhelmingly won the show of hands, but did not go to the poll.[146] At Manchester O'Brien was excluded from the hustings, but following the hustings he and O'Connor addressed the election crowd. O'Brien outlined his plan for establishing a 'People's Parliament'; and O'Connor in an extraordinary speech offered a strong rebuke to the local working class for their conduct at the hustings:

> How . . . can I address you without insulting you? How can I respect you when you will not respect yourselves . . . When a show of hands was taken for Poulett Thomson, almost every hand was held up. What principle — what decency is there in this? Again, you are too prone to treat with levity and mirth the counsels of those who you are assumed are friends. . . . Your moral influence can only be established by straightforward and consistent conduct, and by proper demeanour.[147]

O'Connor was quite prepared to forego the traditional rhetoric of mutual flattery associated with the popular platform, in an effort to dispel working-class political apathy, indifference or levity. From Manchester O'Connor travelled to the West Riding, where there was considerable interest within the RAs in the CNA plans, and where Oastler had only barely lost the Huddersfield election contest. The Huddersfield radicals accompanied Oastler and O'Connor to the West Riding hustings at Wakefield, in order to question the candidates on their attitudes to the new Poor Law and to place O'Connor in nomination, but the nomination proceedings ended in riot.[148]

Following the general election the CNA faded out of existence. However, as the most active London organisation in the agitation against the new Poor Law, in conjunction with its role at the 1837 election, the CNA did make a contribution to the growth of working-class radical national unity. O'Connor was now determined to base

his agitation on the northern districts, convinced that the mass movement for universal suffrage would have to be rolled up to the capital
from the provincial manufacturing districts. He had already launched
plans to establish a radical newspaper based upon the West Riding.
By winter 1837, he dominated the anti-Poor Law platform, alongside
Oastler and Stephens, but always widening the protest to include the
demand for the suffrage.

O'Connor's open break with Lovett and a section of the LWMA
leadership developed over the LWMA's continued cooperation with
middle-class reformers, and centred upon the case of the Glasgow
cotton spinners and the LWMA's relations with O'Connell. In autumn 1837, the members of the Glasgow cotton spinners' committee
went on trial on charges of conspiracy, administering unlawful oaths
and the secret transaction of union business — charges which grew
out of the spinners' strike against a 30-40% wage reduction.[149] The
parallel with the case of the Dorchester labourers was immediately
seized upon by working-class radicals. The case was seen as yet
another confirmation of the Whigs' hostility towards the working
class and their alliance with the industrial bourgeoisie. Together with
the new Poor Law, the case was seen as part of a wider attempt to
create a freer market in labour and to hold down industrial wages.
Moreover, the spinners' case was a more distinctly class issue — one
which served to differentiate working-class radicals from middle-
class liberals — than that of the new Poor Law which had proved
controversial within the middle class itself.[150] There was a sharpening
of class rhetoric. Thus O'Connor declared, in early 1838: 'the RUBI-
CON of profit was between them [the middle classes] and the people'.[151] O'Connor immediately placed himself at the head of the
agitation for the defence of the spinners. He toured the country
rallying support, travelled to Glasgow to attend the trial and gave the
case prominence in his new journal, the *Northern Star*.[152] He called
for the united action of the people of England, Scotland and Ireland,
as they 'are struggling for the same object — the protection of their
labour against the dominion of capital'.[153] O'Connor saw the spinners'
cause as a rallying point around which the entire working class could
unite, and more particularly as illustrative of the need for trade
unionists to abandon their pursuit of sectional interests and turn to
united political action as the only means of defending their rights.

Against this background, the LWMA's alliance with parliamentary
radicals, and especially their continued toleration of O'Connell — an
honourary LWMA member and open critic of trade unionism —

brought rebukes from working-class radicals. The Edinburgh RA respectfully, but firmly, chastised the LWMA for inviting O'Connell to their public dinner in favour of universal suffrage:

> we were astonished, dismayed, and alarmed when we saw your recent invitation to Daniel O'Connell to be your guest at a public dinner, merely because he spouts at his convenience 'universal suffrage', whilst he is the very soul and pillar of those Whigs who would give us UNI-VERSAL BANISHMENT in preference.

And the Surrey RA issued an even more censorious address to their London comrades.[154] The LWMA's policy of cooperation with parliamentary radicals upon the purely political question of universal suffrage was rendered more suspect with O'Connell's proposal of a parliamentary commission to inquire into the practices of trades associations. Within the LWMA Harney struggled unsuccessfully to force the Association to disassociate itself from O'Connell. It was over this issue that Harney, Neesom and Ireland eventually resigned from the LWMA; and in March 1838 formed the rival London Democratic Association with O'Connor's support.[155]

Following the sentencing of the spinners to seven years transportation in January 1838, the LWMA decided to petition Parliament to inquire into trade associations, with the intention of their investigating the proceedings of the spinners' trial. It was over this tactical issue that O'Connor clashed with the LWMA leadership, although underlying this was the more fundamental issue of an alliance between working-class radicals and middle-class reformers. In the light of O'Connell's declared intention to call for an inquiry into trades associations, the LWMA move appeared to play into the hands of those hostile to the very existence of trade unions. At a meeting of the London trades on behalf of the spinners LWMA leaders tried to exclude O'Connor from speaking, on the grounds that he was not a trade union member. At this meeting, however, O'Connor implored unionists

> not to court their own destruction; not to invite a Parliamentary inquiry into the construction, rules, objects and results of Trades Associations . . . once constitute such a tribunal of capitalists, and . . . all the power of selecting evidence to prove order, virtue, and good intentions, would be taken out of the hands of tradesmen. . . . he knew the materials of which Parliamentary Committees were composed.— (Cheers.) It would be the Court in hell, and the Devil the judge.

To London O'Connor brought the defiant tone of the northern platform, bristling with the language of class. He told the meeting that he had 'travelled day and night amongst the real friends of liberty — the working men of Yorkshire and Lancashire'; and sharply criticised 'the London sham radicals' and 'their Parliamentary pets'. 'What have the people ever got by cringing, by going with cap in one hand and petition in the other, a posture beneath the dignity of a freeman . . . ?' O'Connor concluded with the accusation that he had been driven 'from the metropolis to the vallies of Yorkshire' by a 'set of Whig Malthusians, backed by working [class] coadjutors'.[156] The following week, in an open letter to John Fraser, secretary of the Edinburgh RA, he pointed to the LWMA as having taken 'the first step on this deadly course' of establishing a parliamentary committee, and condemned the choice of O'Connell as their parliamentary ally. Lovett defended the LWMA's conduct in a letter to the *Northern Star*, in which he also derided O'Connor's pretensions to leadership, dubbing him 'the great I am of politics, the great personification of Radicalism'. In reply O'Connor recommended 'real working men' to take note of the occupations of those who signed the LWMA letter: 'The greater of those gentlemen . . . belong to the Fine Arts . . . I do more real work in a week than they perform in a year.'[157] The London trades responded to the appointment of a parliamentary commission on trade unionism by appointing their own general committee to watch developments, to which Lovett was chosen secretary.

O'Connor's confrontation with the LWMA should not be construed as a break on his part with wider London radicalism. Under the banner of the anti-Poor Law movement, as champion of the Glasgow spinners' cause and with his newspaper published from Leeds, he propelled himself into the cauldron of northern radicalism. But he left London reluctantly, and dismissed it only as an unsuitable local base from which to organise a mass national movement in 1838. If his future fame as a leader lay in the handloom villages and factory towns of the industrial North and Midlands, O'Connor had established a much respected place for himself within the sphere of London artisan politics. Thus, as I. J. Prothero has noted, the support which O'Connor maintained among London's radical artisans 'casts doubt on the argument that his supporters tended to be deferential'.[158] It was in the Metropolis that he served his political apprenticeship. His association with London's radical artisans was significant for his future Chartist leadership; for the artisan values of independence and respectability, so prominent in London, had a great attraction throughout the industrial districts. Even where many workers' artisan status and way of life had been undermined by factory, sweat shop or the low wages of outwork, this artisan consciousness remained. Nor should O'Connor's early concern for working-class education and self-improvement, expressed during the struggle for a free press, in the attempt to establish the Universal Suffrage Club and in the educational character of the *Northern Star*, go unnoticed. He was always a more complex and wide-ranging radical than is usually acknowledged.

O'Connor was the only London radical leader continually in the industrial North from 1835 to 1838, agitating for an independent working-class movement. In the absence of any national radical organisation his constant touring helped to impart an important sense of national coherence. He was known personally by the most active local radical leaders throughout the industrial districts. The establishment of the *Northern Star*, crucial to the emergence of a national radical movement, developed out of this pre-Chartist agitation. When Cleave and Vincent went north as the representatives of the LWMA in August 1837, and the Birmingham Political Union launched its campaign for the National Petition from Scotland early in 1838, they were building largely upon O'Connor's earlier organisational endeavour. On the northern platform his adherence to a traditional radical programme distinguished him from his fellow anti-Poor Law leaders, Stephens and Oastler, who shared neither his commitment to universal suffrage nor his conception of the establishment of working-class ascendancy. No leader was more important in mediating the juncture between a traditional artisan radicalism and the more spontaneous, mass movement of working-class protest developing in the industrial districts. His insistence on the need for an independent working-class movement, his determined opposition to middle-class 'sham' radicalism and the Whigs, and perhaps most importantly his unshakable confidence in the prospects of radicalism in the years before the flourishing of a mass movement for universal suffrage earned him the respect of local radicals.

> When the working-classes scowled upon him — when the middle-classes insulted him, and the aristocracy endeavoured to destroy his power, he stood it well, and for three years opposed the dominion of faction till at last the millions of England flew to his succour and enabled him to maintain the position he now occupied. [159]

With this tribute George Binns, local Chartist leader, introduced O'Connor to a Sunderland meeting in 1839. The image of the lone champion of radicalism standing firm against hostile class forces was one of O'Connor's favourite. But the powerful impact of this idealised image derived from the real achievement of these years of pre-Chartist leadership.

NOTES

1. 'Homage to Tom Maguire', in A. Briggs and J. Saville (eds.), *Essays in Labour History*, London 1967 ed., p. 314.

2. J. T. Murphy, *Preparing for Power*, London 1972 ed., p. 141.

3. See R.R. Madden, *The United Irishmen, Their Lives and Times*, Dublin, 2nd ed. 1857-60, II, pp. 228-358, 590-612; W.J. O'Neill Daunt, *Ireland and Her Agitators*, Dublin 1845, pp. 121-24; id., *Eighty-Five Years of Irish History, 1800-1885*, London 1886, I, pp. 224-29; F. O'Connor, 'Life and Adventures of Feargus O'Connor . . .', in *National Instructor*, 25 May 1850; D. Read and E. Glasgow, *Feargus O'Connor, Irishman and Chartist*, London 1961, ch. 1; T. Pakenham, *The Year of Liberty*, London 1969, *passim*; F. MacDermont, 'Arthur O'Connor', *Irish Historical Studies*, 15, 1966, pp. 48-69.

4. *NS*, 11 July 1846.

5. M. W. Patterson, *Sir Francis Burdett and His Times, 1770-1844*, London 1831, II, *passim*; Bodleian Library, Oxford, Burdett-Coutts Papers; British Library, Add. MSS 27850, fos. 151 ff.; Add. MSS 27809, fos. 129-46; *Cobbett's Weekly Register*, 14 Apr. 1810, cols. 555-57; 12 May, cols. 721-36; 3 Jan. 1818, col. 6; 17 Jan. cols. 65 ff; O'Connor, 'Life and Adventures', *National Instructor*, 25 May 1850, p. 9; 8 June, p. 41; 15 June, p. 57.

6. Daunt, *Eighty-Five Years*, I, p. 229; *National Instructor*, 29 June 1850, pp. 87-90; 6 July, p. 104; *Dublin Evening Post*, 8 Jan. 1822, p. 4; 15 Jan., pp. 3-4; *Weekly Freeman's Journal*, 19 Jan. 22, p. 3; *Annual Register*, 1822, pp. 9-12, 30-31; G. Broeker, *Rural Discontent and Police Reform in Ireland, 1812-36*, London 1970, pp. 128-37.

7. *A State of Ireland*, Cork, 2nd ed. 1822. According to O'Connor, the first edition was seized and destroyed by the High Sheriff of Cork.

8. British Library, Add. MSS 27818, fo. 492, Hardy to R. O'Connor, 17 June 1822. I am indebted to Dr I.J. Prothero for bringing this reference to my attention.

9. *Southern Reporter*, 3 July 1832, p. 4; 24 Dec., p. 2.

10. *NS*, 9 Nov. 1839, p. 7; *Cork Mercantile Chronicle*, 21 June 1833, p. 3.

11. *National Instructor*, 15 June 1850,p. 58; Read and Glasgow, *O'Connor*, p. 22.

12. *Southern Reporter*, 1 Dec. 1831, pp. 2-3; 6 Dec., p. 4; 30 June 1832, p. 3; 3 July, p. 4; 5 July, p. 1; 27 Oct., p. 2; 30 Oct., p. 3; Daunt, *Eighty-Five Years*, I, pp. 229-32; *National Instructor*, 20 July 1850, pp. 151-54; Read and Glasgow, *O'Connor*, pp. 26-27.

13. Daunt, *Eighty-Five Years*, I, p. 243.

14. *Cork Mercantile Chronicle*, 18 July 1832, p. 3; *Southern Reporter*, 8 Sept. 1832, p. 2; 30 Oct., pp. 2-3; F. O'Connor, *A Letter from Feargus O'Connor, Esq., Barrister-at-Law, To His Excellency the Marquis of Anglesea*, Cork 1832.

15. D. O. Madden, *Ireland and Its Rulers*, London 1843, pp. 179-80.

16. Daunt, *Eighty-Five Years*, I, pp. 237-38.

17. *Southern Reporter*, 28 July 1832, p. 3; 18 Aug., pp. 1-2; 29 Sept., p. 1; 24 Dec., p. 2; 1 Jan. 1833, p. 2; *National Instructor*, 17 Aug. 1850, pp. 201-02; 24 Aug., pp. 215-18.

18. A. MacIntyre, *The Liberator, Daniel O'Connell and the Irish Party, 1830-47*, London 1965, pp. 53-57, 101.

19. *Southern Reporter*, 22 Dec. 1832-1 Jan. 1833; *Freeman's Journal*, 11, 27, 29

Dec. 1832.

20. J. O'Connell, *Recollections and Experiences During a Parliamentary Career from 1833-1848*. London 1849, I, p. 24.

21. E. P. Thompson, *The Making of the English Working Class*, Penguin ed., Harmondsworth 1968, *passim*; A. W. Smith, 'Irish Rebels and English Radicals, 1798-1820', *Past and Present*, no. 7, 1955, pp. 78-85; M. Elliott, 'The "Despard Conspiracy" Reconsidered', *Past and Present*, no. 75, 1977, pp. 46-61.

22. T. Cooper, *The Life of Thomas Cooper*, Leicester 1971 (first published 1872), p. 180.

23. Carlile's *Gauntlet* and *Cosmopolite*, Watson and Cleave's *Working Man's Friend*, and to a lesser extent the *Poor Man's Guardian*, all published Irish news. ·

24. I. J. Prothero, *Artisans and Politics in Early Nineteenth-Century London: John Gast and His Times*, Folkestone 1979, pp. 275, 293-95; P. Hollis, *The Pauper Press: A Study of Working-Class Radicalism of the 1830s*, Oxford 1970, pp. 263-66.

25. *PMG*, 23 Mar. 1833, pp. 91-93; PRO, HO 64/13, fos. 29-48.

26. *PMG*, 18 May 1833; *Cosmopolite*, 18 May 1833; *Working Man's Friend*, 18 May 1833.

27. *Working Man's Friend*, 2-23 Mar. 1833; *Cosmopolite*, 16 Feb.-6 Apr. 1833; *Destructive*, 9 Mar. 1833, p. 47; 6 Apr., p. 78; PRO, HO 64/13-14.

28. *McDouall's Chartist Journal*, 31 July 1841, p. 141.

29. *Freeman's Journal*, 4 July 1833; R. B. McDowell, *Public Opinion and Government Policy in Ireland, 1801-1846*. London 1952, pp. 157-58; MacIntyre, *Liberator*, p. 126.

30. *Southern Reporter*, 15 June 1833, p. 4; *Cork Mercantile Chronicle*, 21, 26 June 1833; F. O'Connor, *A Series of Letters from Feargus O'Connor, Esq., Barrister-at-Law, to Daniel O'Connell*, London 1836, pp. 25-28.

31. *Southern Reporter*, 27 June 1833, p. 2.

32. *Freeman's Journal*, 9 July 1833; *Southern Reporter*, 9 July 1833, p. 2.

33. *PMG*, 15 June 1833, pp. 193-94; *True Sun*, 11 July 1833; *Destructive*, 6, 13 July 1833, pp. 182-84, 187, 191, in which O'Brien was very critical of the O'Connellite position.

34. 10 July 1833, p. 3.

35. Read and Glasgow, *O'Connor*, pp. 34-35, probably overemphasise O'Connor's early opposition to O'Connell, as did O'Connor himself. O'Connell continued to regard O'Connor as a trustworthy, if somewhat rebellious, supporter, at least until early 1834. See W. J. Fitzpatrick (ed.), *Correspondence of Daniel O'Connell*, London 1888, I, pp. 370-72, 391, 412, 429-30.

36. McDowell, *Public Opinion*, ch. 6; A. H. Graham, 'The Lichfield House Compact, 1835', *Irish Historical Studies*, 12, 1961, pp. 209-25; MacIntyre, *Liberator*, pp. 139-46, 152-66; N. Gash, *Reaction and Reconstruction in English Politics, 1832-52*, Oxford 1965, pp. 169-72.

37. O'Connor, *Series of Letters to O'Connell*.

38. See K. B. Nowlan, *The Politics of Repeal: A Study in the Relations Between Great Britain and Ireland, 1841-50*. London 1965, pp. 6-8; E. Larkin, 'Church, State, and Nation in Modern Ireland', *American Historical Review*, 80, 1975, particularly pp. 1245-53; M. Tierney, 'Repeal of the Union', in M. Tierney (ed.), *Daniel O'Connell*, Dublin 1948, pp. 151-70.

39. See, for instance, *Hansard*, Parl. Debates, 3rd Series, XIX, 10 July 1833, cols. 471-72; XXVII, 24 Apr. 1834, col. 1350; *NS*, 31 July 1841, p. 1.

40. *Southern Reporter*, 5 Nov. 1833, pp. 2-3.

41. *Hansard*, Parl. Debates, 3rd Series, XXII, 24 Apr. 1834, col. 1348.

42. *Southern Reporter*, 17 Sept. 1833, p. 2; 2 Sept. 1834, p. 2.

43. See, for instance, *Weekly True Sun*, 3 Nov. 1833, p. 74; *True Sun*, 29 Mar. 1834, p. 2.

44. *Southern Reporter*, 17-29 Aug. 1833; Madden, *Ireland and Its Rulers*, pp.

211-13; *National Instructor*, 13 July 1850, pp. 120-22; 20 July, pp. 135-38.

45. *Southern Reporter*, 18 Dec. 1834-27 Jan. 1834; *National Instructor*, 27 July 1850, pp. 152-54; *Hansard*, Parl. Debates, 3rd Series, XXVI, 4 Mar. 1835, cols. 523-24; *Weekly True Sun*, 28 Dec. 1834, pp. 553-54; 4, 25 Jan. 1835, pp. 561-62, 589; 3 May, p. 699; *Leeds Times*, 9 Jan. 1836, p. 3.

46. *London Mercury*, 28 May 1837, p. 298.

47. *Hansard*, Parl. Debates, 3rd Series, XXII, 24 Apr. 1834, col. 1348.

48. Ibid., XVI, 1 Mar. 1833, col. 19; XVIII, 23 May, cols. 32, 59; 17, 21 June, cols. 905-07, 1024; XIX, 2, 5, 10 July, cols. 36, 255, 463; XXI, 17, 21, 25, 27 Feb. 1834, cols. 445-47, 638-39, 815-16, 926; 4 Mar., cols. 1134-36; XXIII, 22 May, col. 1222; XXV, 21, 23 July, cols. 284, 400-03, 422-23.

49. Ibid., XXIV, 18 June 1834, cols. 541, 544; XXV, 11 Aug. 1834, col. 1224; *Mirror of Parliament*, III, 1834, p. 2278; *NS*, 16 Jan. 1841, p. 7; 21 Feb. 1846, p. 1.

50. *Hansard*, Parl. Debates, XXII, 24 Apr. 1834, col. 861.

51. *Weekly True Sun*, 20 Apr. 1834, p. 265; 4 May, p. 282; O'Connor, *Letters to O'Connell*, pp. 65-66; J. Marlow, *The Tolpuddle Martyrs*, London 1971, pp. 115, 123, 168-69.

52. *True Sun*, 23, 30 May 1833; 22 June; Hollis, *Pauper Press, passim*; J. H. Wiener, *The War of the Unstamped: The Movement to Repeal the British Newspaper Tax, 1830-36*, Ithaca, N.Y., 1969, pp. 163, 240.

53. *Weekly True Sun*, 6 July 1834, p. 354; *NS*, 10 Feb. 1838, p. 3; 8 May 1848, p. 1.

54. *Weekly True Sun*, 9 Mar. 1834, p. 222; 22 June, p. 338; 6 July, p. 358; *Hansard*, Parl. Debates, 3rd Series, XXIV, 4 July 1834, col. 1136; XXV, 23 July 1834, cols. 400-03.

55. *Weekly True Sun*, 22 June 1834, p. 338; also see police report, misfiled in PRO, HO 64/11.

56. *Southern Reporter*, 18 Nov.-16 Dec. 1834; 17-29 Jan. 1835; J. O'Connell, *Recollections*, I, pp. 141-42.

57. *Southern Reporter*, 2-11 June 1835; *People's Press and Cork Advertiser*, 6 June 1835, p. 306; *Journals of the House of Commons*, XC, 9 Mar. 1835, pp. 74-75; 5 June, pp. 393-94.

58. *PMG*, 20 July 1834, pp. 185-88; 9, 16 May 1835, pp. 521-23; 529-32; *Southern Reporter*, 18 Nov. 1834, pp. 203; 22 Nov., p. 4.

59. *Weekly True Sun*, 3 May 1835, p. 698.

60. B. Grime, *Memory Sketches: History of Oldham Parliamentary Elections, 1832-52*, Oldham 1887, pp. 12-22; see especially, J. Foster, *Class Struggle and the Industrial Revolution: Early Industrial Capitalism in Three English Towns*, London 1974, pp. 52-56. I am indebted to Dr Foster for information concerning the 1835 by-election.

61. See *Manchester and Salford Advertiser*, throughout 1834; *Cobbett's Weekly Political Register*, 25 July 1835, cols. 146-47; Oldham Public Library, Butterworth diaries, Mar. 1834-Jan. 1835; also Fielden to Knott, 16 June 1834.

62. *Manchester and Salford Advertiser*, 20 June-11 July 1835; *Manchester Guardian*, 27 June 1835, p. 3; *Cobbett's Weekly Political Register*, 11 July 1835, cols. 67-68; *Leeds Times*, 4 July 1835, p. 3; *NS*, 2 Nov. 1839, p. 4; 16 Jan. 1841, p. 7.

63. Oldham Public Library, Butterworth diaries, 26 June-4 July 1835; *Cobbett's Weekly Political Register*, 11 July 1835, cols. 67-68; *Manchester and Salford Advertiser*, 4 July 1835, p. 3; *Leeds Times*, 11 July 1835, p. 3; *True Sun*, 8 July 1835. G.D.H. Cole commented: 'John Morgan Cobbett was hardly a Radical in any real sense of the word . . .' *The Life of William Cobbett*, London 1947 ed., p. 436. O'Connor's committee agreed to Knight's proposal; Cobbett's refused.

64. *Manchester and Salford Advertiser*, 11 July 1835, pp. 2-3; 25 July, p. 3; 23 Jan. 1836, p. 2; *True Sun*, 8, 9 July 1835; Grime, *Memory Sketches*, p. 26. The division at Oldham between O'Connorites and Cobbettites lasted into the Chartist years.

65. *NS*, 16 Jan. 1841, p. 7; also 26 June, p. 4.

66. *Manchester and Salford Advertiser*, 11 July 1835, pp. 203; *True Sun*, 11 July 1835.

67. *NS*, 4 Dec. 1841, p. 4.

68. Ibid., 20 Jan. 1838, p. 4; 4 May 1839, p. 4; 8 May 1841, p. 7; 8 Apr. 1848, p. 1.

69. British Library, Place Newspaper Collection, Set 70, fos. 211a, 246-47, 262; *Weekly True Sun*, 19 July 1835, p. 792; 9, 16, 30 Aug., pp. 811, 821, 835.

70. F.H.W. Sheppard, *Local Government in St Marylebone, 1688-1835*, London 1958, chs. 16 and 17; J.W. Brooke, *The Democrats of Marylebone*, London 1839; Prothero, *Artisans and Politics*, pp. 272-73; 293; 307-08.

71. *Weekly True Sun*, 20 Sept. 1835, pp. 358-59; *True Sun*, 17 Dec. 1835.

72. *True Sun*, 6 Oct. 1835; *New Moral World*, 10 Oct. 1835, pp. 396-97; *PMG*, 17 Oct. 1835, pp. 704-05; also 24 Oct., p. 714; 5 Dec., p. 763; 12 Dec., p. 778.

73. *True Sun*, 27 Oct. 1835; 2, 18 Mar. 1836; *Cleave's Weekly Police Gazette*, 23, 30 Jan. 1836; 5 Mar.; *Twopenny Dispatch*, 19 Mar. 1836, p. 10; *Radical*, 20 Mar. 1836, p. 16; *True Sun*, 10 June 1836, O'Connor formed the West Middlesex RA, at Brentford. O'Connor later claimed fourteen RAs had been formed in London. *NS*, 16 Jan. 1841, p. 7.

74. I.J. Prothero's work on London working-class radicalism has been indispensible for identifying leading RA members in terms of past political activity and occupation.

75. Hassell was a clerk; Huggett, a carpenter and undertaker; Ross, a journeyman carpenter; Simpson, a painter and glazier; Parker, a tailor; Williams, a journeyman baker.

76. *True Sun*, 9 Dec. 1835; also see British Library, Add. MSS 27791, Lovett to Place, July 1835, on the state of the NUWC.

77. *PMG*, 28 Mar. 1835, p. 480; 18 Apr., p. 504; 30 May, p. 550; 6 June, p. 558; 13 June, p. 566; 1 Aug., p. 622.

78. Macconnell worked on the *True Sun*; Grady was an attorney's clerk; Duffey, a tailor; Hoare, a ladies' shoemaker and Grand Master of the Grand Lodge of Operative Cordwainers.

79. *True Sun*, 23, 30 Dec. 1835; 14 Jan. 1836; 4-18 Feb. Radicals such as Goldspink, Hoare, Prior, a tailor, had been active in the GNCTU; Goldspink, Wightman (secretary of the Westminster RA), William Isaacs (type-founder), Barnes were RA members on the Central Dorchester Labourers Committee; Simpson, who became secretary of the Surrey RA in July 1836, was also secretary of the Walworth Dorchester Committee.

80. *Cleave's Weekly Police Gazette*, 5 Mar. 1836. p. 3.

81. *True Sun*, 12, 19, 29 Jan. 1836; 25 Feb.; 18, 22-23, 29 Mar.; *Cleave's Weekly Police Gazette*, 23 Jan. 1836; 13 Feb.; 5 Mar., pp. 3-4; *Twopenny Dispatch*, 5 Mar. 1836.

82. *Cleave's Weekly Police Gazette*, 9 Apr. 1836, p. 3; 23 Apr., p. 4; *Twopenny Dispatch*, 9 Apr. 1836.

83. *Twopenny Dispatch*, 7 May 1836 (copy in British Library, Place Collection, Set 70, fos. 512-13).

84. *Cleave's Weekly Police Gazette*, 23 Apr. 1836, p. 4.

85. *True Sun*, 22 Apr. 1836, p. 4.

86. *Weekly True Sun*, 29 May 1836, pp. 1149-50; *Radical*, 29 May 1836, pp. 2-3.

87. *Weekly True Sun*, 4 Sept. 1836, p. 1259; 18 Sept., p. 1279; *True Sun*, 13 Oct. 1836, p. 2; *London Dispatch*, 17 Sept. 1836, p. 3; 1-23 Oct., pp. 21, 29, 37, 45; 5-19 Feb. 1837, pp. 163, 173, 182; 11 June, p. 308; *Champion*, 31 Oct.-27 Nov. 1836, pp. 51, 64, 66, 69, 72, 82; 16 Jan. 1837, p. 144; *London Mercury*, 18 Dec. 1836, p. 108; 11 June 1837, p. 305.

88. *London Dispatch*, 22 Oct.-12 Nov. 1837, pp. 461, 469, 486; 17 Dec., p. 527; *NS*, 27 Jan. 1838, p. 5.

89. British Library, Place Collection, Set 70. fo. 493.

90. *True Sun*, 20 May 1836, p. 2.

91. *Radical*, 5 June 1836, p. 5; 12 June, p. 8; 26 June, p. 5; For the 'Address and Rules' of the LWMA, see W. Lovett, *Life and Struggles of William Lovett*, Fitzroy ed., London 1967, (first published 1876), pp. 76-80.

92. British Library, Add. MSS 27819, fos. 21-27, 32-35; Add. MSS 35154, fos. 208-22; Place Collection, Set 56 (1836-June 1838), fo. 63, Russell to Place, 30 June 1836, inviting Place to attend the first USC public meeting; Lovett, *Life and Struggles*, pp. 74-80; *Working Men's Association Gazette*, 1 June 1839, pp. 18-22; *Radical*, 22 May 1836; Prothero, *Artisans and Politics*, pp. 313, 315.

93. *Weekly True Sun*, 4 Sept. 1836, p. 1259; *Cleave's Weekly Police Gazette*, 17 Sept. 1836, p. 4; *London Dispatch*, 17 Sept. 1836, pp. 3-4.

94. D. J. V. Jones, *Chartism and the Chartists*, London 1975, p. 64.

95. *Twopenny Dispatch*, 9 July 1836, p. 3; *Cleave's Weekly Police Gazette*, 2 July 1836; *Radical*, 10 July 1836, p. 3; *Leeds Times*, 30 July 1836, p. 4; *London Mercury*, 9 Mar. 1837, p. 214.

96. Thompson, *The Making*, p. 23.

97. For instance, *London Dispatch*, 29 Jan. 1837, pp. 154-55.

98. R. Johnson, ' "Really Useful Knowledge"; Radical Education and Working-Class Culture, 1790-1848', in J. Clarke, C. Critcher and R. Johnson (eds.), *Working-Class Culture: Studies in History and Theory*, London 1979, p. 101.

99. *Weekly True Sun*, 22 Nov. 1835, p. 932; 29 Nov., pp. 939-40; 13 Dec., pp. 954-56; *Manchester and Salford Advertiser*, 2 Dec. 1835, pp. 2-3; *Leeds Times*, 12 Dec. 1835, pp. 2-3.

100. *Leeds Times*, 26 Dec. 1835, p. 3; 19 Dec. 1835, pp. 3-4; also see *True Sun*, 3 Dec. 1835.

101. *Leeds Times*, 19 Dec. 1835, pp. 3-4; 26 Dec., p. 4; *Manchester and Salford Advertiser*, 19 Dec. 1835, pp. 2-3; 26 Dec., p. 3; *Weekly True Sun*, 3 Jan. 1836, p. 983; 10 Jan., p. 986. In an effort to lend credibility to his plan to return independent radicals to Parliament, at the end of his tour O'Connor announced his intention to stand at the Glasgow by-election, although he later withdrew.

102. *Barnsley Times*, 27 May 1882, p. 3; also see John Jackson, *The Demagogue Done Up*, Bradford 1844, p. 2.

103. *Weekly True Sun*, 31 Jan. 1836, p. 1014; also see the address of the Barnsley radicals, *Leeds Times*, 26 Dec. 1835, p. 4.

104. *Leeds Times*, 26 Dec. 1835, p. 4; also see *True Sun*, 4 Jan. 1836, for the remarks of the veteran radical shoemaker, John Jackson, at Hull.

105. *Manchester and Salford Advertiser*, 19 Dec. 1835-2 Jan. 1836; Oldham Public Library, Butterworth diaries, 25 Dec. 1835; 2 Jan. 1836; *Leeds Times*, 19, 26 Dec. 1835; *Sheffield Iris*, 22 Dec. 1835, p. 3.

106. *Leeds Times*, 9 Jan.-21 May 1836; 30 July, p. 4; *Cleave's Weekly Police Gazette*, 9 Apr. 1836, p. 1; 2 July; *Radical*, 7 Mar. 1836, p. 6; 13 Mar., pp. 6-7; 10 July, p. 3; British Library, Place Collection, Set 70, fos. 414, 550.

107. See *Leeds Times*, Sept. 1837-Apr. 1838; *London Dispatch*, 29 Oct. 1837, p. 460; 5 Nov., p. 471; A. J. Peacock, *Bradford Chartism*, York 1969, pp. 11-14; F. J. Kaijage, 'Labouring Barnsley, 1816-1856; A Social and Economic History' (Warwick Univ. PhD. thesis, 1975), pp. 476-86.

108. Oldham Public Library, Butterworth diaries, 15 Aug. 1836; *Manchester and Salford Advertiser*, 27 Aug. 1836, p. 4; *Twopenny Dispatch*, 27 Aug. 1836, pp. 2-3. For a fuller consideration of O'Connor's relationship with Oastler and Stephens, see below ch. 3.

109. *Leeds Times*, 14 Jan. 1837, p. 8; 21 Jan., p. 6.

110. Ibid., 27 Aug.-17 Sept. 1836; *London Dispatch*, 24 Sept. 1836, p. 11; 8, 16, 30 Oct., pp. 26, 33, 50; *Halifax and Huddersfield Express*, 5 Oct. 1836, pp. 2-3; *Halifax Guardian*, 8 Oct. 1836; D. and E. P. Thompson, 'Halifax as a Chartist Centre', (unpublished paper), pp. 15-16.

111. *London Dispatch*, 20 Nov. 1836, p. 73.

112. Ibid., 27 Nov. 1836, p. 82; 11, 18 Dec., pp. 99, 106; 29 Jan. 1837, pp. 154-55; *Bronterre's National Reformer*, 28 Jan. 1837, p. 30; *Nottingham Review*, 25 Nov. 1836, pp. 1-3; *Glasgow Argus*, 8-26 Dec. 1836; A. Wilson, *The Chartist Movement in Scotland*, Manchester 1970, pp. 33-35.

113. *Leeds Times*, 31 Dec. 1836-21 Jan. 1837.

114. *Pilot*, 12, 24 Aug. 1836; 5 Sept.; *Twopenny Dispatch*, 27 Aug. 1836, p. 3.

115. *London Dispatch*, 17 Sept. 1836, p. 6; 1 Oct., pp. 17-18; 27 Nov., p. 83; *Cleave's Weekly Police Gazette*, 17 Sept.-1 Oct. 1836; *London Mercury*, 18 Sept. 1836, p. 4; 2 Oct., p. 20; 16 Oct., p. 36; 4 Dec., p. 93.

116. I. J. Prothero, 'Chartism in London', *Past and Present*, no. 44, 1969, pp. 90-91; R. O'Higgins, 'The Irish Influence in the Chartist Movement', *Past and Present*, no. 20, 1961, pp. 83-96; J. H. Treble, 'O'Connor, O'Connell and the Attitude of Irish Immigrants Towards Chartism in the North of England, 1838-48', in J. Butt and I. F. Clarke (eds.), *The Victorians and Social Protest*, Newton Abbot 1973, pp. 33-70.

117. *PMG*, 20 July 1834, pp. 185-88; 9, 16, 23 May 1835, pp. 521-23, 529-32, 537-38; 26 Sept., pp. 679-80; 3 Oct., pp. 687-91; *London Mercury*, 18 Dec. 1836, p. 106.

118. *New Weekly True Sun*, 19 Mar. 1836 (copy in British Library, Place Collection, Set 70, fos. 402-06).

119. Of course O'Connell's relationship with the Whigs was more complex and difficult than suggested here.

120. See, for instance, O'Connor's comments on O'Connell, *Leeds Times*, 7 May 1836, p. 4; *True Sun*, 19 May 1836, p. 1; 23 May, p. 1; 8 June, p. 3.

121. *Leeds Times*, 2 Apr. 1836, p. 3; 16 Apr., p. 3.

122. O'Connor, *Letters to O'Connell*, pp. iii-iv, 19-20, 83 ff.; *Factory Question: The Sayings and Doings of Daniel O'Connell*, London n.d.; J. T. Ward, *The Factory Movement*, London 1962, pp. 151-58; *NS*, 7 Nov. 1846, p. 1, 'The Factory Bribe!', is still prominent among O'Connell's political betrayals.

123. *Leeds Times*, 5 Nov. 1836, p. 5; 12 Nov., p. 5; 17 Dec., p. 5; 14 Jan. 1837, p. 8; 21 Jan. p. 6, for the address of the Huddersfield radicals in support of O'Connor; *Manchester and Salford Advertiser*, 24 Sept., pp. 2-3; 24 Dec., pp. 2-3; 31 Dec., p. 2.

124. See his address 'To Irishmen, Women and Children who are residing in England . . .', *London Dispatch*, 24 Sept. 1836, p. 10; and his appeal to the Dublin Trades Council, *Cleave's Weekly Police Gazette*, 1 Oct. 1836, p. 3.

125. See Treble, 'O'Connor, O'Connell and the Attitudes of Irish Immigrants'; O'Higgins, 'Irish Influence in the Chartist Movement'; id., 'Irish Trade Unions and Politics, 1830-50', *Historical Journal*, 4, 1961, pp. 208-17; F. A. D'Arcy, 'The Artisans of Dublin and Daniel O'Connell, 1830-47: An Unquiet Liaison', *Irish Historical Studies*, 17, 1970, pp. 221-43.

126. *London Dispatch*, 29 Jan. 1837, pp. 154-55; also see *London Mercury*, 5 Feb. 1837, p. 163.

127. *London Mercury*, 26 Feb. 1837, p. 190; 5 Mar., p. 196; British Library, Add. MSS 28816, fos. 300-04, Place to Grote, 21 Feb. 1837.

128. *London Mercury*, 29 Jan. 1837, p. 153; 5 Feb., pp. 161, 164-65; *Bronterre's National Reformer*, 18 Feb. 1837, pp. 49-50.

129. *London Mercury*, 19, 26 Mar. 1837, pp. 212, 220-21; *London Dispatch*, 19 Mar. 1837, p. 215.

130. According to Place, however, O'Connor and Bell as gentlemen were considered 'intruders' at LWMA meetings. British Library, Add. MSS 27819, fo. 48.

131. See Hollis, *Pauper Press*, chs. 6 and 7.

132. *PMG*, 12, 19 Sept. 1835, pp. 669, 676-77; *Radical*, 10 July 1836, p. 2; *London Mercury*, 18 Dec. 1836, p. 106.

133. *PMG*, 9, 16, 23 Aug. 1834, pp. 209-11, 217-19, 225-28; 25 July 1835, p. 609; 12, 19 Sept., pp. 663-65, 672-74; 17 Oct., p. 704; also see *Pioneer*, 15 Mar. 1834, pp. 242-43.

134. *London Mercury*, 26 Mar. 1837, p. 212; 2 Apr., p. 228; 18 June, p. 313.

135. Ibid., 26 Mar. 1837, p. 217.

136. *London Mercury*, May-July 1837; A. R. Schoyen, *The Chartist Challenge: A Portrait of George Julian Harney*, London 1958, pp. 14-17; Prothero, *Artisans and Politics*, pp. 313-14.

137. For the views of O'Connor, Wade and Ross, see *London Mercury*, 23 Apr. 1837, pp. 249, 253; 18 June, pp. 313-14; 20 Aug., p. 678.

138. *London Dispatch*, 2 Apr. 1837, p. 225; *London Mercury*, 2, 9, 16 Apr. 1837, pp. 227, 236-37, 241-45.

139. See *London Dispatch* and *Mercury*, Apr.-June 1837; Prothero, *Artisans and Politics*, pp. 320-21. For the personal differences between O'Brien and Hetherington, see British Library of Political and Economic Science, Allsop Collection, O'Brien to Allsop, 29 Nov. 1836.

140. *London Mercury*, 30 Apr. 1837, p. 260.

141. O'Brien later accused O'Connor of joining with Hetherington against the CNA leaders — 'treacherously pretending to be neuter'. British Library of Political and Economic Science, Allsop Collection, O'Brien to Allsop, n.d. (c. Sept. 1847).

142. *London Mercury*, 26 Mar.-23 Apr. 1837.

143. *Leeds Times*, 20 May 1837, p. 8; *London Dispatch*, 21 May 1837, p. 283; *London Mercury*, 21 May-4 June 1837, pp. 284-86, 289, 296, 300. The radical press estimated the attendance to be a quarter of a million. Also on the platform were the anti-Poor Law leaders Fielden, Stephens, Pitkeithley, William Stocks; the socialists Fleming and Alexander Campbell; and working-class radicals like the Bradford woolcomber John Douthwaite and Joseph Crabtree.

144. *London Mercury*, 2, 9, 16 July 1837, pp. 332, 337, 340, 349. For O'Brien's most thorough elaboration of this plan, see *PMG*, 24 Oct. 1835, p. 714.

145. *London Mercury*, 23 July 1837, p. 653; P. Searby, *Coventry Politics in the Age of the Chartists*, Coventry 1964, pp. 12-13.

146. *Preston Chronicle*, 22 July 1837, p. 3; 29 July, p. 2; *Manchester and Salford Advertiser*, 29 July, p. 3; *London Mercury*, 23, 30 July 1837, pp. 653, 667.

147. *Manchester and Salford Advertiser*, 29 July 1837, p. 4.

148. *Leeds Times*, 5 Aug.-2 Sept. 1837; *London Dispatch*, 6 Aug. 1837, pp. 370-71; R. Oastler, *West-Riding Nomination Riot: A Letter to Viscount Morpeth . . .*, London 1837.

149. See W. H. Fraser, 'The Glasgow Cotton Spinners, 1837', in J. Butt and J. T. Ward (eds.), *Scottish Themes*, Edinburgh 1976, pp. 80-97.

150. This points is made very forcefully in R. Sykes, 'Early Chartism and Trade Unionism in South-East Lancashire', forthcoming in D. Thompson and J. Epstein (eds.), *Studies in Working-Class Radicalism and Culture*.

151. *NS*, 10 Feb. 1838, p. 3.

152. Ibid., 6 Jan.-17 Mar. 1838; *Northern Liberator*, 28 Oct. 1837-13 Jan. 1838; *London Dispatch*, 12, 19 Nov. 1837, pp. 486, 494.

153. *NS*, 20 Jan. 1838, p. 4.

154. *London Dispatch*, 19, 26 Nov. 1837, pp. 489, 497, 499; 17 Dec., p. 527; also see *Northern Liberator*, 13 Jan. 1838, p. 2, for Beaumont's attack on the LWMA at a meeting of the Leeds WMA.

155. Schoyen, *Chartist Challenge*, pp. 23-26; British Library, Add. MSS 37773, fos. 85, 87, 90-94, 97-98; Birmingham Reference Library, Lovett Collection, vol. 1, fo. 154, O'Connell to Cleave, 25 Dec. 1837.

156. *NS*, 10 Feb. 1838, p. 3.

157. *NS*, 17 Feb.-10 Mar. 1838. It should be noted that the LWMA gave its unqualified support to the spinners and was in close contact with their leaders. See British Library, Place Collection, Set 52.

158. Prothero, 'Chartism in London', p. 86.

159. *NS*, 29 June 1839, p. 1.

2 THE *NORTHERN STAR*

The first edition of the *Northern Star and Leeds General Advertiser* was published on 18 November 1837, with Feargus O'Connor as proprietor, Joshua Hobson as printer and publisher, and the Rev. William Hill as editor.[1] Together with the platform, the *Northern Star* provided the essential medium of national communication and organisation for the Chartist movement. The *Northern Star* was the most important agency for the integration and transformation of disparate local radical agitation and organisation into the national Chartist movement. Throughout the Chartist period the *Star* gave local working-class protest a national focus. It brought national perspective to the localities and gave local radicalism national coverage.

For O'Connor the establishment of the *Northern Star* marked the all important convergence of the powers of the press with those of the platform. By early 1837, he was unable to depend upon press coverage commensurate with his continual radical touring. In reply to a request for a report of his latest northern tour from Bronterre O'Brien's short-lived *National Reformer*, O'Connor noted:

> the fact of being obliged to apply to me, is a very severe sarcasm upon the press, because, if I had been a beardless Tory, or a doating old Whig, every particular of my down-laying and up-raising, would have been a matter of importance: but as I represented feelings, which the united tyranny of both cannot suppress, silence became necessary.[2]

The *Star* became the means through which he broke that silence. Probably no circumstance was more important to O'Connor's eventual establishment of an unrivalled Chartist leadership than his ownership of the movement's newspaper.[3]

The *Star* was the direct heir to a tradition of popular democracy pioneered in the pages of the radical unstamped press.[4] Through his defence of the editors of the *True Sun* while MP for County Cork, and most significantly through his leadership of the Metropolitan Radical Associations during the final stages of the struggle of the unstamped press, O'Connor had already demonstrated his concern for the creation of a free and radical working-class press. The 'pauper press' had been extinguished by the Whig Government's reduction of the newspaper stamp in 1836 which had been accompanied by provisions for the more stringent suppression of illegal journals. Thus the *Northern*

Star was a stamped newspaper; its price was 4½d. While fully exploiting the advantages which the stamp conferred — principally free postal delivery and the legal publication of news — the *Star* incorporated the ideology and much of the spirit and personnel of the unstamped, along with a readership which the unstamped had helped to educate. The remaining penny stamp was a symbol which divided the middle and working classes. The *Star* succinctly summed up the situation: 'The reduction upon the stamps has made the rich man's paper cheaper, and the poor man's paper dearer.'[5] In his introductory address to readers of the *Star*, O'Connor immediately drew their attention to the paper's stamp:

> Readers — Behold that little red spot, in the corner of my newspaper. That is the Stamp; the Whig *beauty* spot; your *plague* spot. Look at it: I am entitled to it upon the performance of certain conditions: I was ready to comply . . . for the present suffice to say, — there it is — it is my license to teach.[6]

Thus, from the outset, O'Connor placed both his paper and himself within the context of a rich tradition of radical consciousness concerned with the working class's acquisition and control of their own channels of learning and communication.

Historians of the Chartist movement have offered a less generous view of both O'Connor and his paper, criticising the manner in which the *Star* was established and O'Connor's subsequent control. It has been claimed that not only was O'Connor's control narrow and undemocratic and his financial contribution negligible, but that he also perverted the paper's original platform and even plundered the idea of starting a journal.[7] Despite such views, there is evidence to support a more sympathetic picture of O'Connor in the role of newspaper proprietor, a picture which also helps to support an impression of a more democratic relationship between O'Connor and the Chartist rank and file. A careful study of the history of the *Northern Star* throws light upon a range of key questions relating to national Chartist leadership, organisation and culture.

I The Establishment of the *Northern Star*

O'Connor first broached the subject of establishing a radical paper in the North to Joshua Hobson, the radical printer of Leeds and veteran of the unstamped, at the anti-Poor Law meeting on Hartshead Moor, in May 1837.[8] A few days later, O'Connor visited Hobson in Leeds to outline his plans for such a paper and formally to propose that Hobson be publisher and printer. O'Connor was staggered, however, when Hobson told him that no provincial printer had the machinery required to produce the kind of paper intended, nor would any risk the initial outlay necessary on a paper which might quickly fail. O'Connor had, therefore, to decide whether to abandon the idea and have the paper printed in London, or to produce the funds needed to launch such an expensive project in the North. Within a few weeks he returned to Leeds to inform Hobson that he was determined to proceed with the plan as conceived, and asked Hobson to suggest an editor. Hobson named the Rev. William Hill, the radical Swedenborgian minister at Hull, who was eventually hired. Throughout these negotiations, O'Connor had given the impression of a gentleman who could afford to sustain the capital costs involved.

Only after the scheme was well off the ground, the print having been delivered and the press under construction in London, did O'Connor suggest his plan for raising £800 in one pound shares on his own security with a fixed dividend of 10%. O'Connor maintained that this would involve other radicals whose interest would help ensure the paper's initial success. The campaign was opened at Hull, where Hill was able to transfer funds raised for an earlier newspaper project of his own to the cause of the *Star*. John Ardill, the *Star*'s clerk and bookkeeper, was able to secure funds in Leeds and Halifax; at Bradford Peter Bussey helped raise funds; and Lawrence Pitkeithley stirred up Huddersfield. O'Connor campaigned throughout the West Riding and South Lancashire with his usual zeal in the cause of the new journal. Eventually £690 was raised, of which about £500 came from Leeds, Halifax, Hull, Bradford and Huddersfield. Money was also raised at Oldham, Ashton-under-Lyne, Rochdale, Keighley and Barnsley.[9] With constant work and little sleep the *Star*'s first edition of three thousand copies was published. 'The first week we could have sold three times three thousand, but we had not the stamps to print more,' wrote Hobson. Within four weeks the *Star* was a profitable concern, and within little over a year it was the most widely circulated provincial paper in the land.[10]

O'Connor's contribution to the establishment of the *Star* has been both undervalued and seriously misunderstood. A major criticism has been that while providing no financial support for the *Star*, O'Connor manipulated the people's funds to his own designs. Most probably, O'Connor found costs for such an ambitious venture higher than anticipated, and saw the share scheme as a quick way to raise funds and involve leading local radicals. Almost certainly £690, the sum raised in shares, was not enough to launch a paper like the *Star*. By 1837 Hetherington's *London Dispatch* press was worth £1,500 alone, according to O'Brien.[11] Although O'Connor may well have exaggerated his initial outlay on the *Star*, there seems little reason to doubt that he invested a considerable sum in its establishment, and no reason to believe that he had no capital to advance.[12] Controversy over financial matters was endemic to a movement as large and often divided as the Chartist movement. The question of the financing of Chartist agitation raises broader issues concerning the nature of Chartist organisation and leadership. The legitimacy of O'Connor's own leadership depended upon his ability to maintain his position as an independent gentleman of the platform and on his repeated boast that 'I never would travel a mile at your expense, or accept a farthing for any poor service which I may be able to render your cause.' The importance of the claims and counter-claims concerning O'Connor and the financing of the 'people's paper' can only be understood within this context.

Whatever O'Connor's direct financial contribution to the *Star*, his importance to its successful establishment is beyond doubt. It is apparent that the money raised through shares was extended on the basis of O'Connor's own financial security and high-standing within the ranks of the northern radicals. Furthermore, considering the careers of almost all other radical working-class or Chartist papers, there was the prospect of a long period of losses before the paper would break even or show a slight profit. The phenomenal success of the early years of the *Star* was the exception to the rule. O'Connor later pointed out that he had expected and had been willing to lose ten pounds a week on the *Star*, which was the sum Hobson, Hill and he had estimated would be lost. When the *Star* proved the most successful paper in the country, the profits were spent on agitation: 'every £10 made, was spent in travelling, agitating, donations, sub-scriptions . . . in the support of the cause'.[13] Nor were the sharehold-ers dissatisfied with the arrangements or the management of the paper.[14] At the end of 1838, O'Connor offered to buy up any shares.[15] The fact that the *Star* was not run by a committee of shareholders did not necessarily mean it was subject to less popular control. O'Connor may have correctly believed that this was neither the most efficient form of management nor the most effective manner of public control. Before it folded in 1840, the London-based, 'moral-force' *Charter*, which was organised upon a joint stock committee basis, attributed its failure to this form of organisation.[16]

If O'Connor had to pose as a man of greater wealth than he was, if he had to incur debts which might have been difficult to repay, if he had to use some Irish bluff and charm, the fact remains that he launched one of the great radical journals of British history. O'Connor was a shrewd leader who saw the imperative need for a national newspaper of the working class. He knew the North and its people, he recognised the problems inherent in organising from London, and he deduced from where he could launch a successful working-class paper. 'Never was a journal started more opportunely. It caught and reflected the spirit of the times.'[17]

The foundation of the *Northern Star* grew out of the general desire of the leading radicals of the West Riding and South Lancashire to reflect the growing militancy of the northern working class, spread the resistance to the new Poor Law and propagate the principles of traditional radicalism. The radicals at Ashton-under-Lyne welcomed the new paper, as they believed it to be:

> highly desirable that the lovers of freedom, throughout the British dominions, should have some common rallying point for the muster of their forces — some common organ for the expression of their otherwise isolated opinions and wishes which might bestow upon them that influence and power which are only to be derived from unity and concentration, and without which all our efforts will be unavailing.[18]

For O'Connor the project marked the culmination of two years of agitation in London, the North of England and Scotland attempting to bring some general coherence to local protest and radical organisation. The establishment of the *Star* was crucial to the generalisation of local radical agitation. As O'Connor observed:

> Antecedently to the establishment of the *Star*, local opinion was organised at great personal expense, and with much labour and uncertainty. Grievances were matter of mere oral tradition; and local grievances were resisted by the brave in their respective neighbourhoods at great risk. STEPHENS was not known beyond the narrow limits of a portion of Lancashire, and even there, not truly known; his eloquence astounded the ear, but never reached the hearts of those who heard not. . . . OASTLER reigned in the hearts of those within his narrow circle; but how much has the *Star* increased its circumference? BUSSEY was but known to Bradford. PITKEITHLEY . . . could see at one glance the limits of his influence. FLETCHER was buried. SANKEY was unheard of. MACDOUALL would have remained unknown. FROST would

never have been heard of. O'CONNOR would have been prematurely
consigned to the grave from over-exertion. The talents of HILL . . .
would have smouldered in the pulpit, and the immediate precincts of
his own locality; and many others would have died unknown . . . had it
not been that all were here represented in one common mirror, truly
reflected.[19]

O'Connor was not the only radical leader who felt the need for a
newspaper in order to intensify and coordinate the rising tide of
working-class protest. Over a year before the first edition of the *Star*,
William Hill had attempted to start a paper at Hull along with a group
of local working men.[20] O'Connor frequently spoke at meetings with
Hill, and not only knew about the scheme but supported it. Both men
were in contact with the same groups of northern radicals. Around
the same time that O'Connor approached Hobson with his idea for a
newspaper, Hobson was himself planning an Oastlerite journal to be
called *The Justifier*, as an alternative to the middle-class radical *Leeds
Times*.[21] The impression has been given that O'Connor merely took
over a scheme of Hill's based firstly upon Hull and then Barnsley. But
there is no reason to confuse the two newspaper projects, nor propagate debates as to whether O'Connor took over Hill's initiative.[22]
Obviously Hill, O'Connor and others were thinking along similar
lines. However O'Connor's plan was of a different order from Hill's.
Whereas Hill's plan was local, the novelty of O'Connor's conception
was that of founding a national working-class organ outside London,
basing a national paper in a local radical stronghold and using it to
mobilise a movement. From the outset O'Connor envisaged something greater than a provincial paper. 'The *Northern Star* is not, nor
was it ever intended to be, *a mere Leeds paper*. 'Tis a national organ;
devoted to the interests of Democracy in the fullest and most definite
sense of the word; and it is, consequently, supported by every true
Democrat in every place where it became known.'[23]

Indeed it is difficult to point to any other radical leader besides
O'Connor who combined the qualities necessary for the establishment of a paper like the *Star* by late 1837. He had been agitating the
country for two years upon radical principles; had won the confidence
of key radical leadership in the most important localities; had been a
thoroughly radical MP. He was a gentleman of some wealth, a personal friend of Oastler and part of the platform triumvirate who fired
the anti-Poor Law movement, while adhering to the primacy of the
traditional radical demand for universal suffrage. Both Hill and

Hobson later paid tribute to O'Connor's crucial role in the launching of the *Star*.[24]

The success of the *Star* depended upon the active support of a group of northern radicals largely centred on the towns and villages of the West Riding of Yorkshire. These were men with whom O'Connor had shared platforms, organised meetings and discussions, and cooperated in founding Radical Associations. From Huddersfield, not only could O'Connor rely upon the support of Oastler and Hobson, but experienced radicals such as Lawrence Pitkeithley, John Leech, Chris Tinker, Stephen Dickenson; from Leeds George White and William Rider; at Bradford Peter Bussey, John Jackson, Samuel Bower, John Douthwaite, James Ibbetson; at Halifax Henry Rawson, William Thornton, Ben Rushton, Robert Sutcliffe, Robert Wilkinson, Thomas Cliff; and at Dewsbury the veteran T. S. Brooke. Barnsley was already the strongest centre of O'Connorite support by 1837. Here O'Connor called upon the support of the Radical Association, led by such men as Peter Hoey, Joseph Crabtree, Joseph Lingard, Aeneas Daley, George Utley, and the veteran radicals John Vallance and Arthur Collins. It may have been O'Connor's original intention to start his paper from Crabtree's large room in Barnsley.[25] O'Connor also looked to South Lancashire contacts for assistance — J. R. Stephens at Ashton, Manchester friends such as the old Huntites James Wheeler and the Rev. James Scholefield. At Oldham Jessie Ainsworth and James Holladay, both members of O'Connor's Oldham election committee in 1835, became the *Star*'s two sureties, and England's 'oldest radical' John Knight became a regular correspondent until his death in 1838.[26] These were just some of the men who since 1832 had been leading the opposition to the Whigs. They had taken prominent part in the unstamped agitation, the defence of the trade unions, the ten-hours movement, the anti-Poor Law agitation and all aspects of local radicalism. It was this group of leaders who linked the struggles of 1832-38 and earlier traditions to Chartism. We can only begin to suggest the enormous contribution in terms of political experience and radical tradition which such men brought to Chartism. To these radicals O'Connor appealed with his newspaper scheme, not only to take up shares, but for propaganda, reports of meetings, agencies of distribution and organisation. Thus the foundations of the *Star* cannot be divorced from O'Connor's earlier radical involvement. In its establishment and initial success can be seen the fruits of several years hard work during the pre-Chartist years which coincided with the aims and activities of many local radicals, especially in the North.

Although the conception of the *Star* was national, it needed a strong local base from which to grow. Leeds and the surrounding district provided such a base. Joshua Hobson's unstamped *Voice of the West Riding*, published from Huddersfield, 1833-34, had drawn on the same areas for support. Almost half the *Star*'s early circulation of over 10,000 copies a week came from Leeds, Bradford, Halifax and Huddersfield.[27] Hobson's *Voice of the West Riding* was an important precursor to the *Star*. 'Its tone was one of extreme class animosity. . . . And in the area of political and social criticism, the *Voice* anticipated "physical force" Chartism . . .'[28] Hobson's earlier journal had been a vital experience in the development of West Riding radicalism, and Hobson's association with O'Connor's new paper, along with that of William Rider who had worked on the *Voice* during Hobson's spells in prison, was no doubt important in securing the allegiance of the West Riding radicals.

The publication of the *Star* coincided with the height of popular resistance to the new Poor Law in the North. This was reflected in both its early circulation pattern and content. South Lancashire provided the other main area of anti-Poor Law protest and early support for the paper. The case of the Glasgow spinners was the other prominent issue which filled the early columns of the *Star*. O'Connor had put himself at the head of both protests, alongside Oastler and Stephens.[29] There was considerable truth in the claim that O'Connor owed the initial success of the *Star* to his reporting of the speeches of Stephens and Oastler.[30] Although the *Leeds Times* and the *Manchester and Salford Advertiser* carried anti-Poor Law news, both middle-class radical papers were exhibiting an increasing alienation from the rhetoric of violence used by the leaders of the anti-Poor Law movement, especially the speeches of Stephens.[31] In contrast, the *Star* filled its pages with the blood-curdling exhortations of Ashton's 'political preacher' and the intimidating letters of the 'Factory King'. Although this helped to sell papers, it was also hazardous. Publishing the revolutionary utterances of Oastler and Stephens was a bold act. By the third edition, Lord John Russell was considering prosecuting O'Connor for the publication of seditious libel.[32] Despite this coverage, the *Star* was never intended principally as a journal of the anti-Poor Law movement, nor was it. Unlike Oastler and Stephens, the *Star* and O'Connor always supported a wider and more traditional radical programme headed by the demand for universal suffrage. For this reason, O'Connor and the *Star* were crucial agents in transferring

the energy of the anti-Poor Law agitation into Chartism.[33] In the early
months of 1838, Hill's editorials, O'Brien's weekly letters and O'Connor's speeches all reiterated the need for working-class unity behind
the single demand for universal suffrage.

II The 'People's Paper' and the Chartist Movement

(i) *The* Star *and its Readers*

In terms of circulation the *Star* was almost an immediate success. By
26 December 1837, they were receiving a regular weekly supply of
10,000 stamps. By the end of 1838, the *Star* had established itself as
the most widely circulating provincial paper in Britain.[34] The arrest of
J. R. Stephens and the gathering of the Convention in the early
months of 1839 increased sales still further.[35] In the hectic weeks
following the Bull Ring Riots at Birmingham, in July 1839, with the
prospect of a call for a national general strike from the Chartist
Convention, sales perhaps reached 50,000 copies a week.[36] No radical
journal since Cobbett's *Twopenny Trash*, with the possible exception
of the 1d *Cleave's Weekly Police Gazette* in 1836, had reached this
number of people.[37] Certainly no working-class newspaper had ever
had so large a circulation. Sales were so great that 'the Post Office
authorities were in some cases obliged to hire carts or wagons for its
transmission, as it occasionally overflowed the restricted accommodation of the mail coaches'.[38] R. J. Richardson's Salford shop was
'thronged on Saturday, as there is upwards of *300 Northern Stars
sold*'.[39] Although sales never reached the level of 1839 again, the *Star*
was always a paper which depended upon high sales.[40]

Circulation figures, however, give an inadequate measure of either
the influence or total readership of the *Star*. The *Star* was available at
clubs and working-class reading rooms, radical coffee houses and
Chartist taverns; copies were passed between friends; radicals combined to subscribe and have their copy read aloud at home, in the
workshop or at meetings. It is obvious from the highly rhetorical style
of the *Star*'s lead articles that the paper was designed to be read
aloud. It is impossible to estimate accurately how many people read
or heard the *Star* read. For the unstamped — cheaper than the
Star — a ratio of twenty readers to every copy has been suggested.[41]
In 1838, O'Brien referred to the paper's 'ten thousand subscribers,
and your one hundred thousand readers'; and by April 1839, the *Star*
claimed 400,000 readers.[42] In terms of distribution, the *Star* was

successful in creating a national audience in less than a year. From the list of agents, reports of meetings and letter columns the national growth of the paper can be followed.[43] The appeal was direct: 'Let every town briefly address the country through the medium of the *Northern Star,* and let one and all know our strength, our union, and our determination to die freemen rather than live slaves.'[44] Unfortunately it is impossible to discover the number of copies sent to each district. But the North was by no means the only stronghold. James Guest, Birmingham's radical bookseller and veteran of the un-stamped, regularly received three thousand copies a week for the Birmingham area for about three years, and sometimes received as many as six to seven thousand copies.[45] Improved transport facilities helped the *Star* create a national character. The *Star,* printed on Saturday, claimed that it could be delivered in London the same evening.

The readership of the *Star* was almost entirely working class. Great pride was taken in this readership:

> It is true that the greater part of our readers are to be found in the humble and useful classes of society. We rejoice to think that it is so. We claim no alliance with any other 'system' — we wish not to move in any other 'orbit' — the *Northern Star* is their luminary, and sincerely do we thank them for having made it shine so brilliantly.[46]

The tone of the paper was stridently class conscious; the language was the razor-sharp rhetoric of class war. The *Star* filled a radical working-class cultural and educational gap, left partially by the fall of the 'pauper press'. It inherited part of its readership, discovered a part and also helped to create its own new readers. The *Star* did not write down to its readers, quite the reverse. It was a serious political journal written by highly skilled journalists. On occasion the education of many an artisan or factory hand must have been taxed in reading its pages. The *Star* was the major institution of Chartist education.

Equally, the *Star*'s readers took pride in its successes, for instance at the well-publicised point at which its circulation surpassed that of its neighbour and arch-rival, the Whig *Leeds Mercury.* Having their own paper was essential to the working-class struggle for a form of cultural independence and control. O'Connor urged a Liverpool meeting to 'never drink a drop of beer where the *Mercury,* or *Sun,* or *Times,* or *Chronicle* were taken . . .' And James Woodhouse, frame-work knitter and Nottingham delegate to the first Chartist Convention, told a meeting in 1840:[47]

> Do without your pint of ale, but buy the *Star;* refrain from drinking spirits, but buy the *Star;* refrain from using tea and coffee and sugar, but buy the *Star;* and avoid the use of all excisable articles, but buy the *Star;* and lessen the value of household property, at least one-half, but buy the *Star.*[48]

The arrival of the *Star* was an important weekly event. Samuel Fielden, the American anarchist, remembered from his early days in Todmorden, his father, 'an earnest champion and admirer of the principles advocated by . . . Feargus O'Connor', relating, 'that on the day when the newspaper, the *Northern Star,* O'Connor's paper, was due, the people used to line the roadside waiting for its arrival, which was paramount to everything else for the time being'.[49] For many working-class radicals O'Connor's weekly letter was the highpoint of the week. W. E. Adams recalled:

> Another early recollection is that of a Sunday morning gathering in a humble kitchen. The most constant of our visitors was a crippled shoemaker . . . Larry . . . made his appearance every Sunday morning, as regular as clockwork, with a copy of the *Northern Star,* damp from the press, for the purpose of hearing some member of our household read out to him and others 'Feargus's letter.' The paper had first to be dried before the fire, and then carefully and evenly cut, so as not to damage a single line of the almost sacred production. This done, Larry, placidly smoking his cutty pipe, which he occasionally thrust into the grate for a light, settled himself to listen with all the rapture of a devotee in a tabernacle to the message of the great Feargus, watching and now and then turning the little joint as it hung and twirled before the kitchen fire, and interjecting occasional chuckles of approval as some particularly emphatic sentiment was read aloud.[50]

The Sunday morning reading of the *Star,* and the informal discussions and debates which arose from its contents, were regular affairs to which thousands looked forward. Ben Brierley, in his youth a handloom weaver of velvet in the South Lancashire village of Failsworth, later wrote:

> The *Northern Star,* the only newspaper that appeared to circulate anywhere, found its way weekly to the Cut side, being subscribed for by my father and five others. Every Sunday morning these subscribers met at our house to hear what prospect there was of the expected 'smash-up' taking place. It was my task to read aloud so that all could hear at the same time; and the comments that were made on the events foreshadowed would have been exceedingly edifying to me were I to hear them now.

These morning readings were followed by afternoons spent turning

his father's grindstone, 'whilst rebelliously-disposed amateur soldiers ground their pikes'.[51] From near-by Oldham, Benjamin Grime
reminisced:

> Very distinctly does the writer remember going weekly on Saturdays,
> from North Moor, across Tommyfield, to 'Owd Knight's,' for a copy of
> the *Northern Star*, which was the joint property of his father and a few of
> the neighbours. The paper would then be read in some retired place, on
> the grass if in summer, or it would be read over the 'tot of whoam-
> brewed' at some of the hush shops which could then be found in every
> street within a few yards of each other.[52]

Ben Wilson of Halifax recalled: 'Amongst combers, handloom weavers, and others politics was the chief topic. The *Northern Star* was the
principal paper, and it was common practice, particularly in the
villages to meet at friends' houses to read the paper and talk over
political matters.'[53] The *Star* was also taken into the workshop. Daniel
Merrick, a Leicester stockinger, described the atmosphere of a knit-
ters' workshop where 'politics were the general theme for discussion
and conversation'. The customary tea break provided an opportunity
for reading and discussion.

> Some would seat themselves on the winders' stools, some on bricks, and
> others, whose frames were in the centre, would sit on their 'seat boards'.
> Then they would commence a general discussion upon various matters,
> political, moral, and religious. After tea a short article would be read
> from the *Northern Star*, and this would form the subject matter for
> consideration and chat during the remainder of the day.[54]

Wherever ultra-radical politics were discussed the *Star* could be
found.

Although a serious political paper, the *Star* adopted some of the
techniques of the popular/cheap press, principally woodcuts and
steel-engraved portraits.[55] A great success was the series of portraits
called the 'Portrait Gallery of People's Friends' which included An-
drew Marvell, Arthur O'Connor, Hunt and Cobbett, along with the
heroes of Chartism. A portrait was distributed free with a copy of the
paper, to be hung in working-class homes or used to decorate Chartist
meeting rooms. Such souvenirs were remembered by Chartists like
W. E. Adams: 'One of the pictures that I longest remembered . . . was
a portrait of John Frost . . . I have been familiar with the picture since
childhood, and cherish it as a memento of stirring times.'[56] There
were other 'give-aways' from the *Star*, like the O'Connor Liberation
Medals to be distributed with the paper at the slightly higher price of
6½d to commemorate the freedom of the 'People's Champion' from

York Castle. It was acknowledged that such gifts boosted sales.[57]

The relationship between the *Star* and its readers was close and the channels of communication were two way. 'If we were to print all the communications we receive, we should, some weeks, want six or seven *Northern Stars*,' commented Hill.[58] Communications were often received from modest working men who were unaccustomed to addressing journals. John Walker rather apologetically concluded his report of the formation of a Working Men's Association in the South Lancashire village of Mossley: 'Gentlemen, as I never attempted to write to public men before, be so kind as to correct my blunders, and let it appear in your "*Star*".'[59] Letters often ended with an expression of gratitude for the space made available by the *Star*, 'the only medium of expression' — the same phrase so often used in letters to the unstamped. Poems were especially popular. 'We have received as much poetry as a donkey could draw; we shall select from it as occasion offers, so let none be jealous, or we will take it by lot.'[60] Chartist readers were not merely passive recipients of knowledge and news. They were part of the learning process and news-collecting force. It was this involvement which was the format of the *Star*'s style of popular democracy. This popularity was not largely dependent on the paper's ability to flatter readers. In the column headed 'To Readers and Correspondents' working-class enthusiasts were rather harshly reminded that their letters were sometimes 'illiterate', often of no general interest, 'overstrained', or had 'not the poetic merit to stand the ordeal of criticism'.[61] The columns of the *Star* were founded neither upon flattery nor strict O'Connorite censorship.

The *Star* was more than a political paper. It was part of a much larger Chartist cultural experience. It was central to most local Chartist activity. Toasts were drunk to the *Northern Star* and the freedom of the press, votes of confidence and thanks were passed at meetings for its services, at mass rallies banners celebrated its name, on the anniversary of its establishment dinners were dedicated to its continued success. Chartist meetings often started with readings from the *Star*, usually the lead editorial or O'Connor's letter, followed by a thorough discussion of the issues raised. By early 1838, the Mossley WMA announced that they had procured their own reading room, 'where they assemble to read the *Northern Star*, and other newspapers'.

> We have no secrets; we admit any body, whether they are members or not; we read the news of the week, and discuss it paragraph by paragraph, as it is read. We have a good fire in the room, and so it is that we

spend our leisure hours, without ever coming in contact with drunkenness or immorality.[62]

Other localities established *Northern Star* reading societies.[63] For
most localities, with no local press or only a hostile press, the *Star*
took on a great significance through reporting a wide variety of local
activity. Even in the exceptional circumstances where a group of local
Chartists produced their own paper, it was often regarded as an
adjunct to the *Star* rather than as a substitute.[64]

For distribution the *Star* depended largely on existing local radical
booksellers and newsagents. Again the debt to the earlier struggles
for a free press is apparent. Many of these agents were veterans of the
war of the unstamped. At Ashton-under-Lyne, Joshua Hobson, one
of the town's oldest and most respected radicals, a republican and
infidel who had sold Carlile's *Republican* and *Lion* before he took
Hetherington's *Poor Man's Guardian* and *Dispatch*, became the
local agent.[65] At Oldham, the position quite naturally fell to 'Owd'
John Knight. Indeed the *Star*'s early list of agents reads like a
catalogue of victims of the unstamped.[66] In London, the *Star* was sold
at the shops and radical coffee houses established before and during
the unstamped agitation. John Cleave was the main distributor for
London, Abel Heywood for the Manchester area and Hobson for
Leeds. At Birmingham, James Guest, radical and Owenite who
claimed to have been the first man to sell the unstamped in Birmingham when he sold *Carpenter's Political Letter* in 1830 from his
'Cheap Book Repository', became O'Connor's agent.[67] Mrs. Smith,
whose husband was imprisoned in 1836 for selling the unstamped,
made the *Star* available in Nottingham at the 'Tradesmen's Mart'.[68]

The agent could also fulfil the role of organiser. Sometimes a local
working-class radical through a combination of reporting and selling
the *Star* could establish enough financial independence to free himself for full-time Chartist agitation. Such was the case for John Deegan, ex-card-room hand and secretary of the Stalybridge Radical
Association.[69] When an existing agent could not be found to sell the
Star, a local radical would take on the job. Thomas Dunning, a
Nantwich shoemaker and leading local trade unionist, related how he
became an agent for the paper:

> I and a dozen or more of my radical associates wished to subscribe to the
> *Star*, and I being secretary of our Chartist association, was requested to
> order of Mr. Griffiths, bookseller, the only newsagent in the town at the
> time, the required number of *Stars*. I requested Mr. G. to supply me
> with fifteen copies of the *Northern Star* weekly, and for which I offered

to pay him a quarter of a year in advance. He declined taking the order in a most contemptuous manner, with, 'Oh! Ah! a Radical paper, I believe. I am a stamp officer and will not order it, etc.' . . . On Mr. Griffiths' refusal to order the *Star* I wrote to the publisher of that paper, requesting him to say whether under the circumstances he would supply me direct from the office. Mr. Ardill, the clerk replied he should be glad to send any quantity I might require at wholesale price. I immediately sent order and cash, and from that moment, thanks to Mr. Tory Griffiths, I became a newsagent.[70]

Comprehensive reporting was one of the major factors in the successful creation of a national medium of Chartist communication. In the *Star*'s columns ordinary working people were accorded the status of men and women who mattered. Gammage noted:

the *Star* was regarded as the most complete record of the movement. There was not a meeting held in any part of the country, in however remote a spot, that was not reported in its columns, accompanied by all the flourishes calculated to excite an interest in the reader's mind, and to inflate the vanity of the speakers by the honourable mention of their names. Even if they had never mounted the platform before, the speeches were described and reported as eloquent, argumentative, and the like; and were dressed up with as much care as though they were parliamentary harangues fashioned to the columns of the daily press.[71]

One of the great differences between the unstamped press and the *Star* was that whereas the unstamped often had little news or had to quote news from London middle-class journals, the *Star* was a real newspaper which could compete with any adversary for coverage.[72] 'This is our strength . . . The *Star* has more original matter than any ten papers in the Kingdom.' It claimed to spend £500 a year on reporting, more than any paper except *The Times*.[73] But reporting was also an activity which involved local radicals who were invited to send in reports of their meetings and discussions. Thus the cost of reporting does not adequately reflect the wide range of coverage, as much of it was dependent on the efforts of unpaid local Chartists.

Through comprehensive reporting, local and national Chartist themes were merged. As well as integrating local and national activity, the *Star*'s reporting also created an all-important reciprocity between the platform and the press. The platform, in itself transient and local, was transformed into a national medium. For O'Connor the heightening of a national working-class consciousness which such reporting helped to evoke was central to national leadership. The *Star* became the major agency for the transmission of a sense of national Chartist unity, and for the consolidation of O'Connor's claims to leadership.

(ii) *Staff*

One of the most distinctive features of the *Star* was the talent and wide radical experience of its staff, who were never merely O'Connorite mouthpieces. O'Connor depended upon a gifted staff of writers. The ex-handloom weaver Joshua Hobson, printer, publisher and later editor of the *Star* (from 1843 to 1845), was a radical of long service. He was prominent in the ten-hours movement; one of the leading figures in the provincial campaign for an unstamped press; a founder member of the Leeds WMA; and an Owenite socialist who, from 1839 to 1841, published Owen's *New Moral World*. J. F. C. Harrison has described Hobson as 'a kind of representative bridge-figure, in that his activities spanned most of the popular radical movements of the time'.[74] The *Star*'s editor, William Hill, had also been brought up as a handloom weaver in Barnsley, was an experienced radical, educationalist and an able journalist. He was particularly active in the factory movement and was the Swedenborgian pastor of the New Jerusalem church at Hull.[75] Until the *Star* moved to London in 1844, John Ardill, an ex-iron moulder and a founder member of the Leeds WMA, served as clerk and bookkeeper.

From its earliest editions came enquiries concerning the activities of James Bronterre O'Brien. In January 1838, the *Star* announced that 'the valuable services of the glorious BRONTERRE' had been added 'to the phalanx of talent already attached to the *Northern Star*'.[76] In O'Brien O'Connor had secured the services of the most talented radical journalist of the day. Although O'Brien had written for, edited and published many journals during the struggle of the unstamped press, it was as editor of the *Poor Man's Guardian* and for his clear class analysis that he was best known.[77] When O'Brien agreed to write a weekly letter for the *Star*, Oastler wrote to Stephens: 'Tell O'Brien to put the *Poor Man's Guardian*'s soul into the *Northern Star*.'[78] Certainly O'Brien brought a vigorous, defiant intellectual tone to the *Star*'s early columns. In late 1838, however, O'Brien discontinued his regular column, on becoming editor of the *Operative*, another Chartist journal.

O'Connor was also able to call upon the services of a number of well-established radical leaders in the role of reporters: men such as George White, ex-woolcomber, founder member of the Leeds WMA

and one of the West Riding's most determined working-class militants.[79] Through the *Star* younger men advanced. G. J. Harney and
Ernest Jones, both of whom became leading members of the international socialist group of Fraternal Democrats and friends of Marx and
Engels, were assistant editors. Harney, who had been a reporter for
the paper since 1841, was editor from 1845 until 1850.[80] The printer
and ex-stuff weaver William Rider — active in radical politics since at
least 1831 as ten-hours agitator, secretary of the Leeds Radical Reform Union, contributor to the *Voice of the West Riding* and founder
member of the Leeds WMA — was associated with the *Star* from its
early days and replaced Harney as editor in 1850. G. A. Fleming —
leading Owenite, for many years editor of the *New Moral World* and
editor of *The Union*, 1842-43 — became assistant editor when the
paper moved to London, and was to be the *Star*'s last editor.[81] At
various times from November 1843, Engels acted as a foreign correspondent for the *Star*.[82]

Unlike many working-class radical journals, the *Star* paid regular
and quite generous wages to its staff.[83] The *Star*'s ability to pay
regular wages was important in securing the services of such a capable journalistic team. The impression is that O'Connor was an excellent judge of talent and attracted extremely able radicals to write for
his journal. He employed writers of ability and independence, not
'yes' men.

Feargus wrote extensively in the *Star*. His main contribution being
his weekly letter styled to appeal to those with 'fustian jackets,
blistered hands and unshorn chins', and whom he often addressed as
his 'political children'. O'Connor wrote other leaders, helped with
sections such as the parliamentary summary and gave a column of
legal advice. During the early years, when not engaged upon one of
his extensive tours of agitation, O'Connor usually spent mid-week in
Leeds helping prepare the paper for press.[84] O'Connor's weekly
letter was the rallying call of the movement, outlining Chartist strategy, drawing attention to the key events of the week, celebrating
Chartist victories, denouncing the enemy without and warning of the
traitors within their ranks. Punctuated with Irish anecdotes, romantic poetry and a fine sense of humour, his letters were intended to be
read aloud. An able journalist, O'Connor could rise above his limitations as a writer through his emotional appeal and self-confident tone.
His romance was essentially of the platform, and his articles were
attempts to transform that urgency and vitality into print. Thomas
Frost, himself a journalist and a good judge of style, observed: 'His

[O'Connor's] style was vigorous, but coarse, being well sprinkled with expletives, often set forth in capitals, and spiced for the taste of the "fustian jackets" of the Midlands and North.' Frost went on to note, however, that O'Connor was quite capable of modifying his tone and style in accordance with his audience.[85] While O'Connor may have been the paper's dominant personality, he was never the only voice or hero to be found in the *Star*'s columns; other writers were able to make an impression and gain their own following. The *Star* was never O'Connor's paper in the way that the *Political Register* had been Cobbett's, the *Republican* and *Lion* had been Carlile's, or even the *Poor Man's Guardian* Hetherington's. It was more the organ of a movement than that of any individual.[86]

(iii) *The* Star, *Chartist Democracy and National Organisation*

'The *Northern Star* was the principal paper', observed Ben Wilson; and Ben Brierley reflected, it was 'the only newspaper that appeared to circulate anywhere'. The *Star* was *the* Chartist paper. In its pages Chartists learned about the proceedings of the National Convention, found accounts of various defence funds, sent their nominations for the National Charter Association, enrolled in the Land Plan. O'Connor's success as a newspaper proprietor was directly linked to the extent to which the *Star* embodied the movement. Francis Place commented that of the Chartist papers 'not one excepting the *Northern Star* paid its expenses even at the time of the greatest excitement'.[87] The success of the *Star* as the recognised organ of the movement left other Chartist papers a much diminished role. As an extreme example, when the National Charter Association Executive decided to start its own paper, *The Executive Journal of the National Charter Association*, at the end of 1841, it readily acknowledged the *Star* as the movement's paper: 'Notwithstanding the existence of the *Journal*, we shall always conceive the *Star* to be the great organ of our party.' The NCA Executive's paper lasted a short four weeks.[88] It had no obvious role. The failure of *The Executive Journal* serves to underline the importance of the *Star* as the central organ of the Chartist movement. The newspaper of the party had predated the party. The ascendancy of the *Star* was not gained through narrow editorial control. Its popularity was contingent upon its wide range of opinions and news, both local and national. Only in this way could the paper have become the forum of discussion for the Chartist movement and the working class.

Engels noted that the *Star* was 'the only sheet which reports all the movements of the proletariat'.[89] O'Connor and the editors always insisted that their paper was a 'mirror', the 'reflector' of the people's mind. Thus Hill wrote, on the occasion of the *Star*'s fifth anniversary in 1842:

> I have ever sought to make it [the *Star*] rather a reflex of your minds than a medium through which to exhibit any supposed talent or intelligence of my own. This is precisely my conception of what a people's organ should be; this was what I saw to be wanting before the *Star* came into existence . . .[90]

The *Star* was never a sectarian journal. For instance, wide coverage was given to Robert Owen's tours and Owenism in general.[91] Always an accurate reflector of the labour movement's trends, in 1844 with the revival of the trade-union movement, it changed its name to the *Northern Star and National Trades Journal* and moved its office to London. Just as its columns were full of the anti-Poor Law movement in 1838, in 1844-45 its pages carried long reports of the miners' struggle. The *Star* declared its willingness to publish all trade-union notices and became the journal of the National Association of United Trades. 'In that [the trade-union] movement we see the salvation of our country from the principles and practices of UNRESTRICTED, UNREGULATED COMPETITION.' The paper had been 'established to aid LABOUR in its struggles against UNBRIDLED CAPITAL', to 'expose the numerous frauds, extortions, oppressions, and tyrannies committed and inflicted upon the labouring classes by RAMPANT CAPITAL . . .'[92] This concern with the trade-union movement was not new, however. For instance, the *Star* fully reported the great stonemasons' strike which lasted from October 1841 until June 1842. In the 1840s, strikers were often completely dependent on the *Star* for coverage and space for appeals for aid. Even after the miners established their own paper, *The Miner's Advocate*, some district committees still preferred to send their reports to the *Star*.[93]

Most historians of Chartism have accused O'Connor of undemocratic management of the columns of the *Northern Star* in which they claim only O'Connorite views found acceptance. Yet one of the most striking qualities of the *Star* was its willingness to publish criticism of both its own policies and those of O'Connor, and the openness of its columns to all brands of Chartism. As for criticism of O'Connor, G. J. Holyoake commented: 'In the *Northern Star* he [O'Connor] let every rival speak, and had the grand strength of indifference to what anyone said against him in his own columns.'[94] In the autumn of 1839, the

Star published a series of letters from Matthew Fletcher, member of the Convention for Bury, denouncing O'Connor in the harshest terms. When O'Connor and O'Brien clashed over the question of Chartist strategy for the 1841 general election, letters were published weekly from both leaders openly arguing their case. And O'Brien's tone was a good deal sharper, more denunciatory and less generous than that of O'Connor and the *Star*. In March 1849, the columns of the *Star* quite openly paraded the divisions between O'Connor and Harney, his editor.[95] At certain points, events strained the *Star*'s more general democratic character—for instance, in spring of 1842, over the issue of an alliance with the Complete Suffrage Union.[96] Naturally letters were sometimes refused insertion, private arguments curtailed, speeches at meetings not fully reported and leaders subjected to criticism. Although O'Connor repeatedly used the *Star* as a medium through which to attack other Chartist leaders, adversaries such as Hetherington, O'Brien, Hill, Thomas Cooper, John Watkins and Dr Peter M'Douall had their letters inserted in the *Star* and usually proved as acrimonious in debate as O'Connor. Significantly, Chartist leaders regarded the publication of their letters in the *Star* not as a courtesy, but as a matter of democratic right.[97] Still, conflict and accusations of unscrupulous control were inherent in a situation in which the movement's principal paper and most influential policy-making institution was in the hands of Chartism's most prominent leader.

If O'Connor's frequent claim that he gave the editor of the *Star* a completely free hand was an exaggeration, the view that the *Star* was an organ conceived and directed solely towards his own glory is also false. While editor, Hill was always ready to point out the freedom and editorial control which he exercised. Nor did Hill show any deference to O'Connor's position when he disagreed with his political opinions.[98] G. J. Harney testified to the freedom O'Connor allowed his editors in a letter to Engels in 1846: 'I must do O'C[onnor] the justice to say that he never interferes with what I write in the paper nor does he know what I write until he sees the paper.'[99] Hill's dismissal, in summer of 1843, was not over the question of editorial control as such or general management of the paper — although O'Connor had been unhappy about the manner in which Hill ran the *Star* for some years. Deep and irreconcilable differences had developed between Hill and O'Connor over important questions of NCA organisation and leadership.[100] Similarly, the point at issue between O'Connor and Harney, over the attitude to be taken towards foreign affairs, reflected fundamental differences over the commitment of the movement to international socialism. But as far as exercising a dictatorial control of the paper, the *Star* became the organ of the Fraternal Democrats and one of Europe's leading international socialist journals, with little commitment on O'Connor's part to international socialism. Despite ideological differences and serious clashes of personal ambition, Harney remained editor until August 1850.[101] Certainly Gammage's assertion that 'Every paid servant of O'Connor's . . . felt himself bound to follow in the wake of his master', must be seriously modified.[102]

Both O'Connor and the *Star* assumed a cordial attitude towards other Chartist papers, demonstrating a sense of cooperation rather than competition. Almost invariably the *Star* gave publicity and support to new Chartist journals.[103] O'Connor contributed to help O'Brien keep the *Operative* alive and later acted as surety for O'Brien and Carpenter's *Southern Star*. The *Star* publicised the campaign for the O'Brien press fund in 1841-42, despite the mounting bad feeling between O'Brien and O'Connor.[104] In 1842, O'Connor wrote a long series of articles on the land for the struggling *English Chartist Circular* in an attempt to boost its sales. He sent a donation to the Leicester Chartists to help start the *Midland Counties Illuminator*, and in 1842 wrote a series of letters to Cooper's *The Commonwealthsman*.[105] While the *Star* remained the organ of the Chartist party, O'Connor always felt the movement needed a far wider range of journals. This was a general Chartist concern.[106] Although the Chartist movement gave birth to a wide range of journals, some of which lasted several years, there was no flourishing of working-class papers comparable to the years of the unstamped press. Instead Chartism brought forth a new type of working-class journal. The *Star* represented a new departure in the history of the working class, in terms of the concentration of the entire strength and variety of a mass movement of working-class protest into the columns of a single national newspaper.

Almost as soon as the *Star* was showing a profit, O'Connor was planning a more ambitious scheme, a daily London paper.[107] O'Connor asserted that the establishment of a daily journal was essential for the successful marshalling of public opinion. Probably lack of funds combined with the tremendous demands being made upon his energies forced O'Connor temporarily to shelve these early plans for a daily paper. Almost certainly 1839 was the only point at which such a paper would have been a real possibility. However, when discussions

were opened upon the question of the reorganisation of the movement in summer 1840, O'Connor outlined a plan of organisation
based upon a daily newspaper, the profits of which were to finance
lecturers, delegates to Conventions, defence funds and Chartist
agitation in general.[108] No doubt wisely, the founding conference of
the National Charter Association did not act upon this proposal. But
what O'Connor clearly demonstrated was that his conception of the
role of the newspaper went well beyond that of mere propagandist
and educator. In 1838, the *Star* had argued: 'The press is at once the
cheapest, the most expeditious, and the most certain means of keeping a party together.'[109] The organisation of the movement centred
around a national paper. O'Connor always sought to impart the
utmost permanency to the movement's national organisation and he
believed, however mistakenly, that a national Chartist daily paper
provided a key to this problem. When he finally did take over the
Evening Star as a Chartist daily, in the role of manager and editor,
during the summer of 1842, it proved a grave disappointment. Chartism's first and only daily paper lasted only half a year, and lost a large
sum of money.[110]

Without a daily Chartist press, the *Star* assumed the role of national organiser. Besides providing the *Star* with news, the full-time
reporters also served as organisers for the Chartist movement. In
1841, Harney became the *Star*'s Sheffield correspondent; T. M.
Wheeler took on the job of London reporter and agent; and George
White was given the difficult task of organising the O'Connorite/NCA
party in Birmingham and reporting for the *Star*.[111] As the *Star*'s
Birmingham reporter, White earned one pound a week.[112] Thus the
Star helped to fulfil the movement's organisational requirements by
providing working-class Chartist leaders with the necessary financial
independence to undertake full-time agitation, to become in effect
'professional revolutionaries'. O'Connor not only owned the major
medium of Chartist communication, his correspondents formed a
political machine. The reporters and staff of the *Star* were frequently
denounced as 'O'Connor's tools'. At the 1842 Convention, O'Connor
defended himself against such accusations:

> It had been stated, that his reporters were hired tools, while the
> reporters of other papers were public spirited individuals. He could
> positively assert that he never wrote a line to Wheeler in his life, that he
> never wrote a line to White, or any of his correspondents; he had been
> particularly careful on this point . . . they had been entirely free and
> unshackled from any restraint . . . The Editor of the paper he had known

for many years, and had never written a line to him to influence his conduct . . . Great latitude must always be allowed to a public newspaper.

George White denied that O'Connor or any man could buy his services at the cost of his principles.

> With regard to the agents of the *Northern Star* being the paid tools of Feargus O'Connor, as one of those agents, he could assert, that he was in the same position for doing his duty fearlessly as before he accepted that office; his actions were equally free as before. It was well known that when he was employed in Yorkshire, he would never be controlled in his opinions or his actions by his employer, and should act now in a similar manner. So far as O'Connor supported the cause he would support him, whether he was called a tool or no; and if he (O'Connor) deserted the cause, he would be one of the first to oppose him.[113]

O'Connor insisted that anyone accepting employment in the National Charter Association organisation could not also work for the *Star*, in order to ensure their independence. Thus O'Connor informed T. M. Wheeler that if he accepted the post as secretary to the NCA Executive, he could no longer be employed by the *Star*. Edmund Stallwood, the West London socialist and Chartist, replaced Wheeler as the *Star*'s London correspondent.[114]

Not only did the *Star* support the activities of some of the movement's most capable agitators, its profits went to provide financial assistance for many Chartist prisoners and their families. O'Connor even suggested financing another convention out of the *Star*'s profits after the National Convention was dissolved in September 1839.[115] The *Star*'s staff was well paid and the profits after 1839 fell off greatly. There was probably much truth in O'Connor's claim that he spent every penny of the *Star*'s profits on agitation and a good deal of his own wealth on the cause.[116] What O'Connor gained through his ownership and earnings of the *Star* was his total independence as an agitator in the people's cause, a factor of incalculable importance to his leadership. The crucial issues concerning the finances of the *Star* relate not to quibbles over how much initial capital O'Connor could or would advance, but to key questions of Chartist organisation and leadership. The importance of the *Star*'s profits was not as a brilliant stroke of financial speculation, but rather as a contribution to the creation of regular and permanent national Chartist organisation, along with the freedom such funds allowed the movement's most gifted agitator constantly to tour the country propagandising, winning new recruits and organising. O'Connor did not become a rich

man from the profits of the *Star;* he became the undisputed leader
and champion of Chartism.

However the question of the role of reporters and profits of the
Star in Chartist organisation highlights the basic contradiction at the
centre of O'Connor's relationship to the paper. While the *Star* was
the organ of a democratic movement and the Chartist party, the
NCA, it was owned by O'Connor. There was no clear line between
O'Connor's private business concern and the finances of the movement. While O'Connor's leadership was very closely linked to both
the *Star* and the NCA, in a sense it remained above them both. When
the profits of the *Star* were placed at the disposal of the movement,
this was regarded as an act of largesse on the part of O'Connor. This
was related to an older tradition of gentlemanly leadership. His claim
that 'The *Star* is mine and the People's, and only ours', embodies the
essence of a style of leadership associated with the 'People's Champion'.[117] As the *Star*'s success was dependent on the wide support of
the working class, there was always an appeal to a vague brand of
popular democratic control. From the platform at Bolton, O'Connor
solicited the working class for a mandate to continue in the role of
journalist, a task he had undertaken

> according to the terms of a contract which had been mutually entered
> into between him and the people; and now he came to ask them whether
> or not that contract was to be renewed for one more year. (Repeated
> cheers, and 'aye, aye'.) Then he would proceed, fearless of all conse-
> quences, when backed by the brave working classes.[118]

The establishment of a national newspaper was a vital prerequisite
to the emergence of the Chartist party. Through the *Star*'s columns
the Chartist movement was brought together and held together for
over a decade. The *Star* played an essential role in keeping Chartism alive during the most difficult times of government repression.
George White maintained:

> The *Star* had been the main cause for keeping the agitation alive when
> there were many of them in prison, and when all their prospects were
> dark and gloomy. When he was in prison, he recollected being asked by
> thirty or forty in the court yard what would become of the cause? He
> asserted that the *Northern Star* would keep them together. It had done
> this; and the people owed to it a debt of gratitude.[119]

Throughout the 1840s, the *Northern Star,* the National Charter
Association and the 'People's Champion' captured the allegiance of
thousands of working people, as the three central rallying points of

national Chartist unity. Many Chartists regarded the establishment of the *Star* as O'Connor's greatest contribution to the cause of popular rights. As a local Chartist from Hull told a meeting:

> If it had not been for the protection which the *Northern Star* afforded, they would still be as slaves in the desert, and their own sounds might echo through the wilderness, but O'Connor threw them with all the force and power of union into the enemies' camp . . . In all ages, we have found that the most difficult object of accomplishment, has been the marshalling of public opinion, and the *Star* has done more to effect that object than ever has been done.[120]

O'Connor himself was in no doubt as to the *Star*'s place in the history of the British working class.

> The first paper ever established in England exclusively for the people; a paper which has given a completely new tone to the whole press of the empire; a paper which may be truly called the mental link which binds the industrious classes together; a paper which has, for the first time, concentrated the national mind into one body.[121]

NOTES

1. For a somewhat fuller version of this chapter, see my article 'Feargus O'Connor and the *Northern Star*', *International Review of Social History*, 21, 1976, pp. 51-97.

2. *Bronterre's National Reformer*, 28 Jan. 1837, p. 29.

3. See W. E. Adams, *Memoirs of a Social Atom*, London 1903, I, p. 204.

4. For the unstamped press, see C. D. Collett, *History of the Taxes on Knowledge*, 2 vols., London 1889; W. H. Wickwar, *The Struggle for the Freedom of the Press*, London 1928; P. Hollis, *The Pauper Press: A Study in Working-Class Radicalism of the 1830s*, Oxford 1970; J. H. Wiener, *The War of the Unstamped: The Movement to Repeal the British Newspaper Tax, 1830-1836*, Ithaca, N.Y., 1969.

5. *NS*, 2 June 1838, p. 1.

6. Ibid., 18 Nov. 1837, p. 1. Only a fragment exists of this first edition of the *Star*, in British Library, Place Collection, Set 56 (1836-June 1838), fo. 155; of the first seven numbers only those of 2 Dec. and 16 Dec. 1837 have been located, in PRO, HO 73/52.

7. M. Hovell, *The Chartist Movement*, Manchester, 2nd ed. 1925, p. 96; E. Glasgow, 'The Establishment of the *Northern Star* Newspaper', *History*, 39, 1954, pp. 54-67; D. Read and E. Glasgow, *Feargus O'Connor, Irishman and Chartist*, London 1961, pp. 56-76; British Library, Add. MSS 27820, fo. 154, for Francis Place's predictably low opinion of the *Star*.

8. The following account is based largely on the letters which Joshua Hobson wrote to the *Manchester Examiner*, Nov.-Dec. 1847, particularly that of 6 Nov.

9. *NS*, 10 Mar. 1838, p. 8; 18 Jan. 1845, p. 4; F. O'Connor, *Reply to John Watkins' Charges*, London 1843, p. 16; G. J. Holyoake, *Life of Joseph Rayner Stephens*, London 1881, p. 181, Stephens contributed £20.

10. *Manchester Examiner*, 6 Nov. 1847; *NS*, 16 Jan. 1841, p. 7.

11. *London Mercury*, 4 June 1837, p. 297, cited Hollis, *Pauper Press*, p. 135.

12. On O'Connor's finances, see *NS*, 10 Mar. 1838, p. 8; 24 Apr. 1841, p. 7; 18 Jan. 1845, p. 4; F. O'Connor, *Reply of Feargus O'Connor to the Charges against His Land and Labour Scheme*, Manchester 1847, p. 10, id., *The Trial of Feargus O'Connor and*

Fifty-Eight Others, Manchester 1843, pp. 295-96; T. M. Wheeler, *A Brief Memoir of the Late Feargus O'Connor*, London 1855, p. 7; J. W. Knapp and E. Omler, *Cases of Controverted Elections in the Twelfth Parliament of the United Kingdom*, London 1837, pp. 393-94.

13. *NS*, 30 Jan. 1841, p. 7.

14. Ibid., 5 May 1838, p. 5; 17 Nov., p. 8.

15. Ibid., 3 Nov. 1838, p. 4; 24 Apr. 1841, p. 7; 18 Jan. 1845, p. 4, by which time £400 of the original £690 in shares had been bought up; O'Connor, *Reply to Watkins' Charges*, p. 16.

16. *Charter*, 1 Mar. 1840, p. 1; 15 Mar., p. 1; for the *Charter*, see also British Library, Place Collection, Set 66, handbills; Set 56 (Jan.-Apr. 1841), correspondence relating to the *Charter*, fos. 15-17.

17. R. G. Gammage, *History of the Chartist Movement, 1837-1854*, Newcastle 1894 ed., p. 16.

18. *NS*, 16 Dec. 1837, p. 3.

19. Ibid., 27 Apr. 1839, p. 4.

20. British Library, Place Collection, Set 70, fos. 619-21.

21. *Leeds Times*, 14 Jan. 1837, p. 8; 21 Jan., p. 5; 11 Feb., p. 5; 18 Feb., p. 5; 13 May, p. 4.

22. Cf. Glasgow, 'Establishment of the *Northern Star*', pp. 60-61; also see Alexander Paterson, 'Feargus O'Connor and the *Northern Star*', *Leeds Mercury*, 24 Feb. 1900, supplement, p. 1; and Paterson's letter in *Newcastle Weekly Chronicle*, 10 Mar. 1883, p. 2. Glasgow has misread the evidence on this point.

23. *NS*, 26 May 1838, p. 4.

24. Ibid., 5 Oct. 1839, p. 4; 18 Nov. 1842, p. 4.

25. Barnsley Public Library, J. H. Burland, MS 'Annals of Barnsley', fo. 71; Paterson, 'O'Connor and the *Star*'.

26. For references to these radicals, see Epstein, 'O'Connor and the *Star*', p. 64, nn 1,3, p. 65, n 1.

27. Hollis, *Pauper Press*, p. 109; *NS*, 31 Mar. 1838, p. 4.

28. Wiener, *War of the Unstamped*, p. 190.

29. See N. C. Edsall, *The Anti-Poor Law Movement, 1834-1844*, Manchester 1971, pp. 169-70. The agents listed in *NS*, 2, 16 Dec. 1837 were mostly from the West Riding and South Lancashire; *NS*, 20 Jan.-17 Feb. 1838 carried a complete account of the spinners' trial; see Place's comments, British Library, Add. MSS 27820, fo. 153.

30. *Champion*, 27 Oct. 1839, pp. 4-5; *NS*, 2 Nov. 1839, p. 4.

31. For instance, see *Manchester and Salford Advertiser*, 27 Jan. 1838, p. 2.

32. PRO, HO 48/32, case 13; HO 49/8, fos. 214-16. Local authorities immediately drew the attention of the government to the 'seditious' speeches published in the *Star*: HO 40/35, fos. 63-64, 76-77, Maj. Phillips to Gen. Jackson, Bradford, 3, 11 Dec. 1837; MH 12/14830, R. Baker to Poor Law Commissioners, Leeds, 5 Jan. 1838. For actual proceedings against the *Star*, see HO 48/33, case 22; HO 49/8, fos. 289-90, 307-08, 312-15; TS 11/813-14, 817; *NS*, 20 Apr. 1839, p. 4; 21 Mar. 1840; 16 May. O'Connor was eventually sent to prison primarily for speeches published in the *Star*, see below ch. 5.

33. *NS*, 13 Oct. 1838, p. 4, the new Poor Law was regarded as 'only one grievance among many'; M. E. Rose, 'The Anti-Poor Law Movement in the North of England', *Northern History*, 1, 1966, p. 88; Edsall, *Anti-Poor Law Movement*, pp. 169-72.

34. *NS*, 3 Feb. 1838, p. 5; 6 Jan., p. 6; 31 Mar., p. 4, a steam press was in operation; 24 Nov., p. 4; for comparative circulation figures, see Report of the Select Committee on Newspaper Stamps, *Parliamentary Papers*, 1851, XVII, appendix 4.

35. *NS*, 2 Feb. 1839, p. 4, claimed the 26 Jan. edition sold 17,640 copies; 9 Mar., p. 4; 20 Apr., p. 4.

36. For estimates of the *Star's* circulation high, see Benjamin Wilson, *The Struggles of an Old Chartist*, Halifax 1887, p. 3; Frank Peel, *The Risings of the Luddites*,

Chartists and Plug-Drawers, London, 4th ed. 1968 (first published 1880), p. 314; Paterson, 'O'Connor and the *Star*'; Hovell, *The Chartist Movement*, pp. 173, 269, n 1; PRO, IR 69/1B, lists the number of stamps purchased every month, April (278,000) and July (223,000) were the highest, but this does not reflect actual monthly sales; *NS*, 1 June 1839, p. 4; 17 Aug., p. 4.

37. G. D. H. Cole, *The Life of William Cobbett*, London, 1947 ed., p. 207; Hollis, *Pauper Press*, pp. 95, 118-19, 124. Hollis has estimated the circulation high of the *Poor Man's Guardian*, the leading unstamped journal, to have been around 15,000.

38. W. J. O'Neill Daunt, *Eighty-Years of Irish History*, London 1886, I, p. 268.

39. PRO, HO 40/53 (file of intercepted letters), fo. 928, E. Richardson to R. J. Richardson, 16 Feb. 1839.

40. Yearly average weekly sales for the *Star* were:

1838	11,000	1842	12,500	1847	8,700
1839	36,000	1843	8,700	1848	12,000
1840	18,700	1844	7,400	1849	7,000
1841	18,700	1845	6,500	1850	5,000
		1846	6,000		

These figures are based on the annual stamp returns, published in Parliamentary Accounts and Papers; up until 1843, advertising duty can also be found in Accounts and Papers. For a comparison of advertising duty paid by various newspapers, 1838-1842, see J. Curran, 'Capitalism and Control of the Press', in J. Curran, M. Gurevitch, J. Woollacott (eds.), *Mass Communication and Society*, London 1977, pp. 208-11. Most provincial papers with much lower circulation had many times the *Star's* advertising revenue.

41. Hollis, *Pauper Press*, p. 119; also see D. Read, *Press and People, 1790-1850*, London 1961, p. 202; A. Aspinall, *Politics and the Press, 1780-1850*, London 1949, pp. 25-32; R. K. Webb, *The British Working-Class Reader*, London 1955, pp. 31-34.

42. *NS*, 9 June 1838, p. 4; 6 Apr. 1839, p. 3.

43. Ibid., 9 Feb. 1839, lists about two hundred agents representing around one hundred localities.

44. Ibid., 24 Mar. 1838, p. 3.

45. James Guest, 'A Free Press and How it Became Free', in W. Hutton, *The History of Birmingham*, Birmingham, 6th ed. 1861, p. 506.

46. *NS*, 26 May 1838, p. 4.

47. Ibid., 29 Sept. 1838, p. 7.

48. Ibid., 13 June 1840, p. 1.

49. S. Fielden, 'Autobiography of Samuel Fielden', in *Knights of Labor*, 18 Feb. 1887.

50. Adams, *Memoirs*, I, pp. 164-65.

51. Ben Brierley, *Home and Memories*, Manchester 1886, pp. 23-24.

52. Benjamin Grime, *Memory Sketches: History of Oldham Parliamentary Elections, 1832-1853*, Oldham 1887, p. 26.

53. Wilson, *Struggles*, p. 10.

54. Daniel Merrick, *The Warp of Life, or, Social and Moral Threads, A Narrative*, Leicester 1876, pp. 18, 22.

55. J. F. C. Harrison, *Learning and Living, 1790-1960, A Study in the History of English Adult Education*, London 1961, pp. 30, 101; also see L. James, *Fiction for the Working Man, 1830-1850*, Oxford 1968, pp. 21, 91-92, 150.

56. Adams, *Memoirs*, I, pp. 163-64.

57. *NS*, 20 Nov. 1841, p. 5; 26 May 1838, p. 4; Guest, 'A Free Press', p. 506; PRO, HO 40/53, fo. 1001, CEH to R. J. Richardson, 14 Mar. 1839.

58. *NS*, 26 May 1838, p. 4.

59. Ibid., 24 Feb. 1838, p. 7.

60. Ibid., 31 Mar. 1838, p. 4.

61. Ibid., 26 May 1838, p. 4; 9 Feb. 1839, p. 4; 15 May 1841, p. 5.

62. Ibid., 3 Feb. 1838, p. 5; 24 Feb., p. 7.

63. Ibid., 26 Feb. 1842, p. 4 (Glasgow and Walworth).

64. See the comments of the Leicester Chartists, *NS*, 14 Nov. 1840, p. 2; *Midland Counties Illuminator*, 1 May 1841, p. 47; also T. M. Kemnitz, 'Chartism in Brighton', (Sussex Univ. D. Phil thesis, 1969), pp. 179-89, for a discussion of the importance of the press to a group of local Chartists.

65. W. Glover, *History of Ashton-under-Lyne and the Surrounding District*, Ashton 1884, p. 322; *NS*, 24 Mar. 1838, p. 6. Ashton's Joshua Hobson should not be confused with the *Star's* publisher of the same name.

66. *NS*, 2 Dec. 1837, p. 8, along with Ashton's Hobson, Knight, Abel Heywood, the West Riding victims Ibbetson, Brooke and Tinker were early agents. Four of Birmingham's six agents in 1839 had been prosecuted for selling the unstamped.

67. Guest, 'A Free Press', pp. 493-507.

68. *Nottingham Review*, 29 Jan. 1836, p. 4; 5 Feb., p. 4.

69. The bourgeois press was scornful of such independence, see *Manchester Times*, 9 June 1838, p. 3.

70. Thomas Dunning, 'The Reminiscences of Thomas Dunning and the Nantwich Shoemakers' Case of 1834', W. H. Chaloner (ed.), *Transactions of the Lancashire and Cheshire Antiquarian Society*, 59, 1947, p. 112.

71. Gammage, *History of the Chartist Movement*, p. 17; also see the comments of C. D. Collet, in Report of the Select Committee on Newspaper Stamps, p. 152.

72. Hollis, *Pauper Press*, p. 152.

73. *NS*, 9 Jan. 1841, p. 4. It seems likely, however, that the major London daily papers spent considerably more on reporting than did the *Star*.

74. Harrison, *Learning and Living*, p. 98; Tolson Memorial Museum, Huddersfield, collection of MSS and newspaper cuttings relating to Hobson.

75. *Newcastle Weekly Chronicle*, 10 Mar. 1883, p. 2; *Leeds Mercury*, 24 Feb. 1900, supplement, p. 1; J. F. C. Harrison, 'Chartism in Leeds', in A. Briggs (ed.), *Chartist Studies*, London 1959, p. 74, n 1.

76. *NS*, 27 Jan. 1838, p. 4.

77. Hollis, *Pauper Press*, ch. 7, and p. 313; also see I. J. Prothero's comments, 'Chartism, Early and Late', *Bulletin of the Society for the Study of Labour History*, no. 24, 1972, p. 52; A. Plummer, *Bronterre: A Political Biography of Bronterre O'Brien, 1804-1864*, London 1971, for O'Brien in general.

78. Holyoake, *Life of Stephens*, p. 86.

79. See K. Geering, 'George White, a Nineteenth-Century Workers' Leader and the Kirkdale Phenomenon', (Sussex Univ. MA thesis, 1973).

80. For Harney, see A. R. Schoyen, *The Chartist Challenge: A Portrait of George Julian Harney*, London, 1958.

81. For Fleming, see obituary in *Manchester City News*, 25 May 1878, p. 3; G. J. Holyoake, *History of Co-Operation*, London 1875, chs. 9, 10, 12.

82. K. Marx and F. Engels, *Collected Works*, vols. 2-7, London 1975-77.

83. Hill was paid £4 a week in 1839, F. O'Connor, *A Letter from Feargus O'Connor, Esq., to the Rev. William Hill*, London 1843, p. 13; *NS*, 26 Aug. 1848, p. 1, O'Connor gave a breakdown of his editorial costs. Regular contributors were paid 10s per column.

84. O'Connor, *Letter to Hill*, p. 14; *NS*, 21 Nov. 1846, p. 1; 10 Mar. 1849, p. 5.

85. Thomas Frost, *Forty Years' Recollections: Literary and Political*, London 1880, p. 181; also see Engels to Marx, 25-26 Oct. 1847, in K. Marx and F. Engels, *Werke*, 27, Berlin 1963, p. 99.

86. This point is made very forcibly in D. Thompson, 'La presse de la classe ouvrière anglaise, 1836-1848', in J. Godechot (ed.), *La Presse Ouvrière, 1819-1850*, Paris 1966, pp. 28-30; see the reminiscences of John Arlom, in *Newcastle Weekly Chronicle*, 27 Aug. 1892; F. P. [Frank Peel?], ibid., 17 Mar. 1883.

87. British Library, Add. MSS 27820, fo. 25; for the careers of other Chartist

newspapers, D. Thompson, 'La presse de las classe ouvrière anglaise'; T. M. Kemnitz, 'Chartist Newspaper Editors', *Victorian Periodicals Newsletter*, no. 18, 1972; Hollis, *Pauper Press*, p. 119, provides some useful comparative circulation figures; Transport House, Vincent MSS, correspondence relating to the finances of the *Western Vindicator*.

88. *NS*, 9 Oct. 1841, p. 8; full set of the *Executive Journal*, 16 Oct.-6 Nov. 1841, in British Library, Place Collection, Set 56 (Sept.-Dec. 1841).

89. F. Engels, *The Condition of the Working Class in England*, in *Marx and Engels On Britain*, Moscow 1962, p. 260. For Marx and Engels's high opinion of the *Star*, see Marx and Engels, *Collected Work*, vol. 3, p. 514; vol. 6, p. 8; vol. 7, p. 129; *NS*, 25 July 1846, p. 1.

90. *NS*, 19 Nov. 1842, p. 4.

91. This is hardly surprising when one notes the number of Owenites on the *Star's* staff: Hobson and later Fleming as editors, and full-time reporters like Edmund Stallwood and T. M. Wheeler.

92. *NS*, 20 Jan. 1844, p. 4; 5 Dec. 1846, p. 4.

93. I. J. Prothero, 'London Chartism and the Trades', *Economic History Review*, 2nd series, 24, 1971, p. 210; R. Challinor and B. Ripley, *The Miners' Association: A Trade Union in the Age of the Chartists*, London 1968, pp. 40-41.

94. G. J. Holyoake, *Sixty-Years of an Agitator's Life*, London 1892, I, pp. 106-07; also see Holyoake's MS notes on O'Connor, Manchester Co-operative Union Library, no. 820 [1855/-56].

95. *NS*, 21 Sept. 1839, p. 7; 5 Oct., p. 6; 12 Oct., p. 1; 12 June-10 July 1841; 3 Mar.-31 Mar. 1849.

96. For Chartist criticism of O'Connor's handling of the *Star*, see R. K. Philp, *Vindication of his Political Conduct and an Exposition of the Misrepresentations of the Northern Star*, Bath 1842; J. B. O'Brien, *Vindication of his Conduct at the late Birmingham Conference*, Brimingham 1842; W. Hill, *The Rejected Letters*, n.p., 1843; id., *A Scabbard for Feargus O'Connor's Sword*, Hull 1844; J. Watkins, *Impeachment of Feargus O'Connor*, London 1843; W. Thomason, *O'Connor and Democracy Inconsistent with Each Other; Being a Statement of the Events in the Life of Feargus O'Connor*, Newcastle 1844.

97. *NS*, 23 Apr. 1842, p. 5.

98. Ibid., 30 May 1840, p. 4; 3 Apr. 1841, p. 4; 4 Feb. 1843, p. 1.

99. F. G. and R. M. Black (eds.), *The Harney Papers*, Assen 1969, p. 241, also see pp. 251-52.

100. *NS*, 4 Feb. 1843, pp. 1, 5; 8 July, p. 4; 15 July, p. 4; 12 Aug., p. 4; F. O'Connor, *Reply to Mr Hill's 'Scabbard'*, London 1843, pp. 2, 4; PRO, HO 20/10, interview with O'Connor. I am grateful to Dr Michael Ignatieff for drawing my attention to this last source.

101. *Harney Papers*, letters 79 and 80; H. Weisser, 'Chartist Internationalism, 1845-48', *Historical Journal*, 14, 1971, pp. 49-66; id., 'The Role of Feargus O'Connor in Chartist Internationalism', *Rocky Mountain Social Science Journal*, 6, 1968, pp. 82-90; Schoyen, *Chartist Challenge*, p. 131; D. Thompson, 'La presse de la classe ouvrière anglaise', pp. 28-29.

102. Gammage, *History of the Chartist Movement*, p. 200.

103. For instance, *NS*, 10 Nov. 1838, p. 4; 18 Sept. 1841, p. 4; 28 Feb. 1846, p. 3.

104. O'Connor, *Letter to Hill*, p. 28; *NS*, 28 Sept. 1839, p. 4; 28 Dec., p. 5; 11 Jan. 1842, p. 4; 9 July; *Southern Star*, 26 Jan. 1840, p. 5; Plummer, *Bronterre*, pp. 140, 164-65.

105. *English Chartist Circular*, no. 57 (1842); *NS*, 18 June 1842, p. 1; British Library, Add. MSS 27835, fos. 165-68, John Seal to Place, Leicester, 15 July 1841; *Commonwealthsman*, 18 June 1842, copy in PRO, HO 45/260.

106. See *English Chartist Circular*, no. 153 (1843).

107. *NS*, 17 Mar. 1838, p. 4; 12 June, p. 6; 23 June, p. 6; 14 July, p. 4; 8 Dec., p. 5; 22

Dec., p. 8; Holyoake, *Life of Stephens*, p. 85.

    108. *NS*, 18 July 1840, p. 6; 9 Oct. 1841, p. 1; see below ch. 6.

    109. *NS*, 23 June 1838, p. 6.

    110. O'Connor was editor of the *Evening Star* from 23 Aug. 1842 to 1 Feb. 1843. As late as 1848, he was planning to start a Chartist daily paper, *NS*, 4 Sept. 1847, p. 1; 13 May 1848, p. 4.

    111. Schoyen, *Chartist Challenge*, p. 105; *NS*, 9 Oct. 1841, p. 7; 30 Jan. 1841, p. 5. For Wheeler, see W. Stevens, *A Memoir of Thomas Martin Wheeler*, London 1862; obituary in *Reynold's Weekly Newspaper*, 8 June 1862. In 1842, G. M. Bartlett was the *Star's* correspondent for the West of England; William Griffin for Manchester; J. Sinclair for Newcastle; James Williams for Sunderland.

    112. *NS*, 24 Apr. 1841, p. 7.

    113. Ibid., 30 Apr. 1842, p. 6. Also see J. Jackson, *The Demagogue Done Up, an Exposure of the Extreme Inconsistencies of Mr Feargus O'Connor*, Bradford 1844; J. H. Parry, *A Letter to Feargus O'Connor, Farmer and Barrister*, London 1843, p. 11; F. O'Connor, *A Letter from Feargus O'Connor, Esq., to John Humffreys Parry, of the Middle Temple, Barrister at Law; But Neither Farmer nor Lawyer*, London 1843; G. White, *An Answer to John Humffreys Parry . . . and an Exposure of the Self-Styled Liberals and Free Traders*, London 1843.

    114. *NS*, 16 Sept. 1843, p. 6; Stevens, *Memoir of Wheeler*, p. 24.

    115. *NS*, 21 Sept. 1839, p. 3; see below ch. 5.

    116. Ibid., 5 Oct. 1839, p. 4; 18 July 1840, p. 6; 30 Jan. 1841, p. 7; 24 June 1843, p. 1; 23 Nov. 1844, p. 1; 21 Nov. 1846, p. 1; 26 Aug. 1848, p. 1; Schoyen, *Chartist Challenge*, p. 133, n 1; Epstein, 'O'Connor and the *Star*', p. 94, n 2.

    117. *NS*, 18 Jan. 1845, p. 4.

    118. Ibid., 3 Nov. 1838, p. 8.

    119. Ibid., 30 Apr. 1842, p. 6.

    120. Ibid., 18 Aug. 1838, p. 3; also see address of the Dewsbury Chartists to O'Connor, ibid., 11 Dec. 1841, p. 7.

    121. Ibid., 16 Jan. 1841, p. 7.

3 THE COMING TOGETHER OF CHARTISM: 1838

I The Demagogue

Perhaps the most misunderstood aspect of O'Connor's leadership is its extremely personalised character, its exuberant egoism, its blatant arrogance and demagoguery. O'Connor never rejected the title of 'demagogue'. On the contrary, he informed readers of the *Northern Star:* 'I say, I am a Demagogue, the word is derived from the Greek words, "demos, populos", the people; and "ago, duco", to lead; and means a leader of the people.'[1] Part of the vigour of O'Connor's appeal as a Chartist leader derived from his self-confident tone and his assumption of the right to leadership. This self-confidence was firmly rooted both within an English radical tradition of gentlemanly leadership which can be traced through Hunt, Cartwright and Burdett as far back as Wilkes, and within an Irish tradition of popular leadership with which O'Connor's own family was prominently connected. However, the role of the demagogue was not antithetical to the needs of organisation, but rather was in itself an organisational manifestation. Initially, in the absence of national Chartist institutions of organisation, such as the National Convention or the National Charter Association, national agitation could only be undertaken by independent gentlemen like O'Connor who could afford to tour the country constantly speaking and organising, who were not vulnerable to the employers' blacklist nor susceptible to the damaging charge of living off the people through trafficking in politics. There also remained legal restrictions upon national radical organisation.[2] In this situation the champion of the platform became a figure around which the forces of radicalism could rally, a symbol of national unity and solidarity.

O'Connor always most directly associated himself with the memory and principles of Henry Hunt, declaring himself on numerous occasions to be a 'Huntite'. According to O'Connor, Hunt and Major Cartwright had been the only demagogues to advance the people's cause, the only demagogues 'whose object had not been to create grievances, and to magnify those already existing, for the purpose of living upon promises to correct them'.[3] From his first northern tour, working-class radicals placed O'Connor within this tradition and identified him with Hunt.[4] Year after year he travelled to Lancashire to celebrate the anniversary of Hunt's birth with local radicals, and often took the platform at the annual meeting at St Peter's Field held to commemorate the 'never to be forgotten' 16 August.[5] The Chartists were intensely conscious of their own roots, and on such occasions O'Connor carefully outlined the significance of Hunt's career to the development of radicalism. Hunt had been the uncompromising champion of the demand for universal suffrage, having made it the demand which all leaders of the radical/working-class cause had to adopt. Hunt was also the symbol of opposition to the Whigs. He had advocated the primary need for the radical movement to assert its independence from the Whigs and had stood out most prominently against the betrayal of 1832. It was the 'ever-to-be-loved Hunt' who 'pushed the principles of Radicalism beyond Whig convenience'. O'Connor considered the final break with Whiggery which Hunt had initiated to have been the central achievement of his own pre-Chartist agitation.[6] O'Connor saw himself, as did most Chartists, as Hunt's successor, the defender of radical principles in more auspicious days.

> His (O'Connor's) position was tranquil compared with that of Hunt. He was the first to brave danger. . . . He (Mr. Hunt) told them that the Reform Bill was all farce; he saw it to be a delusion; and while he was thus stemming the torrents of public opinion thus misled, his enemies were too powerful for him, and they broke his heart. (Hear, hear.) His (Mr. O'Connor's) position was neither so dangerous, nor was his work so arduous. He (Mr. Hunt) was the great architect who taught the people what that edifice should be; he (Mr. O'Connor) was only a humble workman endeavouring to raise that edifice to its completion.[7]

Chartism originated as a platform movement. The platform, together with the radical press, played a key role in bringing together the Chartist movement. Throughout his radical career O'Connor organised through the platform, through extensive national tours. No leader since Major Cartwright had toured with the energy and the pace of O'Connor. Even with the establishment of the *Northern Star* which carried most of his speeches, there was no substitute for his charismatic presence, bringing news of the movement's progress from all quarters and emphasising the need for unity. The central figure on the popular platform was the demagogue, an orator of charismatic brilliance and usually a gentleman; for it was such gentlemen who 'knew the forms and language of high politics' associated with the platform.[8] O'Connor was a gentleman. His language, his bearing, his dress marked him as a member of the gentry. Part of his appeal was that of a gentleman of high birth and wealth who had foregone the privileges of his social station and taken up the cause of the working class through motives which could only be attributed to a deep conviction based upon principles, the justness of which transcended class.[9] Perhaps vestiges of an earlier tradition of deference enhanced O'Connor's popularity within certain sections of the working class, but certainly this was of secondary importance. His gentlemanly bearing in conjunction with his extreme radical professions merely served to highlight the righteousness of the radical cause. Despite the social distance which existed between leadership and led, a collective identity developed between the gentleman of the platform and the working class, a sense of shared experience, familiarity and mutual dependence. O'Connor constantly claimed that the working class was 'the only class of society who care for me, or for whom I care a single straw'.[10] In his turn O'Connor came to embody the hopes, the sufferings and the aspirations of a generation of working people.

O'Connor came to typify a style of leadership associated with the independent gentleman of the platform in which the relationship between the leader and his following was direct and unmediated — the champion and the people. This style of leadership demanded a continual legitimisation of the demagogue's claim to leadership. 'Nothing is more necessary than that a Demagogue, which I profess myself to be, should be able to defend his every step in the course of Agitation.'[11] The repeated accounts of his unpaid services, the lengthy reviews of his career, the endless assertions of a willingness to die for the cause of freedom, were indicative of a style of leadership in which no formal channels of accountability existed. To reduce this merely to a question of O'Connor's egotism is to miss the point. The frequent promise never to accept 'pension, place or favour under any Government' was not a hollow protestation, nor some rather eccentric manifestation of extreme egotism. When considered alongside the careers of the popular leaders who had gone before O'Connor such statements constituted a recognition of dependence upon and responsibility to the people, a form of accountability. Even during the Chartist period there was distrust of working-class radicals who made a living through political agitation. O'Connor's financial independence and absolute incorruptibility were essential to his standing within the Chartist movement.

O'Connor was not elected to the platform, he was unpaid and possessed no formal mandate. He was not a local leader closely associated with or dependent upon the support of a particular community. Therefore with ritualised regularity he was expected to rehearse his achievements, his steadfastness, his sufferings, his intention to continue undaunted by persecution, danger, pecuniary loss and regardless of the apathy, desertion or betrayal of others. O'Connor resisted any tendency within the radical movement to reject the need for leadership. He pointed out to a meeting at Hull: 'Vincent had exhorted them to put no confidence in any man; if, however they were destitute of all confidence in their leaders, they must naturally feel a sort of contempt for themselves.'[12] O'Connor was extremely conscious of the necessity continually to outline the foundation of his own claim to leadership. Whenever the movement reached a critical juncture or his leadership was challenged he penned a comprehensive account of his past services and history of the movement, carefully explaining his present position.[13]

Despite this highly personalised form of leadership, O'Connor was instrumental in the establishment of more permanent forms of Chartist leadership and organisation, characterised by democratic election, regular payment and a more formal degree of accountability. Despite the powerful attraction of 'champion-style' leadership, national organisation centred upon an individual lacked permanency; his imprisonment, death or betrayal was a profound psychological and organisational set-back. The vanity of these gentlemen of the platform was notorious. Their frequent and acrimonious squabbles had often left a radical movement, devoid of any means with which to arbitrate between their various claims, bemused and seriously divided. Thus the unity achieved through the person of the demagogue was easily placed in jeopardy. From this very instability arose the images which surrounded the demagogue — the rock, the lion, the champion of liberty and martyred patriot — together with an emphasis on principled consistency and unity.[14] Martyrdom and desertion were themes closely associated with the demagogue. Although identified with this older tradition of radical leadership, much of O'Connor's significance as a Chartist leader lies in his efforts to use his personal popularity as a charismatic demagogue to help lay the foundations for more regular forms of organisation. O'Connor brought the old to the service of the new. He was the key figure in the transition from an older style of leadership and organisation to that of Chartism. While Chartism marked a new departure in working-class politics, it carried within it many of the older traditions and earlier problems of radical organisation and leadership.

II The Coming Together of Chartism

More than any other radical leader, Feargus O'Connor was responsible for uniting the emergent forces of Chartism in summer/autumn 1838, and for continuing to provide national leadership and direction to a movement of great local diversity. He was the obvious leader to give expression to the growing cohesion between various groups of local radicals. His high standing within the ranks of English and Scottish radicals was based upon his radical parliamentary record, his unrivalled command of the platform, his recent establishment of the *Northern Star* and most significantly upon his efforts from 1835 to mobilise an independent radical party in the country. O'Connor consciously assumed the role of national leadership in early 1838, calling upon the support of the radicals of England, Ireland and Scotland and asserting a personal claim upon their allegiance based upon his past services in the radical cause.

> I have a right to speak to you in the language of dictation, because, of all the men (since the passing of the Reform Bill to the present moment) who have represented you, both in, and out of Parliament, I alone have stood by my pledges, and supported you and your cause . . . The day will yet arrive when justice will be done to one, who by his personal exertion, and without a single journal to support him, organised the people of England and Scotland, so as to make their united voices a terror to tyrants. Friends, I address you as founder of the Radical Associations of England and Scotland, as accredited missionary of the radicals of London, and as elected president of the National Association of Scotland. I have a right to expect a response to my appeal. I have laboured, for more than five years in your cause, and am still untried and ready to join with you in the glorious pursuit of liberty and freedom. I know what the people can do — they know what they ought to do.[15]

(i) *O'Connor and the Anti-Poor Law Agitation*

The task of national organisation was preceded by that of consolidating and unifying the North behind the leadership of O'Connor, the *Star* and the Great Northern Union. By autumn of 1837, O'Connor was concentrating his energies on the mobilisation of the North of England. In league with Richard Oastler and the Rev. J. R. Stephens, supported by the *Northern Star,* he campaigned on the two issues which dominated the northern radical platform, the new Poor Law and the fate of the Glasgow cotton spinners. By 1838 these three leaders had established a remarkable dominance over the platform in the North, and had become almost inseparably linked in the popular mind. No radical dinner in Lancashire or Yorkshire ended without toasts to these three gentlemen, no meeting was complete without a hearty three cheers for their united services. 'The three . . . played into each others' hands and had an almost inconceivable command over the people', commented Francis Place.[16] O'Connor played down the differences between his own political position and that of his two co-agitators. At Newcastle, in June 1838, O'Connor declared the basis of his platform alliance:

> He, Mr. O'Connor, was in alliance with two men, the one calling himself a Tory, and the other declaring that he belonged to no political creed, and there did not exist two better Radicals, two more determined haters of oppression, or two more faithful friends of the cause of liberty, and the working classes; he need scarcely name, Richard Oastler, and the Rev. Joseph Stephens. (Great cheering.)[17]

However, significantly, the Newcastle meeting was not principally an anti-Poor Law affair, but was called to endorse the National Petition for universal suffrage drawn up by the leaders of the Birmingham Political Union. O'Connor was the central figure in the transference of the mass support for the anti-Poor Law agitation along with its tone of intransigent defiance to authority into the national Chartist movement.

During the autumn and winter of 1837 the anti-Poor Law movement had been revitalised with tremendous force in the North of England. The South Lancashire anti-Poor Law Association was formed in November, and by 1838 thirty-eight local associations had been organised in Lancashire and Cheshire.[18] In South Lancashire and the West Riding plans were laid for a mass petitioning campaign to demand the repeal of the Act. O'Connor, Stephens and Oastler were the principal speakers at the numerous public meetings connected with this campaign at which the rhetoric of violence reached a new pitch. Stephens's rhetoric and Oastler's letters to the *Star* set the tone. Stephens's inflammatory language electrified audiences with images of fire, blood and divine retribution, and alarmed the bourgeoisie with overt threats to the rights and safety of private property.[19]

Although O'Connor and the *Star* defended the language of Stephens and Oastler, O'Connor's own language was always more restrained than theirs. He rarely matched the reckless abandon of Stephens and never dealt in sustained passages of revolutionary exhortation. Even during this period his speeches were characterised by their cautious threats and constitutional reasoning. The language of the constitutional lawyer was very different to the apocalyptic outrage of the Old Testament prophet. O'Connor sprinkled his speeches with ambiguous hints of 'physical force' calculated to delight his audience. He told an anti-Poor Law meeting at Dewsbury, in December 1837:

> I like to look to the moral force of the people. It is like 'stir about', a good thing in its way (loud laughter), but I also like to look to the substance of which this moral force is only a feeble shadow. . . . Talk not about the shadow, if we are not to see the substance,— that necessary physical force.[20]

O'Connor openly identified himself with the lawless side of anti-Poor Law protest. At Bradford he praised the local resistance to the introduction of the law which had ended in serious riot — 'all England admires you for it; the men of Bradford have done more towards annihilating the new Poor Law . . . than all the moral force we have been able to array against it'.[21] He was actively involved in the riots later in the year at Huddersfield and Dewsbury.[22]

As for the purpose of the new Poor Law O'Connor had no doubts. It had been introduced in order to lower industrial wages. He related its introduction to the labour theory of value and a primitive formulation of the theory of surplus value.

> The great design of the Poor Law was to bring down wages to the lowest possible scale, and thus to leave working men completely at the mercy of their masters. . . . Who, he would ask, made the Poor Law necessary? The capitalists have refused you the just amounts due for your labour. Listen to this, ye men of Bradford; mark it well, and learn it thoroughly. The manufacturer who employs four thousand hands, and works them for two hours per day extra, at the rate of 3d per hour, in the course of one year, realises the enormous sun of £11,000 wrung from their labour.

The new Poor Law was not only a violation of the constitutional and historic rights of the poor to relief, but challenged the natural right of the people to gain a living from the soil.[23] Nor did O'Connor recognise the 43rd of Elizabeth as an adequate substitute for the rights of the poor, although he acknowledged its superiority to the new law. All poor laws were mere substitutes for the people's right to the land. Thus he asked the great South Lancashire anti-Poor Law meeting, in February 1838:

> Why were poor laws necessary at all? They were but a substitute. They but declared the right of the poor to the land; therefore they ought not to be called paupers. . . . The land was theirs, and they were entitled to live out of it. (Cheers.)[24]

The new Poor Law came to epitomise the social philosophy, the ruthless 'Malthusian cant', of the centralising Whigs, their 'sham' radical allies and middle-class supporters. It was regarded not only as a vicious attack upon the right to poor relief, but as a trespass upon the responsibilities of community. Together with the Rural Police Bill it was seen as part of a general onslaught upon popular liberties, as well as a wider system of economic and social exploitation.[25] The *Star* pointed out that it was an error to 'suppose that, in the North, all agitation is directed against the New Poor Law Amendment Act. No; but it is the basis of a new constitution and therefore do we work the battering ram of discontent against it.'

> Its provisions are to give effect to the new system of the political economists and to the new religion of the . . . infidels; and therefore we denounce it. The auxiliaries to this infernal law are the Factory scheme, the rural police, and the complete destruction of the Trades' Associations, which was the last remnant of power in the hands of the working classes by which supply and demand could be wholesomely regulated.[26]

The extent to which working people envisaged Chartism in terms of a defence of existing rights and against possible government repression should not be forgotten.

Certain historians have mistaken O'Connor's close association with Oastler and Stephens and his prominence in the anti-Poor Law agitation as a manifestation of an essentially 'tory-radical' or 'tory-paternalist' social philosophy, as well as indicative of the 'backward' looking or 'deferential' character of northern Chartism.[27] O'Connor was not a tory-radical, although he often struck distinctly populist strains; nor was his leadership in the North based upon working-class deference. He stood for a traditional and widely accepted radical programme based upon the demand for universal suffrage. Injustices such as the new Poor Law were merely part of a larger system of oppression and exploitation which would only be ended when the working class had political power.[28] Although Oastler, and more particularly Stephens, might accept the working class's right to universal suffrage, or acknowledge the importance of the vote as a symbol of dignity, universal suffrage was not central to their politics or analysis of society.[29] Nor did O'Connor's ideal of post-universal suffrage society correspond to a tory-paternalist vision of society based upon the mutual interdependence of the squire or capitalist, the labourer and the minister of the Lord, where the rich were the guardians of the interests of the poor. O'Connor's was an essentially artisan concept of the independent small producer reaping the full fruits of his own labour upon the land of his birth. There are no beneficent squires strutting across O'Connor's land of promise, but independent workers meeting and cooperating upon terms of equality.

Certainly O'Connor shared Oastler and Stephens's anxiety over the erosion of certain social values under the impact of the steady advance of industrial capitalism and government centralisation. They found common cause in their opposition to the displacement of labour through the unregulated introduction of machinery; in their mutual compassion for the impoverished handloom weaver and the overburdened factory hand; in their detestation of the break-up of the traditional structure of the family and home through the process of industrialisation; and in their implacable hostility towards the factory owners — 'the Steam Aristocracy'. The central antagonism between capital and labour was a primary concern of the anti-Poor Law leaders. Stephens told a Chartist meeting that he advocated universal suffrage because he believed he had no right to withold it from his neighbour, but added, 'this was not the question — at least not the first question'.

> There was a principle underneath, around, and above all questions of mere forms of government. . . . That question was the adjustment of the balance between poverty and property — between the fruits of labour laid up in the shape of capital and the prolific energies of labour that first created that wealth, and made it bear the value stamped upon it.[30]

While O'Connor disagreed with Oastler and Stephens on the purely political question of universal suffrage, under the influence of the anti-Poor Law agitation, and even more directly the cause of the Glasgow cotton spinners, his language of class became more clearly defined.

> He knew that the working men were pressed down by the capitalists. He saw that instead of the capitalist being dependent upon the labourer, as he ought to be, his sole attention was directed to the improvement of machinery, while the working classes were to be starved, or punished if they attempted to make a stand against so ruinous a system. . . . he divided society just into two classes — the rich oppressors and the poor oppressed. The whole question resolved itself into the battle between labour and capital.[31]

The common ground between the three leaders was a social programme which O'Connor was instrumental in integrating into Chartism. The experience of the anti-Poor Law struggle and the support which Oastler and Stephens gained from working-class radicals offered Chartism a sort of innoculation against a particularly virulent form of middle-class 'liberalism' or whig-radicalism. It was a final injection which kept the Chartists out of the camp of Daniel O'Connell, the parliamentary radicals and the Anti-Corn Law League. O'Connor's ability to fuse the social content of the anti-Poor Law movement and its class conscious tone with a traditional political radicalism was a fundamental aspect of his early Chartist leadership.

O'Connor clearly shared the northern radicals' deep respect for Oastler and Stephens. But respect is not the same thing as deference, appreciation for services rendered to the people's cause is not the same as uncritical reliance upon the external leadership of gentlemen agitators. The radicals of Huddersfield, Oastler's strongest centre of support, as early as spring 1837, clearly outlined the reasons for their support of Oastler in an address entitled 'Why do the Radicals Support Mr. Oastler, Who Designates Himself an Ultra-Tory?' It had nothing to do with tory-radicalism. Their support was based on Oastler's cooperation with the radicals, his opposition to the Whigs, his championship of the cause of the factory children and his position as the foremost opponent of the new Poor Law.[32] Earlier the same year the Huddersfield radicals had published an address to O'Connor, utterly rejecting the label 'tory-radical', and proclaiming their continuity with a radical tradition associated with Cartwright, Hunt and Cobbett.

> In addressing you, sir, we wish to settle another point; we disclaim every such title as Whig-Radical or Tory-Radical. If such political hybrids exist at all, we beg leave to tell our countrymen in general, that any application of such name to the Radicals of Huddersfield is a misnomer. Our creed is the old one professed by Cartwright, Hunt and Cobbett; not the worse for being republished and illuminated by yourself, sir, as with a sunbeam from Erin![33]

The support which O'Connor gained in the North of England and which he brought into Chartism was related primarily to a working-class tradition of independent radicalism as described by E. P. Thompson, and not to the last vestiges of a tradition of tory-paternalism and deference. Henry Vincent, agitating on behalf of the LWMA in 1838, was deeply impressed by the degree of radical feeling which existed in the North.

> Ever since the year 1818 the Yorkshire and Lancashire people have been peacefully struggling for Universal Suffrage. They were the only two counties in which the principle existed to any extent — and the choicest spirits have become almost worn-out by their continuous

exertions. . . . You have no idea of the intensity of radical opinions here. You have an index from the numerous public house signs —full length portraits of Hunt holding in his hands scrawls [sic] containing the words Universal Suffrage, Annual Parliaments, and the Ballot.— Paine and Cobbett also figure occasionally —[34]

At Macclesfield in autumn of 1838, O'Connor and Stephens shared the radical platform with no fewer than ten local radical leaders who had been imprisoned between 1817 and 1820. O'Connor dubbed it 'a meeting of martyrs': 'we have many on this platform, who twenty years ago, were hurled into dungeons . . . for expressing the very same sentiments that we are here assembled to express this day'.[35] In Yorkshire and Lancashire Chartism found a rich tradition of radical politics and culture firmly intact. Despite the tremendous popularity of Oastler and Stephens among northern radicals, the principles represented by O'Connor accorded more closely with the political creed of the majority of working-class radicals. O'Connor based his national leadership upon the support of the most advanced radical localities.

The anti-Poor Law protest was not an autonomous movement, but part of a wider working-class opposition to a series of attacks from the Whig Government on presumed democratic rights. The local leaders who took up the resistance to the new Poor Law were often radicals who had taken part in the reform struggle; organised the ten-hours campaign; sold the unstamped; initiated petitions for the return of the Dorchester labourers and defence funds for the Glasgow spinners; protested against the coercion of Ireland and demanded freedom for the Canadians. Among them were the seasoned radicals with whom O'Connor had cooperated in establishing Radical Associations, men who played such a vital role in launching the *Northern Star* and were to emerge as Chartism's local leaders. In early 1838, the resistance to the introduction of the new Poor Law, however, was the most immediate concern of these radicals. Although the anti-Poor Law movement was the most intense and best organised of these pre-Chartist protests, it was merely the last of this series of overlapping protests which culminated in the emergence of the more generalised agitation for the People's Charter.

What northern Chartism inherited from the anti-Poor Law agitation was its organisation and tone. The organisation of the South Lancashire anti-Poor Law Association and the West Riding Delegates Committee, the links established between Lancashire, Cheshire and Yorkshire leaders, the mass demonstrations and the attempt at a single mass petition to Parliament were important to the coming together of Chartism. Anti-Poor Law riots at Huddersfield, Bradford, Dewsbury and Todmorden and the widespread willingness to defy the law found expression in Chartism's early spirit of intimidation and a sense of imminent confrontation. Constant appeals to authorities above the law and the government of the day — to the 'real' constitution, 'the good old laws of English freedom', natural right, the Bible and the word of God — underpinned a sense of righteousness and legitimation. The earliest recommendations for the people to arm came from the anti-Poor Law platform; and in autumn 1838 Stephens brought to the Chartist platform the rhetoric of violence pioneered at mass anti-Poor Law demonstrations and ten-hours meetings. Much of the strength, tone and forms of protest — a tendency towards direct action — indicative of early northern Chartism derived from the merging of a defensive movement based primarily upon local communal resistance to the encroachments of a modernising central state upon traditional rights with a mass national movement concerned with the acquisition of political rights.[36]

(ii) *The Great Northern Union and the National Petition*

In February 1838, the Commons overwhelmingly rejected Fielden and Lord Stanhope's motion for the repeal of the Poor Law Amendment Act which had been backed by petitions signed by over one hundred thousand men and women. Throughout northern England there was a general resolve 'never to petition again'. With the rejection of their petitions the anti-Poor Law movement had reached an impasse. As a distinct movement the anti-Poor Law agitation was on the wane by spring 1838, although local resistance continued.[37]

During the height of the anti-Poor Law campaign O'Connor had kept the question of universal suffrage before working-class radicals, arguing the pointlessness of petitioning a body elected upon any other basis.[38] He told a meeting at Bolton: 'he had ceased to think of any other question but universal suffrage'.[39] Throughout early 1838, the *Star* emphasised the central importance of the demand for universal suffrage as opposed to partial reforms such as the ballot, corn-law repeal or an eleven-hours bill.[40] With the failure of Fielden's parliamentary efforts O'Connor took the opportunity to bring forward his own plan to establish the Great Northern Union. The *Star*, so crucial in initiating O'Connorite organisation, expressed the hope that those disappointed with the failure of Fielden's parliamentary attempt would now 'join us and the people in chaunting the dirage [sic] of infamy, by raising one loud and universal cry for UNIVERSAL SUFFRAGE'. The editorial called for the formation of 'Anti-Poor Law Associations and Universal Suffrage Associations . . . in every city, town, and village throughout the Northern Hive'. A meeting of representatives would shortly be called at Leeds to plan a mass campaign of agitation, 'after which we shall expect to see the hive swarm, when summer comes, in order to sting the drones'.[41] O'Connor seized the moment to redirect the energies of radical agitation in the North. Although he was periodically drawn back into the arena of strictly Poor Law protest, as during the riots at Huddersfield and Dewsbury, universal suffrage was now the key issue.

O'Connor's initiative corresponded with a reorientation of radical activity in Yorkshire and Lancashire. Even during the height of the anti-Poor Law agitation meetings were held linking the demand for universal suffrage with the repeal of the new Poor Law.[42] At Oldham the radicals revived the Radical Association on the basis of the traditional radical programme. Both the Dewsbury and Barnsley Radical Associations, strongholds of O'Connorite support, held meetings and dinners in April to petition for universal suffrage.[43] At Dewsbury O'Connor was the main speaker, but he was surrounded by local radicals who were crucial to the emergence of northern Chartism — T. S. Brooke, Dewsbury's radical bookseller, in the chair; Peter Bussey from Bradford; William Thornton and Robert Wilkinson from Halifax; Morritt Matthews from Liversedge; Joseph Crabtree from Barnsley; Pitkeithley and Oastler from Huddersfield; James Quarmby from Oldham and James Taylor from Rochdale. While praising the local radical organisation represented at the gathering as 'specimens of united determination', O'Connor continued:

> it was still necessary to have a union based on such principles as would not only enable Radicals to think alike, but, also to *know* that they did think alike. Nothing . . . was so necessary as that they should know how each other thought and with that knowledge they might almost attain any object which they set their wishes.

The generalisation of radical agitation was O'Connor's primary aim in early 1838.

The Great Northern Union has often been seen as an association contrived by O'Connor in order to offset the influence of Lovett and the LWMA in the North. More to the point, the GNU was an organisational expression of O'Connor's efforts to redirect the forces of the anti-Poor Law movement into the emerging Chartist movement. The

Union was a loose federation of local Radical and Working Men's Associations. It lasted only a short time and was never a particularly effective centralised organisation. Although its influence was widespread, the GNU was largely based on O'Connor's West Riding stronghold. Throughout South Lancashire radical associations expressed confidence in its programme and general tone, and some associations like the one at Stalybridge adopted the name of the Northern Union. Branches were also established at places as distant as Carlisle and Loughborough.[44] To some extent the GNU merely superimposed a new label upon existing radical and anti-Poor Law associations. However, it did serve the purpose of consolidating O'Connor's leadership in the industrial North, as well as amalgamating these radicals however incoherently into one body. It also provided the organisational basis from which O'Connor committed these northern localities to the National Petition, the Charter and the plans for the Convention at the demonstrations which launched the Chartist movement in summer and autumn of 1838. The GNU grew steadily with the affiliation of the radicals at Halifax, Barnsley, Leeds and Stalybridge.[45] By the time of the great Birmingham meeting — the official 'beginning' of Chartism — the GNU boasted a membership of fifty thousand. By December it claimed 56,000 members, 1,500 of whom were at Bradford; and by the time the Convention met numbers had risen to 62,000. However, this largely reflects affiliations of associations which were in existence prior to the GNU formation. The criteria for membership are also difficult to determine.[46] Still the Union fostered a sense of identity and allegiance which went beyond the immediate Chartist locality, and offered a framework for O'Connor's constant agitation, especially in autumn 1838. In the West Riding, in conjunction with the stimulus of the great Peep Green demonstration, it facilitated the rapid absorption of large numbers of new recruits into the radical ranks and the integration of outlying villages into a wider organisational structure. It was no coincidence that the West Riding was the most highly organised Chartist district by 1839.[47]

Yet progress was gradual. Nothing apparently came of O'Connor's proposal to convene a four-day conference in Leeds of the Lancashire and Yorkshire districts. A committee was appointed to draw up the objects, rules and regulations of the GNU. George White and William Rider, who became secretary of the Leeds NU, took the lead in composing this document, as well as rallying support in Leeds.[48] The objects of the GNU, published in early May, included a clear statement on the relationship between 'moral' and 'physical' force.

> Before joining the union every member should distinctly understand, that in the event of moral force failing to procure those privileges which the constitution guarantees, but which a party would abrogate; and should the constitution be invaded, it is resolved that physical force shall be resorted to if necessary, in order to secure the equality of law, and the blessings of those institutions which are the birth right of freemen.[49]

This explicit, though well-qualified, statement of a willingness to resort to 'physical force', 'if necessary', was later popularised in the slogan 'peaceably if we can, forcibly if we must'. This found almost universal acceptance among the radicals of the North.[50]

On 5 June 1838, the Great Northern Union was officially established at a meeting on Hunslet Moor, outside Leeds. White, Rider, Abraham Hanson of Elland and Joseph Crabtree were the principal speakers along with O'Connor and Birmingham's John Collins. The GNU was established to counter 'the present disorganised state of the working classes'. Significantly, the Birmingham petition was adopted at this first meeting of the GNU. John Collins, the Birmingham Political Union's hard working missionary, gave the meeting an account of his tour since the Glasgow rally to launch the petition, and outlined plans for mass meetings throughout the country. O'Connor moved a vote of thanks to Collins, and declared: 'he would pledge himself for Leeds and the North. The petition . . . had no ambiguity about it, it bore the imprint of the manly Attwood and his manly followers . . .'[51] Thus, from the outset, the GNU was linked to the National Petition for universal suffrage.

The National Petition was not just another petition. The radicals of Yorkshire, Lancashire and other areas had been petitioning continually since 1832 against government measures and for the right to vote. The ancient right of petitioning had itself been recently weakened. Through a change in the procedural rules of the Commons petitions were no longer allowed to be introduced by a speech. This meant the Commons could no longer be brought to a stand-still through massive petitioning campaigns as during the reform agitation or the great radical campaign of 1816-17.[52] This rather effective constitutional method of focusing public opinion upon radical protest was not available to the Chartists. There was no point in flooding the Commons with numerous small local petitions. Following the overwhelming rejection of their anti-Poor Law petitions the radicals of the North were clearly weary of petitioning. O'Connor summed up this feeling. He asked what had happened to their petitions to the Reform

Parliament:

> Many of them were never read, and when read they were thrust into a
> bag and for-ever forgotten. For his own part he was weary of petitioning,
> — and he would recommend that the next petition sent from that place
> should be to this effect:— 'We the workingmen of Dewsbury, consider
> that we're entitled to Universal Suffrage as a right, and we therefore
> demand it.' (Hear, hear, cheers and laughter.) The right of petitioning,
> which Brougham had designated as the greatest right was now little
> better than a mere farce, and the right of appeal had virtually been taken
> from the people.[53]

The novel nature of the Birmingham petition, the presentation of
one mass national supplication for universal suffrage, made it an ideal
vehicle for the final test of the contractual relationship between
government and people. At meeting after meeting at which the
National Petition was adopted radicals affirmed their resolve 'never
to petition again', a pledge O'Connor often reiterated.[54] For instance
at Newcastle, Thomas Doubleday, chairman of the meeting called to
adopt the Petition, announced: 'They had assembled to petition for
the last time . . .' And James Ayr was certain the National Petition
would be signed 'the more willingly *as it was to be the last document
in the shape of a petition*'.[55] The concept of 'the last petition' was
pregnant with revolutionary overtones. It represented but a thinly
veiled threat to the government. Within the Chartist ranks it also
helped foster the impression that the rejection of the Petition would
mark the point after which alternative action of great consequence
would ensue as a legitimate constitutional response to tyranny. This
was to be the last peaceful attempt to change the basis of government.
Henry Vincent captured the prevailing mood among working-class
radicals, especially in the industrial North, in a letter to his brother-
in-law:

> I tell you . . . plainly — that if we fail in our present efforts to obtain a
> peaceful Radical change, *one of the most bloody revolutions the world
> ever saw will take place in England.—* . . . That a change *must come*, and
> *come quickly,* all men who have *eyes* must *see.*[56]

This sense of the imminence of either great change or great social
upheaval distinguished the first period of Chartist agitation and was
embodied in what was to prove the first rather than the last Chartist
petition.

Throughout the summer of 1838 radical associations throughout
the North adopted the National Petition. O'Connor immediately acted
upon this pretext for agitation and organisation. With single-handed

determination he undertook to unite the national radical movement. The Great Northern Union having been established he headed north to Durham, Northumberland, Cumberland and Scotland. He told the radicals of Carlisle, who soon afterwards joined the GNU with one thousand members:

> He could not conclude without expressing his great delight at having thus perfected the great chain between London and Edinburgh and Glasgow. All the links were now perfect. London, Birmingham, Sheffield, Manchester, Leeds, Newcastle, Carlisle, Glasgow and Edinburgh, had now become forged as it were together . . . a spirit was now growing up which nothing but justice could put down.[57]

O'Connor analysed the reasons for the increased radical coherence and growth in the numbers at their meetings, drawing particular attention to the effect of the government's attack upon the trades as a unifying factor.

> Our meetings of late . . . have been more numerous and more numerously attended, and more strongly characterized by determination of expression than public meetings are wont to be. You will naturally seek a reason. It is not then, that a new spirit has arisen, but that an union of different spirits has taken place. Antecedently to the attack upon, and the threatened destruction of Trades Unions by the Government, the different bodies of Trades considered their order sufficiently protected by the rules of their respective associations, and they rested satisfied with the protection which those rules yielded to their society, and therefore became negligent of their political duties . . . The system of our government, however, cannot afford the surrender of any portion of industry, that can be ceded to the money-mongers as the price for their political support, and consequently at the instance of that party . . . war was made against all labour-protecting schemes, the effect of which has been to throw the whole body of the hitherto disunited and different plan-trying community into one general force, for the assertion of their political rights by which alone their social and class regulations can be protected.[58]

Further north O'Connor joined his old radical ally Dr John Taylor in an extensive three-week tour of Scotland. Dr Taylor later referred to O'Connor as 'the kind of connecting link between England and Scotland'.[59] He came not only to extend and invigorate the agitation to which the BPU had given an impetus, but to consolidate the support for his own and Taylor's leadership and to preempt any attempted alliance between sections of the radical party with the Whig-radicals. O'Connor's reputation was already well-established in Scotland. He had helped to found the Scottish Radical Association and had gained the gratitude of Scottish trade unionists and working-class radicals for his championship of the Glasgow spinners' cause. Thomas Gillespie, secretary of the defence committee for the Glasgow spinners and later secretary of the Glasgow Universal Suffrage Association, moved the vote of thanks to O'Connor at the Glasgow meeting.

> When they saw him at the outset of his public career — when they saw him at Rathcormac, and defending the Dorchester Labourers, they would be prepared to feel towards him that respect and esteem to which such an advocate of their interests was entitled. But there was a subject connected with this city — the Cotton Spinners Trial, in which he had rendered such services as they ought never to forget. (Cheers.)[60]

O'Connor's services during less auspicious times were not forgotten by local working-class leaders like Gillespie, men who were trusted in their own localities. At the Palace Yard meeting, organised by the LWMA in September 1838, the Scottish delegate to the meeting, John Fraser (a veteran of 1819 who soon afterwards clashed with O'Connor), claimed that no leader had done more for radicalism in Scotland.

> Their first obligations were to those men who had stood by them in evil hours — to those who were with them in season and out of season — so far as regarded Scotland, that man had been Feargus O'Connor. (Cheers.)[61]

Here was the basis of O'Connor's leadership. Throughout England and Scotland he was regarded as the prime mover in the agitation which led up to Chartism.

Throughout his tour O'Connor stressed the need for unity behind the single demand for universal suffrage. At Kilburchan:

> I say again, first get universal suffrage, and don't be putting the cart continually before the horse, then when the reins are in your hands, you will be enabled to guide the chariot of the State in peace and safety.

He reminded his Glasgow audience of his own efforts to create a national movement. Before it had been his task to unite the scattered forces of radicalism, now it was to ensure that the unity achieved was not jeopardised. Over and over O'Connor rallied support around his personal claim of unwavering loyalty to a set of traditional radical principles. He challenged his audience to match his own consistency. O'Connor also defended Stephens's threatening language with references to Brougham, Attwood, Fielden, O'Connell and Milton. This was a common device employed to justify the increasingly revolutionary tone being adopted by speakers on the northern platform.

However, O'Connor carefully balanced his support for Stephens with hyberbolical humility before the figure of Thomas Attwood, declaring his willingness to become 'a drummer' in Attwood's 'army'.[62] Such gestures reflect O'Connor's desire to cement national unity by emphasising the common ground which existed between supporters of the Northern Union and those of the BPU.

(iii) *O'Connor and the Birmingham Political Union: August 1838*

The conversion of Thomas Attwood and the BPU Council from the middle-class radical programme of mere suffrage extension to agitation for universal suffrage brought the Birmingham radicals in line with popular radicalism nationally. Attwood's conversion marked the final act in the process of the demystification of the 1832 Reform. The greatest figure in the agitation for that measure now conceded its abject failure. 'The charm of the moral "Reform Bill" is broken; the spell has vanished; the shadow is gone, and the substance is seen', rejoiced the *Star*. Attwood's prominent part in the passing of the Reform Bill and his social position — a wealthy banker and Member of Parliament — lent a certain respectability and legitimacy to the move for universal suffrage.[63]

At the Birmingham demonstration of 6 August 1838, the National Petition and the Charter were presented together for the first time and the Birmingham delegates to the National Convention were elected.[64] O'Connor took the platform as the representative of the Yorkshire radicals. He became the connecting link between the northern radicals and the Birmingham radicals. Uppermost in his mind were the prospects for a united national movement; he came in the role of unifier. During private discussions with leaders of the LWMA and BPU O'Connor exerted his great personal charm in an effort to convince them of his sincere intentions of cooperation.[65] Publicly he adopted a tone of unqualified cordiality. After the 6 August demonstration, the *Star* announced the terms of the new 'Union': 'That we have conferred executive power upon the Birmingham Union. That we of the north shall support them with all our heart, with all our mind, and with all our strength.' Such enthusiasm was tempered only by the reminder that it had been the radicals of the North who had stood by universal suffrage.[66] O'Connor's welcome for an alliance with the Birmingham leaders contrasted with the more guarded tone of other leaders. Many radicals, especially in the North, distrusted the Birmingham leadership. After all, these middle-class politicians had only recently been aligned with Daniel O'Connell and the household-suffrage party. Thus the week before the Birmingham demonstration, the *Champion*, a Cobbettite, anti-Poor Law journal, expressed the hope that the proceedings would be 'so decided . . . as to wipe away the suspicion of wavering and Whiggery, that has been cast upon them by their too long protracted tolerance of O'Connell'.[67] In his weekly letter to the *Star*, O'Brien raised doubts which must have been prevalent among working-class radicals about the paper's rapturous support for the BPU leaders and questioned the wisdom of conferring 'executive power' upon the BPU Council.[68]

Similarly, northern radicals distrusted the LWMA leaders because of their close links with Place and the parliamentary radicals who were acknowledged Malthusians.[69] The publication of the Charter went largely unnoticed within most working-class circles (and in the *Star*) because, on the one hand, it contained nothing novel and, on the other, because the signatures of parliamentary radicals like O'Connell and Roebuck only created suspicion. Matthew Fletcher, Bury's delegate to the Convention, recalled: 'In this neighbourhood we had our doubts, and they were not concealed, as to the source and motives of the agitation, but it was deemed most advisable to join in it. We did so, and made it our own.'[70] Radicals who had been active in the anti-Poor Law and ten-hours movement were apprehensive lest the BPU/LWMA move might challenge the tone and social content of the northern agitation. Historians of Chartism have exaggerated the importance of the role of both the LWMA and the BPU in 1838.

No doubt O'Connor shared many of the anxieties of his comrades, but he also recognised the importance of integrating the Birmingham radicals into the ranks of the national movement which was taking shape. Chartism was in its infancy, its precise character was as yet undefined. No doubt O'Connor believed that it would be possible to embrace sections of the middle class within the movement. Thus he undertook to balance his platform alliance with Stephens and his popularity among the northern radicals with an alliance with the BPU leaders. O'Connor was the only leader in a position to mediate a juncture between these radical forces in summer 1838. However, by late 1838, O'Connor was unable to maintain the alliance between the northern platform and Birmingham's middle-class radicals. When their unrelenting attacks upon Stephens's rhetoric proved divisive to the national unity of Chartism, and when it became clear that the BPU Council no longer commanded the respect of their own working-class following, it was O'Connor who with consummate political skill undermined their local and national pretensions to leadership. But in the summer of 1838 the Birmingham leadership had committed the Birmingham radicals to the universal-suffrage movement. The launching of the National Petition and the election of the Convention were associated with the BPU initiative. An optimistic atmosphere prevailed.

III The Birth of the Chartist Platform

(i) *The Mass Demonstration*

In the wake of the great Birmingham meeting mass demonstrations were convened throughout the country in the late summer and autumn of 1838. The Chartist 'monster' demonstrations were a cross between the eighteenth-century county meeting and the Methodist camp meeting. They were called in order to elect delegates to the National Convention, to sign the National Petition and to parade Chartist strength and unity. O'Connor and the *Star* welcomed the prospect of a National Convention. During these months O'Connor maintained a remarkable pace of agitation, attending nearly every meeting of importance from August through to December. The physical stamina required to travel and speak night after night, often out of doors to thousands and sometimes hundreds of thousands, was tremendous. O'Connor's exertions during these months were equalled in the history of the British platform only by his own extensive touring following his release from prison in late 1841. He undertook personally to connect and unify the national movement through the platform. He was the common denominator at the mass demonstrations which marked the coming together of Chartism, bringing national perspective to local agitation. If the Convention was a move proposed by the Birmingham radicals, it was O'Connor who mounted the platform at almost every meeting in England at which a delegate was elected; not as a local leader committing the forces of a town or district to the national movement, but as a national leader coordinating, connecting, unifying the agitation to which he had given an impetus. He took the platform in order to agitate for the establishment of a more permanent and representative form of national leadership. At these demonstrations O'Connor extended the legitimacy of his personal leadership to the collective leadership of the Convention. Increasingly his personal leadership became identified with that of the Convention.

O'Connor sought to impart a continuity to the agitation of these months through his own ubiquitous presence, together with the comprehensive reporting of the *Star*. A sense of omnipresence was evoked, an image of O'Connor superintending the movement's progress. Wherever he spoke he announced where he had been the previous day and the distance he had journeyed in order to be with them. He travelled two hundred eighty miles to join the working-class radicals of Lancashire at Kersal Moor. Only forty hours before he had been addressing the Brighton radicals who had deputed him to represent them at this meeting, as had the London Democratic Association. Thus he told the Kersal Moor meeting: 'I represented the men of the north in the south the other day, and now I represent the men of the south in the north.' He presented himself to the Palace Yard meeting, organised by the LWMA, as the representative of between forty and fifty towns in England and Scotland. O'Connor reminded the London radicals that it had been three years since he had established the Great Marylebone Radical Association, and 'ever since he had been doing nothing but laying Radical eggs all over the country — (laughter) — which had been hatched and fledged, and were now flying in every corner of the kingdom in the shape of unions'. He told the demonstration at Peep Green that the union now lacked only his own countrymen, the Irish.[71] O'Connor came to symbolise the movement's national dimension. He regarded the development of a mass national radical movement as the culmination of his own endeavour, and repeatedly linked past services to the promise of continued loyalty to the cause which he had nurtured.

At the centre of the mass demonstrations of 1838 stood O'Connor, the popular champion around which the movement rallied. 'The political platform was his natural element', commented the Chartist leader Thomas Martin Wheeler. He was the perfect popular leader. Harney, in a letter to Engels, observed: 'A popular chief should be possessed of a magnificent bodily appearance, an iron frame, eloquence, or at least a ready fluency of tongue. . . . O'Connor has them all . . .'[72] His very appearance on the platform was something extraordinary — as was the demonstration itself — something symbolic, larger than life. There was a dignity about his presence on the platform, a charismatic vitality which placed him outside the ranks of ordinary speakers and which charged any meeting with a sense of expectancy and excitement. George Weerth, a German socialist who spent several years in England, noted:

> In O'Connor's bearing there is dignity and firmness; when he speaks, his
> motions are lively and meaningful, the tone of his voice powerful and
> metallic. One can see at once that he does not belong to the ranks of the
> ordinary, one can divine that there is something wild and ungovernable
> in the man, one is convinced that one is going to listen to an extraordi-
> nary speech when one sees him mount the rostrum with joy shining in
> his eyes. There is his proper place![73]

When O'Connor began to speak a hush descended over the largest
gatherings, the inattentive were called to silence, those on the fringes
of the mass meeting rushed from the booths and beer tents to listen,
and a feeling prevailed that something of great importance was
imminent. O'Connor's charismatic presence, boundless energy and
his magnificent tone of voice enabled him to dominate the great
outdoor demonstrations.[74]

O'Connor's talents as a popular orator were unsurpassed. The roots
of his popular appeal are to be found in his tone and style of address,
as well as the content of his speeches. He brought to the radical
platform the sureness of tone which Cobbett had brought to radical
journalism. With an unfailing instinct he struck the right chord with
working-class audiences, relating the political demand for universal
suffrage to a common working-class sense of daily social and economic
injustice. Possessed of a rare ability to embody and direct collective
feelings and aspirations, O'Connor transformed his presence on the
platform into a symbol of unified mass defiance, and inspired thousands of listeners through his own self-confidence, vitality and enthusiasm for agitation. As a personification of the working-class movement he regularly engaged the class enemy in a form of mock battle
from the platform in which the people's oppressors were vanquished
in a theatrical prefigurement of their eventual defeat in society at
large. A brilliant social satirist, O'Connor was at his best when
subjecting his listeners' 'social betters' to merciless ridicule. In one of
his favourite set-pieces he turns the tables on Lord Brougham,
sending 'Lord Harry and Lady Harry' to the gates of the work house.

> Harry Brougham said they wanted no poor law as every young man
> ought to lay up a provision for old age, yet while he said this with one
> side of his mouth, he was screwing the other side to get his retiring
> pension raised from £4,000 to £5,000 a year. But if the people had their
> rights they would not long pay his salary. Harry would go to the treasury,
> he would knock, but Cerberus would not open the door, he would ask,

'Who is there?' and then the luckless Harry would answer 'It's an ex-chancellor coming for his £1,250, a quarter's salary;' but Cerberus would say 'There have been a dozen of ye here to-day already, and there is nothing for ye,' then Harry would cry 'Oh! what will become of me! what shall I do!' and Cerberus would say 'Go into the Bastile that you have provided for the people.' Then when Lord Harry and Lady Harry went into the Bastile, the keeper would say, 'This is your ward to the right, and this, my lady, is your ward to the left; we are Malthusians here, and are afraid you would breed, therefore you must be kept asunder.' If he witnessed such a scene as this he might have some pity for Lady Brougham, but little pity would be due to Lord Harry.[75]

This brand of social levelling from the platform delighted working-class audiences. For while O'Connor denounced the nation's rulers as parasites and reduced them to figures of fun, he elevated the stature of working people by emphasising that it was their labour only which created the country's wealth. Most importantly, he convinced working men and women that through their own united efforts they had the power to overthrow the existing social order. He told his listeners that he had entered the battle for political rights with no other allies but the working class and that he was determined to fight that battle to a successful conclusion.

Although the demagogue remained at the centre of the mass Chartist demonstrations of 1838, the platform was crowded with local radical leaders. At Peep Green, the great Yorkshire rally, the Halifax leather cutter Robert Wilkinson took the chair and O'Connor was surrounded by West Riding radicals with whom he had agitated for several years. These demonstrations were important not merely in generating a mass consciousness, but provided points of contact for local leaders and future delegates to the National Convention. For instance, the Newcastle radicals delegated Robert Lowery, who also became their representative at the Convention, to attend the Palace Yard and Kersal Moor meetings. The Palace Yard platform included no less than fourteen future members of the Convention.[76] Through representation at such meetings communication between various districts was facilitated.

The demonstrations themselves were not spontaneous gatherings, but events which required much local preparation, expense and regional coordination.[77] The elaborately detailed order of procession, programme of speakers and resolutions, the well-disciplined men, women and children dressed in their finest clothes and marching in file attest to this organisation. The demonstration offered a mass exhibition of the rich traditions of radical politics and culture, a celebration of working-class solidarity. The tricolours and caps of liberty, the green and white flags, the defiant banners inscribed with the demand for universal suffrage and familiar quotations from Paine, Shelley and the Bible, the scenes depicting the Peterloo massacre, full-length portraits of Henry Hunt — along with those of the new champion of the platform — represented a consciousness of the continuity between Chartism and an established radical tradition. On the platform were men like James Wheeler, 'an old man who had been more than thirty years a republican', and who placed in nomination the South Lancashire delegates to the Convention at Kersal Moor.[78]

While mass demonstrations had obvious limitations, those which launched the Chartist movement had far-reaching significance. They announced the emergence of a movement which was prepared for a sustained, organised struggle. Thus the *Spectator* observed, following the Kersal Moor meeting:

> It is plain that the working classes have discovered the advantage of combination and submission to leaders. Their conduct excites respect, and real apprehension . . . There has indeed been nothing like it in the history of the people of this country. . . . At present we may observe the operation of a well-organised plan for rousing the people to *persevering* exertion. It is for a *long struggle* that the masses are preparing. The first campaign only is in progress; the warfare is not begun. It would be foolish to imagine that nothing serious will arise from this movement of the working population — that it will pass away and leave matters as they were. No living man can calculate its effects . . . but millions were never set in motion for months together, as the universalists now are, without some impact, result, more or less visible in the institutions and government of the country which gave birth to the manifestation.[79]

'Public opinion' was a key political concept of the period and there was a widespread feeling that as in 1832 something had to come from such a vast marshalling of public opinion.

O'Connor often reminded Chartists of the three necessary stages of agitation — the creation, organisation and direction of public opinion. Possessed of a sure grasp of the dynamics of popular agitation, he became the movement's foremost advocate of the mass demonstration as essential to the development of radical opinion and organisation. Such demonstrations directly involved hundreds of thousands of working men and women in the movement. The enthusiasm generated stimulated local organisation and recruitment. A consciousness of belonging to a class and the demonstration of the potential strength of that class when organised together fostered an increased awareness of the possibility for fundamental social and political change.

O'Connor's commitment to mass demonstrations corresponded with his reliance upon open-constitutional agitation to carry universal suffrage. The constitutional right to assemble in order to petition provided the pretext for such demonstrations. The reform agitation of 1830-32, especially the BPU's campaign, and O'Connell's campaign for Catholic emancipation in 1829, served as models of socio-political change.[80] In both instances, government was forced to concede reform to organised public opinion which was marshalled outside Parliament and which threatened recourse to violence. Overwhelming displays of popular strength and preparedness linked to intimidating language had forced fundamental political concessions without an outbreak of civil war. The 'moral force' of the mass demonstration warned of the potential 'physical force' which could be unleashed if peaceful demands were ignored. Although the Chartist meetings of 1838-39, even the torchlight ones in South Lancashire, were characterised by their relative peacefulness and extreme discipline and control, they were threatening by sheer virtue of their organisation and size.

The mass demonstration also presented a point of possible confrontation between the people and the forces of law and order and a means of testing government reaction to the emergent Chartist movement. The spectre of Peterloo pervaded the Chartist demonstrations of 1838-39. The anticipation of attack charged these meetings with a tense excitement, transforming them into an overt challenge to authority. In its nature the mass demonstration was vulnerable, open to attack. It presented a target for government repression.[81] Any such interference, which was clearly expected, would be seized upon as a legitimation for popular retaliation. Apprehensions had been reinforced when troops appeared at the Newcastle meeting in June 1838, called to adopt the National Petition, at which O'Connor spoke. From the platform Robert Lowery demanded: 'Who ever saw such an exhibition? Foot and dragoons, actually marched into a public meeting of Englishmen.' In future they must come armed to public meetings, for 'This was an omen of the new reign . . . Let them remember Peterloo and Canterbury.' At a meeting held the following week in Newcastle to discuss the implications of this incident Peterloo was on most speakers' lips.[82]

Lowery's reference to Canterbury was also significant. Only a few weeks before, troops had engaged 'Sir William Courtenay' and his following of Kentish labourers in a bloody pitched battle at Blean Wood. Courtenay was a millenarian prophet who preached resistance to the new Poor Law. Radical leaders such as O'Brien, O'Connor and Harney did not dismiss Courtenay and his followers as primitive rural fanatics. They related the affair to the opposition to the new Poor Law and interpreted the government's actions as a sign of more general intent.[83] O'Brien maintained that the government was trying to precipitate a premature outbreak in the North in order to put down their movement. 'The ruling classes of England, would . . . shed the blood of half the human race, rather than permit the working classes to enjoy equality of rights with themselves, *if they could do so with impunity.*'[84] Throughout the North there was a sense of possible confrontation between the forces of authority and the working class. It was this which underpinned the violent tone of Chartism's early rhetoric. Robert Lowery later commented:

> Even my wildest outbursts always had a semblance of reason, being based on a supposition of some illegal action which the authorities might commit, or some evil consequences most likely to ensue from their conduct to the people.[85]

In August a visit from Oastler and O'Connor to Dewsbury was followed by serious riot aimed at thwarting the efforts of some local guardians to set-up the machinery of the new Poor Law; in November troops and police were introduced into Todmorden to quell anti-Poor Law disturbances.[86]

(ii) *The Rhetoric of Violence and the Right to Arm*

By late 1838 recommendations to arm had become commonplace on the northern platform, especially at the torchlight meetings over which O'Connor and Stephens presided, and where arms were openly displayed. However, the question of arming had been raised earlier by the leaders of the anti-Poor Law movement, most prominently Stephens, Oastler and Fletcher.[87] The recommendation to arm was always placed within a defensive context, as a response to provocative violence from the authorities, thus placing the responsibility for any bloodshed upon the government.[88] The open display of arms was emphasised, as arming was regarded as a constitutional right, and intended as an intimidating gesture calculated to preempt government repression. Stephens reminded audiences that at Ashton and Bury, where he and Fletcher had recommended the people to arm, the new Poor Law did not exist.[89]

The right to arm was supported by a wealth of constitutional precedent. The Chartists borrowed heavily from the eighteenth-century 'Commonwealth' tradition which clearly asserted the established right of armed resistance to tyranny.[90] According to the *Northern Liberator*, the Constitution did not merely say that there was a time to arm, 'but it says that Englishmen *always ought to be armed;* It is perhaps the oldest right the people possess.'[91] R. J. Richardson maintained that the Commons, 'the noblest institution that was ever designed for the good of the commonwealth', had ceased to be the organ of the people. In this situation 'the virtue and intelligence of the people must be manifested in FREE ASSEMBLIES, such as the present demonstrations'. And should that fail, 'the only hope of the nation will be an ARMED PEOPLE'.[92] Magna Carta, Alfred the Great and the famed Anglo-Saxon Constitution, the 'Glorious Revolution', judicious quotation from Blackstone, Locke and such Whig authorities as Lord Henry Brougham, were all used to illustrate the contractual relationship between government and people, and to warn of the dire consequences of any tyrannical severance of that contract.[93] In the name of Queen and Constitution, working men were being instructed to arm with daggars and pikes, pistols and muskets. While it may be argued that the constitutional rhetoric of the Chartist platform held in abeyance the potentially insurrectionary side of Chartism, it seems more likely that the assertion of the right to arm in defence of the Constitution provided a real impetus to Chartist arming. Nor does this reflect the conservative nature of Chartism, but rather underlines the general tendency for revolutionary movements to seek legitimation for their challenge to the existing social order through reference to an idealised past.[94]

Stephens, 'the apostle of armed resistance', was the most persistant and colourful advocate of arming and violent confrontation. He told his Ashton followers that he intended to go to the National Convention 'as the armed delegate of an armed people'.[95] Although his career on the Chartist platform was confined to a mere few months in the autumn and winter of 1838, Stephens did much to shape the image and tone of Chartism. Unlike Oastler, he joined O'Connor on the universal suffrage platform. Despite differences of political principle, strategy and tone, O'Connor and the *Star* unequivocally identified themselves with Stephens. In the middle-class press O'Connor and Stephens were indistinguishably linked as agents of anarchy and revolution.[96]

However, O'Connor avoided direct recommendations to arm in

the autumn of 1838, although he had no objections to the exhortations of Stephens and others. The *Star* hinted at the subject and defended Oastler's letters recommending arming which were published in its columns.[97] Although he did not advise arming, O'Connor continually addressed himself to the subject of the relationship between 'moral' and 'physical' force. He constantly drew attention to the 'moral force' of the middle classes in 1831-32.

> When Bristol was in flames, Newcastle in a blaze, and Nottingham threatened, or when the middle classes followed in the mournful procession of departing monarchy — when upon their banners were exhibited the drooping head of a king, and the bloody axe of the executioner — when the State was threatened to its very centre by the brawling faction panting for power to abuse it — (immense cheering) — when the Infidel Fitzwilliam, and the Malthusian Brougham, led on the assault against the national exchequer, and threatened a national bankruptcy, unless their party were the bankers — (cheers) — that was moral force, peaceably, discreetly, and constitutionally used. (Uproarious applause.)

Although quite prepared to try moral power, in the event of its 'not producing the anticipated result, he had no hesitation in saying that rather than submit to the reign of tyranny and lewd domination of a faction, he would lead the people to death or glory'.[98] The threatening tone of such rhetoric was exhilerating, but it was also highly ambiguous and well calculated. Language such as O'Connor's was part of a rhetorical style which was common among Chartist speakers in late 1838 and 1839.[99] The same well-worn phrases punctuated O'Connor's speeches — the declaration that it was better to 'die freemen rather than live slaves', the exaltation of universal suffrage as 'an object at least worth living for, and dying for', the snatches of romantic poetry hinting at revolutionary deeds to come. Such points of reference were charged with emotive contemporary connotations, however imprecise. Ambiguity was inherent to platform agitation. The public meeting was not the agency through which to plot revolution, but rather to rally, test and prepare opinion. Few speakers trod the line between legality and sedition, moderation and insurrectionary zeal, as finely as O'Connor. Clearly he expected to face government prosecution, but as a barrister he had no intention of making the Whigs' task any easier. If Stephens wished to bid defiance to legal considerations, he would share the platform with him, publish his speeches, defend him in all quarters and welcome the challenge which he presented to the government. However, he had no inclination to echo the unqualified language of civil war. O'Connor's more threatening passages were characterised by conditional phrases and hypothetical developments the results of which he allowed his audience generally to infer. While generating the passions of huge audiences, he usually kept a cool head, even amid the pistol volleys and burning torches. The impression which did emerge was that at a certain point if peaceful means should fail, he would be prepared to resort to violence of some undefined nature. But this was nothing extraordinary among working-class radicals in late 1838, especially in the North. Henry Vincent who had been touring the country for the LWMA noted the widespread resolve of the radicals in Lancashire and Yorkshire to resort to stronger means if peaceful agitation failed.

> One feeling prevails in every town — or rather I should say two, feelings — the *first* a general and almost universal radical opinion — resolved to aid in *one more attempt* to obtain by peaceful means a full recognition of the universal rights of the people — and *second* an apparent fixed resolution to appeal to *arms* should this last moral effort fail.— I regret the prevalence of opinions of this physical nature — but we cannot wonder at them.[100]

The torchlight meetings held first in South Lancashire in autumn 1838, and directly associated with the leadership of Stephens and O'Connor, pushed the boundaries of the right to public assembly to their limit. At these meetings the rhetoric of violence coupled with the recommendation to arm reached a crescendo. Not convened on the distant moors but in the town centres, the torchlight processions toured the town's perimeter where the cotton mills were situated. The spectacle of torches and the sound of pistol shots which punctuated Chartist speeches lent substance to Stephens's language of 'war to the knife', causing understandable alarm among the 'respectables'.[101] Torchlight meetings were not a new phenomenon, but O'Connor and Stephens embarked upon a sustained torchlight campaign in which the threat of violence and destruction of property was always close to the surface. Gammage commented: 'for a short period the factory districts presented a series of such imposing popular demonstrations, as were perhaps never witnessed in any previous agitation'.[102] At Macclesfield O'Connor announced their intention to meet by torchlight the following night at Stockport, 2 October. The threats of certain cotton masters, particularly at Stockport, to victimise radicals who attended the Kersal Moor demonstration and their refusal to stop their mills for the day formed the pretext for this initiative. This move reflected the difficulties which factory workers encountered when they tried to meet during the day.[103]

Torchlight demonstrations followed throughout Lancashire, and to a lesser extent in the West Riding.[104] O'Connor, the initiator of these proceedings, attended nearly every one of the meetings accompanied by Stephens and joined by local Lancashire leaders such as Peter M'Douall, Matthew Fletcher, R. J. Richardson, John Deegan, James Taylor and James Mills. At these meetings the National Petition was ratified, local delegates elected to the Convention and an undertaking to collect national rent (for the Convention) agreed. These were the follow-up demonstrations to the great Kersal Moor and Peep Green meetings, the final integration of the forces and spirit of the Poor Law resistance into the Chartist movement. For O'Connor the torchlight campaign served to further consolidate support for his leadership in Lancashire. He was determined to keep agitation at fever pitch. 'If we allow Universal Suffrage to cool, we shall never get it up to the same temperature again.'[105] O'Connor looked to the North to set the tone of agitation for the national movement. The danger of over-committing the forces of northern radicalism was out-balanced by the need to sustain an atmosphere of urgency which O'Connor trusted would permeate through to less militant localities. The awesome spectacle of torchlight processions and the threatening tone of Stephens's rhetoric were in keeping with O'Connor's general strategy aimed at carrying universal suffrage through open intimidation. He believed that 'These demonstrations, when carried to Melbourne would compel him to yield to fear.'[106]

For a brief few weeks in November 1838, during the height of the torchlight campaign, O'Connor's own language became noticeably more threatening. On several occasions he ventured to name a day after which peaceful agitation would be superseded by physical confrontation. At Bolton he stressed the prospect of the imminent political emancipation of the working class, rejecting Fielden's view that it would take four years of constitutional agitation to carry universal suffrage.[107] The following week at Rochdale, again surrounded by torches, he actually named 29 September 1839 as the date 'for the manumission of the white slaves'.

> If the Whigs did not concede their liberty on the 29th, the people should take it by force on the 30th. They would have their Michaelmas goose on the 29th, and on the 30th their opponents should have the gander. He had preached peace all his life, but at the same time he was always prepared for war. One of those torches (pointing at one near at hand) was worth a thousand speeches: it spoke a language so intelligible that no one could misunderstand.[108]

Such an explicit commitment contrasted with O'Connor's more usual guarded ambiguity. But he was at pains to establish that they had not embarked upon a campaign of endless agitation. O'Connor gave expression to a general feeling that events must soon came to a head, a feeling which characterised the early Chartist years. O'Connor soon qualified his position, however, conceding that although he still favoured establishing a date for ulterior action, such a decision must be left to the collective leadership of the National Convention.[109] When the Convention met O'Connor proved the most forceful advocate for an immediate consideration of the question of 'ulterior measures'.

While Stephens's language was more violent than O'Connor's, it centred upon resistance to the implementation of the new Poor Law. He offered no general strategy for the obtainment of the Chartists' political demands. O'Connor's violent language was largely a platform device. More significant was his attempt to advance a strategy, albeit unsuccessful, to force the government to change the basis of political power. Publicly proposing a date for 'physical force' was a form of intimidating gesture, rather than a serious insurrectionary ground plan. It was also a manifestation of O'Connor's commitment to open agitation. However, the care with which O'Connor phrased his public utterances lent weight to his pronouncements of November 1838. Taken in conjunction with the repeated promise to lead the people to 'death or glory', his readiness to set a date for the termination of peaceful agitation gave rise to misunderstanding among some Chartists concerning O'Connor's commitment to insurrectionary action in the months following the disbanding of the Convention. Here was the contradiction at the heart of O'Connor's strategy of intimidation: it was impossible to intimidate the government without at the same time fostering the impression within Chartist ranks that some course of positive action would follow the failure of constitutional protest. O'Connor was willing to appear more of an insurrectionist than he really was in an attempt to force the propertied classes to concede Chartist demands. The full ramifications of this strategy became clear following the rejection of the National Petition.

By early December, Whig liberality had worn thin and torchlight meetings were declared illegal.[110] Chartists saw this as a blatant denial of the right to public assembly. As the initiator of these meetings, O'Connor called upon radicals to cease meeting by torchlight. Fearing that a riot or partial outbreak might now arise from such proceedings, he warned: 'when a struggle is to be made, even legally, it must be simultaneous. The whole cause should not be jeopardized by partial display.' Government spies or *agents provocateurs* might easily turn their meetings into an excuse for government repression.

> We are ready to face our enemies in human shape, and in open day; but we are not prepared to risk our cause by placing a virtuous people at the disposal of fiendish spies, covered by the cloud of night.

As a gesture of defiance and as evidence of his conviction that such gatherings were legal, O'Connor declared that he would attend one of the last scheduled torchlight meetings at either Wakefield or Bury.[111] At Bury he recommended that they proceed carefully in view of the national unity which the radical movement had achieved during the year. He reminded his audience of what had happened in 1819, when 'the Cause was progressing until it was beaten down by the spy system'. On no account must they allow this to be repeated. They had elected a Convention which was soon to meet in order to propose a concerted national plan of action and nothing must endanger its assembling. O'Connor declared his absolute faith in the Convention.

> From that Convention I expect much and the object of the Government in establishing the Spy System just on the eve of the Convention is to prevent its meeting at all. This shall never be effected for if no other man is there I will go and open the Convention myself. I am determined to go there and until then I will take no step calculated to weaken my hand or take any step that may strengthen the hands of the 'base, brutal and Bloody Whigs' and the no less 'base, brutal and bloody tories.'[112]

The experience of an earlier generation of radicals weighed heavily upon the minds of Chartist leaders. Thus O'Connor gave expression to a recurrent Chartist fear that a partial outbreak or local confrontation induced by government spies might jeopardise the organised strength of the entire movement. He repeatedly emphasised the need to rely upon open, legal agitation as the only means to guarantee national unity. It was essential to devise and coordinate a national plan to ensure unified action. This was the task of the Convention. One of the main reasons for the disciplined and contained nature of Chartist protest in late 1838, in the face of great privation and considerable government provocation, was the prospect of the establishment of the National Convention.

In retreat O'Connor was defiant. The week after the ban on torchlight meetings, and under heavy censure from the BPU leadership for his association with Stephens, he issued his first unequivocal, though carefully worded recommendation to arm.

> The arming of the whole community capable of bearing arms would be the finest means of preserving peace abroad, and harmony and satisfaction at home. . . . By reference to my speeches and writing it will be found that I have never so much as said 'arm'. But now I say 'arm'; and I having said it, the fulfillment shall rest with the whole people. 'Arm'; but in nowise use those arms — offensively nor defensively as individuals. . . . They must in nowise be used against the constitution even in your united strength.[113]

The torchlight demonstrations had two further related repercussions. First, Stephens's participation in these proceedings led to his arrest in late December and his retirement from the Chartist platform. With the arrest of Stephens the Whigs had crossed a threshold.[114] This ,action merely reinforced the Chartist belief that the government was trying to provoke a premature revolt. The *Star* called for restraint in the face of repression: 'THE TIME FOR FIGHTING HAS NOT *YET* COME.'[115] Chartism had its first martyr. Perhaps Robert Lowery was correct in his belief that Stephens's whole purpose was to force the government to arrest him for seditious opposition to the new Poor Law.[116] Certainly nothing was more potent in unifying and rallying the forces of radicalism than government persecution. Identified with Stephens's violent rhetoric, O'Connor was now linked with his co-agitator in his martyrdom. The image of the demagogue was inseparable from that of the patriotic martyr. Throughout 1838 O'Connor had discussed the prospect of a government attack on their leaders. Oastler had been victimised by his employer, Stephens by the Whig Government, it followed that O'Connor would be next. Already Feargus courted the image of the people's martyr. He joined Oastler in leading the campaign in defence of Stephens. Yet while promising never to desert his friend, O'Connor explained to Chartists that universal suffrage was their primary concern.

> Although we go on to assist Mr. Stephens under present circumstance, we will never forget our motto, 'universal suffrage'. This was the object to be obtained, and this we must keep in view; for he would tell them that the government would rather repeal the Poor Law tomorrow, than grant the suffrage to three out of every six of the labouring classes.[117]

IV Moral Force/Physical Force

Secondly, the torchlight demonstrations, and in particular Stephens's persistent recommendations to arm, formed the pretext for the clash between O'Connor and the BPU leaders along with sections of the radical leadership in Scotland and London. The bugbear of 'moral force'/'physical force' emerged briefly as a divisive issue in late 1838, when the BPU leadership, certain members of the LWMA and the Scottish radical leaders Abram Duncan and John Fraser, in association with the Rev. Patrick Brewster, denounced O'Connor's close association and support for Stephens. The dispute surrounding the question of 'moral force'/'physical force' has been a focal point of much Chartist historiography, neatly corresponding with what has been regarded as the central dichotomy betwen O'Connor and Lovett's leadership. In fact it was an issue of relatively little concern or disagreement among either rank-and-file Chartists or the majority of Chartist leaders. The more general question of Chartist violence is one of far greater interest and complexity.[118] The distinction between 'moral' and 'physical' force was never absolute. Most radicals regarded the terms not as diametrical opposites but as part of an interrelationship. O'Connor explained: 'Moral force and physical force were man and wife. Moral force was the wife, and knew when to call in her husband to her aid.'[119] 'Physical force' was the 'substance' which lent weight to the 'shadow' of 'moral force'. 'Moral power is the deliberative reasoning quality in man's mind, which teaches him how to bear, and when forbearance becomes a crime.' All 'moral' means at their disposal must be exhausted before any consideration of 'physical' measures. According to O'Connor, to marshal 'physical force' was to destroy it. In fact the perfect organisation of 'moral' power obviated the need for 'physical' action, since government witnessing their potential power would accede to their peaceful demands. 'Moral' and 'physical' force were two sides to the same coin, part of the same strategy of open intimidation. This formulation was not particularly novel in 1838. O'Connor merely repeated well-worn clichés of the radical platform and press.[120]

Even moderate radicals were unwilling categorically to dismiss the possibility of a resort to 'physical force'. Thus George Edmonds, O'Connor's sternest critic at Birmingham, had stood alongside him at Liverpool in September and proclaimed the Englishmen's right to use 'physical force' in the face of tyranny.[121] At the Convention, 'moral-force' advocates like William Carpenter denied the distinction altogether. 'They were all moral force men, and all physical force men. . . . There could not be an exhibition of moral force without physical force.'[122] Following the attack of the BPU councillors upon the language of the northern platform, the *Northern Liberator* complained that the Birmingham leaders wanted Chartists to believe that procurring arms and 'physical force' were synonymous.

> Asserting, by implication, that *Moral Force* must of necessity and the nature of things be a naked, helpless, Cokneyfied thing, that never smelt gunpowder without fainting, nor knows what a gun is except by report! Now this is a monstrous mistake.

According to the *Liberator*, a poor man with a gun asking a gentleman for his money was an example of 'moral force'. However, should the gentleman refuse and as a consequence be shot and robbed that indeed was a 'physical-force' highway robbery.[123]

The underlying issue was not the abstract question of the relationship between 'moral' and 'physical' force, but the related question of the class nature of Chartism, its tone and social programme. The denunciations of Stephens, Oastler and O'Connor's language were in part a reaction to the hostility shown in the 'liberal' middle-class press; an attempt to convince sections of middle-class opinion that the Chartists were peacefully intentioned and worthy of support. The rhetoric of the northern platform and Stephens's recommendations to arm were seen as undermining the BPU's national strategy of class cooperation by frightening away potential middle-class support.[124] Although the question of viable terms for an alliance between Chartists and sections of the middle class was a recurrent theme throughout the Chartist years, such an alliance seemed unlikely in late 1838. O'Connor, with an appreciation of the essentially working-class basis of Chartist support and the militancy of the northern radicals, had no intention of moderating his tone, renouncing his association with Stephens and Oastler nor compromising principle in an attempt to woo middle-class support. He relied upon independence, firmness of purpose and awesome organisation backed by determined threats to carry universal suffrage.

The brunt of the BPU, LWMA and Scottish attack on the northern platform was aimed not primarily at O'Connor, but at the anti-Poor Law leaders Stephens and Oastler.[125] This was because of O'Connor's political radicalism, his conciliatory tone towards the BPU, his refusal to recommend arming (until December) and his stature within the national radical movement. The moves at Birmingham and later Edinburgh were attempts to separate the social core of Chartism from its political shell. By directing their attacks at Stephens and Oastler, these leaders threatened the fusion of political radicalism with a socio-economic-moral critique of industrial capitalism which was central to Chartism. They also rejected the spirit of confrontation and direct resistance to authority which had characterised the anti-Poor Law agitation. Just before his arrest, Stephens told his Ashton congregation that the Charter, universal suffrage and the repeal of the corn laws were all "Whig juggles, to draw them away from Tory Oastler, and bloody Stephens, who alone stood firm to the factory question, and against the new poor law being introduced'.[126] At its most extreme this antagonism found expression in the 'conspiracy' theory of the origins of Chartism, propagated by Oastler, Stephens and other anti-Poor Law leaders. Oastler maintained that the movement had been concocted by London middle-class radicals and whig-radicals to divert the lawless forces of the anti-Poor Law movement into supine political agitation. He went so far as to allege that certain members of the BPU were 'agents employed by the Government to silence the Northern cry against the new poor law'.[127] Matthew Fletcher told his Bury supporters, in late 1839: 'It was under the expectation that the agitation for universal suffrage would be carried on in the most quiet manner that the agitation for the Charter commenced.' Unlike Stephens and Oastler, Fletcher supported the demand for universal suffrage, but he explained: 'This right had been so long neglected that they stood in a different position to that in which they stood in reference to those encroachments upon their liberties which they have had to encounter.'[128] It was this sense of the need to resist an immediate threat to popular liberties that O'Connor sought to bring to the agitation for universal suffrage. Whereas it was precisely this element of northern radicalism, its tone of urgency, that alienated the BPU leadership.

O'Connor could no longer maintain the compromise between the northern platform and the Birmingham leaders. The northern radicals' earlier doubts which O'Connor had tried to allay about the nature and tone of these middle-class leaders' radicalism were confirmed. In December several BPU leaders welcomed Daniel O'Connell's overtures of cooperation.[129] There can be little doubt that O'Connell deliberately set out to split the Chartist ranks. In his reply on behalf of the Precursor Society to the LWMA address to the Irish people, O'Connell balanced denunciations of O'Connor, Stephens, Oastler and 'the language of intimidation and violence' with praise for Attwood, the BPU Council and their motto of 'peace, law and order'.[130] O'Connor and the northern radicals were outraged that the BPU leaders should respond with the suggestion of a reconciliation between the Chartists and O'Connell. O'Connell symbolised the archetypal apostate, the gentleman leader who had traded in popular politics to his own benefit and deserted the ranks of radicalism for an alliance with the 'bloody' Whigs. The Radical Association at Radcliffe, in Lancashire, declared:

> We do not know of any one man in modern times who has behaved with so much duplicity, treachery, and sordidness [as O'Connell] . . . and shall we throw away the persevering and high-minded Feargus O'Connor, the eloquent and much abused Stephens, or the philanthropic Oastler, for such a man as this? . . . If the Birmingham council wish to shake hands with this hypocritical dictator, let them do so and be ruined, but the men of the North will not . . .[131]

O'Connell's political programme was the epitome of 'sham' radicalism, his social philosophy the embodiment of middle-class political economy. For the Chartist demands he substituted the ballot, triennial parliaments and 'the greatest possible extension of the Suffrage that can be practically obtained'. Furthermore, he insisted on support for the Whigs in preference to the Tories, as did the Rev. Brewster at Edinburgh. This was basically the whig-radical programme which the BPU had earlier abandoned and which middle-class reformers were to offer the Chartists more than once. If O'Connor's leadership was based on anything, it was his implacable hostility to any form of Whig alliance and his insistence upon the independence of working-class radicalism. Although an Irish alliance was central to his general strategy, this was to be achieved not by means of a reconciliation with the 'Liberator', but through an exposure of his betrayals. He cautioned Chartists against any compromise, warning them that overtures from leaders like O'Connell and Lord Durham merely reflected the growing stength of their own movement.[132]

Finally, there was a strong belief among Chartists that the carping censures upon the northern proceedings had opened the door for O'Connell's Whig associates to ban torchlight meetings. This sense of bitter betrayal was deepened with the arrest of Stephens, the object of their attacks.[133] Dissensions from within their own ranks had yielded the Whigs their first Chartist victim. O'Connell's influence was seen at work. Peter Bussey attributed Stephens's arrest to the 'Dictator of the Whig Cabinet, the base, bloody and brutal traitor, Daniel O'Connell'. The Halifax radicals likened him to 'Satan amongst the Angels in Heaven'. And at Hull the Chartists resolved publicly to burn the portrait of the 'arch traitor of the people' at the next meeting of the WMA, concluding with the prayer 'that such may be the fate of all such apostates'. The *Champion* summed up the sentiments of most Chartists:

> This is a matter which does not admit of mincing, and the man, be who he may, who hankers after a reconciliation with Daniel O'Connell, must be himself utterly unworthy of confidence — must be destitute of all self-respect, and cannot merit the respect of other men.[134]

In so diverse a movement the call for unity in the ranks had powerful force. Conversely, the charge of engendering disunion was a grave indictment of one's political character. Already O'Connor's personal leadership was regarded as paramount to the national unity of Chartism. The moves at Birmingham and Scotland, linked with O'Connell's advances, represented a direct challenge to the leadership of O'Connor, Stephens and the Great Northern Union. Most Chartists regarded this as a threat to the national movement itself. The Chartist press was overwhelmed by resolutions and addresses from local Chartist groups affirming their support for O'Connor and Stephens, and expressing deep resentment towards those who had attacked their leadership.[135] In a full page editorial in the *Operative*, headed 'TREACHERY IN THE CAMP', O'Brien argued: 'the blow aimed ostensibly at FEARGUS O'CONNOR and STEPHENS is practically levelled at our organisation . . . under the pretence of opposing moral to physical force, the latent intent is to leave us without any force at all, moral or physical'. By denouncing O'Connor and Stephens, they were abusing the two most trusted leaders of the people.

> The two men who had done most, who had sacrificed most, who had dared most for the present movement: in a word the two men most capable of serving the people, because the two most confided in by them, and most capable of rallying them in a moment of danger. To denounce two such men was to denounce every Radical who trusted in them; to resolve to cast off three-fourths of the radical strength of England . . .[136]

Under attack O'Connor, as usual, fell back upon a highly idealised account of his own radical career and an intense personalisation of political differences. He put his political conduct up for judgement. Wherever he was attacked O'Connor promised to present himself for 'trial' before the local Chartists, 'as I think my character is of some importance to the working classes'.[137] Direct accountability to the Chartist rank and file became his standard means of countering any challenge to his leadership. In the winter of 1838/39, the ascendancy of O'Connor's national leadership became dramatically evident at Birmingham, London and Scotland, where he confronted local leaders who opposed his leadership and routed them in their own localities. He set out to reassert the national unity of the radical movement on the basis of confidence in his leadership.

O'Connor attended a series of meetings at Birmingham in the latter half of November, during the height of the torchlight campaign, in order to defend his position on the question of 'physical-force'. At these meetings the members of the BPU demonstrated their overwhelming support for O'Connor. Middle-class fears about Stephens's language of class war were not shared by the 'constitutional Jury of working men of Birmingham'. It was not merely the excited tone of northern working-class radicalism which alarmed the BPU's middle-class Council. The Union's own working-class membership was gravitating towards an independent working-class party. The programme of a union between the middle and working classes had become increasingly difficult to actualise; there was a diminishing social reality associated with the middle-class concept of the 'productive classes'. The changing social relations of production within Birmingham's small workshops had had crucial implications for Attwood's rhetoric of mutual class interest.[138] Having demonstrated the ascendancy of his leadership, O'Connor sought to reconcile his differences with the BPU leaders in an attempt to ensure their presence at the Convention. Although he defended his association with Stephens, his reticence to recommend arming may have been a concession, a last effort to maintain some sort of unity with the BPU leaders. That fragile unity was soon shattered with the BPU Council's welcome for O'Connell, the government ban on torchlight meetings, O'Connor's open recommendation to arm and the arrest of Stephens. However, the confrontation with the BPU leaders was a superb example of the skilful manner in which O'Connor could transform a local situation into a matter of over-riding national Chartist concern centring upon his own person.

In both London and Scotland, O'Connor established, as in Birmingham, that he possessed the support of the vast majority of Chartists. He had agreed to a sustained tour of London arranged by the London Democratic Association. 'We shall now . . . have something like "real" agitation in London', commented O'Brien.[139] At a rate of a meeting a night, he addressed and chaired gatherings which involved members of the LWMA, LDA and local radicals. At a meeting chaired by Hetherington, at which the leading LWMA members Hartwell and Vincent along with his old associate Thomas Macconnell spoke, O'Connor contrasted the 'complete and overwhelming' organisation of Lancashire and Yorkshire with that of London, 'the least active and least organised' centre.[140] This early apathy in London was to remain a concern throughout 1839. In the familiar company of the Marylebone RA, O'Connor took the chair at a meeting at which the shoemaker, William Cardo, was elected to represent Marylebone at the Convention. Cardo was to be the only official representative of a London district and the only London delegate who was not a LWMA nominee.[141] O'Connor saw the need to balance the large LWMA bloc at the Convention. Therefore, he also attended the Bristol meeting which chose Charles Neesom, a veteran Spencean and member of the LDA, among its delegates for the Convention.[142] At all these meetings he defended Stephens who had now retired from the agitation. A confrontation between William Lovett and O'Connor ensued at a meeting at the Hall of Science, City Road. Lovett, a rare speaker at public gatherings, condemned O'Connor's approval of Stephens's language, on the grounds that recommendations to arm kept potential supporters from their ranks. His speech was constantly interrupted by disapproving jeers. Lovett's isolation upon this issue was demonstrated as the overwhelming majority of the meeting sided with O'Connor.[143]

O'Connor told the St Pancras WMA not to be alarmed about the state of the movement at Edinburgh: 'for I intend . . . to try the real feelings there early next month . . . I am going to see in Dr. Brewster's own town whether the real radicals or the sham and "Philosophical Radicals" are the strongest.' O'Connor posed in the role of unifier and conciliator of differences within the movement. Thus he assured Chartists: 'When I go amongst the men of Scotland, it will not be to divide, it shall be to unite them. . . . I am going to be more active in reconciliation than others have been in making me a bone of contention.'[144] From late November, Abram Duncan and John Fraser had been campaigning to bring the Scottish radical movement in line with the BPU's policy of 'moral, constitutional agitation'. This culminated in a conference held at Edinburgh and a meeting held on Calton Hill where Duncan and Fraser allied with the Rev. Patrick Brewster to pass resolutions opposed to the use of 'physical force'. These moves coincided with O'Connell's attempt to split off the moderate wing of the radical movement and an initiative to bring Lord Durham into the movement.[145] However, resolutions

from Chartist associations throughout Scotland had already indicated
the relative weakness of support for Fraser, Duncan and Brewster's
opposition to the tone of the northern platform and O'Connor's
leadership.[146] O'Connor's whirlwind tour of Scotland, in early January 1839, placed the matter beyond doubt. In person he was invin-
cible. Brewster was humiliated in his alleged strongholds of Edinburgh and Paisley where motions were passed rescinding the Calton
Hill resolutions.[147] As usual, O'Connor gave a detailed account of his
tour to the readers of the *Star*, in a letter addressed 'To the Moral
Philosophers and Philosophic Radicals'.

> Thus, Gentlemen, ends my eight days tour, during which time I at-
> tended nine public meetings, travelled over seven hundred miles,
> slept, on average, three hours a night, and once again united the
> Scottish and English radicals, in a union more lasting than brass, and
> one which I trust, even your malicious ingenuity will not be able to
> break.[148]

Between 18 December and 15 January, he had addressed twenty-two
public meetings and travelled more than 1,500 miles in an effort to
preserve the unity of the radical movement.

Before the Convention met, O'Connor and the Lancashire delegates organised a meeting of all the northern delegates at Manchester, presumably to discuss the general prospects of the movement
and the Convention. From this meeting a delegation was sent to
Birmingham to discuss their differences with the BPU leadership and
receive assurances that the Birmingham delegates would attend the
Convention.[149] The *Star* appealed for unity among the members of
the Convention, 'we do hereby forgive and forget the past . . . the
time for union has now arrived . . .'[150] However, the friction between
various leaders which surfaced in the months before the Convention
prefigured the splits and defections which were to mar its course.
O'Connor had already hinted, 'Mayhap there will be men there [at
the Convention] who will have to be weeded from it'.[151] This dissension was counter-balanced, however, within the mass movement by a
general closing of the ranks behind O'Connor's leadership and Stephens's martyrdom. Throughout 1838 O'Connor had kept the message of universal suffrage in the forefront of mass agitation. He was
the central figure around which the movement came together. When
the Convention met in February 1839, O'Connor could justly claim
that no leader had worked as diligently in advancing the Chartist
cause, defending the movement from its detractors, uniting and
organising its forces.

NOTES

1. *NS*, 17 Feb. 1838, p. 7.
2. The Seditious Societies Act under which the Corresponding Societies were suppressed in 1799 was still on the books.
3. *NS*, 22 Oct. 1842, p. 1.
4. See above ch. 1, pp. 23-24, 34.
5. *Manchester and Salford Advertiser*, 20 Aug. 1836, p. 4; *NS*, 10 Nov. 1838, p. 8; 9 Nov. 1839, p. 1.; 20 Aug. 1842, p. 1; 19 Aug. 1843, p. 5; 24 Aug. 1844, p. 1.
6. *NS*, 4 May 1839, p. 6; also see 22 June 1839, p. 8.
7. Ibid., 9 Nov. 1839, p. 1. Innumerable examples could be cited of Chartist recognition of O'Connor's successorship to Hunt, but see *NS*, 17 Nov. 1838, p. 6 (Wigan); *Manchester and Salford Advertiser*, 2 Oct. 1841, p. 4, for the painting carried at the Manchester demonstration to welcome O'Connor from prison which depicted Hunt's spirit appearing to O'Connor with the inscription: 'Feargus, thou has been tried and found faithful; on lead my people to victory.'
8. E. P. Thompson, *The Making of the English Working Class*, Penguin ed., Harmondsworth 1968, p. 682; also see J. C. Belchem, 'Radicalism as a "Platform" Agitation in the period 1816-21 and 1848-51: With Special Reference to the Leadership of Henry Hunt and Feargus O'Connor', (Sussex Univ. D.Phil thesis, 1975); id., 'Henry Hunt and the Evolution of the Mass Platform', *English Historical Review*, 93, 1978, pp. 739-73.
9. See John Jackson's first reaction to O'Connor, *The Demagogue Done Up*, Bradford 1844, p. 2; or the comments of the Nottingham knitter James Simmons, *NS*, 31 Dec. 1842, p. 2.
10. *NS*, 16 May 1840, p. 6.
11. Ibid., 17 Feb. 1838, p. 8.
12. Ibid., 16 Oct. 1838.
13. For instance, *NS*, 24 Apr. 1841, p. 7; 13 May 1848, p. 1.
14. Such images were particularly common in Chartist poetry. See Y. V. Kovalev (ed.), *An Anthology of Chartist Literature*, Moscow 1956.
15. 2*NS*, 20 Jan. 1838, p. 4.
16. British Library, Add. MSS 27820, fo. 151.
17. *NS*, 30 June 1838, p. 8.
18. *Champion*, 25 Nov. 1837, cols. 912-14; *NS*, 20 Jan. 1838, p. 1; *Manchester and Salford Advertiser*, Dec. 1837-Jan. 1838; N. C. Edsall, *The anti-Poor Law Movement, 1834-44*, Manchester 1971, pp. 121 ff.; M. E. Rose, 'The Anti-Poor Law Agitation', in J. T. Ward (ed.), *Popular Movements, c. 1830-50*, London 1970, pp. 82, 86-87.
19. For Stephens at his most violent, see his New Year's day speech at Newcastle, *Northern Liberator*, 6 Jan. 1838. p. 2.
20. *NS*, 16 Dec. 1837, p. 3.
21. Ibid., p. 5.
22. Ibid., 21 Apr. 1838, p. 5; 28 Apr., p. 5.; 5 May; 12 May, p. 6; 4 Aug., p. 8; 11 Aug., p. 8; PRO, MH 12/14830 (Dewsbury); HO 40/38, fos. 512-14, Mott to HO.
23. *NS*, 16 Dec. 1837, p. 5.
24. *Manchester and Salford Advertiser*, 10 Feb. 1838, p. 4.
25. The new Poor Law and Rural Police Act were but the two most outstanding examples of the centralisation to which radicals objected. See R. J. Richardson's letter, 'The Centralizing System', *NS*, 9 Mar. 1839, p. 7; D. Thompson, *The Early Chartists*, London 1971, p. 11; for the continued opposition to the police, R. D. Storch, 'The Plague of the Blue Locusts: Police Reform and Popular Resistance in Northern England, 1840-57', *International Review of Social History*, 20, 1975, pp. 61-90.
26. *NS*, 23 June 1838, p. 3.
27. Most notably, R. N. Soffner, 'Attitudes and Allegiances in the Unskilled North, 1830-50', *International Review of Social History*, 10, 1965, pp. 429-54; cf. D.

Thompson, 'Notes on Aspects of Chartist Leadership', *Bulletin of the Society for the Study of Labour History*, no. 15, 1967, pp. 28-33. Even in the latest narrative history of the movement (J. T. Ward, *Chartism*, London 1973) there is a tendency to reduce radicalism in the North to 'tory radicalism' and to label basic radical demands 'Oastlerite' for no clear reason.

28. See, for instance, *NS*, 13 Jan. 1838, p. 7, meeting of Leeds WMA.

29. See C. Driver, *Tory Radical: The Life and Times of Richard Oastler*, New York 1946; J. T. Ward, 'Revolutionary Tory: The Life of Joseph Rayner Stephens of Ashton-under-Lyne, 1805-1879', *Transactions of the Lancashire and Cheshire Antiquarian Society*, 68, 1958, pp. 93-116; T. M. Kemnitz and F. Jacques, 'J. R. Stephens and the Chartist Movement', *International Review of Social History*, 19, 1974, pp. 211-27. Stephens and Oastler's views on universal suffrage were not the same. While Stephens might not accept the vote as the primary concern, he often sounded like a radical advocate of universal suffrage — eg. *NS*, 6 Oct. 1838, p. 3. Oastler was much less inclined to support universal suffrage, although he regarded it as preferable to the 1832 franchise.

30. *NS*, 6 Oct. 1838, p. 3.

31. *Bolton Free Press*, 24 Feb. 1838, p. 3.

32. *Leeds Times*, 6 May 1837, p. 8; also see the correspondence between the Bradford and Huddersfield radicals on this issue, ibid., 12 Aug.-Sept. 1837. George White later commented: 'Richard Oastler was a Tory, but he was an individual universally respected by the Chartists, because they believed him to be a humane man. . . . He had exerted himself nobly against the accursed Factory Bill, and the people respected him for it.' *Northern Liberator*, 5 Dec. 1840, p. 6. O'Connor and Oastler remained on friendly terms throughout life.

33. *Leeds Times*, 21 Jan. 1837, p. 6; also see Halifax radicals' address to O'Connor, ibid., 14 Jan. 1837, p. 8.

34. Transport House, Vincent MSS, 1/1/10, Vincent to Minikin, 26 Aug. 1838.

35. *Manchester and Salford Advertiser*, 6 Oct. 1838, p. 4.

36. Cf. C. Tilly, 'The Changing Place of Collective Violence', in M. Richter (ed.), *Essays in Theory and History; An Approach to the Social Sciences*, Cambridge, Mass., 1970, pp. 139-64; C. Tilly, L. Tilly and R. Tilly, *The Rebellious Century, 1830-1930*, London 1975, pp. 49-51, 54. Whatever heuristic value Tilly's categories may have, Chartism provides a good example of a movement which defies neat sociological categorisation.

37. *Champion*, 24 Feb. 1838, cols. 1313-21, 1327-28. While rejecting Fielden's recommendation to petition again, the South Lancashire Association campaigned for Oastler, Stephens, O'Connor, the Rev. G. S. Bull, George Condy and John Cobbett to be received at the Bar of the House of Commons.

38. For instance, *Manchester and Salford Advertiser*, 23 Dec. 1837, p. 4.

39. *Bolton Free Press*, 24 Feb. 1838, p. 3.

40. *NS*, 10 Feb. 1838, p. 4; 17 Feb., p. 5; 24 Mar., p. 3; 12 May, p. 3.

41. Ibid., 24 Mar. 1838, pp. 3, 8.

42. Ibid., 6 Jan. 1838, p. 6; 13 Jan., p. 6; 27 Jan., p. 3; *Halifax Guardian*, 23 Jan. 1838.

43. *Manchester and Salford Advertiser*, 17 Mar. 1838, p. 3; *NS*, 24 Mar. 1838, p. 1; 21 Apr., pp. 3-4, 6.

44. *NS*, 30 June 1838, p. 5; 1 Sept., p. 8; 8 Sept., p. 4; 20 Oct., p. 4.

45. Ibid., 9 June 1838, p. 5; 23 June, p. 5; 30 June, pp. 4-5.

46. Ibid., 4 Aug., p. 4; 25 Aug., p. 3; 22 Sept., p. 4; 22 Dec., p. 8; *Bradford Observer*, 17 Jan. 1839. It appears that the purchase of a GNU medal, with the likeness of O'Connor on one side and the five radical principles on the other, was the symbol of membership.

47. See *NS*, Sept.-Nov. 1838; A. J. Peacock, *Bradford Chartism*, York 1969, p. 18.

48. *NS*, 17 Nov. 1838, p. 5.

49. *NS*, 5 May 1838, p. 8.

50. The slogan 'peaceably if you may, forcibly if you must' was adopted in the Convention's first address to the people. *Charter*, 17 Feb. 1839, p. 54.

51. *NS*, 9 June 1838, p. 8. The *Star* of 16 June 1838 published the Petition.

52. P. Fraser, 'Public Petitioning and Parliament Before 1832', *History*, 48, 1961, pp. 195-211; C. Leys, 'Petitioning in the Nineteenth and Twentieth Centuries', *Political Studies*, 3, 1955, pp. 45-64; J. Cannon, *Parliamentary Reform, 1640-1832*, Cambridge 1973, pp. 168-72.

53. *NS*, 21 Apr. 1838, p. 6.

54. Ibid., 23 Feb. 1839, p. 4; 9 Mar., p. 4; 16 Mar., p. 4; 23 Mar., p. 4; 24 Aug., p. 2; *Charter*, 17 Feb. 1838, p. 50. Fielden and the Cobbettites were critical of the policy of the 'last' petition and recommended continual petitioning of Parliament.

55. *NS*, 30 June 1838, p. 8.

56. Transport House, Vincent MSS, 1/1/9, Vincent to Minikin, 18 Aug. 1838.

57. *NS*, 21 July 1838, p. 3.

58. Ibid., 7 July 1838, p. 3.

59. Ibid., 26 Oct. 1839, p. 3; also see A. Wilson, *The Chartist Movement in Scotland*, Manchester 1970, pp. 54-56.

60. *NS*, 28 July 1838, p. 8.

61. Ibid., 22 Sept. 1838, p. 2.

62. Ibid., 28 July 1838, pp. 6, 8.

63. Ibid., 2 June 1838, p. 4.

64. *Birmingham Journal*, 11 Aug. 1838; *NS*, 11 Aug. 1838, p. 4; R. G. Gammage, *History of the Chartist Movement, 1837-1854*, Newcastle 1894 ed., pp. 41-46.

65. Transport House, Vincent MSS, 1/1/8, Vincent to Minikin, 7 Aug. 1838.

66. *NS*, 11 Aug. 1838, p. 4; also see ibid., 28 July, p. 8; 18 Aug., p. 3, for O'Connor's praise of the BPU leadership.

67. *Champion*, 5 Aug. 1838, p. 4.

68. *NS*, 18 Aug. 1838, p. 4.

69. *Northern Liberator*, 30 Dec. 1837, p. 3; G. Wallas, *The Life of Francis Place*, London 1925 ed., p. 373.

70. M. Fletcher, *Letters to the Inhabitants of Bury*, Bury 1852, letter 4, p. 5; *NS*, 28 July 1838, for the paper's first mention of the Charter; also see D. J. Rowe, 'The London Working Men's Association and the "People's Charter"', *Past and Present*, no. 36, 1967, pp. 73-86; and I. J. Prothero's rejoiner, ibid., no. 38, pp. 169-73.

71. *Manchester Guardian*, 26 Sept. 1838, p. 2; *Champion*, 30 Sept. 1838, p. 1; *London Dispatch*, 23 Sept. 1838, p. 846; *NS*, 22 Sept. 1838, pp. 2-3; 16 Oct.

72. T. M. Wheeler, *A Brief Memoir of the Late Feargus O'Connor*, London 1855, p. 8; *The Harney Papers*, F. G. and R. M. Black (eds.), Assen 1969, p. 241, Harney to Engels, 30 Mar. 1846.

73. Reprinted in *Bulletin of the Society for the Study of Labour History*, no. 24, 1972, p. 22.

74. Gammage, *History of the Chartist Movement*, pp. 45-46.

75. Ibid., p. 26. Also see M. Vicinus, '"To Live Free or Die": The Relationship Between Strategy and Style in Chartist Speeches, 1838-1839', *Style*, 10, 1976, pp. 481-503.

76. R. Lowery, 'Passages in the Life of a Temperance Lecturer', (first published in *Weekly Record of the Temperance Movement*, 1856-57), reprinted in B. Harrison and P. Hollis (eds.), *Robert Lowery: Radical and Chartist*, London 1979, pp. 107-11.

77. For the preparations for the Kersal Moor meeting, see *Champion*, 19 Aug. 1838, p. 4; *Manchester and Salford Advertiser*, 1 Sept. 1838, p. 1.

78. *Manchester Guardian*, 26 Sept. 1838, p. 2.

79. *Spectator*, 29 Sept. 1838, p. 909; also see Place's comments to Hume, 14 Sept. 1838, Wallas, *Life of Place*, pp. 368-69.

80. Most radicals credited Attwood and the BPU with carrying the Reform Bill. See

O'Brien's judgement, *Destructive*, 2 Mar. 1833. For a full discussion of this question, see T. M. Kemnitz, 'Approaches to the Chartist Movement: Feargus O'Connor and Chartist Strategy', *Albion*, 5, 1973, pp. 67-73; for a rather unsatisfactory reevaluation of the role of the BPU, C. T. Flick, *The Birmingham Political Union and the Movements for Reform in Britain, 1830-1839*, Folkestone 1978.

81. See C. Tilly, 'Collective Violence in European Perspective', in H. D. Graham and T. R. Gurr (eds.), *The History of Violence in America*, London 1969, pp. 24-25; John Berger, 'The Nature of Mass Demonstrations', *New Society*, 23 May 1968.

82. *NS*, 30 June 1838, pp. 4, 8; 7 July, p. 8; *Northern Liberator*, 30 June 1838, p. 4; 7 July, p. 4; W. H. Maehl, 'The Dynamics of Violence in Chartism: A Case Study in Northeastern England', *Albion*, 7, 1975, p. 107.

83. P. G. Rogers, *Battle of Bossendean Wood*, London 1961; Thompson, *The Making*, pp. 880-81; *NS*, 9 June 1838, pp. 3-4, 7; 16 June, p. 4; 30 June, p. 4.

84. *NS*, 14 July 1838, p. 4.

85. 'Passages', in *Robert Lowery*, p. 171.

86. *NS*, 4 Aug. 1838, p. 8; 11 Aug., p. 8; 24 Nov., p. 5; 1 Dec., p. 5; *Manchester and Salford Advertiser*, 24 Nov. 1838, p. 3; J. Holden, *A Short History of Todmorden*, Manchester 1912, pp. 190-92; Edsall, *Anti-Poor Law Movement*, pp. 156, 159-60.

87. *NS*, 9 June 1838, p. 8; 4 Aug., p. 6.

88. See, for instance, O'Brien's recommendation, *Northern Liberator*, 8 Dec. 1838.

89. PRO, TS 11/815, no. 2687, report of Bury torchlight meeting.

90. See C. Robbins, *The Eighteenth Century Commonwealthman*, Cambridge, Mass., 1959.

91. *Northern Liberator*, 17 Nov. 1838, p. 3. The *Liberator* actually advertised places where arms could be purchased.

92. *Champion*, 4 Nov. 1838, p. 5.

93. See the list of authorities which Richardson drew up for the Convention's statement on arming, *Charter*, 14 Apr. 1839, p. 188; R. J. Richardson, *The Right of Englishmen to Have Arms*, London 1839.

94. See Marx's comments, *The Eighteenth Brumaire of Louis Bonaparte*, in *Karl Marx and Frederick Engels Selected Works*, one vol. ed., London 1968, p. 97.

95. PRO, HO 40/38, fo. 658.

96. Kemnitz and Jacques, 'Stephens', pp. 226-27.

97. *NS*, 10 Feb. 1838, p. 3; 7 July, p. 8; 1 Sept., p. 4; 24 Nov., p. 4.

98. *NS*, 30 June 1838, p. 8.

99. Thompson, *Early Chartists*, pp. 18-19; Lucy Vincent, Henry Vincent's wife, later commented: 'The "strong language" was a necessity of the time.' Introduction to W. Dorling, *Henry Vincent: A Biographical Sketch*, London 1879, p. viii.

100. Transport House, Vincent MSS, 1/1/10, Vincent to Minikin, 26 Aug. 1838.

101. See report of Hyde meeting, in PRO, TS 11/815, no. 2687. Throughout November and December 1838, the *Manchester Guardian* complained that the government was doing nothing to stop these outrageous proceedings and continually demanded the arrest of Stephens.

102. Gammage, *History of the Chartist Movement*, p. 94.

103. *Manchester and Salford Advertiser*, 6 Oct. 1838, p. 4; C. A. N. Reid, 'The Chartist Movement in Stockport', (Hull Univ. MA thesis, 1974), pp. 110-111; *NS*, 29 Sept. 1838, p. 5, reported two-hundred hands had been dismissed at Heywood for attending Kersal Moor. Similar attempts at dismissal were made at Ashton, Hyde and Stalybridge.

104. For reports of these meetings, see *NS*, 6 Oct.-15 Dec. 1838; *Manchester and Salford Advertiser*; *Manchester Guardian* and the Lancashire press in general; PRO, HO 40/36-38; TS 11/814-15; TS 11/817.

105. *NS*, 6 Oct. 1838, p. 4.

106. *Manchester and Salford Advertiser*, 3 Nov. 1838, p. 4.

107. Ibid., p. 8; also at the Preston torchlight meeting, *NS*, 10 Nov. 1838, p. 6.

108. *Manchester Guardian*, 10 Nov. 1838.

109. *NS*, 17 Nov. 1838, p. 8.

110. *Manchester Guardian*, 1 Dec. 1838, p. 2; *NS*, 22 Dec. 1838, p. 6; PRO, HO 41/13; F. C. Mather, 'The Government and the Chartists', in A. Briggs (ed.), *Chartist Studies*, London 1959, pp. 376-77.

111. *NS*, 8 Dec. 1838, p. 4. Even Melbourne doubted whether torchlight meetings were illegal.

112. PRO, TS 11/815, no. 2687; *Manchester and Salford Advertiser*, 15 Dec. 1838, p. 4; *NS*, 15 Dec. 1838, p. 6; T. Middleton, *History of Hyde and Its Neighborhood*, Hyde 1932, p. 102.

113. *NS*, 15 Dec. 1838, p. 8. The same week the GNU adopted a resolution in favour of arming.

114. *Manchester Guardian*, 29 Dec. 1838, pp. 2-3; PRO, TS 11/817; HO 49/8; *Report of the Trial of the Rev. J. R. Stephens at Chester Assizes*, Leeds 1839; J. Prest, *Lord John Russell*, London 1972, p. 141.

115. *NS*, 29 Dec. 1838, p. 5; also see *Operative*, 6 Jan. 1839, p. 8.

116. 'Passages', in *Robert Lowery*, p. 112.

117. *NS*, 5 Jan. 1839, p. 8. The assertion that 'O'Connor instantly deserted Stephens' (Ward, 'Revolutionary Tory', p. 105) is incorrect. While not as active in his defence as Oastler, O'Connor attended his court hearings, addressed meetings on his behalf and brought his case before the Convention. He never criticised Stephens publicly, even after his disavowal of all Chartist connections at his trial, but blamed his defection on the hounding of the 'moral-force' men.

118. See I. J. Prothero, *Artisans and Politics in Early Nineteenth-Century London: John Gast and His Times*, Folkestone 1979, p. 322; J. F. C. Harrison, 'Chartism in Leicester', in *Chartist Studies*, pp. 133-35; T. M. Kemnitz, 'Chartism in Brighton', (Sussex Univ. D.Phil thesis, 1969), pp. 327-28; G. Barnsby, 'The Working-Class Movement in the Black Country, 1815-1869', (Birmingham Univ. MA thesis, 1965), p. 438; Maehl, 'The Dynamics of Violence'; Thompson, *Early Chartists*, pp. 16-27, for the best general discussion of Chartist violence.

119. *Charter*, 24 Mar. 1839, p. 130.

120. *NS*, 25 Aug. 1838, p. 4. The same logic, phrases and examples were used at nearly every meeting O'Connor addressed in the latter half of 1838. He could have been quoting Hunt's 1816 Spa Fields address, the vocabulary, tone and formulation were almost identical.

121. *NS*, 29 Sept. 1838, p. 7; *Champion*, 30 Sept. 1838, pp. 3-4, 6. As for arming, see R. K. Douglas's speech, *Birmingham Journal*, 9 June 1838.

122. *Charter*, 17 Feb. 1839, p. 53.

123. *Northern Liberator*, 8 Dec. 1838, p. 3.

124. See *London Dispatch*, 28 Oct. 1838, p. 3; *Morning Chronicle*, quoted in H. Jephson, *The Platform, its Rise and Progress*, London 1892, II, p. 252; W. Lovett, *Life and Struggles of William Lovett*, Fitzroy ed., London 1967, p. 143.

125. Lovett, *Life and Struggles*, pp. 161-62; Wilson, *Chartist Movement in Scotland*, p. 63.

126. *Manchester Courier*, 22 Dec. 1838, p. 2.

127. *NS*, 27 Apr. 1839; *Fleet Papers*, 20 Mar. 1841, pp. 94-95; Thompson, *Early Chartists*, pp. 17-18.

128. *NS*, 18 Oct. 1839, p. 1; *Champion*, 20 Oct. 1839, p. 2; also see Fletcher, *Letters to the Inhabitants of Bury*, letter 4, pp. 5-7.

129. *Birmingham Journal*, 8 Dec. 1838; *NS*, 15 Dec. 1838, p. 4.

130. *The Times*, 3 Dec. 1838, p. 2; for O'Connell's earlier attacks on O'Connor, Stephens and Oastler and the English radicals, see *Pilot*, 19 Sept. 1838, p. 2; 30 Nov., p. 4; *Freeman's Journal*, 20 Sept. 1838, p. 3; 26-30 Nov.

131. *Champion*, 30 Dec. 1838, p. 3.

132. *NS*, 15 Dec. 1838, p. 3; for Lord Durham's overtures for a household suffrage

alliance, see *The Times*, 15, 18, 20 Dec. 1838.

133. See the speeches of Oastler and Stephens, *NS*, 17 Nov. 1838, p. 6; 15 Dec., p. 6; 22 Dec., p. 5; *Manchester and Salford Advertiser*, 5 Jan. 1839, p. 3.

134. *NS*, 5 Jan. 1839; *Champion*, 30 Dec. 1838, p. 5.

135. See *NS*, 8 Dec. 1838-12 Jan. 1839; also see *Operative*; *Champion*; *Northern Liberator*.

136. *Operative*, 16 Dec. 1838, p. 97.

137. *NS*, 17 Nov. 1838, p. 6; 15 Dec., p. 3; PRO, TS 11/815, no. 2687.

138. *NS*, 17 Nov. 1838, p. 8; 24 Nov., p. 8; 1 Dec., p. 8; *Birmingham Journal*, 17 Nov.-1 Dec. 1838; T. R. Tholfsen, 'The Chartist Crisis in Birmingham', *International Review of Social History*, 3, 1958, pp. 463-65; Kemnitz and Jacques, 'Stephens', pp. 222-24. For an important reevaluation of the socio-economic conditions which rendered an alliance between middle-class and working-class radicals at Birmingham inoperative, see C. Beehagg, 'Custom, Class and Change: the Trade Societies of Birmingham', *Social History*, 4, 1979, pp. 455-80.

139. *Operative*, 4 Nov. 1838, p. 9; 25 Nov., p. 56.

140. Ibid., 23 Dec. 1838, pp. 116-17; 30 Dec., p. 129; *NS*, 22 Dec. 1838, p. 8; 29 Dec., p. 8; *Champion*, 23 Dec. 1838, p. 6; 30 Dec., p. 5.

141. *Champion*, 23 Dec. 1838, p. 6; 30 Dec., p. 5; D. J. Rowe, 'The Failure of London Chartism', *Historical Journal*, 11, 1968, pp. 472-87; I. J. Prothero, 'Chartism in London', *Past and Present*, no. 44, 1969, pp. 76-105.

142. *NS*, 29 Dec. 1838, p. 8.

143. Ibid.; A. R. Schoyen, *The Chartist Challenge: A Portrait of George Julian Harney*, London 1958, p. 41. Chartist associations at Hammersmith, Chiswick, Kensington and Wandsworth passed resolutions adopting the slogan 'peacefully if we can, forcibly if we must'. *Operative*, 13 Jan. 1839, p. 3; 27 Jan., p. 3, for the resignations of J. C. Coombe and James Chapman from the LWMA over this issue.

144. *NS*, 22 Dec. 1838, p. 8; 15 Dec., p. 3.

145. *True Scotsman*, 24 Nov.-15 Dec. 1838; *NS*, 15 Dec. 1838, p. 7; British Library, Place Newspaper Collection, Set 56 (July-Dec. 1838), fos. 284-85; Wilson, *Chartist Movement in Scotland*, ch. 4.

146. *NS*, 1 Dec.-22 Dec. 1838; *Operative*, 23 Dec. 1838, p. 113; 30 Dec., p. 133; *Champion*, 30 Dec. 1838, p. 3.

147. *NS*, 12 Jan. 1839, p. 8; 19 Jan., pp. 2, 4; *True Scotsman*, 12 and 19 Jan. 1839.

148. *NS*, 19 Jan. 1839, p. 4.

149. Ibid., 15 Dec. 1838, p. 1; 5 Jan. 1839, p. 1; 12 Jan., p. 4; 19 Jan., p. 8. There are no reports of the proceedings of this delegates meeting which may indicate a desire to keep their discussions secret.

150. *NS*, 19 Jan. 1839, p. 1; however, cf. *Charter*, 27 Jan. 1839, p. 11.

151. PRO, TS 11/815, no 2687.

4 THE QUEST FOR WORKING-CLASS POWER: THE NATIONAL CONVENTION OF 1839

I

The concept of a National Convention of the people was not a new idea, but a familiar Painite element of radical ideology, conjuring images of the French and American Revolutions, as well as asserting a constitutional legitimacy through the precedent of the Conventions of 1660 and 1688 which had restored the English monarchy.[1] The Chartist National Convention of 1839 marked the climax of a radical convention tradition. Conventions had been convened by radicals in 1794 and 1817; and the prospect of the election of a national convention in 1819 prompted government repression.[2] In the wake of the reform agitation, plans for a convention were again propagated by radicals like James Lorymer, Richard Lee and William Benbow, and supported by the National Union of the Working Classes.[3] The Cold Bath Fields meeting of 1833, regarded by many working-class radicals as the Whig sequel to Peterloo, had been called by the NUWC to discuss plans for a convention.[4] On his first missionary tour, in winter 1835-36, O'Connor had drawn attention to the need for a convention; and in the *Poor Man's Guardian*, O'Brien first elaborated his election strategy, whereby radicals elected at the hustings were to assemble in London in order to confront the Commons as the true representatives of the people — a variation on the 'legislative attorney' scheme of 1819.[5]

The National Convention embodied the concept of a rival authority to Parliament, an alternative government or 'anti-parliament' of the people facing the corrupt and unrepresentative institutions of the ruling class.[6] Throughout the country, Chartists regarded the Convention as an alternative government to which they declared their allegiance. W. Barnett, veteran of Peterloo, told a meeting in his home town of Macclesfield:

> I declare . . . that I owe the British Government no allegiance, but what I am obliged to give it. I declare, that I will obey the Convention; nor death nor hell shall prevent me from being obedient to them. They are my Government. I had a hand in chusing them. I will not be governed by the House of Commons in any respect, but what I am obliged.[7]

At a Bolton meeting, called to elect a delegate to the Convention, a local working man declared that they were assembled to select a representative 'to the *real* Parliament — the working men's Parliament — the National Convention'. James Fenny, the Wigan delegate and another veteran of Peterloo days, maintained: 'There are now, for the first time, in London, two Parliaments sitting at one time. One was the mock, the self-elected, the Whig and Tory Parliament — the other the real, the universal-suffrage, the People's Parliament.'[8]

O'Connor was among the most ardent proponents of the concept of the Convention as an alternative government. He regarded the Convention as 'the only constituted authority representing the people of this country', and dismissed the 'present House of Commons' as 'an unconstitutional authority'.[9] The precipitation of a confrontation between these two bodies was central to his strategy for obtaining the Charter. O'Connor also maintained that the existence of the National Convention distinguished the Chartist agitation from previous movements and revolutions, as it offered an alternative to the existing political system and ensured unified national action.

> To the existence of that Convention, you are to attribute the difference between our present revolution and any revolution which has hitherto taken place among nations. (Cheers.) Look to the several French revolutions. They failed of producing the promised result because men attacked abuses, and fought for a shadow, without being prepared with a substitute (Cheers.) Your case is now different, for, upon an emergency, you have a Parliament which would act, and one whose orders you would obey, or to appoint *instanter* another, whose orders you could more cheerfully obey. (Loud cheers.) Herein then lies all the difference: you cannot move partially, because you are one link in the great chain. (Cheers.) There is an end to sectional agitation; you are each answerable to the other for the manner in which you shall handle this cause. (Cheers.)[10]

O'Connor, and most Chartists, envisaged the Convention not merely as a petitioning body, but as an institution for formulating a strategy for the attainment of universal suffrage, following the inevitable rejection of the National Petition. However, the heterogeneous composition of the first National Convention militated against any early agreement upon such a policy. In several respects the Convention was something less than a truly representative body. Less than half of the original delegates were working men.[11] (See Table 4.1) This was inevitable before the establishment of the National Charter Association. Few working men could afford to leave their employment, even if supported by their constituents. Victimisation was a very real threat. After the Convention, the knitter James Wood-house, who replaced the Rev. Arthur Wade as Nottingham's delegate to the Convention, could find no employer willing to rent him a frame.[12] Often Chartists had to rely upon middle-class radicals from outside their own districts, whose independence freed them for service at the Convention. Peter Chappell, a factory worker and leading local Chartist, explained why the Stockport Chartists were unable to send a local radical to the Convention: 'Independently of the expense, it was not easy to get working men who could sacrifice everything to represent them in London, and independent gentle-men had not come forward as they had elsewhere.'[13]

In other localities, especially in Lancashire and Yorkshire, local middle-class radicals who had taken the lead in radical protest since the reform agitation, or before, came forward. Local middle-class radicals such as Dr Matthew Fletcher of Bury, Peter Bussey of Bradford, Lawrence Pitkeithley of Huddersfield, James Taylor of Rochdale, R.J. Richardson of Salford and John Frost of Newport remained at the Convention, faithfully representing their localities. Unlike Birmingham's middle-class delegates, these men were closely tied to the local working-class community; although there was a tendency for such leaders to drop out of the movement following the dissolution of the Convention and the Newport rising.[14] What these leaders had in common was a measure of independence denied most working men, although a delegate like Bussey, a beerseller, was only marginally outside the ranks of the working class. Such leaders usually placed great importance upon their independent status and unpaid services as a guarantee of political honesty. Richardson told a Chartist meeting:

> He was not a paid political advocate, perambulating the country to excite the people to disaffection; he was an elector of the township of Salford in the county of Lancaster, and a freeholder of the same county; and he held a station in society which enabled him to employ his time and his humble talents in endeavouring to ameliorate the condition of the people . . .[15]

Chartism never again possessed such a wide range of middle-class leadership. This was partially to do with the way in which the move-ment had come together. Dr Fletcher recalled:

> no one need be ashamed at having been associated with them [the members of the Convention]. It was a very different affair to the subse-quent gatherings of Mr. Feargus O'Connor's tramping lecturers. There were barristers, clergymen, merchants, as well as members of my own

profession, and literary men, and a considerable proportion of honest and intelligent working men . . .[16]

There was an air of middle-class 'respectability' about the first Chartist Convention.

At the Convention certain localities were both over represented and unrepresentative of local Chartist rank-and-file support. Birmingham 'elected' seven BPU councillors, three of whom never attended the Convention, and of the rest only John Collins, the sole working-class delegate, did not resign. These Birmingham merchants also presumed to represent a constellation of towns around Birmingham, including the militant Black Country. Before the Convention met, local Chartists had withdrawn support from their leadership. About a quarter of the delegates to the Convention lived in London. This reflects the preponderance of radical journalists and publishers among the delegates. More significantly, the LWMA, a relatively insignificant radical association, had manipulated the election of eight delegates at the Palace Yard meeting, thus denying the various metropolitan districts and other radical groups any real choice in their representation. With some justification O'Connor later claimed, in his own defence, that it was the LWMA leadership who had tried to 'fix' the membership of the Convention.[17] Certainly the first Chartist Convention was not an O'Connorite body. At the beginning of the Convention, the LWMA delegates were regarded with some suspicion, especially by the northern members who believed that the LWMA men were under the control of Place, the parliamentary radicals and the political economists, and allied with the BPU leaders in an attempt to overshadow O'Connor's influence.[18]

O'Connor's leadership was integrally linked with that of the Convention. Together with the *Star*, the Convention provided the central focus of national Chartist unity, organisation and leadership which O'Connor endeavoured to strengthen. His standing within the Chartist movement placed him in a unique relationship to the Convention. No leader rivalled his influence either outside or within the Convention. O'Connor controlled the movement's most influential journal; he had attended nearly every meeting at which a Convention delegate was chosen; he was known personally and respected by most local radical leaders. Yet O'Connor carefully avoided forming a 'party' as such within the Convention. Dr Taylor commented:

> The only man who could be said to have a party was O'Connor; he was known personally to almost every delegate; with the constituencies of most of them he was acquainted; he had been in Parliament and was

Table 4.1: Delegates Elected To The Chartist National Convention of February 1839

Name	Occupation	District(s) Represented
William G. Burns	shoemaker	Forfarshire; Aberdeenshire
Peter Bussey	beerseller	West Riding
William Cardo	shoemaker	Marylebone
William Carpenter	journalist	Bolton
William Carrier	gig-man or hatter	Wiltshire
John Cleave	publisher	London; Reading
*J.P. Cobbett	lawyer/journalist	West Riding
**R.B.B. Cobbett	lawyer	Manchester
John Collins	tool maker	Birmingham
Hugh Ballie Craig	draper/newspaper owner	Ayrshire
John Deegan	newsagent (ex-card room hand)	Stalybridge/Hyde/Glossop
*R.K. Douglas	journalist	Birmingham
Abram Duncan	pirn maker	Dumfries
**George Edmonds	lawyer	Birmingham
James Fenny	shoemaker	Wigan
Matthew Fletcher	surgeon	Bury/Heywood
John Frost	draper	Newport, S. Wales
**William Greenwood	—	Todmorden
*William Gill	journeyman scale cutter	Sheffield
*John Good	hairdresser	Brighton
*Benjamin Hadley	button manufacturer	Birmingham
Alexander Halley	working man	Stirling/Dunfermline/Alva
G.J. Harney	journalist (ex-seaman)	Northumberland; Norwich; Derby
Robert Hartwell	compositor	London
Henry Hetherington	publisher	London; Stockport
Charles Jones	middle-class	Newton/Welshpool/Llanidloes
Robert Knox	slater	Durham County
**George Lovelace	small farmer (ex-agricultural labourer)	Dorset

Name	Occupation	District(s) Represented
William Lovett	cabinet maker	London
Robert Lowery	tailor	Newcastle
Peter M'Douall	surgeon	Ashton-under-Lyne
Richard Marsden	weaver	Preston
*Patrick Matthew	grain dealer/tree planter	Perthshire and Fife
Richard Mealing	plumber/glazier	Bath/Trowbridge/Frome
James Mills	hatter	Oldham
James Moir	tea merchant	Glasgow
Richard Moore	woodcarver	London
**G.F. Muntz	merchant and metal manufacturer	Birmingham
**Philip Muntz	merchant and metal manufacturer	Birmingham
Charles Neesom	tailor	Bristol
**Edward Nightingale	—	Manchester
James. B. O'Brien	lawyer/journalist	London; Leigh; Stockport; Newport; I. of Wight
Feargus O'Connor	landowner/lawyer/newspaper owner	W. Riding; Bristol
*John Pierce	timble manufacturer	Birmingham
Lawrence Pitkeithley	draper	W. Riding
John Richards	shoemaker	Potteries, Staffs.
R.J. Richardson	shopkeeper/master joiner	Manchester
*William Rider	printer/journalist (ex-stuff weaver)	W. Riding
*George Rogers	tobacconist	London
*T.C. Salt	lamp manufacturer	Birmingham
W.S. Villiers Sankey	gentleman/doctor	Edinburgh
John Skevington	hatter/shopkeeper	Loughborough/Leicester
T.R. Smart	schoolteacher	Loughborough and Derby
**Thomas Smith	—	Liverpool
James Taylor	Unitarian minister	Rochdale/Middleton
John Taylor	surgeon	Renfrewshire; Tillocoultry; Wigton; Alva; Newcastle; Carlisle
Benjamin Tight	middle-class	Reading

Name	Occupation	District(s) Represented
Henry Vincent	printer/journalist	London; Hull; Cheltenham; Bristol
*Arthur Wade	Anglican vicar	Nottingham/Mansfield/Sutton
*James Whittle	journalist	Liverpool
*Hugh Williams	lawyer	Swansea; Carmarthan
*Joseph Wood	tea dealer	Bolton
*James Wroe	bookseller/journalist	Manchester

*denotes delegates who resigned (or ceased to attend) before the Convention adjourned on 17 May.

**denotes delegates elected to the Convention who never attended.

Note: The replacements for those who resigned and additions to the original delegates were usually local working men. For instance: Edward Brown (journeyman silversmith) replaced the middle-class Birmingham delegates; James Woodhouse (framework knitter) replaced the Rev. Wade for Nottingham; Christopher Dean (stonemason) replaced Richardson for Manchester in May. Other additions included: Robert Tilley (bricklayer) for Lambeth; John Stowe for Colne; John Warden (gardener) for Bolton; James Wolstenholme (file manufacturer) for Sheffield; James Osbourne (currier) for Brighton; John McCrae (schoolteacher) for Ayrshire.

For a comprehensive (and most accurate) analysis of the personnel of the Convention, see T.M. Kemnitz, 'The Chartist Convention of 1839', *Albion*, 10, 1978, pp. 152-70. I am indebted to Dr Kemnitz and to Dorothy Thompson for providing information about several of these delegates.

looked upon as competent to arrange the proceedings; he was a lawyer as well, and could point out the methods of avoiding the meshes of the law; he possessed the most powerful press in the world . . . more than one member of the Convention was connected with the sale of his papers; and it is known that his recommendation had gone a good way in the appointment of others; from all these circumstances if any one could presume to have a party, it was him; but the proceedings of the very first day showed that neither was he anxious to extend any influence, nor they inclined to permit it if he had been so.[19]

The delegates to the Convention exhibited a spirit of independence. The northern representatives by no means voted as an O'Connorite bloc. O'Connor assumed the role of unifier and reconciler of differences within the Convention, rather than the leader of a clearly defined group.

More than any other leader, O'Connor linked the popular agitation in the country to the Convention; he was a national figure rather than a local representative. William Ashton of Barnsley considered O'Connor 'to be the mainspring of the agitation'. According to George Binns at Sunderland: 'They all knew that Feargus O'Connor was the life and soul of these proceedings.'[20] O'Connor's duties at the Convention prevented him from embarking upon the sort of whirlwind tours which had characterised his agitation in 1838, although he still maintained an impressive rate of activity. He continued to intervene in key local situations which required the projection of a national outlook. Upon the resignation of the BPU delegates, he immediately travelled to Birmingham to organise and oversee the election of new delegates.[21] His presence at local Chartist meetings still generated tremendous enthusiasm. Following one of O'Connor's flying visits, the Barnsley Chartists reported:

The spirit of O'Connor seems to be hovering around us, and giving us a new impulse every day. We could wish that others of the same influential *caste*, would now and then, like aerial spirits, pay us a visit.

In the wake of this visit so many new recruits joined the ranks of the Barnsley Chartists that new premises had to be found for their weekly meetings.[22]

O'Connor regularly assumed the role of mediator between the Convention and the Chartist rank and file. He called for their indulgence in the face of the Convention's vacillations and squabbles. He was at pains to preserve working-class confidence in the Convention as the central institution of collective Chartist leadership. Thus, following the Convention's decision to delay the presentation of the National Petition, it was O'Connor who assumed the responsibility of explaining their action to the movement at large. Delay was absolutely necessary in order to marshal their forces, especially as this was to be the last petition. He assured Chartists that all was well at the Convention. O'Connor's ultimate appeal, however, was to the people's confidence in his own leadership, clothed in personal sacrifice and unquestionable integrity of motive.

> I have worked when you have been all sleeping. I have worked for nothing, except illness, a broken-down constitution, and the premature old age, now saddled upon me; and I tell you the Convention was right, and those who censure, are either wrong, or they are enemies. . . . Do you suppose that I would consort with them for an hour, if there was even reasonable doubt as to their honesty and their intentions? Do you suppose that I would be willing to hazard the laurels which I have honestly acquired by being party to delay, if that delay was to operate against your interests? No! I would perish first.[23]

In appearance there was a contradiction between a tradition of gentlemanly leadership and new forms of collective, national working-class leadership. In practice the one complemented the other. There was a sense in which O'Connor stood above the Convention, extending the legitimacy of his personal claim to leadership to the collective actions of the Convention. Nothing more clearly illustrates the way in which O'Connor transcended the traditional image of the spontaneous demagogue.

Within the Convention O'Connor continually struggled to force the assembly to assume a position of positive leadership, to direct the mass movement outside its walls. No institution of national Chartist leadership again captured such a wide spectrum of working-class allegiance. Yet there was a distinct note of caution about the Convention's early proceedings. From the outset there was confusion over the posture which the Convention should assume. O'Connor's clarity and firmness of purpose during these early months contrasted with the general hesitancy of the Convention, especially over the central issue of ulterior measures.

II

When the Convention convened its proceedings the National Petition had been signed by just over an half-million people.[24] There was a general feeling that the Petition should be more widely signed before its presentation to Parliament. The Birmingham delegates were already using this as an excuse to call in doubt the whole authority of the Petition and the Convention.[25] Therefore, one of the first debates concerned the proposal that the Convention send out missionaries to agitate and collect more signatures to the Petition. This debate reflected the delegates' early uncertainty about their status as a body. Fletcher questioned the role of the Convention as a national agitating body. He opposed sending out missionaries on the grounds that such a step would lend substance to their opponents' accusations that 'we send out paid agitators to stir up the people to discontent and disaffection', and argued that agitation should be carried out by local leaders. Many delegates were still rooted primarily in their own localities and dominated by established concepts of legitimate agitation in which travelling politicians and demagogues with no local interest were regarded with suspicion. O'Brien countered that delegates sent out under the authority of the Convention 'would be able to find larger masses of the people together, than could be got together by any merely local agitation'; and asked: 'For what purpose had the Convention been elected if not to agitate?' Doubts were raised, however, about the legality of such a step. R. J. Richardson, supported by Peter Bussey, urged 'caution and deliberation'; they must 'most carefully abstain from doing or saying anything that could bring the Convention into danger'.[26] The fears of radicals like Richardson and Bussey concerning the government's intentions were hardly surprising. This was the first time any government had allowed such a body to meet openly. Both men had willingly recommended defiance of the new Poor Law, but were understandably apprehensive about jeopardising the legal standing of the Convention. This sort of uncertainty goes a long way to explaining the Convention's early moderation.

O'Connor was relatively unconcerned over the number of signatures to the Petition. While he called on Chartists to support the drive for more signatures, he reminded them: '*It is the last, the very last* [petition].'

> I know your wants and your feelings: I have communed with you, and have learned them through other channels than inanimate petitions. Those, however, who have not so frequently mixed with you, require your sign-manual as proof of your devotion to liberty. To silence them, give it to them: let every man, woman and child sign the Petition; disarm all your enemies at once. If it can be done by a dash of the pen, it is worth the experiment.[27]

The central problem which was to remain before the Convention, however, was the formulation of a plan of action to follow the rejection of the Petition. O'Connor was the most prominent and forceful advocate of an early resolution of the question of 'ulterior measures', in order that both the movement at large and the government knew what to expect in the event of Parliament rejecting their peaceful overtures. He reasoned that government concessions would only be forthcoming if it were understood that the Chartists were prepared to act decisively in the event of their demands not being met.

Within the Convention it was argued that a premature discussion of ulterior measures would provide the Commons with an excuse to dismiss their petition. O'Brien reflected the majority view in the early weeks.

> The duty of the Convention, at the present time, was to expediate by every means it could devise, the signing of the petition. They had made the signatures to the petition the test of the feelings of the country, and it would be absurd to talk of ulterior measures unless they had two or three millions of signatures . . .

'At present, the Convention stood as mediator between the suffering people and the House of Commons', argued O'Brien.[28] Plans were made to hold interviews with Members of Parliament. Although few delegates believed there was any prospect of the Commons accepting the Charter, it was felt that they must place the Convention formally in the right by having done all in their power to ensure a favourable reception for the Petition. In his account of the Convention, Dr Taylor explained:

> The great majority thought that it was their bounden duty to their constituencies, since a petition was to be presented, to do so under the best auspices, and that however little reason they had to hope from the House of Commons any favourable result, it was still their duty to exhaust every resource, and take from their opponents or pretended friends the power of saying they had neglected anything.[29]

Although O'Connor supported the plans to interview sympathetic MPs in order to convince them that 'they were not all rebels, desirous of anarchy and bloodshed', he believed that the adoption of ulterior measures would make little difference to their potential parliamentary support. On the other hand, the failure to make it clear that this was the last petition, and that consequences would immediately follow its rejection, would seriously weaken the resolve of their working-class supporters.

His opinion was that they would be equally successful with the members of that house, whether they addressed them with 'You scoundrels, will you vote for Universal Suffrage?' or with 'Good sir, representative for so and so, will you have the condescension to support the "People's Charter" for Universal Suffrage?' All the courtesy in the world would not gain the Convention a single vote. The best way to make an impression upon them was to go with the petition in one hand and the ulterior measures in the other. If anything could give increased energy to the people it would be the knowledge of the fact, that as soon as the petition was rejected . . . the Convention would do something, within the law, which would afford a demonstration of the people's strength and determination. — (Cheers.) If there were any apathy in the hearts of the people now, it was because they believed another petition would follow this. He anticipated other duties would fall on the Convention when their petition should be rejected in the house.[30]

O'Connor had one eye closely fixed on the movement in the country. Working-class aspirations, raised by months of frenzied agitation, were now embodied in the Convention. In a typical address, the Barnsley Chartists reminded their representatives at the Convention: 'A faint glimmering of hope has kept them [the people] from desperation: and this hope is now fixed upon you and your colleagues.'[31] O'Connor was concerned lest radical enthusiasm and confidence in the Convention should be dissipated through over-cautious deliberations.

Discussion of ulterior measures most clearly highlighted the central question of the function of the Convention and the nature of the National Petition. J. P. Cobbett moved a series of resolutions asserting that the sole purpose of the Convention was to superintend the presentation of the Petition.[32] Very few delegates accepted this limited conception of the Convention. The presentation of the Petition was merely the pretence upon which the Convention sat. It had been a means of rallying support at mass demonstrations under a constitutional veneer; its rejection would extend a legitimacy to recommendations for further action. Matthew Fletcher admitted: 'They sat under the cloak of being a petitioning body, and the men of the North held their meetings under this cloak, because the right of petitioning was almost the only Constitutional right they had left.'[33] O'Brien likened the Petition to 'a notice to quit, and if the parties did not obey the notice, why, then, the people must follow up their notice by what was called a process of ejectment'. According to the *Star*, the Petition was 'our last notice of the House of Capitalists'. O'Connor claimed, 'it

is well known that their labours, only commenced with the presentation of the petition'.[34] He told the Convention that if they appeared
before the people

> and appealed to nothing but the force of petitioning, they would have
> lost with the people that hold and confidence which had brought this
> Convention together. — (no, no, and yes, yes.) . . . the Convention
> would not be sitting if the people had thought that petitioning was to be
> the last remnant of hope to the people.[35]

Dr Peter M'Douall declared that the people of Ashton would not sign
petitions. 'He did not come to the Convention merely to present a
petition — if they were not allowed to recommend ulterior measures
he had better go home.' And the Preston weaver, Richard Marsden,
one of the Convention's rough working-class diamonds, put the
matter bluntly: the people of the North expected a general strike to
follow the rejection of the Petition.

> The people were told that this was to be the last petition (hear), and that
> if it were rejected, there was to be a sacred week.— (No, no.) The
> working men of the north signed the petition for the Charter, under the
> impression that the men who spoke for them of the holy week were
> sincere. None of the industrious classes who signed the petition in this
> belief, ever thought for a moment that the legislature would grant the
> Charter. The people expected nothing at the hands of the government
> — they looked to the determination of this Convention. . . . If they were
> sincere, all they had to do, was to let the country know when the sacred
> week was to commence.

This was the first call for the 'sacred week' at the Convention.[36]

Cobbett's resolutions found little support, except among a small
group of Cobbettites.[37] As a consequence of the overwhelming rejection of his resolutions, Cobbett resigned from the Convention, a
precedent about which O'Connor expressed foreboding. However,
while most delegates concurred in O'Connor's opinion that such a
circumscription of the Convention's role 'would have amounted to
suicide', there was relatively little support for his argument for an
immediate consideration of ulterior measures contingent upon the
denial of their demands, except from a small group of delegates,
including Marsden, Harney, M'Douall and John Skevington. Even
delegates such as Dr Taylor and Bussey opposed what they considered a 'premature' discussion of this matter. Thus the Convention
left itself in an ambiguous position, having affirmed that its function
transcended that of a mere petitioning assembly, while having refused to commit itself to any immediate policy beyond petitioning.

The issue of ulterior measures remained at the centre of the Convention's discussions into the summer.

The campaign to collect more signatures resulted in the postponement of the date intended for the presentation of the Petition until early May. In the event, the Petition was not presented until June and was rejected in mid-July. Such a delay posed a difficult tactical problem. The movement had to be kept in a state of heightened excitement over an extended period without prematurely committing itself. On the other hand, had the Convention assumed a role of positive leadership for which O'Connor argued and been prepared to act resolutely over the issue of ulterior measures, these months could have provided a vital period for the organisation and preparation of a plan of alternative action.

III

Within the Convention the delay over the presentation of the Petition and the refusal to discuss plans for ulterior action precipitated an open split between the extreme left wing, composed of Harney, Rider, Marsden and Charles Neesom, and the majority of the Convention. Before it had even assembled, Harney had publicly expressed his own doubts, and those of the London Democratic Association, about the Convention.[38] The left now called in question the authority of the Convention. This challenge stemmed from a series of provocative resolutions adopted at a meeting of the LDA: first, that if the Convention did its duty the Charter would be law within a month; secondly, that there should be no delay in the presentation of the Petition; thirdly, that every act of injustice and oppression should be met immediately by resistance. These resolutions, submitted to the Convention, met with severe and near universal censure. R. J. Richardson thought such resolutions constituted 'an insult to the Convention'. The efforts of Harney and his confederates to introduce 'matters at once criminal and dangerous . . . looked like a conspiracy to destroy the Convention'. Dr Taylor thought such resolutions tended to injure the Convention in 'public opinion'. Even M'Douall, who supported an early discussion of ulterior measures, saw this move as an affront to the authority of the Convention, an attempt by politically inexperienced youth to dictate to the representatives of the people, 'many of them grey haired veterans'.[39] Harney's small group was generally isolated from the views of the majority of the

Convention. Their consciously revolutionary rhetoric, steeped in images of the French Revolution, remained unwelcome among delegates concerned about the legal standing of the Convention.[40] As for the LDA, Fletcher commented, somewhat unjustly, 'the politics of this body were purely foreign'.[41] The conspiratorial air which surrounded the LDA's proceedings aroused suspicion. Harney and his confederates were seen as irresponsibly playing into the hands of government agents.[42]

While O'Connor did not share Harney's insurrectionist strategy for 1839, he did not censure the LDA. He assumed rather the role of peacemaker, intent upon preserving at least the image of unanimity at the Convention. He reassured Chartists:

> Everything is going on well in the Convention. Ryder, Marsden, and Harney are as good men as we have, and pray allow us the privilege of man and wife, to fall out among ourselves, so long as we are ready to join against the intruders and meddlers.[43]

Within the Convention, just as outside, O'Connor played a key unifying role. He regularly came to the defence of the extreme left. In April, in the face of considerable opposition, O'Connor welcomed the admission of Joseph Williams, journeyman baker and LDA member, as the newly elected delegate from East Surrey — for 'he appeared in the dress of a working man'. To Fletcher's claim that there was a conspiracy of 'self-styled Jacobin clubs' to swamp the Convention, and Cleave's denunciation of the 'Marats' of the Convention, O'Connor replied that 'if Jacobin clubs or the Democratic Association could infuse fresh zeal into the Convention, so much the better'.[44] O'Connor was a good deal more tolerant of Harney's 'Jacobin', ultra-revolutionary behaviour than a staid constitutionalist like Fletcher who found Harney's dagger waving at meetings and predilection to don a cap of liberty utterly repugnant.[45] O'Connor had been closely associated with both Harney and Rider in the agitation which led up to the Convention and sympathised with their concern over the Convention's equivocal leadership. No doubt he hoped the sabre-rattling of these young revolutionaries would enliven the Convention proceedings and force a clarification of the issue of ulterior measures.

In response to the LDA resolutions, O'Connor proposed that the Convention convene meetings throughout the country a week before the presentation of the Petition to discuss the question of ulterior measures; thus linking the demand for ulterior action with a call for simultaneous meetings. He also moved that the Convention immediately convene a meeting at the Crown and Anchor to dispel any dissatisfaction surrounding the delay, especially in order to clarify their position to the militant northern Chartists.

> It was not surprising that the working men of the north, who were now compelled to subsist for six days upon three days' scanty wages, should be somewhat impatient, but it was necessary that those who were capable of looking at the aspect of the thing through the country, and therefore knew what the state and capabilities of the people generally were, should show those who were more impatient and ardent in their pursuit of reform, the necessity of restraining their impetuosity and impatience, until they could take the proposed step with a greater certainty of success.[46]

Significantly, Harney seconded this motion, conceding now that delay was necessary and trusting that all differences within the Convention were at an end. Thus O'Connor was able to secure a temporary rapprochment between Harney's 'Junta' and the Convention. However, the threatening tone of the Crown and Anchor meeting which contrasted sharply with the cautious tone of the Convention proved the pretext for the resignation of Birmingham's middle-class delegates and the Rev. Wade.[47] At this meeting O'Connor dwelt upon a familiar theme, the duty which the rejection of the Petition would impose upon the Convention.

> It was now out of the nature of things that the Convention should break up without making some attempt for securing the Charter; or if they should, the people would know how to deal with them. . . . The people should recollect that a million of petitions would not dislodge a single troop of dragoons . . .

He also observed: 'The great difficulty which he saw in the present case was, that it was not dealt with by men who laboured all day themselves'.[48] The resignation of the Birmingham delegates marked the beginning of the 'purging' of the Convention which reached alarming proportions by the time the assembly moved to Birmingham in May.[49] Defections were overwhelmingly from the ranks of the middle-class delegates who were invariably replaced by working men.

O'Connor's principal concern in spring of 1839 was to prevent the Convention's isolation from militant local Chartist opinion and to avert the possible degeneration of the movement into sectional agitation through disillusion with the Convention's inaction. He feared that the delay in the presentation of the Petition, the vagueness over the issue of ulterior measures and the steady desertion of middle-class delegates might undermine Chartist confidence in the Convention and result in premature outbreaks of violence in the most advanced localities. Already at Bolton, a centre of Chartist militancy, Alderman Joseph Wood, a local tea-dealer who had resigned from the Convention and become a Poor Law guardian, told a meeting that the Convention was 'doing nothing, had done nothing, and could do nothing. . . . If the people wished to have a physical revolution they must elect another Convention, as the present one was determined not to do anything to promote the object.'[50] O'Connor sought to avert a physical revolution through a strategy of open intimidation and mass pressure. He looked to the Convention not only to set the tone for such a campaign, but to contain the insurrectionary zeal being exhibited in certain northern localities. He warned that although the Convention had been in advance of the people when it first met, that now the situation was reversed.

> The cowardice of some, the lukewarmness of others and the neglect and imputations of others had thrown a damp on the cause of the people. They had been a long time talking of moral force, but he would tell the Convention that unless they exerted themselves, the people in spite of them would have recourse to physical force . . . In Lancashire and Yorkshire the people asked him if he thought the Convention would recommend physical force, and he told them he did not think they would . . .[51]

By late April, it had become apparent that the Convention had to give a more decisive lead to the mass movement. O'Connor urged the mobilisation of simultaneous demonstrations throughout the country upon the authority of the Convention, in order to discuss ulterior measures. He argued the necessity to mount demonstrations greater than those of 1832 in order to carry the Charter. One and an half million people 'assembled in one day for the same important purpose, will show at once what is to be expected from men with arms in their hands, determined to defend their lives, their country and their liberty to the last'.[52] O'Connor used all his influence and persuasive talents to impress upon his fellow delegates the paramount need to transform their debating chamber into a more dynamic agitational force, initiating and directing Chartist policy. He continually stressed the importance of keeping the movement under the control of the Convention as the central institution of national Chartist leadership. In speech after speech he reiterated with all his eloquence the pressing necessity for the Convention to assume a positive character.

While O'Connor appealed to the Chartist rank and file for indulgence on behalf of the Convention, within the Convention his tone became increasingly one of impatience. In a debate over Bussey's motion for an immediate decision on the question of ulterior measures, Fletcher proposed an amendment for a further committee to sit to consider the issue. O'Connor, who had seconded Bussey's move 'because I thought a clear understanding with the country was necessary', vehemently opposed any such delay.

> Let us, then be prepared in time. (Cheers.) You see the position into which delay has brought this country. . . . I tell you that the country will look upon your Charter as a mere fiction, if it is not ready as a substitute for the system you seek to destroy. (Question) What, is that not the question? If not, what is the question? Let those who cry question go to Manchester, and see the men over whose lot they so recently professed to mourn, now reduced to double want and destitution, and tell them that this is not the question. (Hear, hear.) I was in Manchester on Saturday, and there the people are reduced to half that pittance which before was insufficient. (Shame.) Aye, shame, but shame upon us if we allow it to continue. Does this Convention suppose that those persons whose condition Mr. Richards of the Potteries, has described, will wait for reports of select committees? (Hear, hear.) No: I contend for it that if the Convention wishes to prevent revolution, we must take prompt and speedy means.[53]

This was O'Connor at his best, chastising the Convention, riding roughshod over interruptions from the floor and placing the vacillations of the Convention in the context of the daily hardships of their working-class constituents. The following week he returned to the same themes in a discussion of Lowery's moderate address on the people's right to arm, emphasising the need for positive leadership in order to avert the possibility of a partial outbreak. The address he thought was rather one-sided, 'as it merely went to tell what they ought not to do, and never said what they ought to do . . .'

> It was time — aye, more than time for the Convention to speak out to the brave people of England . . . The Convention should step forth and use its power manfully, in order to guide the physical power of the people, for no better check could be had on the physical power of the country than the Convention exercising to its full extent the moral power with which it was entrusted, to prevent anything like partial outbreak. (Hear, hear.)[54]

In the weeks directly preceding the Convention's move to Birmingham, it was O'Connor who persistently urged members to recognise their corporate responsibilities of leadership and, with the exception of the ultra-left, was the one leader who projected a consistent programme of action.

O'Connor's determination to bring the Convention into closer contact with rank-and-file Chartist opinion prompted his campaign to move the Convention out of London. He moved that all members be immediately recalled to the Convention until the presentation of the Petition, noting that nearly half the members either had deserted or did not attend the proceedings. He proposed that the Convention become a perambulating body, sitting for a week at a time in one provincial town after another. O'Connor 'thought that some of the gentlemen required a little fresh air; that the Convention required a little more popular control'. He reminded them that the funds to finance the Convention were collected 'at very great risk' by working people; and insisted that the money be spent in agitation.

> If they sat there a mere money parliament, holding money in their hands, and boasting of the economical manner in which they had done their duty, while much labour remained unperformed, then the people would say they have sent men who simply lived on the pay they had given them — who merely wished to prolong the agitation in order that they might prolong their pay . . .[55]

There was a general feeling that the Convention would be safer in the provinces than in London. O'Connor underlined the need to ensure the safety of the Convention, 'because it involved the safety of the people'; without the Convention the people 'would fall into disorder'.[56] The proposal to move the Convention to Birmingham also was linked to the prospect of ulterior action, and again raised the issue of the Convention's status. According to O'Connor, it would be the duty of the Convention to appoint a permanent chairman upon the presentation of the Petition; for 'The Convention would then be looked on as the only constitutional representative body of the people'. A move to Birmingham which by spring of 1839 was a hotbed of Chartist discontent, O'Connor maintained, would clarify the Convention's true status as 'the true fountain of all law and justice' — a claim they dare not make in London. The moderate wing of the Convention — which included Sankey, Collins, Whittle, Mills, Carpenter, Hartwell, Rogers — objected not merely to the move to Birmingham, but to O'Connor's concept of the role of the Convention. George Rogers, who resigned when the Convention moved to Birmingham, reintroduced the Cobbettite line, that the Convention's 'strength consisted in their sitting as a petitioning body' — a view supported by Carpenter, Whittle and Sankey. Collins did not feel that they were endowed with the powers which O'Connor claimed. The majority of the members were, however, in favour of the move. Rider advocated moving to 'where the men were ready and had tools in their hands'; and added: 'What did the Parliament care for a handful of men sitting in Bolt Court, it was only taken among the millions that they could be effective.' O'Brien, just returned from a tour of Lancashire, reported: 'The people were very anxious that the Convention should meet in Birmingham under the shelter of the guns made by the people there, especially when the time came for ulterior measures . . .' Yet O'Connor's motion for an immediate move to Birmingham was narrowly defeated by O'Brien's amendment in favour of the Convention remaining in London while it fulfilled its petitioning function.[57] When during the next week the government dissolved Parliament, further delaying the presentation of the Petition, the Convention voted overwhelmingly to adjourn its sittings to Birmingham.[58]

O'Connor's efforts to press the Convention to adopt a more bellicose stance conformed with his general strategy for attaining the Charter through intimidation and the mere threat of violent conflict rather than revolution. Such a strategy had a tendency to make his own position appear at times more revolutionary than it was. O'Connor sought to create focal points of confrontation between the government and the Chartists. The Convention, like the mass demonstration, was envisaged as a point of potential confrontation. O'Connor told the Convention that 'if it did not bring itself morally into collision with other authorities it would do nothing. Until they came into collision with some authority, it would be impossible for them to show their own importance.'[59] Just as the torchlight meetings of 1838 had proved an extreme test of the legal right to public assembly, O'Connor's proposal for the Convention to assume a perambulating character, to appoint a permanent chairman, to adopt ulterior measures from the outset and to convene simultaneous meetings were all calculated to bring the Convention into direct confrontation with the government. Through such a confrontation he hoped the Convention would be able to assert its own status as an alternative government.

Once assembled in Birmingham, the Convention at last issued its Manifesto, recommending specific ulterior measures to be put to the Chartist rank and file at the Whitsun meetings. Along with the proposal for a 'sacred month' or general strike, were included the withdrawal of funds from savings banks, the conversion of paper money into gold, the abstinence from the purchase of all excisable goods, exclusive dealing, arming and the support for Chartist candidates at the next general election. This represented a familiar catalogue of ultra-radical tactics, regarded as complementary measures designed to provoke confrontation between government and people.[60] Thus O'Connor maintained 'that every one of those things mentioned in the Manifesto must follow, before the cause of the people would be gained — he believed that confusion would have to be created . . .' He opposed, however, the plan to put these measures before a show of hands at public meetings, as this 'would only create a delusion throughout the land!'[61] There was still confusion within the Convention as to whether these measures were to be implemented simultaneously, or whether some or all of them were to precede a call for a national holiday. O'Connor favoured the withdrawal of money from savings banks as 'the beginning of the battle, because it would be a war of capital against labour, and capitalists would soon find that labour was the only real capital in the world'.[62] The vulnerability of the monetary system, which was considered to derive from the artificial divorce between paper money and the only real source of value — labour — was a central tenet of radical economics. Thus a series of measures aimed at the banks and sources of government taxation was intended to precipitate severe economic crisis, as a prelude to revolutionary political change. Like the national holiday, a concerted attack upon the nation's financial institutions was conceived as a practical assertion of the validity of the labour theory of value. There was also a growing number of delegates resigned to the necessity for a national holiday.[63] The Convention adjourned until 1 July, however, having established no clear priority regarding the list of ulterior measures. Although democratic in appearance, the decision to leave this matter to the will of the simultaneous meetings represented an abnegation of the Convention's leadership responsibilities.

IV

The adjournment of the Convention heralded a renewed phase of sustained platform agitation. O'Connor and the national Chartist leadership were looking for means of escalating the scale and increasing the revolutionary implications of their agitation. The simultaneous demonstrations called for Whitsun to consider ulterior measures and to memorialise the Queen to dismiss her ministers were part of this controlled escalation of constitutional protest. The National Memorial to the Queen represented the next constitutional stage in platform agitation. However convening simultaneous meetings, linked to ulterior measures, had revolutionary overtones reminiscent of earlier radical protest. The *Star* suggested that the Memorial from the simultaneous meetings

> be presented by a deputation of five hundred thousand men from all different counties, proceeding in peaceful and orderly procession, each with his musket over his arm, pledged to the preservation of 'peace' — and the enforcement of 'law', and the establishment of 'order' . . .

The *Star* invited workers to 'let the looms, the lapstones, the anvils, the spinning-jennies, the spades, and the ploughs, have another holiday . . .' The concept of simultaneous meetings was closely associated with both the National Convention and the idea of the national holiday.[64] It was a symbolic gesture, separating the productive classes from the unproductive in a dramatic moral display of national solidarity; it was a preparatory exercise in the creation of mass revolutionary consciousness and organisation. Like ulterior measures, simultaneous meetings were a confrontationalist tactic, an ideal vehicle for testing the temper of the mass movement and government reaction to growing Chartist strength. Both O'Connor and the *Star* regretted that the Whitsun demonstrations, although referred to as 'simultaneous', were not all to be held on the same day; as 'It would at least prevent ALL the military force of the country from being concentrated in one place against the people.' This conformed with O'Connor's strategy of pushing forms of open-constitutional agitation to their limit. Such a demonstration of united determination would shake 'the nerves of the conservators of property', and force them 'to concede that which they can retain no longer'.[65]

There was a general feeling that the simultaneous meetings would provide the government with an opportunity to make mass arrests of members of the Convention. From the outset O'Connor had raised the possibility of the arrest of the Convention and continually stressed the danger which surrounded its sitting.[66] By spring 1839, Chartist leaders increasingly anticipated either the arrest of the Convention *en masse* or a repetition of Peterloo at a meeting convened by the Convention.[67] Henry Vincent became the first delegate to be arrested, in late April, and before the Convention adjourned the Birmingham delegate Edward Brown was arrested along with another local working-class leader, John Fussell.[68] At Llanidloes serious riots and numerous arrests had followed the introduction of special constables from another district along with metropolitan police in late

April and early May; there were riots and Chartist arrests in Wiltshire; in South Lancashire Chartists were arrested for drilling; and thirteen Chartists were seized in a police raid of the LDA headquarters.[69] The government also issued a proclamation against 'illegal' arming and drilling and decided to arm local voluntary defence forces. This accompanied a change in government attitude to Chartist meetings. Magistrates were instructed that meetings were 'illegal' when attended by numbers 'calculated to excite alarm and to endanger public peace'.[70] Against this background, Carpenter told the Convention that he would undertake the mission of attending one of the simultaneous meetings 'with the full persuasion that he would never come back. (Hear, hear.) And every delegate should go out with the same feeling.' Plans were discussed for the election of alternative delegates in case members were arrested. And before the adjournment, O'Connor had successfully moved that if the government interfered with their meetings, the Convention would reconvene and declare its sittings permanent. Furthermore, he accepted Marsden's amendment that if arrests were general, ulterior measures would immediately go into effect. Marsden argued that mass arrests of the movement's leaders would destroy Chartism. He thought 'it rather absurd while arrests were going on day after day, that they should be talking of peace, law and order'; and reminded delegates of the fate of an unarmed people at Peterloo. Although Marsden's recommendation to attend meetings armed was rejected, with the expectation of massive government repression the tone of even the most moderate delegates became more threatening.[71]

Naturally O'Connor was delegated to attend the most important demonstrations at Peep Green and Kersal Moor. Members of the Convention were the principal speakers at all the Whitsun meetings. Throughout June members of the Convention toured the country taking the pulse of the movement.

The mounting number of Chartist arrests, and the expectation of more, prompted O'Connor to establish the National Defence Fund in mid-June. The defence of victims of government repression was always an important point of radical solidarity. Characteristically, O'Connor opened the Defence Fund himself, with a donation of twenty pounds, and then embarked upon a two week tour to coordinate a national plan to provide legal defence for those who had placed themselves in the line of fire. O'Connor assured the Newcastle meeting at which he launched the fund:

The rights of the poorest, though over-zealous, shall be equally protected as those of the rich and discreet — (loud cheers) — and this is the only practical opposition which I can offer to the law's injunction till we are strong enough to tread upon the corns, or the bunions, or the heels of the law.

The movement's acknowledged national leader, O'Connor was well placed to secure the confidence of Chartists in the national defence scheme. He volunteered his services as both treasurer and 'Attorney General' to the radicals.[72] But although O'Connor was the initiating force and his personal standing was vital to the scheme's success, the National Defence Fund was placed under the control of a committee of the Convention.

In spring and summer of 1839, there was a general feeling that some form of violent confrontation would be the inevitable result of Chartist agitation.[73] However, the possibility of violent conflict was invariably placed within a defensive context. Thus O'Connor told a meeting at Leeds that he intended:

> to make them an army not of offence, but of reserve, which though it might not agress, would be quick to return an assault; and the wadding of the first cannon which might be fired upon the people would ignite suddenly all the property of the country.[74]

Such threats of mass incendiarism were well calculated to heighten the fears of factory owners and local authorities, but they also implied a recognition of Chartist vulnerability in the face of a disciplined military force. O'Connor demonstrated a keen awareness of the military might arrayed against the Chartists and grave anxiety over the damaging effect which a failed rising might have on Chartist morale.

> But did they think that he was going to counsel the people with pikes, and pistols without barrels, and guns without locks to unfold their breasts to an armed soldiery? No: when the people made their attack it would be upon property. . . . They were not going to hazard their cause by one skirmish, or by one pitched battle without arms in their hands . . . but let them but fire one shot upon the people, and he would not give them two-pence for all the property within two miles march. . . . They were in high glee, expecting that the people were going to march out against soldiers. They knew very well that a few legs, arms, and heads of patriots hung up by the road side might have the effect of deterring others uniting in their ranks. But that was not the kind of battle they were going to fight.[75]

Many Chartists felt they would not have to fight soldiers. Lowery told workers at Carlisle: 'the soldiers would not fight against the people;

and when the people fought, they would not fight against the soldiers, but against those who employ them'.[76]

Despite some indications of disaffection within the army, neither
General Napier nor O'Connor seriously believed that the army would
hesitate to put down a Chartist rising.[77] This was to prove crucial to
O'Connor's calculations in summer of 1839. While never questioning
the people's right to stage an offensive insurrection, the prospect of
the certain defeat of an undisciplined and poorly armed people at the
hands of a well-trained army mitigated against any such attempt. The
Star explained:

> We have never for a single moment entertained the notion of the
> people, in their most over-heated moments, assuming other than a
> defensive position, while we assert their right, if the chances of success
> warranted, to take a stand of physical resistance against acts of moral
> aggression. It so happens, however, that none are trained to arms in a
> country, where tyrants live by force of arms, save those upon whom the
> tyrants can depend for implicit obedience to the forms of discipline and
> to the word of command; setting life against life, therefore, the odds are
> fearful against those who are not trained to arms.[78]

Along with O'Connor, most Chartist leaders rejected an offensive
rising as an alternative in summer of 1839. Harney's insurrectionist
strategy, modelled upon the French Revolution, captured little support at the Convention. However, the distinction between appeals
for defensive violence and offensive violence cannot be drawn too
sharply, especially in connection with the proposal for a sacred
month. Still, there was a qualitative difference between Harney's
injunction of 'the sacred right of insurrection' and the tone of defensive constitutionalism which characterised the rhetoric of violence
brought into Chartism by leaders of the anti-Poor Law protest.[79] Few
Chartist leaders denied the people's right to arm in their own defence.[80] But the Convention's recommendations to arm, couched in
defensive terms, contrasted with exhortations published in the *London Democrat*, edited by J. C. Coombe, to arm for an offensive
insurrection. The Convention and the *Star* advised Chartists to
attend the simultaneous meetings unarmed, so as not to provoke
attack.

> Parade not your arms at public meetings, but keep them bright and
> ready at home, so as to be ready at all times and all seasons to defend
> your Queen, your country, and your liberty. Give your oppressors no
> excuse for invading your inviolable right to meet and discuss your
> grievances by needlessly carrying arms to public places, but at the same

time fail not to be prepared to resist any and every unconstitutional attempt to suppress your peaceable agitation by physical violence.[81]

O'Connor and most Chartist leaders deprecated any action which might incite partial or premature outbreaks.

Two other possibilities seemed more likely in summer 1839 than that of an offensive rising: a defensive insurrection or a general strike.[82] The widespread expectation of government repression was linked increasingly to the prospect of a spontaneous, defensive insurrection. This conformed with the defensive tone of most Chartist 'physical-force' language and recommendations to arm. O'Connor and O'Brien were the leading advocates of the strategy of a defensive insurrection centred around the simultaneous demonstrations.[83] In a typical address published in May, O'Connor argued the advantages of assuming a defensive position.

> Your position is one of invincible strength. The moment you are attacked, that instant oppression dies, usurpation ends, and the reign of liberty commences. While upon the other hand, should you partially attack and suffer defeat, though ever so trifling, panic seizes our ranks, apprehension divides our forces, and want of confidence in ourselves, would make us an easy prey to our enemies.

And the *Star* claimed that although 'No true lover of the Charter contemplates, for one moment, the offensive position',

> let them be all this time preparing for the physical attack, whenever it might come. Their adversaries — the enemies of right — will soon be compelled either to succomb [sic], or to attempt the sustentation of their power by physical violence; and then, when the attack is made, the people being ALL well armed, the question of 'physical force' will speedily be decided. It will come like the shock of an earthquake, and the issue will be — liberty; or to many — death; and to the rest — eternal slavery.

Such a rising was to develop with apocalyptic suddenness, like a 'thunderstorm', 'the shock of an earthquake' or an 'electric shock'.[84] An outrageous act of government repression was to constitute an open signal to the working class, ensuring a simultaneous, national Chartist response. Certainly the arrest of the Convention or an attack upon Chartists engaged in constitutional protest would have imparted an all-important legitimacy to Chartist violence. At Peep Green William Ashton, one of Barnsley's veteran radical leaders, declared that he had 'swore in Barnsley that the day the Convention was disorganised, should be the day of justice and retribution . . .'[85] The open, spontaneous and unifying qualities attributed to the defensive rising contrasted with the conspiratorial overtones and difficulties of national coordination associated with an offensive rising. The emphasis on counter-attack and the ambiguity which surrounded talk of a defensive rising allowed leaders like O'Connor to discuss the possibilities for insurrection openly from the platform and to recommend the necessity of arming as a pre-condition to confrontation. The Chartists found it extremely difficult, however, to cross 'the threshold of violence'. The experience of earlier radical movements and the fear of infiltration by spies; the distance separating the main centres of militancy in the industrial North from the capital; and most important, the care which the authorities took not to provoke violent confrontation were all contributory factors.[86]

The limitations inherent to a strategy of defensive action are obvious. While the Chartists could create points of potential confrontation, ultimately the initiative remained with the authorities. Although the Chartists faced serious government repression, Lord John Russell and General Napier carefully avoided any blatant transgression of popular liberties comparable to Peterloo.[87] The simultaneous meetings went off peacefully. Although individual members of the Convention were arrested, there was no move to arrest them as a corporate body or to declare their sittings illegal. The open constitutionalism which had proved a revolutionary threat in 1819 no longer provoked the same responses from government or local authorities. The Chartists faced a far more self-assured ruling-class alliance.

V

No violent confrontation having occurred over the mass meetings of late May and June, the Convention was faced even more urgently with the question of ulterior measures, and in particular the sacred month. Like simultaneous meetings, the National Convention and other ulterior measures, the sacred month was part of the ultra-radical arsenal of revolutionary tactics. It was not a new idea introduced into Chartism by Thomas Attwood, but clearly related to earlier concepts of the general strike or national holiday which emerged through the radical struggles of the early 1830s. As I. J. Prothero has shown, the national holiday relates to a whole range of pre-Chartist ultra-radical ideas and categories of reference.[88] The holiday was linked in the radical mind with both the National Convention and revolution. During the reform crisis the question of a national holiday was widely discussed at meetings of the NUWC. Ideas about the general strike were also explored within the context of the trade union and factory movements, in the pages of the *Herald of the Rights of Industry, Pioneer* and *Crisis*.[89] Thus several overlapping concepts of the general strike emerged from the radical working-class agitation of the early 1830s. The Chartist proposal for a sacred month had more in common with the concept of a radical/political national holiday, most impressively articulated in William Benbow's famous pamphlet, *Grand National Holiday and Congress of the Productive Classes*, than with the concept of an industrial/'syndicalist' general strike as outlined by John Doherty or James Morrison. Benbow's pamphlet appears to have circulated widely among Chartists, particularly in Lancashire.[90] The sacred month was envisaged as the final political confrontation between the mass of the People, the producers of all wealth, and the small minority of the Privileged, the consuming parasites of society. Abram Duncan asked a Newcastle meeting in June 1839: 'Were they ready to make a sacred month of it, and take to the hillside? (shouts of "We will".)'

> If they did, they would soon be glad to give them what they wanted. The Convention was at the head of three million of men and as many women, and all they had against them was a fraction of the basest of the community, and if battle they must, he well knew on what side the victory would declare. (renewed cheers.)[91]

The national holiday was not regarded as a peaceful tactic. As Robert Lowery later explained:

> Whatever might have been meant by it [the national holiday] at first, it meant in the people's minds the chances of a physical contest; not an insurrection or assault on the authorities, but that by retiring from labour, like the Roman plebians of old to the Aventine-hill, they would so derange the whole country that the authorities would endeavour to coerce them back, and that they would resist the authorities unless their rights were conceded, and thus bring the struggle to an issue. Hence the *Northern Star* and speakers had advised the people to arm.[92]

There was no doubt among Chartist leaders that a call for a sacred month was tantamount to revolution. R. J. Richardson predicted that a sacred month 'woud be a great revolution in the country'. Harney, the most persistent advocate of a national holiday as a prelude to insurrection, insisted that 'a national holiday would be nothing more or less than a civil war'. M'Douall, among the earliest and most ardent supporters of the sacred month, asked delegates to consider the effect which such a move would have upon the working class.

The majority of the working classes were in debt, and if they were thrown out of work there would be nothing left but starvation, and the country would be thrown into a beautiful state of disorganisation. How were the people to sustain themselves in this condition?[93]

Yet, despite such revolutionary implications, the sacred month struck a fine balance between an offensive initiative and the defensive stance which most Chartist leaders wished to preserve. Although a general strike would almost certainly have led to violent confrontation between the authorities and the working class in many localities, the initial cessation from labour was a peaceful and legal act. Conflict would arise only through an attempt to coerce the people back to work. It was also a completely open form of action.

Despite later disclaimers, O'Connor alluded to the possibility of a Chartist national holiday on several occasions before July. His most explicit reference was at the Convention in April:

If they were refused their just demands . . . they would have recourse to their silent monitor — they would light their torches and repair to the hill-side, and there remain until the prayer of their petition was granted. . . . But that there might be no doubt of what he meant . . . he would say that the resistance of the people would consist of their abstinence from labour, and the men who derived their property from that labour would find that they could not long maintain so unequal a contest.[94]

More important than any particular statement, however, was the general tenor of O'Connor's speeches throughout 1838 and 1839, and his role at the Convention. As late as 27 April, he had predicted they would have the Charter within three months.[95] Militant Chartists had every reason to expect O'Connor to give the lead at the Convention for decisive action in summer 1839. He had openly dared to name 'the day' at the torchlight meetings; he had argued from the outset that the Convention should resolve the question of ulterior measures; and whatever the qualifications and ambiguities in his platform speeches they never lacked the impression that given the opportunity he was willing to risk all in an attempt to gain universal suffrage.

The Convention reconvened in Birmingham amid an atmosphere charged with anticipation of violent conflict, as growing numbers attended nightly Chartist meetings in the Bull Ring in defiance of the magistrates' opposition to such proceedings.[96] In line with his confrontationalist policy, O'Connor opposed Moir's motion that the Convention immediately reassemble in London and proposed instead that they remain in Birmingham for another week: 'It had now become the duty of the Convention to recommend, and not to receive instructions. The question was whether their instructions would be more effective if given from London or Birmingham.' The Convention's decision to remain in Birmingham was to have important consequences. During the first days of July, delegates reported upon the state of Chartist opinion with reference to ulterior measures and upon the degree of organisation in the districts where they had been agitating. O'Connor assured the Convention that 'they were in the last stage of the agitation'.

> He was firmly convinced that they were now in a position to take a bolder stand than they had hitherto been able to do. They now stood in such a commanding position that they could say to the Whigs, 'you must give us Universal Suffrage or we will *take* it!' that was really the position in which the people stood . . .

Yet his pronouncements in early July combined a boldness and confidence in Chartist success with an important note of caution; thus O'Connor warned against directing Chartist opinion before it could be 'irresistibly' directed.[97]

On 3 July, the delegates squarely faced the issue which their very existence as a National Convention had raised: that of political power.[98] Marsden moved that the Convention consider fixing a date for ulterior measures to go into effect. Dr Taylor, an advocate of the sacred month, reported that he had put the Convention's recommendations for ulterior measures to twenty-six meetings in Scotland and found general agreement, 'but with respect to the sacred month, they felt it would be nothing short of physical revolution that would be caused by it . . .' Taylor, therefore, proposed that the Convention leave the question of the sacred month aside for the time being and call on Chartists immediately to begin the withdrawal of money, run on gold, exclusive dealing, boycott on excisible goods and constitutional arming. O'Connor seconded Taylor's proposal. He repeated his conviction that ulterior measures were 'the most important subject before the Convention', and 'that till they had a sacred holiday, they should never have Universal Suffrage'. O'Connor qualified his commitment to the sacred month, however, with a warning:

> Not to hazard their cause, by prematurely forcing forward the people, which would leave them an easy prey to a powerful Government. They should not press their power over the people, as defeat of a section would be the total overthrow of the Chartists.

The complexion and tone of the Convention had gradually changed with the resignation of many middle-class delegates and their replacement from the ranks of local working-class radicals. O'Connor was concerned that the Convention which had lagged behind the enthusiasm of its mass support might now suddenly force militant sections of that support into a premature or partial confrontation against superior government forces.

The Taylor/O'Connor proposal met with considerable opposition. Bussey claimed that his West Riding constituents were armed and ready to strike for the Charter. On this basis, he moved an amendment for the entire recommendations of the Manifesto, including the sacred month, to take effect from 15 July. Support for an immediate call for a sacred month came from the representatives of key northern localities along with several London delegates. M'Douall wanted to see the sacred month commence as soon as possible, and reminded the Convention that 'July was a celebrated month for revolution'. At Ashton, the Chartists had adopted a plan to provide themselves with arms. John Warden of Bolton supported Bussey's amendment, 'because he thought that a national holiday was tantamount with a national insurrection'. Cardo, Marsden, Neesom, Edward Brown, Christopher Dean and John Stowe all supported Bussey. Fletcher noted that at the meetings he attended people did not attach much importance to any ulterior measures except the run on the banks and the national holiday. Even William Lovett was in two minds. He agreed with Dr Taylor's original motion, while 'at the same time . . . entertaining the opinion of Mr. Bussey and others that a holiday, or sacred month would be found to be the only effectual remedy for the sufferings of the people'.[99]

There was general agreement that a national holiday was now the only viable strategy for obtaining popular rights. The point at issue was whether the movement was prepared for such a step. Frost 'agreed with a sacred month being held, but he did not think that they were prepared to give advise to the people of England to act upon it'. Richards reported that the working class in the Potteries would respond to the call for a sacred month, 'but they would rather that the Convention was not over hasty in appointing it to be held till the people had had a few weeks opportunity of preparation . . .' The East Midlands delegates — Skevington, Smart and Woodhouse — concurred in the view that nothing hasty should be concluded. Rather surprisingly, John Deegan reported that the Stalybridge radicals were in favour of leaving the question of the sacred month aside for the moment. Many radicals had waited twenty years for the reconstruction of a mass, independent working-class movement. There was understandable concern that premature action might again set back working-class radicalism. Pitkeithley, veteran Huntite and close to O'Connor, advised the Convention to proceed with caution, emphasising the need to seize the right moment for confrontation.

> He believed there was not a member of the Convention but what was anxious for the consummation of that business, but he would have them recollect that if the people made a struggle when they were unprepared to sustain it, they would only rivet their chains the faster, as the French people did in the two struggles which they had made. It was their duty to do all they possibly could, and that appeared most essential for the safety and progression of the cause, and they had all the chances in their favour if they did not act with indiscretion, for the Government was sinking lower and lower every day, while the people were rising in their dignity, and if they were only a few days beforehand with any measure, it would very likely put them twenty years back.

In the light of conflicting opinion, Dr Taylor proposed that they meet on 13 July, the day after Parliament was to vote on the Petition, in order to set a date for the sacred month. Bussey withdrew his amendment and Taylor's motion was accepted unanimously. The Convention had taken a clear step towards revolutionary confrontation.

Following the debate on ulterior measures, O'Connor set out on a tour of Lancashire on behalf of the Defence Fund. Already he was trying to extricate the movement from a commitment to an early general strike and put forward an alternative interim strategy. At Rochdale, O'Connor told Chartists that if the agitation continued until autumn/winter 1839, he would ignore royal proclamations and reconvene torchlight meetings; as 'nothing had made so great an impression on their enemies as the silent monitor'. But the time was not right for the national holiday.

> If they relied on a sacred holiday, they might depend on it they would do nothing. If they demanded that now, they would do the very thing the masters desired. (Hear, hear.) Their storehouses were well filled, and they had so much machinery that population was a mere drug in the market, and they would do without the people during the sacred month very well. Let their labour become valuable, and then let the whole country strike on a given day, and never return to their calling until they had worked out their political and social salvation.[100]

Here was a clear rejection of the sacred-month strategy for summer

1839 in favour of continued platform agitation.

The pace of events, however, prevented O'Connor from developing an alternative course of agitation. On 4 July, the day after the Convention had taken its decision on ulterior measures, the introduction of London police into Birmingham and their violent dispersal of a peaceful Chartist meeting in the Bull Ring ended in riot. The police had to be rescued by the military.[101] Immediately returning to the Convention, O'Connor pointed to the role of the military at Birmingham as a vindication of his view that Chartists could not place confidence in the soldiery siding with the working class. Through the *Star* he pressed for the transformation of the Convention into a permanent body. It was now the duty of the Convention to declare its sittings in London permanent, electing thirteen members to form a National Council. The remaining delegates should be dispatched to the principal towns of Britain to counsel the people.[102] Thus, while attempting to contain the movement within the bounds of threatening platform agitation, O'Connor sought to create a permanent, centralised national institution of Chartist leadership and organisation.

The events in Birmingham represented the sort of collision with authority which O'Connor had expected the Convention to provoke. The Convention's presence in Birmingham transformed a local incident into a matter of national Chartist outrage. Four members of the Convention were arrested — Dr Taylor, M'Douall, Lovett and Collins. Lovett and Collins were arrested for signing and having printed the Convention's resolutions condemning the action of the authorities. These arrests were regarded as an open attack upon the Convention, and the intervention of the 'blood thirsty and unconstitutional force' of London police as a gross infringement of popular liberty.[103] This confirmed the apprehensions of many local Chartists such as John Gillespie of Bolton, who noted: 'There seemed to be a disposition arising to murder the people, as at Peterloo.'[104] Cardo believed the attack was in response to the Convention's recommendations for ulterior measures, and denounced it as 'a most flagrant outrage . . . almost as bad as Peterloo, or Cold Bath Fields massacre'. According to the *Star*, the Convention 'had now been wantonly, violently, and illegally attacked . . . There is a suspension of all law . . . the rule of military despotism and uncontrolled sway of spies, informers, jurymen, and murderers.' The paper warned: 'But let one attack be made on the Convention as a body, and in 24 hours after, Universal Suffrage will be the law of the land, and the great disparity between man and man will cease.' At Newcastle, O'Brien declared that the arrest of the Convention 'should be the signal for one general strike'.[105]

However, the Birmingham events were as near as the forces of law and order came to an outright attack upon the Convention or to the precipitation of a Peterloo-type incident. Although this was not the signal for spontaneous insurrection, the behaviour of the Birmingham authorities served to intensify Chartist resolve and strengthen support for the sacred month. According to Thomas Devyr, the Newcastle Chartist, the attack at Birmingham 'exasperated the Democracy all over the country. . . . Then commenced the work of "preparation" '.[106] From Cheltenham, Vincent observed in a private letter:

> A desperate feeling is now abroad — You have no conception of its intensity — even in this aristocratic town of Cheltenham the people are *ripe* and *ready* . . . The Crisis has now come. A few weeks must bring the opposing powers into dreadful collision.[107]

Throughout the country meetings were called to condemn the authorities and discuss ulterior measures. From Bolton it was reported:

> The events of the last few days have produced in this town the utmost agitation of the public mind. The subject of every conversation, from the 'peaceful precincts' of the Parish Church Sunday School, to the riotous benches of the pot-house, is the 'State of the Country', embracing the exciting topics of Chartism, the National Holiday, the people and pikes, *versus* the soldiers and sabres, social evils and popular remedies, and others of a similar nature.

The Bolton Chartists were holding nightly meetings and within a week of the news of Birmingham the WMA had three hundred new members. The local Chartist leaders were busily organising the new recruits into classes and launching a plan for exclusive dealing.[108] At Barnsley, 'in unison with our friends in Birmingham', Chartists renamed May Day Green 'the Bull Ring'.[109] The attack at Birmingham had a profound effect upon the movement and was a crucial influence in the Convention's decision to set the date for the commencement of the sacred month.

The mood of the Convention hardened in the wake of the Bull Ring riots, as delegates reassembled in London to await the Commons' decision on the Petition. Following the rejection of the Petition, on 12 July, the Convention began to debate Lowery's motion calling for the sacred month to commence on 12 August.[110] Opinion was by no means unanimous. Reports from Lowery and Dr Taylor suggested that the northern manufacturing districts were prepared to strike.

But other northern delegates raised doubts about their prospects nationally. Moir argued that the move had to be general, 'otherwise they might pull down the houses of those opposed to them, and sacrifice many lives, and yet not succeed in obtaining their rights'. Opinion was in flux. Bussey, who had led the opposition to Taylor and O'Connor's earlier move to delay setting the date for the holiday, was now opposed to an immediate decision.[111] Warden,[112] who had welcomed the national holiday as the first step to insurrection, refused to vote for the strike until he was satisfied that the people were prepared and the Convention had matured a plan of action.

> He could not vote for the measure until every delegate was ready to show . . . first, that the people were prepared for the measure; and next, that they had matured some plan of action during the existence of the holiday. The majority of his constituents were quite prepared to adopt the measure upon the condition, but upon no other. He would not consent to sacrifice them, however; he would rather incur any odium than do that.— (Cheers.) A partial strike would lead to extreme and indescribable misery.

Considerable uncertainty and skepticism surrounded the Convention's decision on the sacred month. Private doubts came into the open, as the delegates tried to form a realistic assessment of the movement's chances of success. Although Fletcher stated his intention to vote for the sacred month, he confessed: 'That the evidence they had collected was by no means satisfactory, or even encouraging. . . . There might be zeal, and no doubt there was much of it; but zeal only was not adequate to the urgency of the case.' The Convention found itself in a false position. While most delegates had serious reservations about the holiday, they saw no alternative course of action. Thus William Burns, a Scottish delegate, complained 'Of those who objected to the sacred month, and yet admitted that a bold step was necessary in order to avert revolution, while they abstained from suggesting anything relative to this bold step'. Burns summed up the dilemma: 'In his mind, if we went forward we were lost, and if we stood still or retreated, we were lost.' But he did not see how the Convention 'could get out of the national holiday, without covering itself with disgrace'.[113] Events in the country also influenced the Convention's decision. Throughout July arrests continued. During the debate further riots occurred at Birmingham; while affairs at Newcastle were also reaching a point of crisis.[114]

Only the ultra-left expressed unqualified support for setting the date for the holiday. In fact, Cardo, Neesom, M'Douall and Marsden had attempted unsuccessfully to force a discussion of the sacred month several days before the Petition had been rejected. Neesom now moved an amendment to Lowery's motion, calling for the holiday to commence a week earlier, on 5 August. James Osbourne, Brighton's delegate, put the ultra-left case, advising 'them to begin the sacred month to-morrow; for the sooner they begin the more chance had they of success'.

> After the state of things at Birmingham and Newcastle, to recede would be to ensure their defeat . . . He assured Mr. Fletcher and Mr. Bury that the feeling in favour of the Charter was much more extensive and uniform than what they thought. As for supplies, he could assure them that ten thousand fellows met together without breakfast would not endure a long fast. (Cheers.) He knew the cessation from labour would be the first step towards a revolution, but the result would not deter him. They had been *coming to the point* long enough.

Neesom's amendment was overwhelmingly defeated.[115] More crucial was the defeat of an amendment proposed by Bussey, calling for a committee to be set up to examine the best time for the commencement of the holiday. This move to delay the decision on the sacred month was lost only on the casting vote of the chairman, Richard Mealing.[116] On 16 July, the Convention adopted Lowery's original motion by a majority of thirteen votes to six, with five abstentions.[117]

O'Connor was present at none of these crucial sessions of the Convention. On the day the Convention made its decision on the sacred month he was answering libel charges brought against the *Northern Star* at York assizes. When the Convention moved to London he travelled north to prepare his defence. Several other key leaders were also absent. Both Frost and Dr Taylor were also involved in preparing their defences against government prosecution.[118] And O'Brien was touring the most militant districts of the North in a last minute attempt to assess the movement's strength and preparedness.[119] Obviously it is impossible to know for certain what difference these leaders' presence at the Convention might have made to the decision to set a date for the sacred month, however, it seems likely that they would have influenced the Convention in favour of some form of delay, perhaps along the lines of Bussey's amendment. Probably only Taylor would have supported an immediate call for a national holiday. O'Connor had already indicated his opposition to calling a holiday under the prevailing conditions; Frost sent a letter to the Convention urging delay until late August or September;[120] and although O'Brien continued to use extremely violent language and referred to the national holiday throughout his tour, his subsequent actions suggest that he also favoured delay.[121]

Until July, O'Connor had provided the clearest and most consistent lead over the question of ulterior measures at the Convention. He had insisted that the Convention must issue an early declaration of ulterior measures, as a necessary preparatory step, and take positive control of the movement. The Convention, however, had not acted upon his persistent advice, nor had they laid the groundwork for a national holiday. In summer 1839, O'Connor concluded that the movement was unprepared for a decisive confrontation with the government. Only by remaining uncommitted over the question of the sacred month could the movement avoid defeat while maintaining its threatening tone and essential ambiguity. The major criticism of O'Connor's leadership in summer 1839 is not that he opposed the sacred month, but that given his assessment of the situation he failed to make his position clear before the Convention came to its decision. His failure to provide clear leadership left him in a very difficult position and had disastrous consequences for the movement. O'Connor placed great emphasis upon the need for a centralised national leadership and organisation. Yet the reversal of the Convention's decision on the sacred month, for which he was largely responsible, left the movement without a strategy and resulted in the collapse of the Convention.

O'Connor's position contrasted with expectations in the most militant Chartist localities. Throughout the northern manufacturing districts great expectations had been raised by the Convention. Under the impetus of government repression, the rejection of the Petition, and especially the Convention's decision to call a sacred month, local Chartists anticipated some form of decisive confrontation. The events at Birmingham and then at Newcastle, where Chartists clashed with police and troops, seemed to reinforce such prospects.[122] Isaac Johnson, veteran radical and local smith, told Stockport Chartists following the Bull Ring riots: 'The sacred month was near at hand (not ten days off); and, if properly followed up, would unquestionably save the nation.' At Sheffield, William Ashton declared that the Barnsley radicals were determined 'not to go to work again until the Charter was the law of the land'.[123] Activities such as Chartist exclusive dealing and the spontaneous Sunday occupation of churches throughout the country were preparatory exercises in the build-up to the sacred month.[124] John Gillespie assured the Bolton Chartists before they attended church in mass, that the day of reckoning was near:

They had two more Sundays to go to Church before the struggle commenced; and he thought, after three weeks' praying and fasting, if any of them should fall in the struggle, they would be prepared for heaven, and he was *almost sure they would be received into it* . . . Many of them were afraid to join in the procession because the eye of their taskmaster was upon them . . . They had, however, only another fortnight to endure such tyranny, and then they would remember the masters who had inflicted such miseries on them, and *would pay them for it*.[125]

At Bradford the Chartists held nightly meetings to discuss the sacred month; the Barnsley Chartists formed a committee of public safety. At district level the West Riding Chartists were organised through regular delegate meetings held at Heckmondwike, where plans for the sacred month were discussed in private. Alternate Convention delegates were elected in case the government should arrest their representatives.[126] Retreat in the face of such enthusiasm was not easy and was bound to lead to disillusion.

In summer 1839, O'Connor demonstrated a strong sense of organisational conservatism. Believing there was little prospect of immediately realising their aims, he sought to prevent the Chartist movement being jeopardised through an abortive or partial general strike. His strategy of intimidating open-constitutionalism was not necessarily incompatible with the national holiday nor did it preclude the possibility of armed conflict.[127] What remains difficult to determine are the circumstances under which O'Connor would have been willing to turn from propaganda and organisation, preparation and threatening agitation, to armed struggle. Unlike the reform crisis the ruling classes showed few signs of a loss of confidence and the army remained loyal. O'Connor clearly stressed that he had no intention of precipitating a struggle between an untrained and poorly armed people and a well-disciplined army, although the ambiguity central to his strategy of intimidation led to misunderstanding within sections of the movement. There is considerable evidence of widespread Chartist arming in Lancashire, the West Riding, the Newcastle area and South Wales, although the real extent of such preparations is difficult to estimate.[128] Thus Devyr later maintained that thousands of pikes were manufactured and sold on the Tyne and Wear, while Harney informed Engels that 'Notwithstanding all the talk in 1839 about "arming", the people did not arm'.[129] There also remain doubts about the effectiveness of Chartist arms and the popular strategy of pike-warfare.[130]

But whatever the extent of arming in the most advanced Chartist localities, O'Connor was almost certainly correct in the belief that they were not in a position to carry their demands by means of a national holiday. Napier could have handled a series of local strike confrontations isolated in the industrial North, although such a situation might have developed into full-scale insurrection in certain areas. What appeared unlikely was that the Chartists could mount more than a partial general strike, even in the northern and midland manufacturing districts. Chartism faced a serious problem of uneven and uncoordinated national development. The swiftness with which the movement had come together meant that Chartism lacked the coherent national organisation and mutual understanding between districts necessary to a successful national holiday. One of the tragedies of Chartism was that its point of highest militancy and most widespread support preceded the establishment of a permanent organisational structure. Perhaps this was inevitable, as the need for such organisation was the principal lesson of this earlier period. What must be stressed, however, is that the failure of the Chartists to carry through a revolution in summer 1839 cannot be reduced merely to poor leadership. The divisions within the Chartist leadership reflected the dilemma which faced a revolutionary working-class movement in what was essentially a non-revolutionary situation. Only one side of the equation for revolution was fulfilled, as the ruling classes remained essentially confident in their power to rule and united in their opposition to reform. While John Saville has overestimated the stability of the ruling classes in 1839, his general formulation of the situation remains correct:

> There was often anxiety and unease: of that there is much evidence; but there was never any serious dent in the massive confidence of Government or the propertied classes. It was upon this rock of confident power that the Chartist movement, which came near to the point of armed uprising in certain areas, broke and was defeated. Their failures in 1839 as in later years, were naturally much assisted by the differences within their own ranks and by the differences as well as the distinctions between different social groups in different parts of the country; but it cannot be insisted upon too strongly that for a revolutionary situation to prevail there must be a breakdown or the beginnings of a breakdown, in the confidence of the ruling classes; and of this, throughout the whole Chartist period, there was no sign.[131]

On their return to the Convention, O'Connor and O'Brien joined forces in a move to have delegates reconsider their decision. On 22

July, O'Brien moved that while the Convention continued in the opinion 'that nothing short of a general strike . . . will ever suffice to re-establish the rights and liberties of the industrious classes, we nevertheless cannot take upon ourselves the responsibility of dictating the time or circumstances of such a strike . . .' Instead, the Convention was to issue an address on the question, but was to leave the ultimate decision with the people themselves. This was an implicit rejection of the Convention's role as the formulator of national Chartist strategy. O'Brien explained that he did not believe that the people were generally prepared for the national holiday.[132] O'Connor supported O'Brien's move. He told the Convention that had he been present he would have opposed their decision 'with all his might and main'. O'Connor maintained, however, that O'Brien's motion did not alter the day for the sacred month, but was intended only to devise the best means for rendering the national holiday effective. He moved an amendment calling on all delegates to return to the Convention, on 31 July, 'prepared with the views of their constituents', in order to take 'into consideration the most effectual means for carrying out the ulterior measures for the accomplishment of universal suffrage'. This would have the effect of leaving the final decision with the Convention and delaying any definite pronouncement on the sacred month. In retreat O'Connor was concerned to preserve the credibility of both his own leadership and that of the Convention. He argued that delegates from unorganised and thinly populated districts had prematurely forced the measure upon the movement. The defeat of the national holiday would place the entire movement in jeopardy.

> Once let them be defeated in this, and they were lost forever; while if done with general concurrence, it was the gaining of the great battle . . .
> If thousands were arrested, it should not expediate our movement. (Hear.) No power on earth, but the folly of the Convention, could impede the progress of universal suffrage.

O'Connor appealed to the authority of the people, claiming that the Convention had acted 'before they had the sanction of the millions, who were to be vitally affected by the vote'. It was now the movement that was to instruct the Convention. He denied that either he or the *Star* had ever given the impression that the country was armed and ready; quite the reverse, they had continually expressed regret that the people were not generally armed.[133]

The debate which continued for three days retraced familiar ground. There was a feeling that the Convention had been either inadequately informed or, in some cases, misled about the degree of preparedness in certain districts. Several delegates accused M'Douall of having deceived the Convention with regard to the extent of Chartist arming in South Lancashire.[134] Most delegates agreed with O'Brien's maxim, that 'if you strike universally, you strike successfully; but if partially, fatally'. Northern delegates like Fletcher, Bussey and Warden, who were closely linked to the communities they represented at the Convention, were reluctant to commit the most advanced sections of the movement to a partial attempt. Central to the concept of the national holiday was the image of the whole people, the nation, rising against their rulers. It was not conceived as a move on the part of the most advanced localities alone, but represented a form of non-sectional, national confrontation. Nor was success believed to be possible on any other basis.

Opinion remained deeply divided. O'Connor's amendment was narrowly defeated and O'Brien's motion was carried by a majority of twelve votes to six, but with seven abstentions.[135] An analysis of the voting reveals that there was no dramatic change in opinion among the delegates. No member who originally voted for the sacred month reversed his stand and voted for O'Brien's motion. Yet many delegates who supported the Convention's initial decision no doubt felt that O'Connor and O'Brien's united opposition had jeopardised any chance of establishing the national unity necessary for a successful strike. All those who abstained had voted previously for the sacred month, and with the exception of Robert Tilley, they all represented important manufacturing districts. The debate was marked by serious differences and bitter recriminations.

Despite the divided state of the Convention, O'Connor was able to reimpose at least the image of a united leadership. He was concerned to counter the impression that the Convention had cancelled the national holiday. Thus the day after the Convention adopted O'Brien's resolution, he moved that 12 August remain the provisional date for the national holiday, but that a central council be set up to receive information from the localities. This council, acting on advice from local Chartist groups, would then make the final recommendation concerning the national holiday. According to O'Connor, his proposal 'went to equalize the responsibility between the Convention and the people'. O'Connor's motion was adopted with only one dissentient, as delegate after delegate expressed satisfaction at the reestablishment of unity at the Convention. Only Harney still openly denounced the retreat from the sacred month. On 26 July, the Convention adjourned. Affairs were left in the hands of the council, composed of O'Connor, O'Brien, Fletcher, Carpenter, Lowery, Smart and Burns, who put the finishing touches on the Convention's vacillations and retreat.[136] Lowery later commented: 'This was the finishing stroke. From that time the Convention, as a body, had only to wind up its affairs; its prestige was gone.'[137]

The national holiday had been a real possibility only if the Convention had provided a clear lead. The very reopening of the issue of the sacred month at the Convention by the movement's two most influential national leaders destroyed the confidence essential to such a national move. Few localities were willing to strike unless they felt they were part of a larger national effort to gain political power. The appeal to the Chartist rank and file at this point by O'Connor and the Convention was a move designed primarily to legitimate retreat. The devolution of responsibility from the Convention to the localities represented an abandonment of national leadership. It reemphasised the fragmentation and localism of working-class radicalism. The letters which came into the council from local Chartist leaders in late July and early August reflected this breakdown of national confidence. The result of the survey of local Chartist opinion, under the circumstances, was a foregone conclusion. Most localities were opposed to an immediate sacred month.[138] There were a few exceptions. Ann Sidwell, secretary of the Bath Female Radical Association, assured the council:

> that the Chartists of Bath both Male and Female are not only prepared but they were determined that come what — come may they would strike on 12 August and would not resume their labours until success should have crowned their exertions . . .

More typical was the response of the Hyde Chartists, among the most militant radicals in the country, who reluctantly passed a resolution instructing Deegan, their delegate, to recall his vote in favour of the sacred month. 'For although we in Hyde are fully prepared, yet we believe the whole country is not — and in consequence we had better put off the day than have a failure.' The Chartists at Colne, mainly handloom weavers, called on the Convention to devise a plan of organisation and cooperation 'whereby the people may have sufficient confidence in each other to carry out and prosecute their plans with some certain hope of success'. James Wolstenholme informed the council that although the Sheffield working class was not generally prepared for a sacred month, there was a feeling of great disappointment over the Convention's proceedings, and he stressed the urgent need for decisive action.

> Many feel greatly disappointed at the abandonment of the Month, some
> fearing that it will do the cause a great injury in damping the ardour and
> the hopes of the zealous, and deprecating the Convention in the estima-
> tions of the People; it was a premature and unwise step to fix the day at
> first without the fullest evidence [of] deliberate preparation of the
> People. . . . In fact the Convention must begin to *act* decisively, in some
> way or other, or the faction's strength will get so strong that our cause is
> lost, and the Nation destroyed . . . we must either have the Charter now,
> or England will become a heap of ruins, and that soon, and if we get the
> Charter the Convention must act *firmly.*

The strongest rebuke came from the West Riding, the most thoroughly organised district in the country and O'Connor's stronghold.
The delegates meeting at Heckmondwike resolved:

> That the representatives in the general Convention assembled have in
> their late vacillating conduct with regard to the feeling of the day for the
> commencement of the sacred month done infinite injury to our noble
> cause and we most earnestly request them on the earliest opportunity to
> fix permanently a certain day for that purpose without swerving there-
> from.

Confidence in the Convention was clearly shaken.[139]

In his letter to the people, published in the *Star* of 3 August,
O'Connor preempted the council's decision on the sacred month. He
called on Chartists to abandon the sacred month and proposed a
three-day strike in its place. His argument was punctuated with
appeals for continued confidence in his personal leadership. His
direct appeal to the Chartist rank and file was reinforced by an
editorial which declared: 'ANY ATTEMPT TO BRING ABOUT THE
SACRED MONTH BEFORE AN UNIVERSAL ARMING SHALL
HAVE TAKEN PLACE, WILL RUIN ALL.'[140] Nothing more clearly
demonstrates the importance of O'Connor's control of the movement's main organ of communication, as well as his unique relationship to both the Convention and the Chartist rank and file. He was
the one leader who could assume responsibility for the Convention's
retreat and still hope to preserve the unity of the movement behind
his leadership. On 6 August, the council officially called off the
national holiday, on the grounds that the movement was unprepared.
Instead, they followed O'Connor's lead and recommended 'making a
grand moral demonstration' on 12 August, consisting of a three-day
cessation from labour. Great emphasis was placed upon the need to
keep the peace. During these three days, Chartists were to hold

meetings in support of universal suffrage from which addresses were to be forwarded to the Queen calling on her to dismiss her ministers. Motions in favour of the repeal of the Union between England and Ireland were also proposed as part of a general move to win Irish support for Chartism.[141] This was a final attempt to contain Chartism within the bounds of constitutional platform agitation. In practice, the three-day holiday merely provided the government with an opportunity to make further arrests of Chartist leaders.

VI

With the cancellation of the sacred month O'Connor's leadership, for the first time, was called seriously into question by sections of the Chartist rank and file. From Bradford, Bussey reported difficulty in keeping the radicals under control: 'O'Connor's letter in the *Star* of last week has done infinite mischief here.'[142] John Jackson recalled the effect of O'Connor's letter on his Bradford supporters:

> [it] came like a simoon wind to the out-and-out O'Connorites, who had been anxiously waiting the arrival of the day of deliverance . . . never dreaming but that the 12th of August would not only set them straight, but would put them in possession of their fair share of everything the land produced.[143]

In the Rochdale district, where the local Chartists felt the working class was unprepared for a general strike, the Convention and O'Connor's leadership, in particular, also came under severe criticism.

> The fact is the discussion on the holiday has done much harm, it has raised great expectations which must be disappointed. This disappointment is already manifesting itself thro' even this district where it was not so generally approved as in many others. The Convention is suffering in character with the people thro' it. And Mr. O'Connor is getting a good share of the blame which is thrown upon the Convention in this matter, for his leading article in the *Star* of last Saturday on this subject. I am told that in 2 or 3 districts it was suggested to have the *Star* burnt.[144]

By August Heywood, Middleton and Bolton were the Lancashire localities most committed to the sacred month and in these towns disillusion with O'Connor's leadership was widespread.[145] This was particularly evident at Bolton, where the three-day holiday led to large-scale rioting and mass arrests. Bolton's local leaders, including their delegate to the Convention, Warden, were among the most outspoken critics of O'Connor's actions over the issue of the sacred month.[146]

But although his leadership came under attack, O'Connor was still able to secure the confidence of most Chartists at this crucial period. In many of the most militant localities, such as Halifax and Barnsley, Chartists apparently accepted the need to call off the holiday and reaffirmed their support for O'Connor.[147] Although he disappointed many and earned the resentment of a few, O'Connor generally escaped the charge of apostasy over his conduct in August 1839. Even where he was denounced in the heat of the moment, this usually represented only a short term rupture between leadership and led. O'Connor reacted with great sensitivity to rank-and-file Chartist criticism and opinion. Thus, in response to local criticism, he addressed a letter to the 'Working Men of Bolton', again outlining his position over the sacred month. His ultimate appeal was to his steadfastness to the working-class cause.

> I am ever among you, and will remain among you until the work is done; but no hunting for false popularity will ever make me place you in a wrong position. For seven long years I have been at my post, not seeking leadership, but doing my duty . . . Suppose I was wrong, in your opinion, do you think that so old a friend should not be allowed a fault?[148]

The tone was altogether different to the invective reserved for middle-class critics and leaders who had deserted the movement. Although he disagreed with the Bolton Chartists and their leaders, he was prepared, indeed he was compelled, to argue his case with them and establish an understanding. His leadership was based upon this sort of open relationship with the rank and file. He promised to present himself at Bolton at the first opportunity to discuss their differences. When he did face his Bolton critics, in winter 1839, local Chartists openly stated their opposition to his stand over the national holiday. But their general regard for his national leadership had been restored.[149]

On 12 August, the day set for the commencement of the three-day holiday, O'Connor shared the platform at Kennington Common with Dr Taylor, O'Brien, Cardo, Hartwell and the Polish revolutionary Major Beniowski. The meeting was called to petition the Queen to extend a pardon to Jones, Roberts and Howell, sentenced to death for their part in the Birmingham riots. O'Connor declared his intention to resign from the movement, if they allowed these men to die at the hands of the Whig Government. He also dwelt on the theme of organisation and the need for unity. It was only the disorganised state of their movement which allowed the government to send 'their blue coated underlings' into their homes to seize the arms which they had a legal right to possess. He announced: 'The moment your disunion has disappeared, then will I issue the word of command, "March".'[150] With the sacred month cancelled, O'Connor was again able to adopt his familiar threatening tone, but it now represented little more than a flourish of platform rhetoric. Following this meeting, O'Connor embarked upon a two-week tour of Scotland, where there had been relatively little support for the sacred month. He had been deputed to attend a conference of Scottish delegates at Glasgow as the representative of the Convention. The Scottish conference had been called to discuss the best means of organising Chartism in Scotland, a subject which O'Connor considered particularly important. Improved organisation was the main task which now faced the movement.[151]

The Convention reassembled at the end of August. But although there was discussion about organising Chartist election clubs and the defence of Chartist prisoners, the cancellation of the sacred month had marked the end of the Convention's effective career. The Convention had failed to resolve the recurrent dilemma of British working-class radicalism, the formulation of a strategy to follow constitutional protest. For those delegates who anticipated a decisive confrontation with the government, the Convention was seen as totally discredited. Thus, on 4 September, Dr Taylor moved the dissolution of the Convention, along with a self-denying ordinance recommending the people not to return any of the delegates from the present body to any future convention. He explained that he had brought forward this motion because 'I consider the Convention, as a body chosen by the people, has failed to do its duty towards them.' Bussey seconded Taylor's motion. O'Connor came to the defence of the Convention's character. He denied Taylor's allegation that the Convention had been dominated by personal squabbles, and stressed the difficulties which faced a body 'composed . . . of discordant elements — of men from different parts of the country entertaining their own peculiar views and influenced by local prejudices'. Under the circumstances they had accomplished much. O'Connor's concern was to prevent the breakdown of national Chartist organisation and direction which he regarded as implicit in Taylor's move to disband the Convention.

> What I fear is that . . . there would be no Convention at all to guide and direct public opinion, and then the country would be left to local discussions and sectional power, which above all things must be avoided

because nothing is more necessary than that all the currents of public opinion should so harmonise and blend together as to bring them in one overwhelming tide against the enemies of the people.[152]

On several occasions, O'Connor had intimated his desire to see the Convention transformed into a permanent body. He now offered a series of counter-proposals to Taylor's resolution. He agreed that the Convention should dissolve on 7 September, but they should recommend to the country the appointment of another body 'to watch over and carry onward the cause of the people'. O'Connor was now resigned to the view that the movement, lacking the preparedness and organisation necessary to defeat the government in a 'physical' confrontation, must brace itself for a period of defensive agitation, reorganisation and consolidation. Some form of Convention or national leadership council was essential, not only as a symbol of solidarity, but in order to superintend the movement's progress and stimulate organisation and propaganda. The Chartist movement must not be allowed to stagnate; agitation must go forward.[153]

The central point at issue between O'Connor and Dr Taylor concerned the course of Chartist agitation over the coming months. Taylor believed that only armed insurrection could now settle the question: 'in these times the only place of safety is at the head of a band of armed men determined to work out their own salvation — and I am determined to put myself there in a very short time'. Leaders such as Taylor, Harney and Bussey, now regarded the Convention as an impediment to the organisation of insurrection. Taylor feared that a central body like the Convention, or even a permanent national council under O'Connor's influence, could again call off any potentially revolutionary move, or at least render it ineffective through dividing the movement's ranks. Thus he vehemently opposed the proposal for a committee or council to sit in place of the Convention. 'A single letter issuing from such a Council might throw the whole country into a blaze — or a letter might quench the blaze which I might wish to see spread a little faster . . .'[154] There was a strong feeling that any effective action must now emanate from the localities. Bussey told delegates that he saw no danger to the Convention: 'I see it in the country where the struggle must finally take place, and where I am willing to go rather than remain here and do nothing.'[155] O'Connor remembering the fate of earlier mass working-class movements, sought to prevent the degeneration of Chartism into sectional agitation and underground organisation by maintaining an open national centre around which the movement could rally. A fundamental breach had opened up between Dr Taylor and his former allies O'Connor and O'Brien. Taylor realised that O'Connor had no intention of leading an armed insurrection.

Mutual recrimination and accusations of cowardice were bandied across the floor of the Convention in its last days. The decision to dissolve the Convention was a narrow one. Taylor's original motion was easily defeated, and an amendment from Hartwell for the Convention merely to adjourn was lost on the chairman's casting vote. O'Brien then moved a straight-forward resolution that the Convention dissolve by 14 September which was carried on Frost's casting vote as chairman.[156]

Despite the failings of the Convention, and although there was a drawing back from the conception of the National Convention as an 'anti-parliament' or alternative government in the 1840s, most Chartists still recognised the break-through marked by the Convention of 1839. Thus, in summer 1840, the West Riding delegates declared:

> The most superficial observer must have seen, that the late National Convention — ill-chosen as it confessedly was; heterogeneous as was its composition; unwise and precipitate as were many of its acts — still, it must be acknowledged by all, formed such a nucleus of public opinion as this country never saw . . . Even bad as it was . . . it created a power which made the best guarded system of corruption, yet on record, tremble to its very core.[157]

Upon its dissolution, O'Connor offered his own evaluation of the Convention:

> It had forced a consideration of our principles upon the monarch; upon both Houses of Parliament; upon the judges of the land; upon all classes of society; upon all the states of Europe; upon the press; and above all, upon the people themselves.

The Convention had given Chartism concreteness. 'Chartism previous to the meeting of the Convention, was spoken of as a thing in the clouds.' Furthermore, O'Connor claimed that the Convention had established the all-important 'right of its successor to sit'. Nor was he alone in this view. The *Northern Liberator* declared:

> If, a few years ago, it had been affirmed by any one that a NATIONAL CONVENTION would sit in London, assuming to itself many of the powers of Parliament, being, in fact a Rival Parliament; and looked upon by the people as their representatives, to the exclusion of the assembly at St. Stephens . . . such a man would have been set down as insane. It would have been answered that no Government . . . could permit such a thing; and yet this, the half awakened energies of the people, have

achieved without difficulty! This, as a precedent, is invaluable. Here is a vantage ground gained that can never be lost, and which gives to the people a moral power, of which, till now, they were destitute. Do the tools who oppose them imagine that this CONVENTION IS TO BE THE LAST? . . . this Convention is only the first of a series of Conventions, which will assemble as duly as Parliament, go on increasing in influence, power and moral effect and ability to rule . . . The movement is neither 'checked' nor 'driven back!' IT HAS ESTABLISHED A PARLIAMENT.

The other fundamental right which both O'Connor and the *Liberator* claimed the Convention had established was that of the people to possess arms.[158]

The inglorious end, the squabbles, the failure in its ultimate goal to provide a strategy to carry universal suffrage, none of this should overshadow the substantial working-class achievement which the Convention represented. An assembly elected upon democratic principles and financed almost entirely by working men and women had openly deliberated for seven months in the face of government represssion and the hostility of the other classes in society. The independence, organisational capabilities and discipline of working-class radicalism, as well as the intelligence and courage of many of the movement's national and local leaders, had been dramatically demonstrated. The Convention represented a most outstanding example of the potential of the working class to generate alternative political institutions within early industrial capitalist society. For Chartists the Convention was a prefigurement of the realisation of their demand for universal suffrage and working-class political power. The failure to realise this end in 1839 was the result of the speed with which the movement had come together, the great local and occupational diversity of working-class support, the disparate composition of the Convention's membership, but most significantly it was the result of the powerful class forces arrayed against the Chartists. However, despite the achievement which the Convention embodied and whatever the rights and precedents which it may have established, its dissolution and failure to provide a strategy for 1839 resulted in the decentralisation of Chartist leadership and organisation in autumn 1839 and culminated in the abortive risings of that winter.

NOTES

1. T. M. Parssinen, 'Association, Convention and Anti-Parliament in British Radical Politics, 1771-1848', *English Historical Review*, 88, 1973, pp. 504-33; I. J. Prothero, 'William Benbow and the Concept of the "General Strike" ', *Past and Present*, no. 63, 1974, particularly pp. 135-41; C. Robbins, *The Eighteenth Century Commonwealthman*, Cambridge, Mass., 1959; *NS*, 29 June 1839, p. 1; 26 Oct., p. 3.

2. E. P. Thompson, *The Making of the English Working Class*, Penguin ed., Harmondsworth 1968, pp. 134 ff., pp. 697-99; J. Gerrald, *A Convention the Only Means of Saving Us from Ruin*, London 1793.

3. J. Lorymer, *A National Convention, the Only Proper Remedy*, London 1833 (copy in PRO, HO 64/19); R. E. Lee, *A Whisper to the Whigs, or, What is Treason?*, London 1833; W. Benbow, *Grand National Holiday and Congress of the Productive Classes*, London 1832; *Radical Reformer*, 28 Oct. 1831, p. 1; *Cosmopolite*, 7 Apr. 1832; *Man*, 8 Aug. 1833, pp. 49-50.

4. *Cosmopolite*, 18 May 1833; *PMG*, 18 May 1833, pp. 155-60; *Working Man's Friend*, 18 May 1833, pp. 169-73; PRO, HO 64/19.

5. *Leeds Times*, 18 Dec. 1835; *NS*, 9 Feb. 1838, p. 4; *PMG*, 24 Oct. 1835, p. 714.

6. Parssinen, 'Association Convention, Anti-Parliament'; Prothero, 'Benbow and the "General Strike" ', p. 135.

7. *NS*, 3 Aug. 1839, p. 7.

8. *Bolton Free Press*, 20 Apr. 1839, p. 3.

9. *Charter*, 24 Feb. 1839, p. 76; 24 Mar., p. 130.

10. *NS*, 22 June 1839, p. 8; also ibid., 4 May, p. 1.

11. According to Place, of the original fifty-three members who attended, twenty-nine were 'middle-class', i.e. men who did not work for wages, and twenty-four were working men. British Library, Add. MSS 27821, Appendix D. fo. 161.

12. PRO, HO 40/50, fo. 752, Napier to HO, 5 Sept. 1839.

13. *NS*, 22 Dec. 1838; also see Frost's comments, *Western Vindicator*, 28 Sept. 1839, p. 1.

14. D. Thompson, *The Early Chartists*, London 1971, p. 27. For biographical sketches of both Fletcher and Bussey, see *Charter*, 31 Mar. 1839, p. 151; 5 May, p. 229.

15. *NS*, 1 June 1839, p. 8.

16. M. Fletcher, *Letters to the Inhabitants of Bury*, Bury 1852, letter 4, p. 7. Also see the description of the reporter from the *London News* of his visit to the Convention, quoted *NS*, 2 Nov. 1839, p. 6; and that of Flora Tristan, *Promenades dans Londres*, Maspero ed., Paris 1978, (first published 1840), pp. 98-102.

17. *NS*, 8 May 1841, p. 7; for objections to the LWMA's handling of this 'election', see *Charter*, 3 Feb. 1839; *Operative*, 14, 28 Apr. 1839. In general, I do not concur in the opinion that Chartists 'made a mockery of their principles' in the election of Convention delegates. Cf. K. Judge, 'Early Chartist Organization and the Convention of 1839', *International Review of Social History*, 20, 1975, p. 376.

18. *NS*, 26 Oct. 1839, p. 3; 9 Nov., p. 6; Fletcher, *Letters to the Inhabitants of Bury*, letter 4, p. 9. The LWMA originally asked J. A. Roebuck and Francis Place to be among the London delegates. British Library, Place Collection, Set 56 (July-Dec. 1838), fo. 34, Lovett to Place, 30 Aug. 1838.

19. *NS*, 26 Oct. 1839, p. 3.

20. Ibid., 25 May 1839, p. 1; 29 June, p. 1.

21. Ibid., 30 Mar. 1839, p. 4; 6 Apr., p. 5.

22. Ibid., 13 Apr. 1839, p. 6; 20 Apr., p. 4; 27 Apr., p. 4.

23. Ibid., 16 Mar. 1839, p. 4.

24. Ibid., 9 Feb. 1839, p. 4; almost £2000 had been raised by this time in national rent.

25. *Birmingham Journal*, 16 Feb. 1839; *NS*, 23 Feb. 1839, p. 4; *Charter*, 24 Feb.

1839, p. 73; *Champion*, 24 Feb. 1839, p. 4; British Library, Add. MSS 34245 A, fos. 41-42, Salt to Lovett and Douglas to Lovett, 17 Feb. 1839.

26. *Charter*, 10 Feb. 1839, pp. 45-46. The *Charter, Northern Star* and *Operative* carried reports of the Convention proceedings, as did the *Sun*, a 'liberal' daily which the Convention paid to carry daily reports. Place gives a very full narrative of the proceedings in Add. MSS 27821; there are also some very full government reports in PRO, HO 40/44.

27. *NS*, 23 Feb. 1839, p. 4.

28. *Charter*, 17 Feb. 1839, pp. 50-52.

29. *NS*, 2 Nov. 1839, p. 6.

30. *Charter*, 17 Feb. 1839, p. 50.

31. Ibid., 3 Mar. 1839, p. 93.

32. Ibid., 17 Feb. 1839, p. 53.

33. Ibid., 28 Apr. 1839, p. 220. Lord John Russell told the Commons that the Convention 'was a body for the sole purpose of preparing and presenting petitions to Parliament'. *Hansard*, Parl. Debates, 3rd Series, XLV, 11 Feb. 1839, col. 220. Also see law officers' reports, PRO, HO 48/32; HO 49/8.

34. *NS*, 6 Apr. 1839, p. 5; 20 July, p. 4; 4 May, p. 5.

35. *Charter*, 17 Feb. 1839, p. 53.

36. Ibid., pp. 54, 50.

37. Cobbett's resolutions were defeated by a vote of 36-6; Whittle, Wroe and probably James Mills voting with Cobbett.

38. British Library, Add. MSS 27821, fo. 5. However, most LDA members supported the Convention and Harney's condemnations generally lost him radical support in London. See J. Bennett, 'A Study in London Radicalism: The London Democratic Association, 1837-41', (Sussex Univ. MA thesis, 1968), pp. 23, 26; I. J. Prothero, *Artisans and Politics in Early Nineteenth-Century London: John Gast and His Times*, Folkestone 1979, p. 324.

39. *Operative*, 10 Mar. 1839; *Charter*, 10 Mar. 1839, pp. 108-09; *NS*, 9 Mar. 1839, p. 5; Schoyen, *Chartist Challenge*, pp. 57-59.

40. Sankey actually moved a resolution: 'That the present movement, being essentially English, and not having in view any theoretical innovations, but a recurrence to the first principles of the original Saxon Constitution, this Convention do deprecate any language or expression which would appear to associate our objects to those of the French Revolution, or to take it as our model.' *NS*, 4 May 1839, p. 5.

41. Fletcher, *Letters to the Inhabitants of Bury*, letter 4, p. 9.

42. By early 1839, the LDA had been infiltrated by several government agents. See reports in PRO, HO 40/44. As early as March, it was rumoured that Harney was a spy. *Chartist*, 15 Mar. 1839.

43. *NS*, 16 Mar. 1839, p. 4.

44. *Operative*, 28 Apr. 1839, p. 3; *Charter*, 28 Apr. 1839, p. 219; Schoyen, *Chartist Challenge*, pp. 65-66. The Convention refused to seat both Williams and William Drake, another LDA man.

45. *Charter*, 28 Apr. 1839, p. 221; *NS*, 22 June 1839, p. 8.

46. *NS*, 16 Mar. 1839, p. 5.

47. Ibid., 23 Mar. 1839, pp. 4-5; 6 Apr., pp. 3, 6; 13 Apr., p. 8; *Charter*, 31 Mar. 1839, p. 157; 7 Apr.; British Library, Add. MSS 34245 A, letter of resignation from the Birmingham delegates; *Morning Chronicle*, 19 Mar. 1839, p. 4, for Wade's letter protesting the language used at this meeting.

48. *NS*, 23 Mar. 1839, p. 4; *Morning Chronicle*, 18 Mar., p. 3.

49. *NS*, 21 Sept. 1839, p. 3, O'Connor reckoned there had been twenty-one resignations from the Convention.

50. *Charter*, 21 Apr. 1839, p. 205.

51. Ibid., 28 Apr. 1839, p. 219.

52. Ibid., 21 Apr. 1839, p. 204; *NS*, 20 Apr. 1839, p. 1.

53. *NS*, 4 May 1839, p. 1.

54. Ibid., 11 May 1839, p. 1.

55. Ibid., 27 Apr. 1839, p. 1; *Charter*, 28 Apr. 1839, p. 219. It was privately acknowledged that the call to move the Convention to Birmingham stemmed from an apprehension of arrests. British Library, Add. MSS 27821, fo. 93.

56. *Operative*, 12 May 1839, p. 3.

57. Ibid., 28 Apr. 1839, p. 3.; *Charter*, 28 Apr. 1839, p. 220; *NS*, 4 May 1839, p. 5; British Library, Add. MSS 34245 A, fos. 414-15, Fussell to the Convention.

58. *NS*, 11 May 1839, p. 5; *Charter*, 12 May 1839, p. 252. For the Convention's arrival in Birmingham, see *NS*, 18 May 1839, pp. 1,4; PRO, HO 40/50, fos. 108-11, Scholefield (mayor) to Russell, 13 May 1839.

59. *Operative*, 28 Apr. 1839, p. 3.

60. For discussion of the Manifesto, see *Charter*, 19 May 1839, p. 268; *NS*, 18 May 1839, p. 5; *Sun*, 13-18 May 1839; also see Prothero, 'Benbow and the "General Strike"', pp. 153-55. O'Connor strongly objected to the original proposal to recommend the non-payment of rent and taxes.

61. *Sun*, 13 May 1839, p. 4; *Charter*, 19 May 1839, p. 268.

62. *Sun*, 15 May 1839, p. 1.

63. Among these were M'Douall, Osbourne, Harney, Neesom, Rider and Fletcher. *Sun*, 13 May 1839, p. 4; 15 May, p. 1; *Charter*, 19 May 1839, p. 268.

64. *NS*, 11 May 1839, p. 4; 18 May, p. 4. For earlier calls for simultaneous meetings, see Thompson, *The Making*, pp. 765 ff.; Prothero, 'Benbow and the "General Strike"', pp. 151-53; *Man*, 8 Aug. 1833, pp. 49-50, proposed the election of a National Convention by means of simultaneous meetings.

65. *NS*, 11 May 1839, p. 4; 18 May, p. 4.

66. For instance, *Charter*, 17 Feb. 1839, p. 60.

67. In fact, on the arrival of the Convention in Birmingham, the mayor made just such a suggestion to Russell, proposing they seize the opportunity to suppress totally the Convention by arresting members in their separate quarters. PRO, HO 40/50, fo. 112, Scholefield to Russell, 13 May 1839.

68. *NS*, 11, 18, 25 May 1839; *Birmingham Journal*, 18 May 1839.

69. E. Hamer, *A Brief Account of the Chartist Outbreak in Llanidloes*, Llanidloes 1867; *Western Vindicator*, 6 Apr. 1839, p. 4; 13 Apr., p. 1; R. B. Pugh, 'Chartism in Somerset and Wiltshire', in A. Briggs (ed.), *Chartist Studies*, London 1959, pp. 185-86; *NS*, 11 May 1839, p. 1; *Manchester and Salford Advertiser*, 4 May 1839, p. 3; 11 May, p. 4; *Manchester Guardian*, 4 May 1839, p. 3; 8 May, p. 3; 12 May, p. 2; PRO, HO 40/47; *Sun*, 11 May 1839, p. 1; Schoyen, *Chartist Challenge*, pp. 67-68.

70. F. C. Mather, 'Government and the Chartists', in *Chartist Studies*, pp. 378-79; J. Prest, *Lord John Russell*, London 1972, pp. 145-46; PRO, HO 41/13; *NS*, 11 May 1839, p. 4; 18 May, p. 4.

71. *Sun*, 13 May 1839, p. 4; 16 May, p. 1; 17 May, p. 2; 18 May, p. 2. See Lovett's speech, *NS*, 18 May 1839, p. 6.

72. *NS*, 15 June 1839, p. 4; 22 June, p. 8; *Northern Liberator*, 22 June 1839, p. 4. O'Connor had already appeared as defence attorney for Brown and Fussell; given legal advice to Vincent; and gone bail for five Lancashire Chartists arrested for drilling in the amount of £350.

73. See, for instance, Harney's reflections, *Newcastle Weekly Chronicle*, 5 Jan. 1890.

74. *NS*, 6 Apr. 1839, p. 6.

75. Ibid., 4 May 1839, p. 8; report in PRO, HO 40/43, fos. 164-66.

76. *Carlisle Journal*, 13 July 1839, quoted in B. Harrison and P. Hollis, 'Chartism, Liberalism and the Life of Robert Lowery', *English Historical Review*, 82, 1967, p. 514.

77. W. F. P. Napier, *The Life and Opinions of Sir C. J. Napier*, London 1857, II, pp. 5-6. Throughout 1839 and 1840, Napier never lost his confidence in the army's ability

to put down a Chartist rising, although he certainly took the problem of disaffection in the ranks seriously. See ibid., pp. 54-55, 64. There is some evidence of Chartist sympathies on the part of soldiers in the radical press. *Charter*, 17 Feb. 1839, p. 57; *London Democrat*, 4 May 1839, pp. 30-31; *NS*, 11 May 1839, p. 4.

78. *NS*, 6 Apr. 1839, p. 3.

79. See Fletcher's speech, *Charter*, 10 Mar. 1839, p. 108.

80. See the debate on Richardson's report on the question of arming, *NS*, 13 Apr. 1839, p. 1; *Charter*, 14 Apr. 1839, pp. 188-89.

81. *NS*, 18 May 1839, pp. 6, 4; cf. *London Democrat*, 11, 18, 25 May 1839, pp. 36, 41, 44, 51-52.

82. See D. Thompson, *Early Chartists*, pp. 22-23; Parssinen, 'Association, Convention, Anti-Parliament', pp. 527-29; Prothero, *Artisans and Politics*, p. 289.

83. At both Peep Green and Kersal Moor, O'Connor raised the prospect of being attacked at the meeting. *NS*, 25 May 1839, p. 1; 1 June, p. 6.

84. Ibid., 4 May 1839, pp. 6, 4; 11 May, p. 4; 18 May, p. 4; *Operative*, 28 Apr. 1839, p. 3.

85. *NS*, 25 May 1839, p. 1.

86. See E. P. Thompson's comments, *Bulletin of the Society for the Study of Labour History*, no. 20, 1970, p. 13.

87. Napier, *Life and Opinions*, II. p. 40, for Napier's handling of the Kersal Moor meeting.

88. Prothero, 'Benbow and the "General Strike" ', offers the most lucid discussion of this whole question

89. *Herald of the Rights of Industry*, 5, 12 Apr. 1834; *Pioneer*, 29 Mar.-3 May 1834; *Crisis*, 19 Apr. 1834; Prothero, 'Benbow and the "General Strike" ', pp. 166-70; W. H. Oliver, 'The Consolidated Trades' Union of 1834', *Economic History Review*, 17, 1964, p. 83; J. Saville, 'J.E. Smith and the Owenite Movement', in J. Salt and S. Pollard (eds.), *Robert Owen, Prophet of the Poor*, London 1971, p. 137; R. G. Kirby and A. E. Musson, *The Voice of the People, John Doherty, 1798-1854*, Manchester 1975, particularly ch. 8.

90. Copies of Benbow's pamphlet were found among the papers of Chartists arrested at Stockport and Ashton-under-Lyne in 1839. PRO, Assizes 65/2. Benbow toured Lancashire in spring and early summer of 1839 addressing meetings on the question of the national holiday.

91. *NS*, 16 June 1839, p. 7.

92. R. Lowery, 'Passages in the Life of a Temperance Lecturer', reprinted in B. Harrison and P. Hollis (eds.), *Robert Lowery: Radical and Chartist*, London 1979, p. 142.

93. *Sun*, 13 May 1839, p. 4; 15 May, p. 1; also see *London Democrat*, 4 May 1839, p. 29.

94. *Operative*, 28 Apr. 1839, p. 4. In August, O'Connor gives the impression that it was Attwood who brought the idea of the national holiday into Chartism; and by the early 1840s, the entire affair is put down to a conspiracy of Birmingham merchants. *NS*, 3 Aug. 1839, p. 4; 7 Aug. 1841, p. 1; 23 Sept. 1843, p. 1.

95. *NS*, 4 May 1839, p. 8.

96. *Birmingham Journal*, 29 June 1839; 6 July; *Sun*, 4 July 1839, p. 2; T. R. Tholfsen, 'The Chartist Crisis in Birmingham', *International Review of Social History*, 3, 1958, p. 471.

97. *NS*, 6 July 1839, p. 1.

98. This account is based on reports in *NS*, 6 July 1839, p. 1; *Sun*, 4 July 1839, p. 2; *Charter*, 7 July 1839. Part of the session was held *in camera*.

99. Lovett suggested they test the movement by calling out a few of the best organised trades first.

100. *NS*, 13 July 1839, p. 7.

101. *Birmingham Journal*, 6 July 1839; *Times*, 5 July 1839; *Charter*, 7 July 1839; *NS*,

13 July 1839; *Borough of Birmingham Report of the Committee Appointed by the Town Council . . . to Investigate the Causes of the Late Riots*, Birmingham 1840, pp. 18-21.

102. *NS*, 13 July 1839, pp. 6,7, 4.

103. PRO, TS 11/815, case no. 2687; *NS*, 13 July 1839; *Birmingham Journal*, 6, 13 July 1839; W. Lovett, *Life and Struggles of William Lovett*, Fitzroy ed., London 1967, pp. 180-81; Birmingham Reference Library, Lovett Collection, II, fos. 50ff.

104. *Bolton Free Press*, 13 July 1839, p. 3; also see the factory worker James Mitchell's remarks at Stockport, *NS*, 20 July 1839, p. 1.

105. *NS*, 13 July 1839, pp. 7, 4; 20 July, p. 3; *Charter*, 14 July 1839, p. 396.

106. T. A. Devyr, *The Odd Book of the Nineteenth Century*, New York 1882, p. 177.

107. Transport House, Vincent MSS, 1/1/19, Vincent to Minikin, 19 July 1839; also see *Western Vindicator*, 13, 20, 27 July 1839.

108. *Bolton Free Press*, 13 July 1839, p. 2; *NS*, 13 July-3 Aug. 1839, for reports from throughout the country.

109. Barnsley Public Library, J. Burland, MS 'The Annals of Barnsley', fos. 110-11; *NS*, 13, 20, 27 July 1839 — cited in F. J. Kaijage, 'Labouring Barnsley, 1815-1875', (Warwick Univ. PhD. thesis, 1975), p. 493.

110. *Hansard*, Parl. Debates, 3rd Series, XLIX, 12 July 1839, cols. 220-78. For reports of the Convention's deliberations, see *Charter*, 21 July 1839, pp. 412-13; 28 July, p. 429; *NS*, 20 July 1839, pp. 5, 7; July 27, p. 1. Part of these sessions was held *in camera*.

111. Bussey had been touring the industrial districts, *NS*, 13, 20, 27 July 1839.

112. There is some confusion in Convention reports as to whether the speaker was Warden or Marsden.

113. *Charter*, 21 July 1839, p. 412.

114. *Birmingham Journal*, 20 July 1839; *Borough of Birmingham Report*, pp. 25-41; *Dundas Report, Riots of the 15th of July*, Home Office, London 1840; *Northern Liberator*, 20 July-3 Aug. 1839; W. H. Maehl, 'Chartist Disturbances in North-Eastern England, 1839', *International Review of Social History*, 8, 1963, pp. 395 ff; id., 'The Dynamics of Violence in Chartism: A Case Study in Northeastern England', *Albion*, 7, 1975, pp. 112-13.

115. *NS*, 20 July 1839, pp. 7, 5; Only Marsden, Neesom, Stowe, Osbourne and Tilly voted for this amendment.

116. Burns, Bussey, Carpenter, Duncan, Hetherington, Jones, Knox, Lowery, Pitkeithley, Smart, James Taylor, Woodhouse voted for the amendment; Cardo, Deegan, Fletcher, Hartwell, Marsden, M'Douall, Neesom, Skevington, Stowe, Tilly, Osbourne, Richards against.

117. Carpenter, Duncan, Hetherington, Knox, Pitkeithley and James Taylor voted against the motion; Burns, Bussey, Smart, Skevington and Woodhouse abstained. All voting details from *Charter*, 21 July 1839, p. 413.

118. *NS*, 20 July 1839, p. 5; 27 July, p. 6; *Charter*, 28 July 1839, pp. 418-20; D. Williams, *John Frost: A Study in Chartism*, Cardiff 1939, pp. 171-75.

119. *NS*, 13, 20, 27 July 1839.

120. British Library, Add. MSS 34245 B, fo. 49, Frost to Convention, 19 July 1839.

121. *Bradford Observer*, 18 July 1839; *Northern Liberator*, 13 July 1839; *Manchester and Salford Advertiser*, 20 July 1839, p. 2.

122. Maehl, 'Chartist Disturbances', pp. 401-02; *Northern Liberator*, 27 July 1839, p. 3; 3 Aug.; PRO, HO 40/46, Northumberland to Russell, 23 July 1839, also Fife to Russell, 31 July; Devyr, *Odd Book*, pp. 192-93.

123. *NS*, 20 July 1839, pp. 1, 5.

124. H. U. Faulkner, *Chartism and the Churches*, New York 1916, pp. 35-41; *NS*, 27 July-10Aug. 1839.

125. *Bolton Free Press*, 3 Aug. 1839, p. 2.

126. *NS*, 13 July 1839, pp. 7, 8; 27 July, pp. 4, 5; 3 Aug., p. 6; 17 Aug., p. 3; *Sheffield Iris*, 6 Aug. 1839; 'Life and Times of John Vallence', in *Barnsley Times*, May-June 1882;

also see J. L. Baxter, 'Early Chartism and Labour Class Struggle: South Yorkshire 1837-1840', in S. Pollard and C. Holmes (eds.), *Essays in the Economic and Social History of South Yorkshire*, Barnsley 1976, pp. 141-42.

127. Cf. T. M. Kemnitz, 'Approaches to the Chartist Movement: Feargus O'Connor and Chartist Strategy', *Albion*, 5, 1973, pp. 67-73.

128. See reports in PRO, HO 40/37, 38, 40, 43-46, 50, 51, 53. For South Lancashire, reports of arming appear in the press by late 1838 and are commonplace by spring 1839. *Manchester Guardian*, 29 Dec. 1838, p. 3; *Stockport Advertiser*, 28 Dec. 1838, p. 3; 17 May 1839, p. 4; *NS*, 11 May 1839, p. 5; *Champion*, 24 Mar. 1839, p. 4; 7 Apr., p. 1; 5 May, p. 3; also see C. A. N. Reid, 'The Chartist Movement in Stockport', (Hull Univ. MA thesis, 1974), pp. 115-22. When Timothy Higgins, the Ashton Chartist, was arrested, his house was discovered to be a small arsenal, TS 11/1030, no. 4424 A.

129. Devyr, *Odd Book*, p. 177; Harney to Engels, 30 Mar. 1846, *The Harney Papers*, F. G. and R. M. Black (eds.), Assen 1969, pp. 239-40.

130. See A. Somerville, *Dissuasive Warnings to the People on Street Warfare*, London 1839; id., *Public and Personal Affairs Being an Enquiry into the Physical Strength of the People, in which the Value of Pikes and Rifles is Compared with that of the Grape Shot . . . of the Woolwich Artillery*, London 1839.

131. J. Saville, intro. to Merlin reprint of *The Red Republican and The Friend of the People*, London 1966, I, p. v.

132. *Sun*, 23 July 1839, p. 3; *Charter*, 28 July, p. 428.

133. *Sun*, 25 July 1839, p. 3; *Charter*, 28 July 1839, p. 428; *NS*, 3 Aug. 1839, p. 4.

134. *NS*, 27 July 1839, pp. 1, 5; Lowery, 'Passages', in *Robert Lowery*, p. 143.

135. On O'Brien's motion: Cleave, Carpenter, Knox, Burns, Hetherington, O'Brien, O'Connor, Pitkeithley, Smart, Skevington, James Taylor, Woodhouse (for); Lowery, Mealing, Marsden, Neesom, Osbourne, Wolstenholme (?) (against); and Deegan, Fletcher, M'Douall, Richards, Stowe, Tilley, Warden (abstain). *Charter*, 28 July 1839, p. 429.

136. *NS*, 27 July 1839, p. 4; *Charter*, 28 July 1839, p. 429; *Sun*, 26 July 1839, p. 2.

137. Lowery, 'Passages', in *Robert Lowery*, p. 144.

138. *NS*, 17 Aug. 1839, p. 8. Of the twenty reports received by the council only four districts (the West Riding, Bath, Middleton and Pontypool) were now in favour of striking.

139. British Library, Add. MSS 34245 B, fos. 80-81, Sidwell to Council, 27 July 1839; fos. 110-111, Deegan to Fletcher, 6 Aug.; fos. 117-118, Stowe to Fletcher, 7 Aug.; fos. 112-13, Wolstenholme to Smart, 6 Aug. 1839, p. 4; fo. 114, Bussey to Smart, 6 Aug.

140. *NS*, 3 Aug. 1839, p. 4; also see O'Brien's letter, ibid., 10 Aug., p. 4.

141. Ibid., 10 Aug. 1839, p. 5. O'Connor claimed that the council had reached this decision before his letter of 3 August.

142. British Library, Add. MSS 34245 B, fos. 103-04, 114, Bussey to Smart, 3 Aug. and 6 Aug. 1839.

143. J. Jackson, *The Demagogue Done Up, an Exposure of the Extreme Inconsistencies of Mr. Feargus O'Connor*, Bradford 1844, p. 16.

144. British Library, Add. MSS 34245 B, fos. 123-24, Taylor to Smart, 8 Aug. 1839.

145. See *Bolton Chronicle*, 19 Oct. 1839, p. 3, for Job Plant's denunciation of O'Connor, O'Brien and the majority of the Convention delegates at Heywood. For earlier criticism of the Convention, see *Heywood Democrat*, 6 June and 5 July 1839 (copies in Bury Public Library). I am indebted to Robert Sykes for drawing my attention to this last source.

146. *Bolton Free Press*, 27 July-17 Aug. 1839; *Bolton Chronicle*, 27 July-17 Aug. 1839; *Manchester Guardian*, 3 Aug. 1839, p. 2; 7 Aug., p. 2; 10 Aug., p. 3; *Manchester and Salford Advertiser*, 17 Aug. 1839, p. 3; 24 Aug., p. 3; W. Brimelow, *Political and Parliamentary History of Bolton*, Bolton 1882, pp. 368 ff.

147. *NS*, 17 Aug. 1839, pp. 3, 5.

148. Ibid., p. 8.

149. *Bolton Chronicle*, 21 Dec. 1839, p. 2; *NS*, 21 Dec. 1839, p. 1.

150. *NS*, 17 Aug. 1839, p. 5; PRO, HO 40/44, fos. 739-48.

151. *NS*, 10 Aug. 1839, p. 5; 24 Aug., pp. 2-4; 31 Aug., p. 6; British Library, Add. MSS 34245 B, fos. 155-56, O'Connor to Smart, 18 Aug. 1839.

152. PRO, HO 40/44, fos. 838-70; *Champion*, 8 Sept. 1839, p. 4; *Northern Liberator*, 8 Sept. 1839, p. 8; *NS*, 7 Sept. 1839, p. 7.

153. PRO, HO 40/44, fos. 858-60, report of 4 Sept. 1839.

154. Ibid., fos. 920-30, report of 6 Sept. 1839; *Champion*, 8 Sept. 1839, p. 4; *Northern Liberator*, 14 Sept. 1839, p. 3.

155. PRO, HO 40/44, fo. 866, report of 4 Sept. 1839.

156. *Champion*, 8 Sept. 1839, p. 4; *NS*, 14 Sept. 1839, p. 1; *Northern Liberator*, 14 Sept. 1839, p. 3; 21 Sept., p. 3.

157. *NS*, June 27, 1840, p. 1; Parssinen, 'Association, Convention, Anti-Parliament', pp. 530-33.

158. *NS*, 21 Sept. 1839, p. 3; *Northern Liberator*, 14 Sept. 1839, p. 4; 17 Aug., p. 4; also 11 Apr. 1840, pp. 5-6. The *Champion* was less enthusiastic, concluding 'THE NATIONAL PETITION WAS NOT A FAILURE: THE CONVENTION IS.' 1 Sept. 1839, p. 1.

5 THE RISINGS AND AFTER

As E. P. Thompson has stressed: 'From 1817 until Chartist times, the central working-class tradition was that which exploited every means of agitation and protest short of active insurrectionary preparation.'[1] Until summer 1839, Chartism was characterised by an unprecedented openness and emphasis upon constitutional forms of agitation and organisation. However, with the rejection of the National Petition, the cancellation of the sacred month and the disbanding of the Convention, small groups of determined Chartists prepared to go beyond such tactics and traditions, to cross the threshold of violence and move towards insurrection. It was a pattern reminiscent of 1817-20, and one to be repeated in 1848. O'Connor was the foremost advocate of open national agitation. An implacable opponent of secret or 'illegal' proceedings, on the grounds that such activity laid the movement open to the intrigue of *agents provocateurs* and invariably led to partial, and therefore unsuccessful outbreaks, he had constantly emphasised the need for united national action which could be guaranteed only through open constitutional methods. O'Connor remained committed essentially to the platform rather than a radical tradition associated with conspiracy and insurrection. Indeed, there is a sense in which the role of demagogue was in itself antithetical to conspiracy. As Chartism entered a short but critical period dominated by secrecy and marked by the development of underground organisation, it became difficult for leaders committed to constitutional agitation to provide effective national leadership. Thus O'Brien, whose position in 1839 was similar to O'Connor's, explained why he retired from active Chartist leadership in the months following the Convention:

> I could do no more . . . I could not conscientiously take part in projects which should imply secrecy, and which in spite of the protractors themselves, would necessarily lead to partial outbreaks and detached movements,— to be as easily crushed as projected, and always followed by increased prosecution of the Chartists generally. In short I could not conscientiously approve of any other than a national movement conducted openly in the broad face of day, under the safeguard of the constitution . . . a movement in which physical force should have no part whatever, unless it began with the oppressor, in which case, the

oppressed would be bound (by the constitution itself), to resort to physical force in self-defence.[2]

During the autumn and winter of 1839-40, O'Connor remained near the centre of Chartist agitation. In the absence of any institution of national Chartist leadership, with large numbers of Chartist leaders either in prison or facing trial and in an atmosphere of profound disillusion, he sought to sustain some form of open national agitation, to provide an alternative to sectionalism and the development of a Chartist underground. Thus, in late August and September, he launched a campaign to establish a system of Chartist election clubs throughout the country in preparation for the next general election. O'Connor elaborated upon O'Brien's scheme for electing Chartist candidates at the hustings, placing particular emphasis upon the need to build a coherent national Chartist organisation and to reconstruct a centre of national leadership. He proposed that as soon as an election committee was formed in a locality that Chartists call a public meeting to consider the propriety of appointing a National Election Convention of twenty-one delegates to sit in London. In this way he linked efforts to convene a new convention with his plan for forming election associations. Most importantly, this plan offered an alternative form of constitutional agitation to follow the failure of petitioning; its adoption 'will at once raise a safe and constitutional standard around which the friends of Radicalism may rally'.[3]

Despite the set-backs of the summer, O'Connor radiated enthusiasm and confidence in the Chartist cause, predicting that the next general election would return between four and five hundred radical members to Parliament. He promised to open up Yorkshire as he had done County Cork, and set out on a tour of Yorkshire to present himself to the electors and non-electors. O'Connor looked beyond the election of Chartist candidates at the hustings towards the achievement of universal suffrage through the disintegration of the Whig Party. He argued that the next election would see not merely the defeat of the Whigs, but a fundamental realignment of political forces which would place Chartism in the ascent. Driven from power the Whigs would again be forced to initiate an intimidating campaign for suffrage extension in order to recapture power. This time the radicals must ensure that unlike 1832 the working class win its political emancipation, a task to be achieved by 'standing alone'. Never again must the working class be 'used to grace the Whig pageant', or serve as the 'reserve army' of Whiggery.[4] But although there was some support among local Chartists for his plans for reorganisation, O'Connor did not provide a strategy for autumn 1839.[5] Chartists had to wait until 1841 for a general election. Furthermore, his proposal for a new convention, and particularly his offer to pay delegates from the profits of the *Star*, met with opposition. Not surprisingly, the Cobbettite *Champion*, in an editorial headed 'KING O'CONNOR'S PARLIAMENT', denounced the proposal for a new convention as a further attempt to subordinate the movement to O'Connor's personal designs.[6] The proposal was undoubtedly misconceived. What O'Connor demonstrated, however, was a concern to formulate an alternative to conspiratorial organisation. In September 1839, he also began to place particular importance upon the worker's alienation from the land and his own ideas concerning the benefits of small farming.[7] Thus we can detect already some of the main lines along which O'Connor tried to redirect Chartism in the early 1840s — the emphasis upon reorganisation, the development of a strategy dependent upon the final break-up of the Whig alliance as a means to working-class political ascendancy and the need for a social programme to complement the political demand for universal suffrage.

Having outlined his plans for a redirected constitutional agitation, O'Connor abruptly cancelled a scheduled tour of Lancashire and departed for Ireland on 5 October, and did not return to England until 2 November; thus placing himself outside the country during the critical month preceding the tragic Welsh rising. David Williams and A. J. Peacock have carefully sifted through the complex and often conflicting evidence and provided lucid accounts of the plotting and insurrectionary organisation which went on both in Wales and England following the Convention. Both historians have exonerated O'Connor from the accusation that he betrayed Frost.[8] What remains in question, however, is the extent of O'Connor's knowledge of the plans for insurrection; his attitude towards the plotting going on throughout the country; the extent to which his earlier rhetoric created the atmosphere for an attempt at insurrection; and why he withdrew from the responsibilities of national leadership during this difficult period of Chartist history. October 1839 stands out as the only period during a long career of radical leadership when O'Connor appears to have voluntarily removed himself from the centre of national agitation.

It is extremely difficult to determine the extent of O'Connor's knowledge about the plans afoot for insurrection in autumn 1839. Certainly he must have had a general awareness and concern about secret plans for insurrection. By summer 1839 there were hints of underground activity, when both the council of the Convention and the *Star* cautioned radicals 'against some who we hear have counselled the holding of secret meetings, and the formation of secret societies. No man will do this unless he is either a spy or a fool. Let no such man be trusted.'[9] There is considerable evidence to suggest that by summer 1839 certain members of the Convention, including probably Dr Taylor, Bussey, Richardson and M'Douall, as well as the Polish revolutionary Beniowski, were meeting privately, perhaps as a 'committee of public safety', to discuss plans for revolution. It is almost certain that the plans which culminated in the Newport rising were laid by a group of Convention delegates, including Bussey, Dr Taylor, Frost and Burns, with the dissolution of the Convention in mid-September.[10] Other delegates, such as Hartwell, Cardo, Warden, Hetherington, Lowery, Pitkeithley and perhaps Harney, knew something of these plans, or soon learned of them.[11]

It is difficult to believe that O'Connor who was in close touch with the movement in the country knew nothing of these plans. On the other hand, there is evidence to suggest that O'Connor, who was held most responsible for the cancellation of the national holiday and who was the foremost advocate of calling another convention, was not only excluded from these plans, but that details of this plotting were carefully concealed from him for fear that he would expose them. Lowery, who in fact believed that O'Connor did know of the plans for insurrection, related in his reminiscences that he learned of the plans for a rising from an ex-member of the Convention, W. G. Burns of Dundee. When Lowery observed that he supposed that this was O'Connor's scheme he was told that 'they had not let him [O'Connor] into their secret, for they did not think he was to be trusted'.[12] William Ashton, the Barnsley Chartist, was admitted into the company of those Convention members discussing plans for insurrection in the closing days of the Convention. Ashton later accused O'Connor of having betrayed Frost, but in early 1840 he claimed that at these meetings 'a base conspiracy was formed to destroy O'Connor's reputation and the *Northern Star*', although these delegates remained outwardly friendly towards O'Connor.[13] Dr Taylor was highly conscious of how O'Connor had used the *Star* and his standing as a national leader to undermine the national holiday, and thus had every reason to ensure that O'Connor did not learn of the plans for insurrection. Certainly O'Connor always claimed that had he known of the plans for the Welsh rising he would have done everything in his power to call it off. One of the criticisms later levelled against O'Connor was that he was the only leader in a position to call off the rising. For this very reason those planning insurrection tried to keep such information from him.[14]

Of course, this does not prove that O'Connor did not learn of these plans, nor does it explain why he left the country. However, it is unlikely that he knew any precise details. By William Hill's own admission Ashton's message about the plotting was not conveyed to O'Connor until after the risings.[15] Although not certain, it is possible that the decision for the English radicals to act in concert with the Welsh was taken at a West Riding delegates meeting held at Heckmondwike, on 30 September. According to Lovett's account, a messenger was sent from this meeting to inform O'Connor of their decision and to ask him to lead an insurrection. A messenger could have reached O'Connor who was by this time in London and who did not decide to leave for Ireland until 2 October. However, it seems almost certain that Lovett, along with several other contemporaries, confused the Dewsbury Chartists later approach to O'Connor in connection with the 'after risings' with the events leading up to the Welsh rising. Two delegates were appointed from the next meeting of West Riding delegates, on 25 October, to wait on O'Connor 'to inform him of the decision of the meeting', but by this time O'Connor was out of the country. Thus it was Bussey, not O'Connor, who sent George White around the West Riding localities to call off the intended simultaneous risings.[16] Shortly after the Welsh rising, O'Connor published the following note 'To The Dewsbury People' in the *Star:*

> I know no more of the matter than the man in the moon. I never even heard of it till Monday last. I had not seen George White for more than two months. I had neither hand, act, nor part in the foul trick played upon the people. They will have no difficulty in putting the saddle upon the right horse.[17]

Why did O'Connor leave for Ireland, if not to avoid the implications of insurrectionary activity? In 1843, O'Connor gave his own account of the reasons for his absence from England during this period:

> Firstly, because I had been convicted in July, 1839, and was under recognizance to appear in the Queen's Bench on the 7th of November, to receive judgement and go to prison; and as I had not been in Ireland since April, 1836, it was not unnatural that I should wish to see my friends, and arrange something about my property before I was incarcerated. . . .

Secondly, because just at that period, Mr. O'Connell, at a dinner at Macroom, asserted that I dare not come to Ireland. I did go, and held large meetings in the county of Cork, and challenged his friends to oppose me. Thirdly, I went because the Cork newspapers stated that the registration then going on was detrimental to the liberal interest. I thought I could assist them, and the first place I visited was the registration court at Cork . . . Fourthly, I went to Ireland to get money to keep the *Northern Star* on its legs . . .[18]

In October 1839, he explained to Chartists that he was concerned by reports that the local aristocracy was using its powers of intimidation to prevent electors from registering in County Cork, in an attempt to reassert political control over a county which O'Connor had been instrumental in opening up in 1832. Furthermore, he announced his intention to establish RAs in Ireland. He had been planning a tour of Irish agitation for some time; from the early days of the Convention he had asserted the importance of winning Irish support for Chartism. Lowery had only recently returned from Ireland, where he had had little success in mobilising support as the missionary of the Convention.[19] Perhaps O'Connor felt that in his own home county, where he had first established his reputation as a popular leader, he might be able to establish a base from which to stimulate Chartism in Ireland. If so, he was mistaken. He did hold several public meetings at which he assured Irishmen that the English working class was not indifferent to the claims of Ireland and urged the initiation of a campaign for universal suffrage and the repeal of the Union. But O'Connell's deputies excluded him from any active part at the registry sessions; and despite his confident reports of having 'been received with open arms' by the people of County Cork, no organisation emerged from this agitation.[20]

The other reasons which O'Connor later gave for his Irish trip were personal and financial. O'Connor faced almost certain imprisonment for several years, and putting his finances in order was no doubt of considerable importance not merely to himself, but for the movement at large. O'Connor's personal finances were closely linked to those of the Chartist movement. Much of the high cost of defending Chartist leaders arrested in 1839 and maintaining the families of those imprisoned was sustained out of profits of the *Northern Star*, and although these profits were high, so were the financial demands of the movement in the closing months of 1839 and throughout 1840. O'Connor's own legal costs must have been very high, as the cases against himself and the *Star* formed the most protracted Chartist prosecution. Against this background, his assertion that he needed money 'to keep the *Northern Star* on its legs' may not appear so extraordinary. As for the timing of this trip, there was probably little choice; O'Connor had just been released on bail at Manchester and had to reappear at the Queens Bench on 7 November. It may be that he also had some interest at this time in the sale of Connerville, his father's old estate.[21] Thus there were substantial reasons for O'Connor's return to Ireland. The movement was in need of finances, as was O'Connor, and with a lull in Chartist activity October might well have seemed an appropriate moment to try to rouse Irish agitation. However, O'Connor's motives at this time must remain a matter of historical speculation. Nor should this preclude the possibility that he left the country in order to allow a very confused situation to clarify itself, particularly as he found it increasingly difficult to provide the movement with direction in autumn 1839.

His departure drew little contemporary Chartist comment, except in the editorial columns of the *Champion* which was in conflict with O'Connor over a range of leadership issues. The *Champion* charged that his visit to Ireland was occasioned by conciliatory overtures from O'Connell, and accused O'Connor of seeking a self-interested accommodation with Whiggery; at the same time, the *Champion* urged an anti-Whig alliance between Chartists and Tories.[22] The *Champion* also reminded readers of O'Connor's promise at the torchlight meetings to have universal suffrage by Michaelmas day, and implied that he was now afraid to face the Lancashire working class. The *Champion* posed the general question of the extent to which O'Connor's earlier rhetoric had raised expectations of violent confrontation and created an atmosphere which encouraged revolutionary plotting. Thus, following the Welsh rising, the paper asserted: 'These Monmouth men are Mr. O'Connor's victims!'[23] John Jackson, the veteran Bradford radical who became one of O'Connor's sternest critics, later maintained: 'I do not think, and I frankly avow it, that O'Connor did betray Frost in the light [John] Watkins has it; but I do believe that he most woefully deceived him by his false representations of the "preparedness and determination of the men of the North" . . .'[24] Yet Frost never accused O'Connor of either betraying or misleading him, and throughout his life retained a deep friendship and affection for O'Connor.[25]

To such charges O'Connor replied that although he advocated arming for self-defence, that he had always expressed a clear recognition of the unarmed state of the working class.[26] Still, there can be little doubt that the threatening platform campaign to which he gave a lead and the contingent strategy of open intimidation were by nature ambiguous and open to misconstruction. However, the logic of O'Connor's strategy had stressed the importance of the development of spontaneous retaliatory action. In this he sought not only a powerful legitimating force, but a means to overcome the tremendous difficulties of national communication and organisation which the abortive risings illustrated only too well. Finally, it must be stressed again that O'Connor was a national leader committed to open national protest. As Dorothy Thompson has noted, the risings were community orientated; had they spread, the responsibilities of leadership would have fallen upon local leaders like Bussey, Richardson and Fletcher rather than leaders such as O'Connor, O'Brien or even Harney.[27] It is by no means clear that rank-and-file Chartists expected O'Connor to play this role, or held him responsible for Frost's fate. Thus, when he came to Barnsley in 1842 and 1843 to face William Ashton's charges concerning the risings, local Chartists and their leaders — in a district deeply involved in the plans for insurrection — sided with O'Connor and rejected the accusations of a much respected local radical leader.[28]

O'Connor returned to England on 2 November, two days prior to the Welsh rising, and on 4 November embarked upon his promised tour of Lancashire, speaking at a Manchester meeting to commemorate the birthday of Hunt. Two days later, with the first news of Newport coming in, he spoke at Oldham. Careful not to pass judgement upon the actions of the Welsh Chartists, placing the blame for the events at Newport upon a system of government which excluded working-class representation, he firmly reiterated his own resolve to act with caution. He had no intention of being forced to lead an unarmed people against a disciplined military force.

> My proper place is with the people, to remain with them; at the same time I should be guilty of high treason to them, if I were to present an unarmed, undisciplined mass of men, to an armed and disciplined army. (Hear, hear.) I think that, though you may be degraded and oppressed, when the widow returned to her desolate hut, and found that her husband had been laid low through me, she would indeed weep tears of blood, and would curse the man who had brought her to that situation. (Hear, hear.) Therefore, I have my wits about me; no irritated followers shall ever make me take a false step, or any step that I would not take in the full possession of my cool judgement. But as soon as ever I see a lane or a road, be it wide or narrow, that seems likely to lead to Universal Suffrage, then the man who gets to the bottom sooner than I do, I will

admit has a stronger claim upon your confidence. (Applause.)

This was to remain O'Connor's position throughout the coming months. He also took the opportunity again to emphasise the paramount need to convene another convention — 'for if we looked at the occurrences of the day, we see that it is only organised bodies that can act with effect'.[29]

With the arrest of the Welsh leaders O'Connor again had a cause around which to rally the national movement. Paradoxically the Welsh insurrection reopened the field of constitutional protest. Thus O'Connor immediately embarked upon an extensive speaking tour throughout the northern districts to raise funds and organise a mass campaign to save Frost. He appealed to Chartists:

> are we to remain idle spectators, while the officers and agents of the Crown are busily engaged in the work of destruction? Is liberty to be kept down by the swords — are its friends to be tied like dogs to swing in the air? No forbid it, nature — forbid it working men. What then becomes our duty? Again I say to strain every point for the liberation of Frost.[30]

He explained the high cost of a defence before a Special Commission and the advantages which this mode of legal procedure afforded the government. He called upon the working class to release funds held by their societies and clubs, offering his personal guarantee of repayment along with a higher interest rate until the money could be repaid through national subscriptions. He also levied a penny donation on readers of the *Star*, raising the paper's price for 21 December to 5½d and donating the profit from this issue to Frost's defence. O'Connor insisted 'that in the first instance' they must 'meet the law's quirk by the law's quibble, and to the raising of sufficient funds for that purpose the minds of the working classes should be roused'.[31] Frost could be saved legally.

Conscious that underground plans for insurrection were being formulated, O'Connor repeatedly warned against secret associations and declared that spies were abroad. In a key letter to the *Star* of 7 December, entitled 'The "Liberal" System of Espionage', he raised the spectre of 1819 and urged that nothing be done which might jeopardise Frost's legal chances. Ominously he noted that he had 'learned much since my arrival in London as to the plans of some infernal devils'. He referred Chartists to the authority of Hunt who had warned the radicals of 1819: 'Our enemies cannot openly beat us, but our friends may secretly do it.' O'Connor wrote: 'I caution you, again and again, against those who give exaggerated accounts of the spirit of one locality to the people of another locality.' He assured Chartists that reports that London was in an advanced state of preparedness were utterly false, and concluded:

> My friends, so long as I live, no man nor society shall dupe you, without being fully exposed; and now I tell you, that many emissaries are actually employed by the Government to entrap and then destroy you. Not a single move is taken that the Government is not apprised of and party to. . . . mark my word, beware![32]

James Harrison's role at Bradford bore out this warning only too well.[33] Yet an extensive underground network continued to exist following the Welsh rising, with local militants constantly travelling between the North East, Yorkshire, Lancashire, Nottinghamshire, Birmingham, Wales and London.[34]

The dismal failure at Newport and the agitation to save Frost highlighted the need to reconstruct some form of national Chartist leadership body. Thus while O'Connor assumed the responsibility for saving Frost in terms of an almost personal crusade, he used his enormous influence to push persistantly for the formation of another National Convention.[35] This priority corresponded with a growing sense among local Chartists that such a move was now necessary and again possible. In fact prior to the Welsh rising, the Newcastle Chartists had initiated a plan for a district convention and made contact with other districts about holding similar conventions in their localities.[36] Dr Taylor, who had been and was to remain deeply involved in the plans for insurrection, was a prime mover in these plans to convene another convention. His tone, in contrast to that of O'Connor, remained that of an intransigent revolutionary. Therefore, while there was now a convergence between the two leaders upon the need for another convention, their objectives remained in opposition. Whereas O'Connor saw the convention as a means for establishing permanent national Chartist organisation, preventing partial outbreaks and coordinating an open and legal movement to save Frost, Taylor and many local militants envisaged the convention primarily as the coordinating body for a revolution which they regarded as the only means of saving Frost. Thus Taylor wrote to his confidante, Mary Ann Groves — secretary of the Birmingham Female Political Union — following the Newcastle Convention:

> *Frost shall not be tried*, or will have companions he little thinks of, keep this in mind and be astonished at nothing, depend upon it there

will be a merry Christmas, all here are already preparing for a national illumination, I presume in anticipation of the Queens Marriage but you know best: these Radicals are terrible fellows, at least half a dozen Emissaries have been sent to see what state the North of England was in and the universal feeling is that there is no Country like xxxx, this is partly to be attributed to the vast extent of Moorland which has generated a race of hardy Poachers all well armed, and who would think themselves disgraced if they missed a moorcock flying seventy yards off; this together with the number of Weavers necessarily in want has made a population ripe for action and its Neighbourhood to the Scottish border, with the facilities for a guerrilla warfare, are said to have xxxx to make it the Headquarters for a winter campaign . . .

Taylor dismissed as useless O'Connor's attempts to raise funds for Frost's defence, and related:

It is said your Irish Friend O'Connor, has proved himself the coward his enemies always called him, and having before betrayed the men of England in the matter of the strikes has now refused to take part with the men of his own county (Yorkshire) — he is agitating for money to pay lawyers, as if money could save Frost when he knows that every Lawyer would give ten years Briefs to hang him, if it is to be done at all, other means must be used and the Chartists are not worth the name of men if they don't try them.[37]

Taylor's letter is one of the few documents existent which provides an insight into the private thinking of the insurrectionary wing of the Chartist movement in winter 1839; it also establishes that O'Connor was approached even before the second Convention with plans for insurrection and refused his cooperation.

The District and Border Convention which met at the beginning of December was attended by delegates not only from the North East but Yorkshire, Wales and Edinburgh. The most important decision to emerge from this Newcastle meeting was to call another convention in London for 19 December. The West Riding delegate reported that 'his people were determined to persevere, and they were determined that Frost should not be sacrificed'.[38] The objectives of saving Frost and obtaining the Charter by force merged in the winter of 1839. While ostensibly the Newcastle Convention, the Manchester delegates meeting held on 10 December and the London Convention were concerned with raising money for Frost and petitioning the Queen, plans were also being formulated for insurrection.[39] Unlike the first Convention the delegates to the second Convention were local working-class militants held strictly accountable to the local movement. The second Convention was not conceived as a permanent organisation, but was only to meet for three weeks. It was closely linked to the underground movement throughout the country, particularly to the northern delegates committee at Dewsbury. The West Riding delegates meeting of 12 December decided to send three representatives to London from Bradford, Dewsbury and Sheffield—all localities involved in the 'after risings'. The Convention was also attended by delegates from Bolton, Hull, Newcastle, Nottingham, Surrey and Tower Hamlets. Dr Taylor did not attend the Convention, but remained in the North waiting for instructions; however, Major Beniowski was the Tower Hamlets delegate.[40]

O'Connor did not attend the London Convention, but continued addressing meetings and raising funds for Frost in the North. His relationship to the second Convention was ambiguous. The Dewsbury Chartists, no doubt in an attempt to tie O'Connor to the plans for insurrection, actually elected him as their delegate to the Convention. When the Dewsbury deputation, Samuel Allatt and William Fox, waited upon O'Connor on 16 December, he accepted the trust, but told them that he was occupied totally until after Christmas. O'Connor clearly distrusted those involved at the Convention.[41] Robert Lowery, a delegate to this Convention, later commented:

> F. O'Connor was in London at first, and although he had urged the formation of the Convention he never attended it. Yet he knew its materials, and still took no steps to pacify it or the more desperate committes who had set it up, except that he induced them to draw the £200 which the former body had left in the hands of Mr. Rogers, for the use of the next Convention, and to hand it over to him to be applied in Frost's defence.[42]

Sometime in late December, however, a deputation from the Convention waited upon O'Connor who was in London conferring with Geach, Frost's son-in-law, before travelling to Monmouth to attend Frost's trial. The deputation asked O'Connor why he had not attended the Convention, requested funds and sought his opinion as to what Chartists should do if Frost were convicted. According to Ashton's account, O'Connor told the deputation that should Frost and the others be convicted and their lives endangered, 'he would place himself at the head of the people of England, and have a b___y r_____n to save them'. This was reported to a secret meeting of the Convention held at Southwark at which Ashton was present. Around the same time a messenger was sent from the delegates assembled at Dewsbury to ascertain the determination of the Convention and O'Connor with regard to a rising to save Frost. The messenger was informed that the Convention supported plans for an insurrection and that O'Connor had promised to take the lead. After returning to Dewsbury, the messenger came back to London with the information that the northern radicals had fixed the date for 12 January. A delegate from the Convention was dispatched to Monmouth to inform O'Connor of the decision. The members of the Convention then returned to their respective localities 'to bring the people out'. However instead of the *Star* of 11 January appearing in 'letters of blood', it carried an editorial denouncing the whole plan.[43]

O'Connor's account of these events corresponds with Ashton's basic outline, although differing upon certain details. Most notably O'Connor denied that he told the deputation from the Convention that he was prepared to lead a 'b___y r_____n' to save Frost, but rather that '*I would rather risk my life* than allow Frost to be hung . . .' Whatever his exact words, and the delegates may well have embellished upon them, this highly ambiguous reply allowed for wide interpretation. According to O'Connor, he also gave the deputation twenty-five pounds in order to send the country delegates home. He confirmed that a delegate from the Convention, Henry Ross, related the Convention's decision to him at Monmouth, and added that Ross '*rejoiced that I had no connection with what was going on in the North*'. Ross told him that Dr Taylor was selling commissions and that Major Beniowski was to be the commander-in-chief; O'Connor claimed, '*I cursed the whole gang.*'[44] O'Connor also related, in later years, that in early 1840 Arran (presumably John Arran of Bradford) and Richardson (presumably the Salford Chartist) waited upon him at Manchester and requested him to come to Dewsbury 'at a moment's notice to take command of Mr. Bussey's army', to which he replied, 'it was never my intention to command troops that I did not marshal myself'.[45] The vagueness in this account with regard to date, and the fact that O'Connor appears to have been in Monmouth attending Frost's trial from late December through mid-January, makes it difficult to determine precisely when this interview took place, although it suggests that O'Connor was certainly approached upon several occasions with plans for insurrection and refused his cooperation.[46] Finally, both O'Connor and Dr Taylor mention a meeting between themselves at Leeds which O'Connor dated 'About the time of the Bradford rising' (26 January), and at which Taylor discussed revolutionary plans. According to O'Connor, he told Taylor, 'I always thought you mad, but I'm sure of it now.'[47]

The importance of O'Connor's ownership of the *Northern Star* in determining Chartist policy was again well illustrated in January 1840. Thus the *Star* of 4 January noted with concern that some Chartists were secretly plotting vengeance, and cautioned: 'This is ill-advised in the extreme, and must be everywhere carefully suppressed. The time for big words and loud talking is gone by.' The surest way to see Frost hanged, argued the *Star*, 'is to let us have just now an *emeute* or two in England'. Again Chartists were warned against the activities of government agents who 'like spirits of darkness, flitting and gliding from place to place with stealthy steps' were plotting their destruction.[48] The *Star* of 11 January, which was published the day before the date set for the intended risings and which carried news of Frost's conviction, recommended peaceful, constitutional action as the only means to save Frost, and warned that those involved in plans for risings 'will find themselves most awfully deceived', as the government was prepared to meet them.

> Is it not evident, that however quietly and silently the 'movement party' may be preparing, the authorities know every 'movement', and are just as quietly and silently preparing to receive them.
>
> We tell them that they are everyman sold; that every single meeting of their committees and their delegates is faithfully reported to those who only wait the 'time' to 'give a good account of them.'[49]

This finished any serious prospects for an extensive insurrection, although abortive risings took place at Sheffield and Dewsbury.[50] Chartists in the localities preparing for insurrection had expected the *Star* to appear printed in red as an open signal for national revolt. For instance, at Barnsley, it was reported:

> as it is well known that preparations have been going on for some time, in the event of Frost being convicted. . . . But on Sunday, when the *Northern Star* came out, with a recommendation to peace and quietness, many Chartists were at a loss to know the meaning of such advice, as they expected seeing one portion of the paper being printed in red, no doubt as a signal for blood.[51]

In fact, the position of O'Connor and Hill had remained consistently opposed to secret meetings and underground preparations for insurrection, and although recommendations to arm continued, it was always stressed that the Chartists were in no position to confront the military.[52] What remained in question was the kind of leadership O'Connor might be prepared to offer in the event of Frost's conviction or, more importantly, the certain prospect of his execution. However, he always felt that Frost had been 'trapped' into leading the Welsh rising, and was determined not to be forced into a similar tragic situation. Clearly O'Connor believed that Frost could be saved through legal tactics combined with mass constitutional protest, and this perspective determined his relationship to the revolutionaries in the country. Nor was this policy ill-conceived, if the priority were merely to save Frost's life. Although he had no illusions about the class nature of British justice, O'Connor was aware of the strict definition of high treason and the difficulties involved in proving such a charge, as well as the potential which the scrupulous regard for legal technicalities in such cases afforded the defence.[53] Indeed, Frost was very nearly acquitted at Monmouth: first on a minor legal technicality which provided the basis for an appeal following the decision at Monmouth, and then, when the Lord Chief Justice Tindal summed up for an acquittal.[54] O'Connor had no intention of giving a lead to insurrection in early January, while there remained a chance that Frost might be saved on appeal. He acted with a sense of responsibility both to the movement in the country and to Frost and his comrades. Sir Frederick Pollock, Frost's lawyer, assured O'Connor that the government would not execute Frost.[55] It should also be remembered that in August 1839, the Chartist campaign to save Howell, Jones and Roberts, sentenced to death for their part in the Bull Ring riots, had been successful. Along with Pitkeithley and Richardson, O'Connor called on Chartists to convene public meetings to memorialise the Queen to grant mercy; and the following week O'Connor called for a delegates meeting to assemble at Manchester to discuss the best plan of action for saving Frost. As he never failed to point out, Frost was not executed, although by 28 January he felt the government was determined to hang Frost.[56] In fact, on 29 January, the Whig Cabinet decided that Frost, Williams and Jones must be executed as an example to the country. The Welsh Chartists were saved neither by Pollock's private pleading with Melbourne nor the mass protest of the Chartist movement, but rather by the last minute intervention of the Lord Chief Justice.[57]

As the final abortive rising at Bradford on 26-27 January illustrated, the insurrectionary spirit was still alive in the northern Chartist localities.[58] The conviction that Frost should not be hanged without some form of retribution upon the ruling class was widespread.[59] The scale and immediacy of the working-class response throughout the country following the news of the death sentences attest to the symbolic significance placed upon Frost's fate, as a measure of the limits of Whig tyranny. At Birmingham more than thirty thousand signatures were collected in six days for a petition to pardon Frost; at

Oldham eighteen thousand signatures were collected in two days; at Sunderland seventeen thousand signatures were collected in three days; at Aberdeen fifteen thousand within three days.[60] The commutation of the death sentences to transportation for life, on 1 February, defused a potentially violent situation, and almost certainly had a profound influence upon the development of working-class radicalism and the nature of social conflict over the next decade. As Dorothy Thompson has commented: 'This act of the government . . . raised doubts about the fundamental violence of the authorities, and also appeared to be the result of peaceful constitutional pressure.'[61] February 1840 marked the end of the first phase of Chartist protest. Despite the substantial achievements of the following decade, Chartism lost something of its earlier spontaneity, optimism and mass support. Never again would Chartism quite recapture the widespread conviction that the achievement of working-class political power was within its immediate grasp, or the feeling of a mass willingness to risk all in a final confrontation to overthrow corrupt government and a system of economic and social oppression. The tone of Chartism changed.

The months between the commutation of Frost's death sentence and O'Connor's imprisonment, in May 1840, marked the reemergence of the mass platform and the first moves towards the reorganisation of the Chartist movement. Within forty-eight hours of an appeal from O'Connor, a large delegates' conference assembled at Manchester, on 3-4 February, and despite an almost universal resolve never to petition Parliament again, the conference adopted O'Connor's recommendation to convene mass demonstrations throughout the country to memorialise the Queen for a free pardon for Frost, Williams and Jones.[62] Following the heady days of August 1839, Chartism had abandoned the mass platform in favour of smaller, more intimate meetings of local hard-core activists, held at the beershop, committee room or homes of class leaders. Suffering from the large-scale arrest of leaders and severe repression by local authorities, the movement had turned in upon itself. In February 1840, Chartism again exhibited its self-confidence, mass support and vitality, as the movement took to the platform in a petition campaign in support of the Welsh martyrs.[63] At the Manchester conference and at the local meetings, O'Connor's standing as the movement's acknowledged national leader was reaffirmed and a debt of gratitude expressed for his exertions on behalf of the Welsh leaders. Frost, Williams and

Jones were transported, but the agitation for their return continued throughout the Chartist years, and in early 1840 provided a cause around which the movement could rally. O'Connor still rejected the strategy of launching another campaign to petition Parliament for universal suffrage, although he called for simultaneous meetings on Easter Monday to petition the Queen to dismiss her present ministers for a government pledged to making universal suffrage a cabinet issue, and for the return of the Welsh leaders and the release of all political prisoners.[64] There was little alternative to a petitioning campaign linked to the mass platform as a means of mobilising Chartism's mass strength.

Delegates meetings, or 'conventions', were held in March and April 1840, at Manchester and Nottingham, to discuss the reorganisation and direction of the Chartist movement, along with the question of Frost's cause; however, the movement in the country was at a low ebb and neither convention was well attended nor able to produce a plan for national reorganisation. O'Connor supported both conventions, but attended neither, as he was preoccupied with his own defence against government prosecution.[65] However, the direction outlined by O'Connor and the *Star* clearly stressed the paramount necessity to organise a united movement which in itself would obviate the need for 'physical-force' measures.

> aggressive violence would ruin all . . . There is in moral force a mighty engine, whose power is irresistible for good; this engine has never been adequately worked . . . We have never yet seen the full development of political combination. Many partial attempts have been made, but they have all failed, because no one course of action has been universal. . . . With such an unanimity, no physical force will be required.[66]

The theoretical position was not new, but the tone had changed. At the Manchester Convention, in March, there was discontent among certain delegates with O'Connor's recent strictures upon the use of force. Nottingham's delegate, George Black, told the Convention that many of his constituents had sold their coats to purchase arms and would welcome a call for a national holiday: 'he would rather die by the sword than perish with hunger'. Black maintained that 'physical force' had not as yet been fairly tried. Black's insurrectionist tone was distinctly out of tune with the spirit of the movement, although supported by the more militant of the radical East Midlands stockingers.[67] The *Northern Liberator* commented: 'this is not policy but dispair'.[68] The general consensus both at the Convention and in most Chartist localities was in agreement with O'Connor—reorganisation, not revolution, was the order of the day. And in many localities the task of reorganisation had already begun by the spring of 1840.

Chartist trials continued through the early spring. O'Connor came up for trial at York assizes in mid-March to face charges of seditious libel for speeches, his own and those of other Chartist leaders, published in the *Star*.[69] Trial and imprisonment provided the acid test of Chartist leadership and commitment. The trial of Chartism's most prominent national leader naturally acquired particular symbolic importance, as O'Connor made the issue of his personal fate and confrontation with authority the focus of national Chartist opinion. O'Connor envisaged his trial as an occasion upon which to redeem his oft-repeated pledge never to desert the working-class cause, and to reaffirm an uncompromising dedication to Chartist principle. His defence stood as a form of guarantee against apostacy; his persecution constituted a form of shared experience with the working class.[70] Defending himself (the Attorney General led the prosecution), O'Connor opened his address to the jury with the observation that he looked for an acquittal not in court, but in the country.

> Gentlemen of the Jury, in the outset let us understand each other. We are of different politics. I neither court your sympathy, desire your pity, or ask for your compassion. I am a Chartist — a democrat to the fullest extent of the word; and if my life hung upon the abandonment of those principles, I would scorn to hold it upon so base a tenure.

His defence was a model of its kind, rooted in an established radical tradition of defiant opposition to government prosecution. His address which lasted nearly five hours was marked by a firmness and dignity with which even the judge was impressed. Combining the talents of the barrister with those of the platform orator, O'Connor moved from points of law and constitutional history to an eloquent condemnation of the Whigs. There was never any doubt that he would be found guilty by the special jury, although O'Connor's request to have his sentencing deferred until after the Liverpool assizes at which he was also bound to appear was granted.[71] From defeat O'Connor snatched a form of moral victory for Chartism. Following the trial he commented: 'I shall console myself with the reflection that I have perfumed the whole atmosphere with a scent — the essence of Chartism. Every day at York was a Chartist meeting, with a judge in the chair. . . .'[72] O'Connor laboured diligently to transform his trial and imprisonment, as well as that of other Chartists, into a focal point of national Chartist unity. Despite the set-backs of 1839-40, O'Connor retained the confidence of Chartism's rank and file. His conduct towards Frost and his own defence at York won widespread respect for his leadership and provided inspiration for a movement which had suffered temporary defeat.

O'Connor was sentenced to eighteen months imprisonment in May 1840. In a series of parting addresses he outlined the achievement of Chartism's early years — the national unity forged within the ranks of working-class radicalism — and pointed to the successes which lay ahead. He prevailed upon Chartists not to be duped into the ranks of middle-class reformers, but to stand firm to their class and universal suffrage. Weary and in poor health, but with characteristic optimism and fortitude, he raised the famous slogan 'UNIVERSAL SUFFRAGE AND NO SURRENDER'.[73] While the Whigs had avoided resorting to the measures of political repression adopted by Castlereagh and Sidmouth, nonetheless, by the spring of 1840 over five hundred Chartists had been sent to prison.[74] Yet, in contrast to the history of earlier working-class movements, the removal of Chartism's national leadership and many of its local militants did not precipitate the collapse of radicalism. When the 'People's Champion' emerged from York Castle in September 1841, he was greeted by a mass movement, a movement which during his imprisonment had laid the foundations of the first working-class political party in world history.

NOTES

1. E. P. Thompson, *The Making of the English Working Class*, Penguin ed., Harmondsworth 1968, p. 735; also see J. C. Belchem, 'Republicanism, popular constitutionalism and the radical platform in early nineteenth-century England', *Social History*, 6, 1981, pp. 1-32.

2. *Southern Star*, 26 Jan. 1840, p. 1.

3. *NS*, 31 Aug. 1839, p. 4; 14 Sept., p. 7; 21 Sept., p. 6; 28 Sept., pp. 4-6; 5 Oct., p. 4.

4. Ibid., 28 Sept. 1839, p. 5; 28 Dec., p. 8.

5. For instance, among the West Riding, Newcastle and Glasgow Chartists. *NS*, 5 Oct. 1839, pp. 1, 5, 8; 26 Oct., p. 1.

6. *Champion*, 29 Sept. 1839, pp. 4, 5. For differences between the Cobbettites and O'Connor at this time, see *Champion* 1 Sept.-6 Oct. 1839; *NS* 21 Sept.-12 Oct. 1839.

7. *NS*, 24 Aug. 1839, p. 2; 21 Sept., p. 6; *Sheffield Iris*, 24 Sept. 1839.

8. D. Williams, *John Frost: A Study in Chartism*, Cardiff 1939, ch. 7; id., 'Chartism in Wales', in 'A. Briggs (ed.), *Chartist Studies*, London 1959; A. J. Peacock, *Bradford Chartism, 1838-1840*, York 1969, pp. 28 ff; also see A. R. Schoyen, 'George Julian Harney', (London Univ. PhD thesis, 1951), Appendix I.

9. *NS*, 10 Aug. 1839, p. 4; 3 Aug., p. 8; also see O'Brien's comments, *British Statesman*, 5 Nov. 1842, p. 1.

10. A Somerville, *Cobdenic Policy, the Internal Enemy of England*, London 1854, pp. 29-30; *NS*, 3 May 1845, pp. 6-7.

11. D. Urquhart, *The Chartist Correspondence*, Sheffield 1856; Balliol College

Library, Urquhart Bequest MSS, series 1E; R. Lowery, 'Passages in the Life of a Temperance Lecturer', in B. Harrison and P. Hollis (eds.), *Robert Lowery: Radical and Chartist*, London 1979, pp. 155-57. Dr Taylor gave his account in a letter to Lovett, Birmingham Reference Library, Lovett Collection, II, Taylor to Lovett, 10 June 1841. One of Hetherington's shop assistants informed the Home Office that he had learned of the plans for an insurrection from the Welsh delegate Charles Jones, noting 'it seems generally known among the Chartist leaders that an outbreak would take place . . .' PRO, HO 40/44, fos. 958-59, R. T. Edwards to HO, 6 Nov. 1839.

12. Lowery, 'Passages', *Robert Lowery*, p. 155; R. G. Gammage, *History of the Chartist Movement, 1837-1854*, Newcastle 1894 ed., p. 267.

13. *NS*, 29 Feb. 1840, p. 1.

14. F. O'Connor, *A Reply to John Watkins's Charges*, London 1843, p. 17; *NS*, 23 Apr. 1841, p. 1; 3 May 1845, p. 7; also see Napier's observations, W. F. P. Napier, *The Life and Opinions of Sir C. J. Napier*, London 1857, II, pp. 88-89; G. D. H. Cole, *Chartist Portraits*, London 1965 ed., pp. 150-52.

15. *NS*, 17 May, 1845, p. 6.

16. Ibid., 5 Oct. 1839, p. 5; 2 Nov., p. 2; W. Lovett, *Life and Struggles of William Lovett*, Fitzroy ed., London 1967, pp. 197-98; Peacock, *Bradford Chartism*, pp. 30-33; also see Bussey's letter in *Leeds Times*, 16 Jan. 1841, p. 7; and Hobson's account in *Manchester Examiner*, 2 Jan. 1848, in which he claims that he took steps which prevented three risings in Yorkshire towns around the time of Newport.

17. *NS*, 23 Nov. 1839, p. 4.

18. O'Connor, *Reply to Watkins's Charges*, p. 17; also see *NS*, 23 Apr. 1842, p. 1; 3 May 1845, p. 6.

19. *NS*, 5 Oct. 1839, p. 4; 29 Dec. 1838, p. 8; 9 Feb. 1839, p. 4; 9 Nov., p. 7; Lowery, 'Passages', *Robert Lowery*, pp. 144-48.

20. *Southern Reporter*, 3 Oct. 1839, pp. 1, 2; 19 Oct., p. 2; *Constitution, or Cork Advertiser*, 3 Oct. 1839, p. 2; 19 Oct., p. 2; 22 Oct., p. 2; *NS*, 19 Oct. 1839, pp. 1, 4; 26 Oct., p. 1; 2 Nov., p. 3; 9 Nov., p. 7. For the situation in Ireland, see W. J. Fitzpatrick, *Correspondence of Daniel O'Connell*, London 1888, II, p. 204.

21. *NS*, 28 Sept. 1839, p. 6; 5 Oct., p. 4; 19 Oct., p. 4; *Southern Reporter*, 22 Oct. 1839, p. 1; *Constitution, or Cork Advertiser*, 5 Oct. 1839, p. 2.

22. *Champion*, 13 Oct.-15 Dec. 1839; *NS*, 19 Oct. 1839, p. 3; 2 Nov., p. 4; 23 Nov., p. 4; *Manchester and Salford Advertiser*, 23 Nov. 1839, p. 3; *Southern Reporter*, 3 Oct. 1839, pp. 1-2.

23. *Champion*, 13 Oct. 1839, p. 1; 27 Oct., pp. 4-5; 24 Nov., pp. 1; 8 Dec., p. 1. Chartists in some of the most militant northern localities, however, came to O'Connor's defence. *NS*, 26 Oct.-23 Nov. 1839; *Manchester and Salford Advertiser*, 9 Nov. 1839, p. 2; *Regenerator*, 26 Oct. 1839, pp. 9, 10; *Scottish Vindicator*, Nov. 1839, p. 27.

24. John Jackson, *The Demagogue Done Up*, Bradford 1844, p. 20.

25. Williams, *John Frost*, p. 201; id., 'Chartism in Wales', p. 242; *NS*, 15 May 1841, p. 8; 22 May, p. 1.

26. *NS*, 2 Nov. 1839, p. 4.

27. D. Thompson, *The Early Chartists*, London 1971, p. 21.

28. *NS*, 23 Apr. 1842, p. 1; 21 May, p. 8; 19 Aug. 1843, p. 1; 3 May 1845, p. 7.

29. Ibid., 9 Nov. 1839, p. 1. O'Connor did not return to Leeds until 6 November, when Hill related Ashton's information.

30. *NS*, 16 Nov. 1839, p. 4.

31. Ibid., 16 Nov.-7 Dec. 1839; 30 Nov. 1839, p. 6 (quotation). O'Connor immediately advanced one-thousand pounds for Frost's defence.

32. *NS*, 7 Dec. 1839, p. 4; also see 16 Nov., p. 4; 30 Nov., p. 6. The government was opening letters to Taylor, Harney, James Arthur, Cardo, Robert Peddie and other key leaders. PRO, HO 79/4, fo. 237.

33. See PRO, TS 11/813; HO 40/51; Robert Peddie, *The Dungeon Harp*, Edinburgh 1844, pp. 6-14. The underground movement was thoroughly infiltrated both at

Birmingham and London. See HO 40/50; 40/44; 40/43, for spies' reports from Manchester.

34. See PRO, HO 40/43-46; 40/50-51; 40/56; 65/10; TS 11/813; 11/815-16; Cardiff City Library, Bute Papers, XX. I am indebted to Dr D. J. V. Jones for references from this last source.

35. *NS*, 23 Nov. 1839, p. 3.

36. *Northern Liberator*, 12 Oct. 1839, p. 5; 19 Oct., p. 5; 2 Nov., pp. 5-6; 9 Nov., p. 5; 23 Nov., p. 5; *NS*, 2 Nov., p. 6; 16 Nov., p. 3; 30 Nov., pp. 3, 5; *Charter*, 10 Nov. 1839, p. 667.

37. Balliol College Library, Urquhart MSS, 1E1, fos. 15-16, letter dated 8 Dec. 1839, reproduced in *Chartist Correspondence*, pp. 3-4. Also see Birmingham Reference Library, Lovett Collection, II, fo. 5, Taylor to Lovett, 10 June 1841; J. Taylor, *The Coming Revolution*, Carlisle 1840 (copy in PRO, HO 40/57).

38. *Northern Liberator*, 7 Dec. 1839, p. 7; *Charter*, 8 Dec. 1839, p. 721; *NS*, 7 Dec. 1839, pp. 1, 4; 14 Dec., p. 4.

39. *NS*, 21 Dec. 1839, p. 2, for Manchester conference; Peacock, *Bradford Chartism*, p. 35, n 228.

40. *NS*, 21 Dec. 1839, pp. 4, 7; 21 Dec., p. 1; 28 Dec., p. 5; 4 Jan. 1840, p. 5; 18 Jan., p. 7; *Northern Liberator*, 14 Dec. 1839, pp. 5, 7; 21 Dec., pp. 1, 6; 28 Dec., p. 6; *Manchester and Salford Advertiser*, 18 Jan. 1840, p. 3; *Bolton Free Press*, 21 Dec. 1839, p. 3; Peacock, *Bradford Chartism*, pp. 35-36.

41. *NS*, 21 Dec. 1839, p. 5; 3 May 1845, p. 6; PRO, HO 40/51, fo. 697, Bradford magistrates to HO, 17 Dec. 1839.

42. 'Passages', *Robert Lowery*, p. 158.

43. *NS*, 3 May 1845, p. 6; T. A. Devyr, *Old Book of the Nineteenth Century*, New York 1882, pp. 199-200; Peacock, *Bradford Chartism*, pp. 35-37. According to Lowery, the decision for insurrection was taken not at the Convention but by the northern committees.

44. *NS*, 3 May 1845, p. 6.

45. Ibid., 6 May 1848, p. 1; *National Instructor*, 4 Sept. 1850, p. 66. Lovett's account of the meeting between a northern delegate and O'Connor must have taken place around this time. Similarly, Thomason, the Newcastle Chartist, confused the pre- and post-Newport attempts at insurrection, but refers to O'Connor's 'betrayal of the Dewsbury Chartists'. W. Thomason, *O'Connor and Democracy Inconsistent with Each Other*, Newcastle 1844, p. 8.

46. Frost's trial opened on 31 December and lasted until 6 January; Williams and Jones's trial followed and sentencing took place on 16 January. O'Connor was speaking at Middleton as late as 25 December and returned from Monmouth on 19 January. I have found no reference to him returning to England during the trial.

47. *NS*, 3 May 1845, p. 5; Birmingham Reference Library, Lovett Collection, II, fo. 5, Taylor to Lovett.

48. *NS*, 4 Jan. 1840, p. 4; also see 28 Dec. 1839, p. 4.

49. Ibid., 11 Jan. 1840, p. 4. Both editorials were penned by Hill who later claimed there was much ill-will directed against him from the Dewsbury Chartists in particular. *NS*, 3 May, 1845, p. 6.

50. *Sheffield Iris*, 14 Jan. 1840, pp. 2-3; 21 Jan., pp. 2-4; *NS*, 18 Jan. 1840, p. 4; Devyr, *Old Book*, pp. 200, 204-05; Peacock, *Bradford Chartism*, pp. 37-39; J. L. Baxter, 'Early Chartism and Labour Class Struggle: South Yorkshire 1837-40', in S. Pollard and C. Holmes (eds.), *Essays in the Economic and Social History of South Yorkshire*, Barnsley 1976, pp. 146-50.

51. *Leeds Mercury*, 18 Jan. 1840, p. 5. O'Connor had told Chartists: 'if they did pass sentence upon John Frost, on the Saturday following the *Star* should appear on one side in red ink — the other side in dark mourning'. *NS*, 7 Dec. 1839, p. 1.

52. *NS*, 25 Jan. 1840, pp. 4, 5; 21 Mar., p. 4.

53. Ibid., 25 Jan. 1840, p. 5, 'The Welsh Patriots and the Value of the Law'.

54. See Williams, *John Frost*, ch. 8.

55. *NS*, 3 May 1845, p. 6; Williams, *John Frost*, pp. 286, 293.

56. *NS*, 25 Jan. 1840, p. 5; 1 Feb., pp. 4-5, 7-8; 8 Feb., p. 1.

57. Lord Broughton, *Recollections of a Long Life*, (ed. Lady Dorchester), London 1909, V, pp. 240-45; Williams, *John Frost*, pp. 290-95. The Welsh rising had taken the government by surprise and the determination to execute the leaders may have reflected genuine fears of Chartist insurrection. The Whigs also had come under heavy Tory criticism for their handling of the Chartists. See L. C. Sanders (ed.), *Lord Melbourne Papers*, London, 2nd ed. 1890, pp. 407-08, Melbourne to Russell, 6 Nov. 1839; Cambridge Univ. Library, Graham MSS (microfilm), Peel to Graham, 8 Nov. 1839; Graham to Stanley, 25 Nov. 1839.

58. Peacock, *Bradford Chartism*, pp. 39-46.

59. See Napier's comments, *Life and Opinions*, II, p. 95; also PRO, HO 40/43, fo. 806, Shaw to HO, 13 Dec. 1839. Devyr claimed the feeling at Newcastle was: 'The Government has just pronounced its own sentence. That on John Frost will never be executed.' *Odd Book*, p. 199.

60. *NS*, 8 Feb. 1840, p. 2; *Manchester and Salford Advertiser*, 15 Feb. 1840, p. 2; *Northern Liberator*, 1 Feb. 1840, p. 1; *Aberdeen People's Journal*, 26 Feb. 1887, cited D. Thompson, *Early Chartists*, n 60; *Hansard*, Parl. Debates, 3rd Series, LII, 10 Mar. 1840, col. 1135.

61. D. Thompson, 'Chartism as a Historical Subject', *Bulletin of the Society for the Study of Labour History*, no. 20, 1970, p. 12; id., *Early Chartists*, p. 27.

62. *NS*, 8 Feb. 1840, p. 1; *Northern Liberator*, 14 Feb. 1840, p. 7; PRO, HO 40/54, fos. 595-98, 599-602, 615-18, Shaw to Phillipps, 4, 5, 6 Feb. 1840.

63. *NS*, 15 Feb. 1840, pp. 7-8, and 22 Feb., p. 2, reported nearly sixty meetings in support of Frost throughout the country.

64. *NS*, 11 Apr. 1840, p. 4; 25 Apr., pp. 3, 8.

65. Ibid., 7 Mar. 1840, p. 4; 14 Mar., p. 4; 28 Mar., p. 4; 18 Apr., p. 2; *Champion*, 15 Mar. 1840, p. 6; 22 Mar., p. 2; 19 Apr., p. 1; *Northern Liberator*, 25 Apr. 1840, p. 3; *Nottingham Review*, 10 Apr. 1840, p .3.

66. *NS*, 22 Feb. 1840, p. 4.

67. Ibid., 14 Mar. 1840, pp. 4, 7; *Champion*, 22 Mar. 1840, pp. 2, 4; 29 Mar., p. 8; *Southern Star*, 29 Mar. 1840, p. 7; PRO, HO 40/55, fos. 59-62, Heyrick to Phillipps, 16 Mar. 1840.

68. *Northern Liberator*, 28 Mar. 1840, p. 3.

69. PRO, TS 11/813; 11/817, no. 2694.

70. See *NS*, 7 Mar. 1840, p. 4; 11 Apr., p. 4; 16 May, p. 4.

71. Ibid., 21 Mar. 1840, pp. 1, 4-5. O'Connor was tried *ex officio*.

72. Ibid., 21 Mar. 1840, p. 4.

73. Ibid., 21 Mar. 1840, p. 4; 28 Mar., p. 1; 11 Apr., p. 4; 25 Apr., p. 4; 16 May, pp. 4,6.

74. Parl. Papers, 1840, XXXVIII, pp. 691-750; L. Radzinowicz, *A History of English Criminal Law and its Administration*, London 1948-68, IV, pp. 243, 245, 247-51. Perhaps as many Chartists emigrated after 1840. See R. Boston, *British Chartists in America*, Manchester 1971, pp. 17, 35.

6 THE PEOPLE'S CHAMPION AND THE PEOPLE'S PARTY

I The Caged Lion

From May 1840 until late August 1841, Feargus O'Connor remained a prisoner in York Castle. Thus he was in prison during one of the most important periods of Chartist history, that which marked the reorganisation of the national movement and the establishment of the National Charter Association. However, O'Connor hardly remained isolated from developments, nor did imprisonment prevent him from maintaining his position as the movement's most influential leader. On the contrary, it was during this period that O'Connor consolidated his unrivalled ascendancy over the national leadership of Chartism which was to last for nearly another decade.

The image of the radical demagogue was inextricably linked to that of the martyr. No image was more powerful, more calculated to rally and unify the ranks of popular radicalism than that of the martyred patriot. With a characteristically sure sense of the roots of popular radical feeling and the traditions of radical protest, O'Connor used his imprisonment and victimisation as a cause around which to unify working-class support behind his personal claim to leadership. The rhetoric and the mass response were rooted in an established radical tradition associated with champion-style leadership. Before he even entered York Castle, in his farewell address to the Chartists, O'Connor had raised the image of his death. In accounts published in the *Star* and in O'Connor's own addresses from prison the prospect of the death of the people's champion was ever present.[1] However, it was his determination not to be broken, to remain loyal to Chartist principles, and his unequivocal identification with the working class alone which inspired the mass movement. From York Castle echoed that defiant tone which thousands had heard so often from the Chartist platform.

> What! do the villians suppose that I am to be bought or bribed? They have tried it for eight years and failed! No! b___t them! — if my body is dragged down these stone stairs, they shall drag with it the very same principles that I brought here! *They may perhaps find slaves* TO MAKE MERCHANDISE OF MARTYRDOM,— but the country, and not myself, shall have the full benefit of mine. The villians sent me here to murder me! — but . . . *I am to Live* . . .[2]

From prison the tendency to personalise issues of Chartist leadership and policy became more pronounced. While O'Connor often adopted a rather paternalistic tone, more important was his class tone and the image of mutual dependence between the gentleman leader and his working-class following. Thus he addressed his first letter from prison 'To the men with blistered hands, unshorn chins, and fustian jackets — you, who spend your youth in rattle boxes, and your manhood in bastiles; to you, and you only, I address myself.'[3] O'Connor's imprisonment served as a source of shared suffering, bridging the social distance between the gentleman leader and his working-class support.

During his early months in prison constant attention was focused upon O'Connor's conditions of imprisonment—in the Chartist press, from the radical platform and on the floor of the House of Commons. 'FEARGUS▸ O'CONNOR HERDING AND FEEDING WITH CONVICTED FELONS', declared the *Star*'s lead editorial.[4] Although convicted only of a misdemeanour, the only privilege allowed O'Connor beyond that of felons was wearing his own clothes. In the Commons radical MPs such as Duncombe, Wakley, Hume, Warburton, Talfourd and even O'Connell supported the Chartist petitions for improved prison conditions for O'Connor and other Chartist prisoners.[5] The campaign for improved conditions for political prisoners provided an area of contact between such middle-class radicals and Chartists in spring and summer of 1840.

Throughout England and Scotland, local Chartists responded to the *Star*'s call for mass meetings and petitions to support O'Connor.[6] As he had been sent to prison primarily for publishing the speeches of other Chartists, for boldly confronting the Whigs with the truth, the campaign to defend O'Connor was also in defence of the *Northern Star* and the freedom of the press. There was a strong feeling within the Chartist ranks that O'Connor had gone to prison for them, that the Whigs had victimised him as Chartism's most prominent leader and defender. For this reason he became, in a sense, *the* Chartist prisoner. At Rochdale the veteran radical Joshua Haigh took the chair.

> Although advanced in years, the barbarous treatment of O'Connor called forth the wonted energies of youth. He had long been battling in the same cause, and during the whole of his political experience, it had never been his lot to witness a circumstance of such barbarity, not even in the bloody days of Castlereagh and Sidmouth. What crime had their friend committed in their estimation. Doubtless the worst of crimes.

When he first came amongst them, they were weak and disunited, but, through his exertions, they had become enlightened to their country's wrongs and interests. (Loud cheers.)

At Bradford the Chartist lecturer Jonathan Bairstow declared: 'O'Connor was the leading agitator, and, therefore, they had met that day to record their sympathy with him.' The themes of self-sacrifice and steadfastness were integral to the rhetoric associated with the gentleman leader. Thus Alexander Campbell, Glasgow radical, Owenite and trade unionist, drew particular attention to O'Connor's gentlemanly status and the fact that he had chosen to abandon a life of leisure to join with the working class.

He might have lived at home on his property — he might have associated with the rich and with the powerful — but he had nobly thrown aside all considerations of this description to promulgate to his poor and suffering fellow-countrymen the great truth — that all men were born equal.[7]

O'Connor had often reminded working-class radicals that Hunt had been prematurely consigned to the grave through their ingratitude and desertion. The meetings and petitions in support of O'Connor were a symbolic affirmation from the ranks of Chartism that the steadfastness of the people's champion would be matched by the support of the people.

By summer of 1840 most of the restrictions had been lifted upon O'Connor's conditions of imprisonment. He was allowed to furnish his own room — now the best in the prison — to supply his own food, wine, candles and coals, books and newspapers; to keep a menagerie of foreign birds; to receive his own doctors, as well as a virtually unlimited number of visitors, and even to have a turnkey wait on him. Class distinction in Victorian society extended to imprisonment. The only restriction upon which the Home Secretary, Normanby, insisted was that O'Connor not be allowed to write political articles for publication.[8] However, inside prison as outside, O'Connor proved irrepressible: the *Star* of 11 and 18 July 1840 carried pages from his pen which had been smuggled out of prison. From early 1841 O'Connor wrote regularly for the *Star*, although even before this he was able to exert influence over the movement, as he met regularly with Hill and Hobson. O'Connor's ability to keep in contact with the movement, to provide direction at critical junctures and to defend himself against political opponents during his imprisonment through the *Star* was of vital importance to his leadership.

Placed alongside the experience of many Chartist prisoners, particularly those at Yorkshire's Northallerton 'hell-hole', O'Connor suffered little. But while certain Chartist prisoners resented the special attention and treatment accorded O'Connor, the fact that his conditions of imprisonment were relatively comfortable was, in a sense, beside the point.[9] For the importance which O'Connor's imprisonment assumed for most Chartists was symbolic. John Watkins, who had himself suffered imprisonment, later explained that his 'romantic idea of performing a pilgrimage to his [O'Connor's] cell, as to the shrine of a martyred patriot' was motivated by the fact that 'I regarded him as a personification of the Cause; nay, more, I identified him with it . . . I meant to pay [respect] to the principle for which he was imprisoned, and not to the man alone.'[10] A similar motivation lay behind the rash of Chartist christenings throughout the country in 1840-41. O'Connor and Frost were the most popular choice of names for 'young patriots'. This inversion of religious ritual was a conscious political affront to the establishment, an attempt to infuse traditional forms of ritual with radical content.[11] Of course the issuing of the O'Connor 'liberation medals', the banners depicting Hunt's spirit appearing to O'Connor, the eulogistic poetry that came into the *Star* and O'Connor's triumphal entry into York upon his liberation dressed in a suit of green fustian, all harked back to older traditions of popular protest.[12] By summer 1840 the standard way to close a Chartist meeting or dinner was with three cheers for O'Connor and all incarcerated Chartists, Frost, Williams and Jones, and the People's Charter.

The campaign to support O'Connor was part of a much broader campaign on behalf of Chartist prisoners. The Chartist press gave constant attention to the plight of the Chartist prisoners and provided space for letters and petitions from prisoners, their wives and families. The radical movement always found it easiest to unite around campaigns of a defensive character, and the campaign to support O'Connor, Frost and other Chartist prisoners provided an important source of unity and revitalisation in 1840-41. Together with the reorganisation of the national movement, the support of Chartist prisoners was the most important concern of the movement in 1840. Localities which suffered large-scale arrests had to organise funds to help support the wives and families of local victims. Thus the Ashton Chartists toured South Lancashire performing a dramatic production of 'The Trial of Robert Emmet', the proceeds from which went to relieve the families of incarcerated Chartists. The Birmingham

Chartists initiated a national campaign of simultaneous meetings for 1 January 1841, to petition for the return of Frost and the Welsh martyrs. From prison O'Connor called for the convening of the Petition Convention which coordinated the mass petition drive for the release of all Chartist prisoners which collected more signatures than the first National Petition.[13] The release of Chartist leaders in summer of 1840, most notably the release of M'Douall, Lovett and Collins, provided a tremendous impetus to the revival of Chartist agitation. Each successive group of released Chartists was greeted by large meetings and dinners. O'Connor's own release — one of the most elaborate and carefully planned demonstrations of popular support in the history of popular radicalism — and exhaustive tour of triumph throughout England and Scotland served to mark the culmination of one of Chartism's finest achievements: the movement's resilience to government repression.

II The National Charter Association and the Reorganisation of Chartism, 1840-42

Much of the significance of the National Charter Association lies in its claim to have been the first independent political party of the working class in history — in terms of its membership, programme and permanence.[14] The NCA was a national organisation which was to remain the dominant organisational and leadership force in Chartism throughout the rest of the movement's history, although after 1842 its membership and influence waned significantly. In a movement in which the balance between local and national interests always remained a delicate matter, the NCA, together with the leadership of O'Connor and the *Northern Star*, provided an essential source of radical working-class unity and direction. There can be no doubt that the establishment and growth of the NCA marked a major qualitative advance in working-class organisation and leadership.

Chartism had come together in 1838 largely as a platform movement; the platform together with the radical press and existing local working-class associations provided the organisational framework at its birth. In 1839, the National Convention became the major national coordinating force for the movement. Despite the acknowledged break-through represented by the Convention, almost all schemes put forward in the first half of 1840 for the reorganisation of the movement started from the perceived failings of the Convention.

The principal lesson of Chartism's first phase was clear, the movement had been defeated through a lack of organisation and united leadership. In the first issue of his *Chartist and Republican Journal,* M'Douall, one of the most intelligent and forceful advocates for the reorganisation of the movement, maintained:

> In my opinion the real cause of failure has not been sufficiently dwelt upon.
>
> There should have been a power behind the Convention, great enough, terrible enough, to have made it dangerous for the government to arrest the least of its members. . . . A national organisation should have been proceeded or have been simultaneous with the Convention. Then direction, judgement, and energy would have carried the Charter. Our associations were hastily got up, composed of prodigious numbers, a false idea of strength was imparted, and enthusiasm was wrought up to the highest pitch, thence originated a sense of security which subsequent events proved to be false, and why? because no real union existed at the bottom. . . . I refer to these events, my friends, not to blame but to correct, not to dishearten but simply to prevent the recurrence of such misery and ruin by convincing you of that which you will be ready to believe, namely, that we never would have sustained the slightest check in the late movement, if we had begun to unite like men, and to organise like a number of brothers. I implore you to unite, unite, unite! organise, organise, organise![15]

By spring of 1840 the reorganisation of the movement at the district and local level was already well under way, and it was this grass-roots initiative which provided much of the impetus towards national reorganisation. As Hovell commented:

> All things considered, this revival in the spring of 1840 was a remarkable tribute to the vitality of Chartism. The movement was much more localised than in 1839, but within its narrower bounds it was stronger and healthier.[16]

For instance, the Newcastle Chartists reconstituted the Northern Political Union in early April and established a system of Chartist missionaries to agitate the surrounding district. The Carlisle Radical Association was revived; and the Sunderland Chartists met in June to revive the Durham Charter Association. The Birmingham Chartists formed a new association in March and also began to regroup around the Frost Restoration Committee. The Metropolitan Charter Union was an unsuccessful attempt to unite all London Chartist societies into one organisation; however, their proposals for a quarterly elected executive council, collection committees and membership cards, paid lecturers and strict financial accounting, all pointed towards a more highly structured system of organisation. The South Lancashire delegates committee formed a district union and established an extensive system of Chartist lecturers which was in full operation by June; and the West Riding delegates committee, active throughout 1839 and early 1840, continued to meet monthly and discuss the prospects for reorganisation.[17] The South Lancashire and West Riding committees were the leading associations in laying the groundwork for the founding conference of the NCA in July.

The Chartist press was inundated with schemes and calls for national reorganisation in spring and summer of 1840. '[I]t is now a most important duty we have to perform, once more to give our movement its original character — nationality of action', declared the Edinburgh Chartists who recommended that a national delegates conference be convened.[18] Harney, who had been lecturing in Scotland, urged English Chartists to follow the example of the Scottish movement which had been reorganised in late summer of 1839, with an emphasis on the need for a system of paid missionaries, a centralised national leadership body, the dissemination of political knowledge through tracts and mobilisation through continual petitioning campaigns.[19] Harney recommended petitioning, 'Not because I imagine petitioning will get the Charter . . . but . . . as a means of furthering their organisation, and of annoyance to their oppressors . . . it affords a legal excuse for assembling together'. Although he still believed that 'physical force' would be necessary, there was no point in talking of 'physical force' while the movement was disorganised. Harney maintained they should move from district reorganisation towards a national reorganisation. Each district should elect paid delegates or leaders. He rejected the idea 'that a new Convention should be formed to sit like the last, week after week, and month after month, a sort of mock Parliament', but suggested that each county select one or more delegates to meet at critical periods as a national delegate assembly to decide upon matters of policy. From such a national assembly twelve should be selected to sit permanently in Manchester as a 'central committee'; the other delegates would return to their districts to act as full-time Chartist leaders. Harney also gave approval to O'Brien's election plan, but argued that it was only a viable policy if the movement were prepared to act nationally.[20] Despite the diversity of schemes placed before the movement at this time, Harney had touched on the central features of national reorganisation which were to emerge from this exchange and were to find form in the plan of the NCA, namely: a system of paid lecturers; strong district organisation; the need for a national delegates conference rather than a Convention on the 1839 model and a full-time national executive; a commitment to O'Brien's election plan as a means of action.

In June a meeting of the West Riding delegates, called to discuss the plans for reorganisation put forward by Robert Lowery and 'A Republican', proposed that a national delegates conference convene in July at Manchester. The South Lancashire delegates immediately endorsed this proposal. The West Riding delegates also submitted a plan for consideration which stressed the need for another National Convention to sit while Parliament was in session and for a three-man executive to sit between Conventions.[21] Few districts still favoured this type of 'parliamentary' Convention, however; several districts, including London and South Durham, did not even support sending delegates to Manchester.[22] In the *Star* Hill gave full support to the plans for the Manchester conference, quoting O'Connor's opinion that such meetings 'went further to create a good understanding between the various towns than any, or all other methods of communication'. The *Star* urged the conference to adopt some general plan of organisation 'whereby the energies of the people may be rallied, concentrated and directed'. Hill maintained that it was not the role of the 'people's paper' to propose its own plan of organisation, but confined himself to a detailed outline of the law relating to the organisation of political associations.[23]

From prison O'Connor encouraged all districts to send delegates to Manchester. He also offered his own plan for the reorganisation of the movement. The central feature of O'Connor's plan was the establishment of a Chartist daily newspaper upon the basis of one-pound shares. Not only would such a paper counter the influence of the middle-class daily press, but the profits from this venture would go to finance Chartist lecturers, delegate conferences, defence funds and provide regular prizes for working-class essays. Twenty paid delegates were to meet for eight weeks as a convention in London and twenty paid lecturers were to tour the country for the same period. Delegates and lecturers were to be elected at public meetings and be responsible to district 'committees of review'. The convention would have a permanent chairman and executive council of five. Although the newspaper aspect of this scheme was largely impractical, O'Connor was grappling with the difficult problem of how to ensure substantial, regular financing for a mass working-class movement in a period in which the working class was generally unaccustomed and often unable to afford regular subscriptions towards a political cause.

He drew on the experience of the *Star* which had provided funding for the movement.

O'Connor also offered his opinion on the various other schemes placed before the movement. Lowery, newly appointed missionary of the Northern Political Union, had proposed that England, Scotland and Wales be divided into districts each with its own elected 'delegate' or 'agitator', and argued that to call a National Convention or adopt O'Brien's election strategy before the groundwork was established at a local level would be useless. While admirable as far as it went, O'Connor believed that the need was for more than just lecturers: 'I have a peculiar horror of sectional agitation, if not tributary to, and directed by, some responsible controlling power.' In contrast to Lowery's emphasis upon district organisation, 'A Republican' argued that 'want of centralised power' was the fundamental weakness in Chartist organisation, and urged the formation of a 'permanent, secret and irresponsible' directory of seven to direct the movement, with powers to call delegate meetings, spend funds and keep a record of all Chartists. While many Chartists recognised the need for a more highly centralised national leadership, they found the insurrectionary connotations associated with the idea of a secret directory contrary to the traditions of open, constitutional protest upon which the movement was based. O'Connor refused even to discuss 'A Republican's' plan, on the grounds that he was unalterably opposed to all forms of secret organisation. Perhaps the most elaborate scheme had come from R. J. Richardson, who proposed a hierarchical masonic structure with a 'Grand Marshal' at the top. While generally approving of Richardson's plan, O'Connor opposed the idea of having a 'Grand Marshal', as it was too easy for a leader to sell a party: 'The loss of a leader strikes great dismay into a party, and worse by treachery than death'. O'Connor noted that he had been one of the most consistent and active proponents of O'Brien's election plan.[24]

All these plans for reorganisation, along with several others from William Benbow, R. K. Philp and T. R. Smart, were placed before the delegates who assembled at Manchester on 20 July. The rules for the organisation of the National Charter Association adopted at this conference reflected the desire of the movement's leadership and rank and file to move towards a permanent, nationally coherent, centralised organisation.[25] Membership in the NCA was to be contingent upon signing a declaration of agreement to the Association's principles and the purchase of a 2d quarterly membership card. The names, employment and residence of all members were to be registered with the Executive Council. Where possible members were to be organised locally into classes of ten under a leader who was responsible for collecting each member's 1d weekly subscription. In each town classes were to be grouped into wards or divisions, and every month ward meetings were to be held at which the business of the district was to be transacted and reports heard from class leaders. There was to be a 'collector' for each ward responsible for forwarding monthly subscriptions to the National Executive. Each large town was to have a council with a local secretary to ensure that the policy of the National Association was carried out; each county or riding was also to have a council. All officers were to be democratically chosen, although they held office formally upon the appointment of the NCA Executive Council, composed of seven full-time, paid members, including a secretary and treasurer.[26] The Executive was to be elected annually by a ballot of all NCA members, each county being allowed to nominate one candidate for the Council. The NCA Executive members were responsible for the coordination of the national Chartist movement and when not in executive session were expected to act as missionaries undertaking agitation throughout the country. As for the means of carrying universal suffrage, approval was given to O'Brien's election plan; members were encouraged to attend all political meetings in order to propose Chartist resolutions and argue their cause; petitioning was again recommended, as were sobriety and the wider diffusion of political knowledge.

In practice, this elaborate organisational structure rarely found full expression at the local level. However, it is easy to lose sight of the break-through represented by the establishment of the NCA. With its establishment the Chartist movement approached the threshold of democratic, mass party organisation. While British political historians have traditionally regarded the Anti-Corn Law League as a major advance and model of Victorian extra-parliamentary political organisation, they have tended to ignore the achievement of the NCA, a much more ambitious and in many respects pioneering venture into the realm of organised socio-political protest. It is easy to forget the tremendous problems involved in attempting to form a national working-class party in the 1840s, problems related to finances, communications, the legal restrictions placed upon national political association, the local and occupational diversity of the working class, and, not least important, traditional concepts of legitimate modes of political leadership.

The Chartist movement obviously drew upon a wider experience of working-class voluntary association, and the formation of the NCA was related to a general trend towards more 'sophisticated' forms of working-class association, characterised by regular subscriptions, and the election and regular payment of permanent officials. For instance, the 1840s also saw the beginnings of a major shift in the organisation of friendly societies, the largest voluntary association of the Victorian period, towards nationwide affiliated orders; and it was no coincidence that, like the NCA, this movement found its greatest support in Lancashire and Yorkshire.[27] On a smaller scale the Owenite movement had reorganised from 1835, with a system of districts, branches, missionaries and social institutes, an annual congress and a Central Board whose members were paid regular weekly wages.[28] Developments in trade union organisation, particularly the attempts to form a national general union in the early 1830s, were also of significance; although trade unionism, especially as defined by the Webbs, was dominated by skilled craftsmen and unlike the NCA tended to be exclusive rather than inclusive organisations. However the Miners' Association, founded in 1842, which had close ties to the Chartist movement, may be viewed as an interesting parallel development to the NCA, with its large membership, durability, regular subscriptions and national executive.[29] The influence of Methodism upon working-class political organisation was also apparent. There was much discussion at the Manchester conference about the advantages of the class system, especially with regard to the difficulties faced in collecting regular subscriptions. According to Philp: 'Since the class system had been adopted [in Wiltshire], the money came in to a considerable extent.' George Black, ex-Primitive Methodist preacher and a stockinger, reminded delegates of the great difficulty in collecting any form of regular subscriptions from impoverished sections of the working class, such as the Nottinghamshire stockingers; and Smart argued: 'they had so much difficulty in getting money, that, without the class system . . . they would not get it in for any purpose whatever'.[30] The Methodist model was also influential with regard to the system of itinerant Chartist missionaries or lecturers. As David Jones has noted, the NCA was often remembered primarily as a lecturing association.[31] This is not to ignore the important differences which existed between all these popular movements, in terms of size, permanence, organisational structure and most importantly objectives, nor the element of competition between them, but there was also an important overlapping experience in the organisation of collective working-class endeavour. The matrix is complex, but it would be mistaken to regard the establishment of the NCA as a discrete social development.

The initial growth of the NCA was only gradual, with perhaps seventy local Chartist associations affiliated by the end of 1840. Lancashire, Yorkshire, the East Midlands and London constituted the districts of considerable early support, with Birmingham and the West Midlands and Scotland the most notable areas of early weakness. County councils or regular district organisations had been established in Lancashire, the West Riding, the East Midlands, Durham County and Gloucester by the end of the year; and full-time NCA missionaries had been engaged for all these districts with the exception of Gloucester.[32] In several localities, such as Bradford, the NCA had already taken on the character of a mass political party.[33]

There were several reasons for the moderate early growth of the NCA, and the hesitation of some Chartists to become members. Following an address by James Leach, president of the NCA Provisional Executive Council, on the objects of the Association, the Shelderslow Radical Association passed three resolutions outlining their objections to the Manchester plan. First, they objected to the principle of centralisation and the loss of local autonomy and control. Secondly, they objected to the recognition of 'paid itinerant orators, which is the worst feature in their plan, as it is setting up a number of acknowledged leaders, which is rather an inducement than otherwise for the Government to prosecute'. Thirdly, they believed the correspondence between NCA secretaries to be 'most decidedly illegal, and the whole of their plan is more likely to retard than forward the cause of freedom'.[34] One of their comrades, Mayall Beaumont, was even more outspoken in a letter to the *Northern Liberator*. He asked whether it was not dangerous to 'Give such monstrous powers into the hands of a set of reckless politicians, sitting in Manchester to determine the fate of any agitation that may be honestly and assiduously taken up by the people?' As for paid lecturers or agitators he was decidedly opposed to men 'making a trade of politics'. Although Beaumont's views were extreme, suspicions about the NCA's professionalism were probably widespread and the problem of exerting control over the increasing number of itinerant lecturers trying to eke out a livelihood through Chartist agitation was quite real. Finally, Beaumont strongly objected to the registration of members' names, suggesting that the name of the NCA Executive be changed 'to that of the Attorney General's Registration Office, for all political offenders'.[35] The fear of victimisation either by the government or employers was probably the greatest deterrent to joining the NCA. At the Manchester conference Black, who had himself faced victimisation for his Chartist involvement, felt that some were disposed to join their ranks who might be frightened of losing their employment if their names were known. It was pointed out, however, that the provision for the registration of names had been included in order to render the Association legal.

The vulnerability and uncertainty which surrounded the NCA's position in law were to remain a concern throughout the Association's existence, but presented a particularly pressing problem with regard to its early development. The early growth of the NCA was definitely inhibited by the widespread fears that the organisation contravened the laws on corresponding societies. Thus, in late February 1841, a national delegates meeting was again held at Manchester to adopt a new plan of organisation. The principal change was to emphasise that all NCA members belonged to one society; there were no branches, divisions, local secretaries. The members of the NCA in each town were to nominate members to a NCA General Council; local secretaries and treasurers were to be 'sub' secretaries and treasurers to the one national society.[36] In this way it was hoped to get around the law, by having all communication within one general association rather than between affiliated branches or localities.

In the *Star* Hill welcomed the revised plan of organisation. National organisation was essential. While Hill noted the organisational superiority of the original plan, he acknowledged the importance of taking every precaution to conform, if possible, with the law. He also recognised, however, that the law, particularly with regard to working-class political organisation, was largely in 'accord with the designs and purposes of the dominant class' in society, a reflection of the existing balance of class forces.

> Yes, this is the very first Association ever yet formed by the fustian jackets, blistered hands, and unshorn chins; and its illegality consists in its 'unfortunately flourishing' position . . .[37]

> The National Charter Association of Great Britain, may then bid defiance to the Government. It shall stand; it shall prosper; it shall flourish; in despite of all their power, in despite of all their sophistry, or they shall do one of two things — they shall make a special law for its extinction, as was done with the London Corresponding Society . . . or they shall at once throw off the mask, which, we have no doubt they will do as soon as they may deem it expedient, and, trampling under foot all semblance of respect for the laws of their own making, try the temper of the people by further experiment of undisguised brute force.[38]

Under such circumstances legal considerations, while important, were regarded as subordinate to the great task of establishing the people's party. However, opposition on the grounds of the NCA's illegality continued from a small section of Chartist leadership, including John Collins and the Rev. Arthur O'Neill at Birmingham and William Lovett. In Birmingham this issue formed the pretext for a split in the Chartist ranks.[39] The legalistic position of these radicals contrasted with the position of O'Connor, the *Star* and the majority of the Chartist leadership.

The tremendous growth in the NCA in 1841 and 1842 would indicate that the revised plan of organisation gave substantial relief to the concerns of most Chartists. From February 1841 to the end of 1841, the NCA grew from eighty associations to nearly three hundred, with twenty thousand members.[40] The election, in June 1841, of the first NCA National Executive — James Leach, Peter M'Douall, Morgan Williams, George Binns, R. K. Philp and John Campbell, secretary — and their extensive touring, along with that of O'Connor, in late summer and autumn 1841 gave a great impetus to the association's growth.[41] When the Executive's term of office ended in June 1842, the NCA boasted more than four hundred local associations and fifty thousand members, although a large proportion were not paying regular dues.[42] The petition for the release of all Chartist prisoners presented in spring 1841, which collected two million signatures, and the second National Petition for universal suffrage in summer 1842, which collected more than three million signatures, attest to this growth and improved organisation. The NCA reached its peak membership probably in autumn 1842, by which time over seventy thousand membership cards had been issued.[43] However, the dispute surrounding the NCA Executive's accounts and Hill's persistent attacks on the Executive in late 1842 and 1843, combined with a general downturn in radical prospects following the defeat of the mass strikes of 1842, seriously eroded the growth and influence of the NCA.

Whatever the difficulties of arriving at a precise estimate of the total membership of the association, during the early 1840s the NCA clearly assumed the character of a mass, national party of the working class. The local strength of the NCA came from the established Chartist centres: Lancashire, Yorkshire, East Midlands, South Wales and London (see Table 6.1). The growth of NCA membership in London marked an important development in terms of metropolitan working-class radicalism and a shift in the balance of regional Chartist support. At London, as well as Manchester, Birmingham and

Nottingham, members of the 'lower' trades — shoemakers, tailors, carpenters, stonemasons — formed trades branches of the NCA.[44] One of the most impressive features, however, was the widespread support for the NCA throughout the country, with towns like Brighton, Bath, Trowbridge and Northampton boasting sizeable membership. Birmingham, with around one thousand members, remained a relatively weak area of NCA support, whereas areas of the Black Country, most notably Bilston, became Chartist strongholds.[45] The early support for the NCA in the North East apparently waned by late 1841. In contrast, the Sheffield NCA membership which remained small throughout 1841 climbed steadily throughout 1842 towards the two thousand mark.[46] The most dramatic growth in membership occurred in the East Midlands, at Leicester and Nottingham, where there were three thousand and one thousand-six hundred members respectively by autumn of 1842.[47] The support for the NCA among the East Midlands stockingers, the weavers of Bradford and Trowbridge, the domestic metal workers of Bilston, underlines the strength of radicalism in districts dominated by declining traditional trades. Also important was the influence and activism of key local leaders: for instance, Thomas Cooper at Leicester, James Sweet at Nottingham, or Harney at Sheffield.

The figures for NCA membership are merely rough approximations of local Chartist strength. On the one hand, they tend to overemphasise the NCA's formal strength (see note to Table 6.1); certainly they do not reflect the number of regular dues-paying members. The Executive constantly complained of the difficulty of collecting regular subscriptions from NCA members.[48] On the other hand, in some districts these figures underestimate the number of active local Chartists. Thus while the NCA lists would suggest relatively little Chartist support at Ashton-under-Lyne and Stalybridge — although large-scale support at the neighbouring factory towns of Stockport and Oldham — the Chartist leadership and mass political radicalism demonstrated during the 1842 'general strike' would indicate mass Chartist support in both towns. As in mining districts, the low NCA membership here may be explicable, at least in part, by the fear of the employers' blacklist.[49] Obviously, NCA membership figures do not indicate the vast numbers who considered themselves Chartists. The influence of a movement like Chartism cannot be gauged by counting dues-paying members. The latent support for Chartism, the powerful force of dreams too long deferred, dramatically reasserted itself at moments like summer of 1842. In a letter to

Table 6.1: NCA Membership in Some Key Chartist Localities

Locality	No. of NCA cards taken out Mar. 1841-Oct. 1842
London	8000
Manchester	2800
Salford	500
Oldham	700-900
Ashton- u.- Lyne	350
Stalybridge	200
Stockport	880
Rochdale	470
Bolton	700
Wigan	150
Liverpool	800
Preston	330
Blackburn	280
Clithero	350-400
Burnley	570
Todmorden	500
Colne	220
Keighley	200
Leeds	1325
Bradford	1500-1900
Halifax	460
Sowerby	170
Hebden Bridge	300
Huddersfield	630
Dewsbury	580
Barnsley	480
Sheffield	2000
Rotherham	150
Hull	550
York	150
Newcastle	1000
Sunderland	750
Bishop Wearmouth	450
Bishop Auckland	190
Carlisle	120
Hanley district (includes Shelton)	1100
Longton	480
Derby	370
Belper	290
Leicester	3100

Locality	No. of NCA Cards taken out Mar. 1841-Oct. 1842
Loughborough	800
Nottingham	1650
Sutton-in-Ashfield	560
Birmingham	1000-1200
Wolverhampton	200-300
Bilston	1000
Coventry	250
Kettering	100
Northampton	600
Norwich	200-300
Ipswich	120-140
Brighton	420
Gloucester	200-300
Cheltenham	270
Trowbridge	500
Bristol	920
Bath	420
Newport (Wales)	300-400
Merthyr Tydvil	1100
Aberdare	440

Source: Balance sheets of the NCA Executive published in *NS*, 20 Mar. 1841, p. 2; 24 July, p. 6; 18 Dec., p. 6; 18 Jan. 1842, p. 1; 9 Apr., p. 6; 12 Nov., p. 8.

Note: There are difficulties regarding these figures as an index of NCA membership in any precise way, although they do provide a rough guide. Based on the number of NCA membership cards issued to each locality over a two-year period, these figures do not take account of those who left the ranks during this time. Nor do these estimates render the number of dues-paying members which must be considerably less. Unfortunately, in the accounts monthly dues paid to the Executive are mixed in with membership fees. The balance sheets themselves are hardly a model of good bookkeeping, and certainly allow for a considerable margin of error. Finally, where it has been possible to check these numbers against other evidence either in the Chartist press or in the work of other scholars who have worked on particular localities, the figures extrapolated from the NCA balance sheets have proved to be remarkably close to other estimates of NCA membership in almost all cases. Still, the claims for such a breakdown must remain modest.

Cooper, written from Birmingham in late July 1842, George White scoffed at the 'card retailers' of the NCA Executive:

> Pshew! What an abominable estimate some of our *intellectual* beings form of a glorious movement like the present. . . . Poor Campbell [NCA secretary] always estimated the progress of the movement according to the number of cards sold and paid for . . .

White went on to report that he was addressing immense meetings throughout the district, 'and the universal cry is "We must have the Charter" — and Wonderful! oh Wonderful not one in a thousand has got a Card . . .'[50]

O'Connor's leadership was inextricably associated with the NCA. He became the greatest agitator in the service of the NCA, its most prominent spokesman and defender. More than any other leader he brought the platform to the service of the party, recruiting thousands to the NCA ranks through his extensive tours of platform agitation. The *Northern Star* became the organ of the NCA. The association was often denounced as 'O'Connor's party'. One of the most consistent themes of O'Connor's career was his belief that the Charter would be gained only through the united struggle of the working class organised within an independent, national party. For the Chartist movement, but particularly for O'Connor, the NCA marked the culmination of a series of efforts to establish permanent, democratic forms of leadership and organisation. Until the final years of his career, O'Connor strove to make the NCA the party of all working-class radicals.

The NCA was intended to serve as a model of democratic leadership. In an address published in 1842, the NCA Executive declared:

> By pursuing on a smaller scale a course which must sooner or later be imitated on a larger one, we have served the people . . . hereby affording a practical illustration of Chartism to our opponents, which they are in general too selfish to admit, or too tyrannical to imitate.[51]

Yet, at the centre of O'Connor's relationship to the NCA and its Executive, there remained a contradiction in terms of democratic leadership. His status as an independent gentleman, his acknowledged preeminence, his ownership of the movement's principal journal, meant that O'Connor stood rather ambiguously outside and above the NCA structure. O'Connor, rather than the NCA Executive, continued to be the most important, although by no means the only, influence in the initiation and determination of Chartist policy. Throughout the 1840s, the NCA Executive was manifestly unable to mediate differences between O'Connor and other prominent Chartist leaders, which meant that differences over Chartist policy often degenerated to the level of debilitating personal disputes. As always O'Connor's ultimate appeal was to the Chartist rank and file. Attacks on his leadership were usually, and often quite correctly, regarded as attacks on the NCA.

During the early years of the NCA O'Connor remained conspicuously off the association's Executive Council. Yet, despite his own continual avowals of independence and promises never to live off the movement, O'Connor was the most forceful proponent of the essential need for paid Chartist missionaries and a permanent, paid Executive, the most controversial aspect of NCA organisation. Thus, in early 1843, when the Executive was under attack in the pages of the *Star* for the mismanagement of the people's funds, he disassociated himself from Hill's denunciations and reaffirmed his confidence in the Executive members M'Douall, Leach and Bairstow. O'Connor was at pains to counter the growing opposition to the NCA Executive: 'I assert that we had no organization before the appointment of an Executive; I contend for it that we now have an organization.' The unpaid gentleman of the platform contended for the absolute necessity for a paid Executive, if they were to have working men as their leaders.

> I am, then, decidedly in favour of an Executive; I think we cannot do without it. I am obstinately opposed to an unpaid Executive, and for this reason. If you have an unpaid Executive, you must have a purely middle-class Executive, because you cannot elect working men as your officers, that moment every door is closed against them, and at once they are marked, and if in work are dismissed. . . . Let us have our paid Executive, our paid lecturers, and our unpaid volunteers confined to their several localities; but let us have no more of this system of unconnected and disorganized agitation.[52]

The payment of Chartist leaders remained, however, a delicate issue. Local Chartists were often reluctant to forward funds to the Executive, preferring to use their limited resources to employ local or district lecturers over whom they had more direct control. There continued to be a distrust of working men who 'traded in politics'. O'Connor constantly sought to contrast the position of those working men who had hired themselves out to middle-class social and political movements with that of the NCA Executive and lecturers. Thus

Vincent, 'the political peddlar', had sold out to the middle-class Complete Suffrage movement for six pounds a week (according to the *Star*); whereas the NCA Executive drew a mere working-man's wage of thirty shillings.[53] In 1840, the Tory advocates of the foreign-affairs movement, led by the Russophobe David Urquhart, had enlisted the services of former Convention delegates such as Cardo, Lowery, Richards and Warden, as lecturers in their campaign against the Whig Government's foreign policy.[54] Such middle-class attempts to 'buy' Chartist leaders, to exploit their popularity in the interests of counter-agitations, became a familiar theme for denunciation from O'Connor and the *Star*. The employment of Chartist missionaries under the auspices of the NCA represented an attempt to establish a coherent, accountable, 'legitimate' system of Chartist lecturers.

In 1843, the NCA once again was reorganised, largely along lines drawn up by O'Connor; and the Executive moved its base to London. In September 1843, O'Connor finally agreed to serve on the NCA Executive, as treasurer, in order to bolster confidence in the association's financial and legal position.[55] The Executive which presided nearly unchanged from 1843 to 1847 was, however, predominately working-class in composition; it included: Philip M'Grath, an East End tailor as president, T. M. Wheeler, a former baker and school teacher as secretary, Thomas Clark (who replaced the carpenter Henry Ross in 1844), cordwainer, and Christopher Doyle, power-loom weaver.[56] Every year O'Connor stood for democratic reelection to the Executive, although he still refused payment for his services. In fact, in 1844, he had to advance payments to the Executive; he also established the policy that any Chartist locality for which he lectured had to forward half the funds raised to the NCA Executive fund and to support NCA lecturers.[57] Yet O'Connor's own leadership remained essentially unincorporated within any formal organisational structure; the legitimacy of his leadership remained rooted in an older tradition of independent gentlemanly leadership. One of the most striking characteristics of the Chartist movement was the way in which older forms of radical protest, culture and leadership coexisted with newer forms and innovations. O'Connor consciously assumed a mediating role in this process of transition, continually extending the legitimacy of his own leadership to that of the NCA and its Executive. Thus, in a peculiar, and perhaps quite necessary way, the independent gentleman of the platform presided over the career of the first workers' party.

III The Question of Chartist Direction, Unity and Democratic Leadership

O'Connor has often been severely criticised for having exerted an undemocratic, 'dictatorial' control over the Chartist movement. However, as David Jones has suggested, 'the problems which he faced deserve greater attention'.[58] The central problem of national Chartist leadership was the maintenance of radical working-class unity. The magnitude of this task should not be forgotten. With remarkable forbearance, energy and enthusiasm O'Connor battled to overcome the divisions and sources of fragmentation within the working-class movement: the gulf between the 'labour aristocrats' and the rest, the antagonism between Irish and English workers, the strong sense of local autonomy and independence, the spirit of individualism among Chartism's leaders, the diffusion of working-class energy in a multitude of self-help activities, the countless middle-class overtures for a reform alliance. Following the defeats of 1839 and early 1840, Chartism lost much of its earlier sense of urgency. With the realisation that the agitation for universal suffrage was to be a protracted one there was a tendency for radicals to drift into other forms of social protest or self-help activity. In the early 1840s, the vulnerability of Chartism's national unity was tested. Both from outside and within the Chartist ranks the movement was faced with a series of 'rival' or alternative agitations. O'Connor's leadership was crucial in determining the Chartist reaction, at both the local and national level, to these moves.

In the early 1840s, Chartist activists turned not only to the task of national reorganisation, but began to broaden the scope of their radical involvement at the local level. Increasingly Chartists turned to the more cultural side of their radical commitment. Throughout the country they formed cooperative stores, temperance societies, burial clubs, schools and democratic chapels. A wide range of leisure activities was also provided locally — regular lectures, debates, communal newspaper readings, soirées and tea parties, annual dinners to celebrate the birthdays of radical heroes like Paine and Hunt. While the movement never fully recaptured its earlier spontaneity and tone, characterised by a sense of imminent and decisive class confrontation, Chartists set about establishing the foundations of an alternative radical culture. This cultural broadening, the creation of what might be termed a 'movement culture', was crucial to binding Chartism together during the early 1840s.[59] In general, Chartism's

challenge at this cultural level was complementary rather than antithetical to the movement's more overt challenge in terms of mass
action. Many Chartists who advocated the need for working-class
temperance, education, cooperation or religion showed their revolutionary colours in 1842 and 1848, when the politics of mass class
confrontation reemerged. Moreover, it would be mistaken to view
Chartism's cultural dimension as simply a holding operation; the
cultural sphere was one of vital class self-definition and continual
conflict. This is not to deny that an artisan tradition which stressed
the importance of collective self-help and 'moral' improvement often
remained ambiguously poised between revolutionary class politics
and a more gradualist, or at times even class-collaborative orientation. Still, Gladstonian liberalism should not be read back into the
Chartism of the 1840s, particularly upon the basis of the careers of a
few Chartist leaders.[60] The strong emphasis upon self-improvement
among many Chartists did not necessarily represent an acceptance of
middle-class social values or concepts of 'respectability'. Chartists
demonstrated a strong sense of independence and a determined
opposition to middle-class efforts to foist their own brand of self-help
upon working people.

While this broadening of Chartism's self-sustaining cultural activities was central to the flourishing of the movement in the early 1840s,
especially in countering any tendency towards degeneration into
sectarian agitation, this trend could also create problems in terms of
the maintenance of both local and national Chartist unity and direction. Such concerns could divert radicals from the central thrust of
Chartism, away from the primary demand for working-class political
power and away from the agency of the mass platform. Thus, in 1843,
George White recalled as a form of cautionary tale the fate of Newcastle Chartism. Following the first Convention, the Newcastle Chartists initiated an extensive system of cooperative associations. White
maintained that the relative weakness of Chartism in Newcastle, an
early stronghold, derived from this diversion of radical energies.

> but the attention of their most active members being almost solely
> engrossed in weighing tea and sugar, and measuring potatoes, they
> neglected the public meetings. The splendid spirit of Chartism, which
> previously existed, was allowed to die away . . .[61]

On the other hand, the incorporation of working-class cooperative,
temperance, educational and religious tendencies within the framework of local Chartism was important in undercutting the attraction
which such alternative movements of working-class improvement

had for many working-class radicals. Activists concerned with educational or temperance goals were able to fulfill this side of their radicalism within the Chartist movement. The key, however, was the subordination of such social and cultural objects to the political struggle for the suffrage. The balance was not always easily maintained.

It is within this context of a general broadening of Chartist concerns and a shifting emphasis in tone and orientation, that O'Connor's effort to sustain Chartism's mass appeal and national unity must be considered. His primary concern, to maintain Chartism's political direction, gave rise to a certain ambivalance in O'Connor's attitude towards the struggle for working-class 'moral' improvement. However, as Eileen Yeo has noted, O'Connor, as well as Lovett, saw the need 'to create a dependable and vigorous radical culture at the grass roots which would sustain agitation over the long term and prepare Chartists to make the most socially beneficial use of the Charter once it was won'.[62] O'Connor espoused the virtues of working-class education and temperance. He enthusiastically supported the establishment of Chartist halls and schools. He made a point of attending Chartist Sunday school recitations, for as he told parents and children at the Chartist Sunday school at Manchester's Carpenters' Hall, it gratified him 'to know that there was a little army coming up, who if the old one was to die before the liberties of the country were gained would take the field and finish the work their fathers had so nobly begun'.[63] His scheme for Chartist reorganisation provided for regular prizes for working-class essays. He also suggested that Chartist delegates and lecturers take the teetotal pledge during the period of their service. At the 1842 Convention O'Connor moved a resolution that all delegates abstain from all intoxicating drink and tobacco, as an example to the movement; in 1843, in a similar vein, he pressed the NCA Executive to take the teetotal pledge and proclaimed his own willingness to take the pledge.[64] O'Connor realised that the image of drunken lecturers and irresponsible leaders living off the movement could damage the radical cause. He appreciated the importance of disciplined conduct to radical agitation and the need to foster a sense of working-class self-esteem. When the *Star* outlined the rules for Chartist conduct at the demonstrations called to petition for the release of Chartist prisoners, working-class radicals were recommended to imitate the conduct of temperance associations: rise early, appear in their best clothes, abstain from all intoxicating liquor, patronise Chartist soirées in the evenings and visit no place of amusement except those open for Chartist purposes.[65] O'Connor was careful to exclude drinksellers from his land plan settlements. The land plan was itself the most obvious example of O'Connor's regard for the virtues of working-class self-reliance.

In the early 1840s, the columns of the *Star* were open to reports and discussions which reflected the entire range of Chartist cultural activity. This is hardly surprising, as the paper's editor, Hill, was a keen educator, temperance advocate and Christian Chartist. It is important to note, however, that this did not imply that O'Connor, Hill or the Chartist movement accepted the middle-class argument that the suffrage should be conditional upon the demonstration of the attainment of a certain educational or 'moral' standard. The suffrage was a natural right to which all men were entitled.[66] Working-class ignorance or insobriety was the result of social conditions, particularly wage slavery, which only a total reordering of society could change. Universal suffrage was the first necessary step on the road to working-class 'moral' improvement. O'Connor's concern for Chartist intellectual and cultural goals has often been ignored in assessments of his leadership, particularly by the early historians of Chartism who portrayed differences between O'Connor and Lovett as fundamental to the development of national Chartist leadership. This central split in national leadership in turn corresponded to a neat delineation in terms of working-class support: between the 'physical-force' proletariat of the North — largely inarticulate, deferential and motivated by economic distress—and the enlightened artisans of London—largely articulate, independent and motivated by democratic idealism. That this picture of both leadership and support is inaccurate and misconceived is one of the central arguments of this study.

Yet the Chartist concern for collective self-improvement remained a problematic issue. If Chartists sometimes failed to defend traditional, 'rough' sport, or denounced heavy drinking, this was, at least in part, because they felt that such pastimes served to obstruct the formation of a disciplined political force.[67] At one level, it reflected the seriousness with which Chartists regarded their activity. Thus R. K. Philp complained of the difficulties in putting over the Chartist message at a tavern meeting, of the 'frequent interruptions' that 'completely break every chain of thought'. He left this vignette of the struggling Chartist lecturer.

'Brethern, we are enslaved, and as we all love liberty, so must we all make sacrifices to obtain it. (Betsey a pint of stout!) Let us arouse, then, with a manly, a patriotic determination to be free. (Bring that screw and pipe, Betsey, push along, order!) Shall we be content to have our homes desolated, and see our wives and children perish for want of that we could easily procure under just government? Rather let the millions arouse, and firmly declare that they will have (a joey of brandy!) the Charter of their freedom. (Bravo! Knocking on the tables, glasses rattling, and clouds of smoke!)'[68]

However, Philp's proposal that Chartists abandon the tavern was neither realistic nor probably widely desired. The strength of the Chartist movement derived from its situation within the popular culture of working people. The important point was not that Philp had to compete with the overworked 'Betsey', but that working people were eager to take a strong dose of radical politics with their glass of stout.

In spring 1841, O'Connor published his famous condemnation of 'Church Chartism, Teetotal Chartism, Knowledge Chartism, and Household Suffrage Chartism'. Until this point O'Connor had offered no real opposition to the development of the first three tendencies within the Chartist movement. In November 1840, Hill co-signed an address, along with Vincent, Hetherington, Cleave and Neesom — all of whom later were exposed as supporters of Lovett's 'New Move' — urging Chartists to form teetotal Chartist associations. Even before this, such associations existed in many localities. The response to this address was immediate and impressive. Support came from local NCA leaders throughout the country, members of the NCA Executive, NCA lecturers and other prominent Chartists. During the early months of 1841, Vincent found an enthusiastic welcome for his temperance message among local Chartists.[69] Clearly the demand for voluntary teetotalism was not seen as inimical to the aims of Chartism or the NCA.

Several weeks before the publication of his attack on the quadruple alliance of church, teetotal, knowledge and household-suffrage Chartism, O'Connor explained his position: 'I do not object to Chartists being religious — to Chartists being teetotallers — to Chartists thirsting after knowledge, or to Chartists voting out of, and living in, their own houses.' His opposition was based rather upon his fears that these various tendencies might become splinter groups, dissipating the movement's strength. He was also concerned to counter any tendency towards elitism or a withdrawal from mass action. His attack was not upon religion, teetotalism or education as such, but rather upon the danger of establishing an exclusive standard for Chartist membership. By grouping these various Chartist tendencies

together with the household-suffrage movement, O'Connor underlined his view of their implicit accommodation to middle-class radicalism. The brunt of his attack, however, was directed at 'Christian
Chartism', particularly as practised by the Rev. Arthur O'Neill's
Birmingham Chartist Church. 'Yours is an exclusive dealing in religion; a kind of spiritual co-operative store.'

> Chartism is, although extensive, yet a well-defined political designation
> of a political party. Christian Chartism, though apparently, all-embrac-
> ing in its meaning, carries with it exclusion of all other sects from whom
> we expect political aid.

Hill maintained that O'Connor had misconceived the issue, gener-
alising from the experience of one untypical group of Christian Chartists, and suggested that imprisonment had left him out of touch with
the movement at large. However, O'Connor had himself made a
distinction between the Scottish Christian Chartists and those at
Birmingham. In Scotland he maintained Chartist preachers 'assume
no distinct religious bearing', and their preaching 'unites the people,
and weakens and disunites the enemy; the funds go to advance
political principles, while no peculiar religious faith is preached or
attempted to be enforced'. Whereas at Birmingham, 'Christian Chartism tends to disunite the great body of Chartists and to increase their
opponents . . .' O'Connor's attitude was determined by the extent to
which he deemed any tendency likely to advance or retard the unity
of the movement. He concluded his address on a conciliatory note,
giving his assurance that should these adherents act to inculcate
'religion, abstinence, and knowledge, as a means to any end which
they may unitedly produce, without establishing man's adhesion to
any of them, as a political test, then I will give them my blessing and
my every assistance . . .'[70]

O'Connor offered little suggestion as to how such improvement
tendencies might legitimately be incorporated within the scope of
local Chartism, and in several localities his admonition created some
confusion within the Chartist ranks.[71] He may also have overestimated the threat posed to national unity. It is important, however, to
see the timing and urgency of his warning as a response to local
developments at Birmingham, where a serious split had developed
between Chartists organised around the Christian Chartist Church
and members of the NCA. From the period following the Bull Ring
riots, when sections of the local movement had assumed an underground character, working-class radicalism at Birmingham remained
fragmented. The radical unity demonstrated in summer 1840, with

the release of Collins and Lovett from prison, was short lived. From autumn 1840 Collins held himself aloof from the activities of those Chartists — many of whom had been involved in the insurrectionary plotting of late 1839 — reorganising around the NCA. He refused to join the NCA on the grounds that it constituted an illegal association. In late 1840, with Collins's support, O'Neill established the Birmingham Christian Chartist Church which increasingly became an alternative to and came in conflict with the local NCA party.[72] George White who arrived in Birmingham early in 1841 in the role of reporter for the *Star*, a job O'Connor had originally offered to Collins, worked hard to win support for the NCA and earnestly sought a reconciliation with Collins, O'Neill and the Chartists of the Christian Chartist Church. However, even after the NCA plan had been revised, Collins and O'Neill refused to acknowledge the legality of the association and maintained the separation between the Christian Chartists and those of the NCA. The task of establishing a strong NCA party at Birmingham remained a priority of leaders like O'Connor, White, M'Douall and William Martin who became the Birmingham NCA lecturer in spring 1841.[73]

Nationally and locally Chartists were displeased not only with Collins and O'Neill's stand on the question of NCA membership but with their equivocal attitude towards middle-class radicalism. Although they formally had opposed the household-suffrage initiative of the Leeds Parliamentary Reform Association, the conciliatory tone which both leaders adopted towards the middle class generated working-class suspicion. Locally NCA members, like T. P. Green and William Smallwood, concluded that Collins had abandoned Chartism. Nationally O'Connor was concerned about the strength of this local challenge to the NCA and the movement's class tone. Here was an example of the dangers of any deviation from 'pure' Chartism.[74]

The week after O'Connor's warning about church, teetotal, knowledge and household-suffrage Chartism, Hill exposed Lovett and Collins's 'New Move'. Lovett and Collins, along with Hetherington, Cleave, George Rogers and Henry Mitchell, had privately circulated an address to 'all the leading Chartists', soliciting their support for the establishment of a 'National Association for the United Kingdom, for Promoting the Political and Social Improvement of the People'. Ostensibly Chartist in character, this scheme to raise an enormous sum of money for educational improvement and the financing of schools, public halls, missionaries and libraries, had much in common with Owenite goals.[75] First, the scheme was denounced in the

Star as an attempt to initiate a rival national Chartist association to the NCA. Secondly, the 'New Move' was linked to the household-suffrage movement and the politics of class collaboration. Certainly Lovett and Collins had sought the advice of Roebuck and Place on the question of the NCA's legality, and Hetherington acknowledged that the leaders of the 'New Move' had met with Hume to discuss the prospects of a middle-class/working-class political alliance, although only Hetherington had been willing to support a household-suffrage move.[76] The enthusiastic welcome for the National Association in the middle-class press and O'Connell's praise served to underline the collaborationist orientation of the 'New Move'. Thirdly, the emphasis on educational and social goals tended to obscure the political aims of Chartism. Hill argued that working-class energies should be concentrated on winning that political power which would ensure that all the educational institutions of the country would be placed at the service of the people. Fourthly, the private or 'secret' manner in which the proposals for the National Association had been circulated created suspicion and emphasised the elitest or 'anti-democratic' character of the move.[77] Correspondingly Lovett had attacked the nature of Chartist agitation, the mass demonstrations and the 'personal idolatry' which had marred their proceedings.

In a letter to the *Star* O'Connor reduced the issue to a test of confidence in his personal leadership. The motives of the 'New Move' men were obvious, they were allied with O'Connell in an attempt to undermine his leadership. While it was necessary to pay lip-service to universal suffrage to gain working-class approval, the plan was to forge a union with middle-class reformers. O'Connor noted that the list of those who had signed the address for the establishment of the National Association included 'Not one man for the hive', Lancashire and the West Riding. In response to the list of eighty-seven Chartists who had endorsed the 'New Move', O'Connor offered his own list of eighty-seven prominent Chartists who had not signed, and called on Chartists to choose between the 'new list' and the 'old': 'I am in the old, my enemies are in the new; declare for one or the other . . . I require a strong, an instant, an unequivocal verdict . . .'[78]

The verdict was never in doubt. Throughout the country local Chartist associations passed resolutions condemning the 'New Move' as calculated to create disunion, and expressed confidence in the NCA, O'Connor and the *Star*. It was reported from Bradford that local Chartists were so embittered against those associated with the 'New Move' that 'several have actually publicly burnt the portrait of

John Collins; others, who are not exactly so severe, and have had him framed, have turned him upside down'. At Birmingham the committee in charge of collecting funds for the relief of the large family of Edward Brown, former delegate to the Convention, expressed concern upon finding Brown's name on the list, as it would be difficult to raise funds, many of his former supporters being NCA members.[79] Many Chartist leaders who had signed the 'New Move' address were quick to renounce their support, explaining that they thought it a plan to complement rather than supplant the NCA organisation. Under pressure from the Bristol Chartists Vincent publicly declared the 'New Move' to have been ill-considered, as it split the movement. Vincent joined the NCA.[80]

The close identification of the NCA and the working-class movement at large with O'Connor's leadership was evident in the local Chartist response to the threat of the 'New Move'. 'To injure O'Connor is to injure the people; he is identified with them', declared John Watkins, one of the sternest opponents of the 'New Move' in London.[81] Still, several Chartist associations were careful to distinguish their support for O'Connor and the NCA from any form of 'personal idolatry'. The South Lancashire delegates meeting censured an attack by Hetherington on O'Connor, but insisted that the NCA, established during his imprisonment, was not O'Connor's 'tail'. Nor did all Chartists relish the loss of former comrades from their ranks. At the same Lancashire meeting, Harney reviewed his earlier differences with Lovett and the LWMA, but noted that Lovett had regained his respect through his conduct at the Convention and with his imprisonment; he expressed personal regret that Lovett was no longer with them.[82] The experience of the Convention and the subsequent imprisonment of so many Chartist leaders had caused a general closing of the ranks of Chartism's leadership in 1840. The breach over the 'New Move' marked a reopening of national leadership differences which were seriously to weaken the movement in 1842. However, in 1841, the dispute surrounding the 'New Move' probably weakened the movement only in London and Birmingham. A fair number of London Chartists, including several former LDA members, continued to support Lovett's plan. But even in London the National Association never commanded widespread support and was completely overshadowed by the NCA.[83] At Birmingham the NCA gained support under White's leadership, and the Christian Chartists were reduced to a marginal Chartist grouping. Often national leadership disputes had little effect upon the day-to-day activities of local

Chartists. At the 1842 Convention, the Rev. George Harrison, Nottingham's delegate and an ardent opponent of the 'New Move', reported that he represented two groups, 'the one teetotal, the other not, but they were both good Chartists'.[84] At Nottingham, in contrast to Birmingham, local Chartists had successfully integrated a whole range of cultural activity — preaching and hymn singing, an adult school and a Sunday school, a library and reading groups, a Chartist temperance association — under the auspices of the NCA. The attack on the 'New Move' did not signal a retreat from Chartism's cultural direction.

While the damaging split within the Chartist movement came not over the 'New Move', but with the middle-class Complete Suffrage initiative, the 'New Move' controversy points to tensions within the movement's leadership in the early 1840s. It was not always easy to persuade all of Chartism's leaders, many of whom were possessed of a strong streak of individualism, to submit to the authority of a national Chartist party or to recognise the NCA's claim to represent all Chartists. At the National Petition Convention, in May 1841, there was opposition to Collins's claim to represent Birmingham, on the grounds that he had not been chosen by the NCA Executive, was not a member of the NCA and was the representative of a sectional interest at Birmingham — this despite his election as a delegate at a meeting of all Birmingham Chartists. John Barmby, the Suffolk delegate whose credentials were also in question, declared he was a member of both the NCA and the National Association. Pitkeithley argued that Collins should be allowed to sit in the interests of unity, and informed the Convention that O'Connor was of the same opinion. M'Douall, who opposed recognising Collins, resented the name of O'Connor or the *Northern Star* being introduced; they had rules which must be followed. Eventually Collins was denied his seat and William Martin, the Birmingham NCA delegate, recognised as Birmingham's sole representative.[85] While a minor incident, it highlights the tensions involved in trying to maintain a united Chartist movement and construct a centralised national organisation. Nor was the problem confined to the NCA's first year. O'Brien, who did not join the NCA, in 1842-43 maintained that the question of whether a Chartist joined the NCA should remain a matter of individual choice.

> To attempt to bully the entire Chartist body into any one particular Association, is not the way to promote union. It is, on the contrary, a certain way to promote and perpetuate disunion. . . . To tell a man he is no Chartist, because he does not choose to take out a card from Mr. John

Campbell, will neither convince him that he is no Chartist, nor make him take out a card.

O'Brien maintained: 'Chartism has been wrecked—frittered away—all but annihilated by the attempt to force the whole Chartist body into one association.'[86] O'Brien's opposition to the NCA, along with his rejection of the agency of the mass platform upon his release from prison, was as important as his attitude towards a working-class/middle-class alliance, and more important than tactical differences over the 1841 general election, to his eventual split with O'Connor.

Differences had also emerged over the character and direction of Chartist protest and the determination of the movement's relationship to middle-class radicalism. A relatively small section of Chartism's leadership, associated with the 'New Move'—including Vincent, Lovett, Hetherington, Collins, O'Neill, Lowery—renounced, to varying degrees, the confrontationalist tone of early Chartism and urged a retreat from mass platform agitation. The emphasis of these radicals upon 'rational' agitation stood in opposition to O'Connor's continued commitment to the mass platform as the principal agency of Chartist protest. Such a perspective also shared much common ground with the aims and style of middle-class radicalism. This change in tone and emphasis is particularly evident in Vincent's correspondence from prison with Place. Having expressed his conviction that the NCA was an illegal association, he wrote:

> I am convinced that the *real practical agitation* now to be carried on is the *forming of societies in the various towns for the raising of Halls in which the members may meet for the acquisition of Political, Moral and Scientific Information* . . .[87]

An address adopted by a meeting of the National Association, in September 1841, declared: 'we felt anxious *to redeem by reason what had been lost by madness and folly*'.[88] Although Lovett continued to stress the need for working-class radicals to rely upon their own exertions, the National Association became increasingly dependent upon the goodwill of middle-class politicians.[89] The Association's failure to support the second Chartist National Petition, in 1842, contrasted with its enthusiastic support for the Complete Suffrage initiative and the prospects for a cross-class alliance.[90]

The 'New Move' controversy also underscores the role of O'Connor and the *Star* in establishing national Chartist policy and direction, and raises an issue which was to reemerge throughout the 1840s, namely the extent to which O'Connor's ascendancy over the movement's national leadership conflicted with the interests of democratic leadership. As the movement's most respected national leader, O'Connor exercised an enormous influence over Chartism. However, the view of O'Connor as the 'dictator' of Chartism has served to obscure the fierce spirit of democracy which characterised Chartist protest. Local activists, as well as national leaders, were prepared to voice criticism of O'Connor's actions and policies, and O'Connor was compelled to take notice. Although never clearly defined, there were limits upon his right to leadership of which he was often reminded. On occasion O'Connor over-stepped the bounds of democratic leadership, but he never did so with impunity. For instance, in March 1841, having urged the formation of the National Petition Convention, O'Connor presumed to put forward the names of several key Chartist leaders whose election to the Convention he deemed imperative. He was quickly rebuked for his presumption. Similarly, his offer to support several local Chartists in the role of NCA lecturers in late 1840 brought immediate rank-and-file opposition. At the 1842 National Convention, O'Connor faced stern criticism concerning the role of the *Star* and the denunciations of other Chartist leaders published in its columns.[91] O'Connor acknowledged the continual need for Chartists to subject the movement's leadership, including his own, to close scrutiny and criticism. In turn, Chartists were particularly sensitive to the charge of being merely the 'dupes' of O'Connor and the *Star*. For instance, the Chartists of Middleton, after expressing their disappointment at seeing O'Brien at the Complete Suffrage conference in April 1842, noted:

> The Chartists have long been taunted with being the slaves of Mr. O'Connor; but, if Mr. O'Connor should deviate one iota from the principles contained in the People's Charter we should be as ready to denounce him as any other man.[92]

Still, the close identification between O'Connor's personal leadership and the need for national Chartist unity, rendered sustained opposition to O'Connor and the *Star* over fundamental questions of Chartist policy and organisation damaging to the status of any Chartist leader. Thomas Cooper later reflected, with regard to his own zealous support for O'Connor:

> The people taught me this attachment. I did not teach it to them. I was assured they had no hope in Chartism, but in him . . . during my Leicester chieftainship . . . I held that union was the absolute requisite of Chartist success; and as the people cleaved to O'Connor as their leader, I became a foe to all who opposed him as the fomenters of *disunion*.[93]

This sense of 'attachment', closely linked to a concern for unity, was the motive force behind the verbal, and on occasion physical, attacks which loyal 'O'Connorites' like those at Leicester brought down upon 'renegades' like O'Brien and Vincent. Behind such demonstrations of loyalty important political questions were usually at issue, such as determining the movement's relationship to middle-class radicalism. The attachment which Chartism's rank and file felt towards O'Connor's leadership was rooted in their respect for his past services and the deep class feeling which underpinned their political commitment and which O'Connor had come to symbolise. The twin themes of unity and working-class independence were those to which O'Connor constantly returned. At Glasgow he called on radicals to stand firm to the cause of 'the good old Chartism'. 'Let us hear no more humbug, but let the man who is not a Chartist without any alloy get his walking papers and tramp.'[94]

Generally speaking, O'Connor did not seek confrontations with other Chartist leaders; on the contrary, he was highly conscious of the damaging effect which leadership disputes could have upon Chartist morale, and tried to avoid them when possible. In June 1841, as differences between himself and O'Brien came into the open, O'Connor wrote: 'I have the fear of Hunt and Cobbett before my eyes!'[95] When leaders such as O'Brien, Cooper or Watkins did clash with O'Connor they found themselves in a difficult position. Having previously acknowledged his rightful preeminence and urged the need to unite behind his leadership, they appeared inconsistent and in turn opened themselves to the charge of engendering disunion.

While there is a sense in which Chartism suffered a closure at the level of national leadership, a loss of diversity, particularly in the mid-1840s in the wake of the Complete Suffrage controversy and the defeat of the 1842 'general strike', Chartism never turned in upon itself. The need for Chartist unity, the drive to have all Chartists join the NCA, the purge of the 'rational' Chartists of the 'New Move' and those leaders favourable to an alliance with middle-class radicals, did not mean that Chartism developed into a sectarian political movement. Throughout the 1840s, particularly at the local level, Chartists took the lead in a whole range of working-class activity — trade unionism, cooperation, the ten-hours campaign, anti-Poor Law agitation, etc. O'Connor urged Chartists to petition against the new Poor Law in 1841; support the stonemasons in 1841 and miners in 1844; put the demand for the repeal of the Union between Ireland and England upon their banners and petitions; and back the demand for a

ten-hour day. In 1844, O'Connor outlined his reasons for urging
Chartists to support Ashley's Factory Bill, drawing a careful distinction between support for this measure and lending support to the
middle-class Anti-Corn Law League or Complete Suffrage movement.

> Some very sincere and enthusiastic, but misguided Chartists, have said,
> 'why not oppose this policy equally as the policy of the League, the
> Feudalists, and the Complete Suffragists'! To that view my answer is:
> because the agitation of each and all of those parties is intended to
> *subjugate labour to capital*; WHILE LORD ASHLEY'S BILL WOULD
> TAKE THE VERY LARGEST RIVET OUT OF LABOUR'S FETTERS.
> Shall I be asked if it would be prudent to move the Charter as an
> amendment upon the Ten Hours Bill? . . . my answer is, that it would be
> equally prudent to move it as an amendment to the formation of the
> Colliers' Union; and yet I am rather of the opinion that such a course
> would be scouted by every Chartist in the land. It would be equally
> prudent to move it as an amendment to the Collieries Regulation Bill;
> and yet no man dreamed of doing so, because that was substantively a
> *Labour question*.[96]

With regard to the trade-union movement, he advised Chartists:

> Attend their meetings, swell their numbers, and give them your sym-
> pathy; but on no account interpose the Charter as an obstacle to their
> proceedings. All labour and labourers must unite; and they will speedily
> discover that the Charter is the only standard under which they can
> successfully rally.[97]

Thus O'Connor sought to formulate a policy of Chartist action
which allowed the movement's activists to participate in other working-class agitations for immediate and sectional gains in the hopes
that the majority of workers through their own experience and the
leadership and propaganda of Chartists would come to realise that the
only protection for labour lay in the acquisition of their political rights
as a class.

IV The Promised Land

> Aye, and when success should have crowned his exertions; when the
> moans of sadness, the only note now heard in this seabound dungeon,
> should be changed into the song of gladness; when the factory discipline
> should surrender some hours from slavery to domestic employment and
> social comfort; when the bloody bastile should close, and for ever, its
> jarring gates against the captive, who should fly to the hearth's revelling,

and the cottage wassel; when the children of freemen should graduate from the mother's breast to the father's knee, from the cottage to the national school, and from the school to take his station in the commonwealth as part partaker of these fruits of which he had been part producer, and when in old age the national savings bank in which in youth he had freely deposited, should as freely discount for comforts in after life; then with equal pride to the Peruvian, he should, if spared to see those halcyon days, walk abroad and exultingly proclaim 'this, this, has been in part my work'.[98] (O'Connor at Peep Green, October 1838)

Though vague, and rarely articulated with great theoretical clarity, the vision of an alternative, post-universal-suffrage society exerted a powerful influence over the imagination of working-class radicals. Following Chartism's first phase of mass agitation, O'Connor placed increased importance upon the need to give definition to this vision, to outline more clearly the social benefits which universal suffrage would bring to working people, and to provide Chartism with a social programme to complement the political demand for the suffrage. Thus it was during the early 1840s that O'Connor began to concentrate upon the development of his ideas on the land and to outline the benefits of small farming; it was through the acquisition of a portion of the soil that working people might regain that measure of social and economic independence lost in the process of capitalist industrialisation. 'Lock-up the land to-morrow, and I would not give you two pence for the Charter the next day, because you would have deprived it of its jewel', declared O'Connor in 1841.[99] Increasingly, he came to link the demand for universal suffrage to the question of the worker's alienation from the land.

O'Connor's views on the land have been widely misunderstood and misrepresented by labour historians, many of whom have dismissed his concern with the land as 'backward' looking and as having constituted a 'diversion' from Chartism.[100] Yet a working-class yearning for the land together with the assertion of the labourer's right to a portion of the soil — 'the people's farm' — represents one of the most powerful and persistent themes in the history of British radicalism. The attack on land monopoly and parasitic landlords, the demand for the abolition of primogeniture and entail, claims to the land based on natural right and historic claims based on the myth of the Norman Yoke were all central features of nineteenth-century popular radicalism. O'Connor's ideas on the land should not be divorced from this more general context. Certainly there were differences between radicals over the question of the land; for instance, between those who demanded nationalisation or some form of communal land ownership and those who advocated small private ownership — a split which went back to Spence and Paine. What stands out in the 1830s and 1840s, however, is the widespread interest of working people in all schemes designed to settle workers on the land. Thus O'Connor's land scheme was welcomed not only by the majority of Chartists, but by many socialists as well. More remarkable than the differences between radicals over the question of the land, whether Owenite socialists, Spenceans or supporters of the Chartist land plan, was their common vision of an alternative society and economy — an egalitarian society of small producers based upon small commodity exchange and some form of labour credit.[101] It was to this essentially artisan vision that O'Connor gave expression and to which he appealed.

From his earliest contact with the English radical movement O'Connor had demonstrated an interest in the subject of the land.[102] In summer 1839, in one of the speeches for which he was prosecuted, he had told the Rochdale Chartists:

> Yes; if they had universal suffrage tomorrow, they would not allow the system to remain a day longer. (Hear, hear.) The people ought to have a portion of their native soil, and the poor squalid wretches who are put up in the close rooms and the noxious alleys of Manchester should have the power of turning out from them, and of enjoying the invaluable blessings of the sun and air. (Cheers.) . . . The land belonged to the people; those who by their labour and capital cultivated it have a right to its productions; but no man had a right to more than his share of the soil itself, which upon every principle of justice belonged equally to all the inhabitants of the country . . . The labourers ought to possess the earth.[103]

The following month, at Glasgow, he returned to the theme of the land and the abuse of machinery. He asked why the working class had not been prepared for the sacred month:

> It was because the abuse of machinery had transformed them from a natural to an artificial state of society, by which means they were compelled to live from hand to mouth, being entirely at the mercy of their employers . . . Why were the laws of olden times better than those of this reforming era? It was because they could test the value of labour by a month's or a year's holiday, until the rights they sought for were granted. (Loud cheers.) . . .
>
> As to Universal Suffrage . . . if you and your children were still immured in the unhealthy rattle boxes, it would not be worth one farthing to you — (cheers) — but your share in law making would ensure for you a share in the distribution of that wealth which you create.[104]

The gaining of the Charter clearly implied a redistribution of property and wealth, and the recognition of the labourer's right to the product of his labour, as well as an amelioration of the social conditions imposed by the rise of industrial capitalism. While favouring a society based upon small private property, O'Connor's notion was of limited and controlled individual ownership and competition. He rejected the assertion of total ownership rights and warned of the increased domination of large-scale capital over the lives and labour of working people. Thus in a parting address, published in March 1840, he reminded Chartists:

> It is now some years since I told you that machinery was man's curse instead of man's holiday. I have . . . repeated the assertion, that the great speculators resembled gamblers round a gambling table — that in the end, those with largest capitals would destroy the less opulent; until at length the extensive improvement in machinery, worked by boundless fictitious money, would concentrate the whole trade of the country into a few hands. This prediction is being worked out; and, in its fulfilment, the ruined small capitalists will be compelled to join your ranks. . . . The man whose machinery is over six years old, cannot compete with his neighbour working with that more recently invented. What must be the natural consequence of this unsettled state of things? Must it not always leave a reserve of unemployed at the mercy and disposal of masters and as a terror to those who are thereby compelled to give their work for the lowest rate of wages?[105]

O'Connor was not opposed to the employment of machinery in itself — although the moral outrage directed at the factory system often obscured this point — but rather to the conditions under which it was employed, to its unregulated introduction, displacement of workers and unequal distribution of the wealth created. He never anticipated a total return to the land, but like many radicals wished to establish a balance between agriculture and industry.[106]

It was during his term in prison that O'Connor began to elaborate upon his theories of the land and its benefits. He directed the attention of the founding conference of the NCA to the question of the land. In a series of open letters to James Leach, former cotton operative and member of the NCA National Executive, O'Connor explained that he had 'never desired a too close investigation into the various results likely to spring from Universal Suffrage' as such a discussion might lead to divisions over particular measures.

> I have, however, at all times kept before my hearers and readers the one paramount advantage which I anticipate from Universal Suffrage. It is the restoration of my fellow man from a too artificial to a more natural state of life. This blessing can only be accomplished by discharging the overgrown and overpopulated towns of their squalid, artificial and

superabundant population, and by once more bedecking the face of nature with the comfortable, modest homes of Nature's children.[107]

Thus he started from the distinction between 'natural' and 'artificial' society, a distinction rooted in the romantic critique of utilitarianism and industrialisation widely assimilated within the working-class radical movement. According to O'Connor: 'All save the land is artificial.'[108] At the centre of his concern with the land was a critique of the nature of work and work discipline in industrialising society. Man was being transformed 'from a natural to an artificial being'. O'Connor appealed to a rugged, outdoor spirit of individualism and hard work. 'I am a beef-and-mutton, a pork and butter and bread and milk and honey Radical. I am an open-air, a work-when-I'm-able-and-work-for-myself-and-my-family-Radical.'[109] He looked to a time 'when the weaver worked at his loom, and stretched his limbs in his own field, when the laws recognised the poor man's right to an abundance of everything'.[110] Like Cobbett, he drew a highly idealised picture of a rural 'golden age' in which there existed an 'organic' community with a sense of mutual dependency and a rough egalitarianism.

> Formerly society was divided into small rural communities, so closely allied in interest, and so mutually dependent upon each other for companionship, as to make them resemble a large family. . . . There were masters and men reciprocally depending upon each other for everything. . . .
> Thus did the machinery work well and harmoniously, and the little community were happy. No policemen — no Commissioners of the Poor — no spies — no informers . . . were known.[111]

It is in such passages that O'Connor comes closest to embracing a tory-paternalistic vision. The power of this myth of a lost paternalistic community was rooted in the deep sense of an absence of community and mutual regard in the industrial towns, a denial of humanity.

However, O'Connor's real aim was not the restoration of a paternalistic community, but the establishment of a community based upon the independence of the worker. His ideal was the small independent farmer, weaver or craftsman. He looked to the land to provide comfort, security and independence to working people. 'The sum and substance of my Chartism is independence and contentment, neither of which can you by any possibility enjoy under the present system.'[112]

> Always keep one fact in view, that by locating you upon the land, I seek to make you masters of your own labour and your own time,— to make your wives housewives instead of slaves,— and to make your children

freemen, instead of serfs,— in short, to make you what you ought to be, '*first partakers of the fruits of your own industry.*'[113]

A strong proponent of the labour theory of value, O'Connor maintained, 'labour is the foundation of all wealth. That is indisputable.'[114] In the present 'artificial' state of society, however, the dominance of capital over labour, particularly in the form of steam-powered machinery meant that the price of labour was constantly being driven down. As O'Connor explained to a meeting of London stonemasons, the employment of steam power in the cotton industry was a matter of concern not only for cotton spinners, as it had the effect of lowering the general price of labour throughout the trades by swelling the ranks of the unemployed.[115] It was necessary to establish a 'natural' standard to determine the real value of a man's labour. This could be realised only through the land, where the worker who owned his own small plot reaped the full fruits of his labour. Once this value had been established, then workers could freely choose whether to enter the factory or work the land. The settlement of unemployed workers on the land would force up industrial wages and bring improved work conditions as employers would have to attract workers into the factory.

> When one man employs another and makes profit of his labour, let others call it what they please, I call it slavery. That is, provided the man employed is *compelled* to work for another because he has not the means of working for himself. The case is far different, when both doors are open, and when the workman may enter at which door he pleases — the natural door, which is the land, or the artificial door, which is the factory. In such case, the standard of wages established in the free labour, or natural market, renders the man who works in the artificial market from choice, just as independent as his neighbour.[116]

It is not always clear whether O'Connor is calling for an abolition of wage labour, of a system in which the worker is forced to sell his labour power as a commodity in the marketplace, or merely some modification of this economic system whereby workers might improve and exert some measure of control over their material conditions of life. Similarly, at one level he offered what he considered to be an immediately realisable, though limited, course of working-class collective self-help, while at another level he raised the prospect of a total reordering of society to be achieved through the political emancipation of the working class. Although O'Connor clearly failed to provide a fully coherent socio-economic theory, his vision was no more utopian or impracticable than, for instance, O'Brien's proposals for land nationalisation without forcible expropriation.[117]

O'Connor's practical experience as a farmer lent authority to his pronouncements on the capabilities of the land and the advantages of small farming and spade husbandry. His book, *A Practical Work on the Management of Small Farms*, published in 1843 and co-authored by T. M. Wheeler, became essential reading for radicals interested in the land question.[118] However, O'Connor was merely continuing a discussion about the advantages of intensive farming initiated by Cobbett and Owen and taken up by others. His interest in the land must be seen within the context of a wide-ranging contemporary debate about agricultural production, scarcity and abundance, population, poor relief and unemployment, home colonisation versus emigration.[119] In opposition to the Anti-Corn Law League, O'Connor maintained that the need was not for free trade, but rather the establishment of England's self-sufficiency in agriculture through a more efficient and intensive system of farming. He asserted the potential of material abundance, rejecting the Malthusian doctrines of the political economists. The country was not overpopulated but undercultivated, the unregulated introduction of machinery was the root cause of unemployment.[120] The land question was closely linked to the debate over provision for the poor and the opposition to the new Poor Law. O'Connor claimed that the right to poor relief was as a substitute for the worker's natural right to the land which had been usurped at an earlier period of English history.[121] He proposed land settlements as a practical solution to the problems of poverty and unemployment, as an alternative to the new Poor Law.

Upon his release from prison, during his extensive tours of agitation in late 1841 and 1842, O'Connor continually returned to the theme of the land. At the Convention of April 1842, he moved discussion of the need to devise a social programme for Chartism:

> The Charter was a new system of government. It was necessary that they continue to secure the continued approbation of the public, that they should produce before them, in tangible shape, the benefits to be derived from the adoption of the Charter. The public mind was now prepared for great changes; the Charter would be the means of giving them a power of increasing the productive resources of the empire; and secondly, the Charter would give them the means of more equitably distributing the wealth.

He urged Chartist lecturers to speak out on the question of the land and outline the potential of small farming, in order to 'show that when they removed the present system they were enabled to supply its place with a better one'.[122] Although the 1842 Convention deferred any decision on whether to adopt the call for land reform, O'Connor's comments were received with much interest and approbation. The following year, the Birmingham NCA conference approved O'Connor's proposal to incorporate a scheme for establishing Chartist land communities as part of the NCA programme, although the Chartist Land Society was not formed until 1845.[123]

As John Saville has argued, O'Connor's concern with the land question should not be viewed as an Irish imposition on the Chartist movement. This is underlined by the deep response which O'Connor's ideas on the land evoked within the working class. Support for the land plan was extremely widespread; there were probably more members of the National Land Company than there were of the NCA at its height.[124] The Chartist land plan represented merely the most outstanding example of a more general working-class concern. If there is a sense in which O'Connor's concern with the land proved a diversion from Chartism's political core, there is also a sense in which it provided an important complementary aspect to Chartist agitation. As Henry Dorman, Nottingham's delegate, explained to the 1845 conference convened to discuss the land plan: 'the people wanted something tangible. . . . The land plan was well calculated to keep up the Chartist agitation, and he did not believe one country delegate would have been present had it not been for the desire to become in some measure possessors of the soil.'[125] In many localities it was the land plan which reinvigorated the movement in the mid-1840s.[126]

An inspired propagandist and agitator, O'Connor advanced no original economic or social theory. His categories of reference — the worker's right to the soil, the labour theory of value, the distinction between 'artificial' and 'natural' society, the assertion that machinery should be man's holiday rather than his curse, the concept of a 'fair day's wage' — were commonplace to working-class radicalism in the 1840s. Furthermore, the points of disagreement between O'Connor's outlook and that of the Owenite socialists should not be exaggerated. O'Connor always expressed the deepest respect for Owen, his ideas and practical work. There was no sharp opposition between O'Connor's advocacy of individual small private property and Owenite communitarianism, both flowed from the same tradition of artisan radicalism.[127] What O'Connor captured was an artisan consciousness concerned with the values of independence and self-reliance. It was this artisan consciousness which lay at the heart of English working-class radicalism from the 1790s to the Chartist period. While the working class was exposed to a general process of proletarianisation, this artisan consciousness remained. During the Chartist period working-class radicals still cherished the ideal of a society composed of small producers. This was a 'backward-looking' ideal in the sense that it implied an arresting of the full development of the emergent forces of industrial capitalism. However, during the 1830s and 1840s, it still appeared as if the dominance of industrial capitalism was by no means an inevitable outcome. When this historical perspective became no longer tenable, the essentially artisan radicalism of Chartism no longer provided a viable alternative vision of society.[128]

NOTES

1. *NS*, 16 May 1840, p. 6; also see J. C. Belchem, 'Radicalism as a "Platform" Agitation in the period 1816-21 and 1848-51; With Special Reference to the Leadership of Henry Hunt and Feargus O'Connor', (Sussex Univ. D. Phil thesis, 1975), p. 7.

2. *NS*, 2 Jan. 1841, p. 1.

3. Ibid., 7 July 1840, p. 7.

4. Ibid., 23 May 1840, p. 4; 23 May-15 Aug., for publicity concerning O'Connor's imprisonment; also *Times*, 26, 28 May 1840; 13 July.

5. *Hansard*, Parl. Debates, 3rd Series, LIV, 27 May 1840, cols. 647-56; 4, 5, 22 June, cols. 908-13, 917-22, 953-54, 1365-68; Parl. Sessional Papers, Commons, XXXVIII, 1840, pp. 613-20; York Castle Museum, O'Connor to Talfourd, 19 May 1840 and n.d. (c. 25 May).

6. *NS*, 30 May-27 June 1840; *Southern Star*, 7 June 1840, p. 1; *Northern Liberator*, 6-20 June 1840.

7. *NS*, 30 May 1840, p. 1.

8. Parl. Sessional Papers, XXXVIII, 1840, pp. 616-20; *NS*, 13 June 1840, p. 4; PRO, HO 20/10, interview with O'Connor.

9. See the complaints of Edward Brown, PRO, HO 20/10, and Timothy Higgins (Ashton cotton spinner), *Stephens Monthly Magazine*, Aug. 1840, pp. 187-92. For the conditions of Chartist prisoners generally, see Parl. Sessional Papers, XXXVIII, 1840, pp. 691-766; PRO, HO 20/10; *NS*, throughout 1840 and 1841; also see C. Godfrey, 'The Chartist Prisoners, 1839-41', *International Review of Social History*, 24, 1979, pp. 189-236.

10. J. Watkins, *John Watkins to the People, in Answer to Feargus O'Connor*, London 1844, p. 4.

11. Chartists merely revived an older tradition. Angus Bethune Reach commented that at Middleton: 'a generation or so back, Henry Hunts were as common as blackberries — a crop of Feargus O'Connors replaced them, and latterly there have been a few green sprouts labelled Ernest Jones'. *Morning Chronicle*, 26 Nov. 1849.

12. For some of the poetry dedicated to O'Connor, see *NS*, 27 June 1840, p. 7; 6 Feb. 1841, p. 3; 19 June, p. 3; 21 Aug., p. 3; 11 Sept., p. 3; 4 Sept., p. 6, for O'Connor's liberation.

13. *Manchester and Salford Advertiser*, 12 Dec. 1840, p. 2; *NS*, 14 Nov. 1840-9 Jan. 1841; 13 Mar., p. 7; 22 May, p. 6.

14. I use the term 'party' here in a loose sense; it is meant to convey neither the image of a modern social democratic party nor a Leninist vanguard party. While following Marx and Engels in the view that the Chartists formed the first national party of the working class, it should be noted that Marx and Engels were inconsistent in their

own use of the term 'party'.

15. *McDouall's Chartist and Republican Journal*, 3 Apr. 1841, pp. 1-2.

16. M. Hovell, *The Chartist Movement*, Manchester, 2nd ed. 1925, p. 196.

17. *Northern Liberator*, 28 Mar.-23 Apr. 1840; 13 June, p. 5 (Newcastle, Carlisle, Sunderland); *NS*, 15 Feb. 1840, p. 5; 28 Mar., p. 5; 24 Oct., pp. 4-5; 31 Oct., p. 4; 5 Dec., p. 7 (Birmingham); *NS*, 25 Apr. 1840, p. 3; 23 May, p. 5 (London); *NS*, 16 May 1840, p. 8; 13 June, p. 8; 27 June, p. 8; PRO, HO 45/46, handbill 'Chartist Plan for Lectures' (Lancashire).

18. *Northern Liberator*, 28 Mar. 1840, p. 6; also 2 May, p. 1.

19. For the Scottish movement see A. Wilson, *The Chartist Movement in Scotland*, Manchester 1970, pp. 114-17; *Chartist Circular*, 28 Sept. 1839, pp. 1-3.

20. *Northern Liberator*, 21 Mar. 1840, p. 7.

21. *NS*, 6 June 1840, p. 1; 13 June, p. 8; 27 June, p. 1.

22. Ibid., 20 June 1840, p. 1; 27 June, pp. 1, 4. Richard Spurr did attend, however, as London's representative.

23. *NS*, 4 July 1840, p. 4; 18 July, p. 4.

24. Ibid., 11 July 1840, p. 7; 18 July, pp. 1, 6 (O'Connor); 2 May, p. 7; 4 July, p. 7 (Lowery); 9 May, p. 7; 30 May, p. 7; 20 June, p. 7 (also for Richardson); 11 July, p. 8 ('A Republican').

25. *NS*, 25 July 1840, p. 1; 1 Aug. 1840, p. 1.

26. The Provisional Executive appointed at the Manchester conference included: James Leach, John Deegan, Richard Littler, William Tillman (secretary), James Taylor, William Smith and Abel Heywood (treasurer). In February 1841, the Executive was reduced to five and Leach, Littler, Tillman, John Campbell and James Cartledge were appointed as a new Provisional Executive to serve until June 1841. Tillman resigned in April and Campbell replaced him as secretary.

27. P. H. J. Gosden, *The Friendly Societies in England, 1815-1875*, Manchester 1961, *passim.*

28. J. F. C. Harrison, *Robert Owen and the Owenites*, London 1969, pp. 216-32.

29. G. D. H. Cole, *Attempts at General Union, 1818-1834*, London 1953; W. H. Oliver, 'The Consolidated Trades' Union of 1834', *Economic History Review*, 17, 1964, pp. 77-95; E. P. Thompson, *The Making of the English Working Class*, Penguin ed., Harmondsworth 1968, ch. 8, also pp. 908-13; S. and B. Webb, *The History of Trade Unionism*, London 1920 ed., ch. 3, pp. 163-78; R. Challinor and B. Ripley, *The Miners' Association: A Trade Union in the Age of the Chartists*, London 1968, *passim.*

30. *NS*, 25 July 1840, p. 1; also see R. F. Wearmouth, *Methodism and the Working-Class Movements of England, 1800-1850*, London 1937, particularly ch. 3; Thompson, *The Making*, pp. 45-48, 427-40; E. J. Hobsbawm, *Primitive Rebels*, Manchester 1971 ed., pp. 129-32, 139-40.

31. D. J. V. Jones, *Chartism and the Chartists*, London 1975, p. 103.

32. *NS*, 22 Aug. 1840, p. 1; 17 Oct., p. 2; 24 Oct., p. 2; 28 Nov., p. 1; 5 Dec., p. 7; 19 Dec., p. 7; 26 Dec., p. 1.

33. Ibid., 19 Dec. 1840, p. 1.

34. *NS*, 3 Oct. 1840, p. 1.

35. *Northern Liberator*, 28 Nov. 1840, p. 6.

36. *NS*, 27 Feb. 1841, p. 1.

37. Ibid., 9 Jan. 1841, p. 3.

38. Ibid., 6 Mar. 1841, p. 4.

39. Behind the scenes Collins was in touch with Place and several parliamentary radicals over this question. British Library, Place Collection, Set 56 (Jan.-Apr. 1841), fos. 315, 339, Collins to Place, 27 Feb. 1841 and Place to Collins, 1 Mar. 1841; R. E. Leader, *Life and Letters of John Arthur Roebuck*, London 1897, p. 134.

40. *NS*, 11 Dec. 1841, p. 5; 24 Dec., p. 7.

41. Ibid., 5 June 1841, p. 5; 7 Aug., p. 7. Heywood remained NCA treasurer.

42. Ibid., 11 June 1842, p. 1.

43. Ibid., 9 July 1842, p. 6; 12 Nov., p. 8.

44. I. J. Prothero, 'Chartism in London', *Past and Present*, no. 44, 1969, pp. 82-84, 86, 97; id., 'London Chartism and the Trades', *Economic History Review*, 24, 1971, pp. 202-04.

45. *NS*, 23 Apr. 1842, p. 6; 30 Apr., p. 6, for the state of the movement at Birmingham; G. Barnsby, 'The Working-Class Movement in the Black County, 1815-1867', (Birmingham Univ. MA thesis, 1965), p. 194, and ch. 7, *passim*.

46. PRO, TS 11/601, Harney to Cooper, 2 Aug. 1842, Harney claimed 1300 NCA members at Sheffield.

47. At the 1842 Convention, in April, 1200 NCA members were reported at both Leicester and Nottingham; J. F. C. Harrison, 'Chartism at Leicester', in A. Briggs (ed.), *Chartist Studies*, London 1959, p. 110.

48. For instance, *NS*, 30 Oct. 1841, p. 1; 27 Apr. 1844, p. 1, O'Connor estimated that only seven thousand out of twenty thousand NCA members would pay regular subscriptions.

49. *NS*, 4 Dec. 1841, p. 6.

50. PRO, TS 11/602, White to Cooper, 27 July 1842.

51. *NS*, 19 Feb. 1842, p. 5.

52. Ibid., 4 Feb. 1843, p. 1. For Hill's attack on the Executive, see *NS*, 19 Nov. 1842-4 Feb. 1843; F. O'Connor, *A Letter from Feargus O'Connor, Esq., to the Rev. William Hill*, London 1843, pp. 23-24. Leaders such as Cooper, Hill and Watkins were becoming increasingly opposed to a paid Executive, desiring only a paid national secretary.

53. *NS*, 4 June 1842, p. 7; 7 Jan. 1843, p. 1.

54. Ibid., 24 Oct. 1840, p. 5; 14 Nov., p. 7; *Northern Liberator*, 7 Nov. 1840, p. 6. For a full discussion of the foreign-affairs movement and Chartism in 1840, see J. A. Epstein, 'Feargus O'Connor and the English Working-Class Radical Movement, 1832-1841', (Birmingham Univ. PhD 1977), pp. 417-25.

55. *NS*, 16 Sept. 1843, p. 6; R. G. Gammage, *History of the Chartist Movement*, Newcastle 1894, pp. 250-51.

56. The 1841/42 Executive included: Leach, powerloom weaver, M'Douall, surgeon, Philp, printer, Morgan Williams, proprietor of a small flannel factory, George Binns, printer and bookseller, Campbell, powerloom weaver. In June 1842, Philp lost his seat to the weaver, Jonathan Bairstow.

57. *NS*, 29 June 1844, p. 1; 27 July, p. 1.

58. Jones, *Chartism and the Chartists*, p. 183.

59. The term 'movement culture' is borrowed from Lawrence Goodwyn's study, *Democratic Promise: The Populist Movement in America*, New York 1976. For an important discussion of 'radical culture', see E. Yeo, 'Robert Owen and Radical Culture', in S. Pollard and J. Salt (eds.), *Robert Owen, Prophet of the Poor*, London 1971, pp. 84-114.

60. Cf. B. Harrison and P. Hollis, 'Chartism, Liberalism and the Life of Robert Lowery', *English Historical Review*, 82, 1967, 503-35.

61. *NS*, 2 Sept. 1843, p. 4.

62. Yeo, 'Owen and Radical Culture', p. 104.

63. *NS*, 20 Apr. 1844, p. 1; for Chartist halls and schools, see B. Simon, *Studies in the History of Education, 1780-1870*, London 1960, pp. 243-53.

64. *NS*, 30 Apr. 1842, p. 6; 16 Sept. 1843, p. 1; B. Harrison, 'Teetotal Chartism', *History*, 58, 1973, pp. 193-217, which includes an excellent discussion of O'Connor's views on drink.

65. *NS*, 26 Dec. 1840, p. 1.

66. Chartists remained ambiguous on the question of female suffrage. O'Connor seemed to support the vote for 'all widows and spinsters'. *NS*, 14 Sept. 1839, p. 7.

67. See G. Stedman Jones, 'Class Expression versus Social Control? A Critique of Recent Trends in the Social History of "Leisure" ', *History Workshop*, no. 4, 1977, pp.

169-70.

68. *Union Advocate*, 1 Nov. 1842, p. 3, copy in British Library, Place Newspaper Collection, Set 56 (Nov. 1842-Jan. 1843).

69. *NS*, 28 Nov. 1840, p. 3; 3 Apr. 1841, p. 1; 10 Apr., p. 1; *English Chartist Circular*, Mar. 1840, pp. 35, 39.

70. *NS*, 13 Mar. 1841, p. 7; 3 Apr., pp. 7, 4; H. U. Faulkner, *Chartism and the Churches*, New York 1916; Wilson, *Chartist Movement in Scotland*, chs. 10 and 11.

71. *Midland Counties Illuminator*, 17, 24 Apr. 1841, pp. 39, 43, for problems at Leicester.

72. See reports in PRO, HO 40/50; 40/56; 65/10; 45/52; 45/102A., pt. 1; *NS*, 21 Nov. 1840, p. 1; 2 Jan.-17 Apr. 1841; *Birmingham Journal*, 2, 9 Jan. 1841; T. Tholfsen, 'The Chartist Crisis in Birmingham', *International Review of Social History*, 3, 1958, pp. 473ff.

73. See the report of a conversation between White, M'Douall and Martin, in PRO, HO 45/52, fos. 34-35.

74. *NS*, 6-27 Feb. 1841.

75. W. Lovett and J. Collins, *Chartism, A New Organization of the People*, Leicester 1969, with intro. by A. Briggs (first published 1840); W. Lovett, *Life and Struggles of William Lovett*, Fitzroy ed., London 1967, pp. 202-07; The *Star's* initial reaction to Lovett and Collins's pamphlet had not been unfavourable, *NS*, 3 Oct. 1840, p. 5.

76. *NS*, 8 May 1841, p. 7.

77. *NS*, 10 Apr. 1841, pp. 1, 5; also 17 Apr., p. 3; 24 Apr., p. 4.

78. Ibid., 24 Apr. 1841, p. 7.

79. Ibid., 8 May 1841, p. 1 (Bradford); 17 Apr., p. 1; 24 Apr., pp. 2, 7 (Birmingham).

80. Ibid., 24 Apr.-15 May 1841; 26 June, p. 4; see B. Harrison's entry for Vincent, in J. M. Bellamy and J. Saville (eds.), *Dictionary of Labour Biography*, London 1972, I, p. 328.

81. *NS*, 1 May 1841, p. 7.

82. Ibid., 22 May 1841, p. 2.

83. Prothero, 'Chartism in London', p. 98; D. Large, 'William Lovett', in P. Hollis (ed.), *Pressure from Without in Early Victorian England*, London 1974, p. 126.

84. *NS*, 30 Apr. 1842, p. 6.

85. Ibid., 8 May 1841, p. 5; 15 May, p. 6.

86. *British Statesman*, 5 Nov. 1842, p. 1; *Poor Man's Guardian and Repealer's Friend*, no. 8 (1843), p. 57.

87. British Library, Place Newspaper Collection, Set 56 (Oct. 1840-Feb. 1841), fo. 47, Vincent to Place, 31 Dec. 1840. For the favourable reaction of the middle-class press, see *Leeds Times*, 8 May 1841, p. 7; *Stockport Chronicle*, 23 Apr. 1841, p. 2, 'Chartists Returning to Reason'.

88. Handbill, copy in British Library, Add. MSS 27821, fos. 354-55.

89. *Receipts and Expenditure of the National Association, Feb. 22-June 24, 1843*. Substantial donations came from middle-class politicians such as Leader, Hume, Bowring, Warburton, J.S. Mill, Grote, Duncombe, Villiers, Milner Gibson, Burdett, John Marshall, etc.

90. See British Library, Add. MSS 37774, National Association Minute Book; *National Association Gazette*, 8 Jan.-23 Apr. 1842; *NS*, 19 Feb. 1842, p. 5.

91. *NS*, 13 Mar. 1841, p. 7; 3 Apr., p. 7; 14 Nov.-10 Dec. 1840; 23 Apr. 1842, pp. 6-8.

92. Ibid., 23 Apr. 1842, p. 1.

93. Gammage, *History of the Chartist Movement*, p. 407.

94. *NS*, 16 Oct. 1841, p. 5.

95. Ibid., 26 June 1841, p. 1.

96. Ibid., 6 Apr. 1844, p. 1.

97. Ibid., 16 Nov. 1844, p. 1.

98. Ibid., 16 Oct. 1838.

99. Ibid., 24 July 1841, p. 1.

100. For an important reevaluation of O'Connor and the land question, see J. Saville's introduction to Gammage, *History of the Chartist Movement*, Cass ed., London 1969; also see J. MacAskill, 'The Chartist Land Plan', in *Chartist Studies*, pp. 304-41; id., 'The Treatment of the Land in English Social and Political Theory, 1840-1885', (Oxford Univ. B. Litt thesis, 1959), particularly pt. 1.

101. Thompson, *The Making*, pp. 176-77, 224-25, 326; I. J. Prothero, *Artisans and Politics in Early Nineteenth-Century London: John Gast and His Times*, Folkestone 1979, *passim*; T. M. Parssinen, 'Thomas Spence and the Origins of English Land Nationalisation', *Journal of the History of Ideas*, 34, 1973, pp. 135-141; T. R. Knox, 'Thomas Spence: The Trumpet of the Jubilee', *Past and Present*, no. 76, 1977, pp. 75-98. A Spencean like Allen Davenport supported the land plan, as did socialists like Hobson and Wheeler, Thomas Frost, editor of the *Communist Journal*, and members of the Fraternal Democrats.

102. See the series of letters signed 'Quintus Cincinatus' (O'Connor), *True Sun*, 24 Sept. 1836, p. 1; 1 Oct., p. 4; 12 Oct., p. 2; 21 Oct., p. 1.

103. *NS*, 13 July 1839, p. 7.

104. Ibid., 24 Aug. 1839, pp. 2-3.

105. Ibid., 28 Mar. 1840, pp. 4-5.

106. Ibid., 23 June 1838, p. 8; 4 May 1839, p. 7; 5 Feb. 1842, p. 4; *English Chartist Circular*, II (1842-43), pp. 29, 37, 57, 101. O'Connor's position was in line with that of other radicals and trade unionists. See M. Berg, *The Machinery Question and the Making of Political Economy, 1815-1848*, Cambridge 1980, ch. 12.

107. *NS*, 16 May 1840, p. 6.

108. *English Chartist Circular*, II (1842), p. 45. The distinction between 'artificial' and 'natural' society was also a prominent theme of Owenism.

109. *NS*, 28 Mar. 1840, p. 5; 11 July, p. 7.

110. F. O'Connor, *The Employer and the Employed; The Chambers' Philosophy Refuted*, London 1843, p. 56.

111. *NS*, 16 May 1840, p. 6; also see *Employer and the Employed*, pp. 15-17, 41-42.

112. *NS*, 29 Aug. 1840, p. 5.

113. *English Chartist Circular*, II (1842), p. 94.

114. *NS*, 31 July 1841, p. 1.

115. Ibid., 18 Sept. 1841, p. 1.

116. Ibid., 13 May 1843, p. 1.

117. The principal difference between O'Connor and O'Brien concerned how the land was to be repossessed by the people. Although O'Brien called for land nationalisation, like O'Connor he favoured a system of private small ownership. O'Brien's opposition to the land plan was to a large degree sparked by personal differences; initially, he had praised O'Connor's views on the land.

118. Also see F. O'Connor, *The Land and Its Capabilities*, Manchester 1842; id., *A Treatise on the Land*, London 1848; id., *What May Be Done with Three Acres of Land*, London n.d.

119. Saville, introduction to Gammage, *History of the Chartist Movement*, pp. 50-59; D. Martin, 'Land Reform', in *Pressure from Without*, pp. 131-58; D. C. Barnett, 'Allotments and the Problem of Rural Poverty, 1780-1840', in E. L. Jones and G. E. Mingay (eds.), *Land, Labour and Population in the Industrial Revolution*, London 1967.

120. *NS*, 30 Apr. 1842, pp. 6-7; 15 Apr. 1843, p. 1.

121. Following Cobbett, O'Connor usually dated this usurpation from the reign of Henry VIII.

122. *NS*, 30 Apr. 1842, pp. 5-6.

123. Ibid., 9, 16 Sept. 1843; 3 May 1845, p. 1; Gammage, *History of the Chartist Movement*, pp. 248-51.

124. See MacAskill, 'Chartist Land Plan', pp. 315-22; Jones, *Chartism and the Chartists*, pp. 10, 134-37.

125. *NS*, 26 Apr. 1845, p. 6. There was a general feeling that Chartism needed a social programme. See, for instance, Cooperative Union Library, Holyoake Collection, Harney to Holyoake, 22 Apr. 1844. According to Holyoake: 'Mr. O'Connor started his land scheme partly to satisfy the longing for social experiment which had begun to show itself in the ranks of his adherents.' G. J. Holyoake, *History of Co-operation*, London 1875, p. 291.

126. See T. Frost, *Forty Years Recollections*, London 1880, p. 96; F. J. Kaijage, 'Labouring Barnsley, 1816-1856: A Social and Economic History', (Warwick Univ. PhD thesis, 1975), pp. 525-26.

127. See O'Connor, *Practical Work on Small Farms*, p. 115.

128. See G. Stedman Jones, 'Class Struggle and the Industrial Revolution', *New Left Review*, no. 90, 1975, pp. 68-69.

7 THE MIDDLE-CLASS CHALLENGE AND CHARTIST STRATEGY

I The Middle-Class Embrace, 1840-1841

During the early 1840s the Chartist movement redirected its energies towards forming a viable national organisation, broadening its cultural sphere and considering the need to incorporate a social programme under its banner. However, the central problem of how to achieve the desired goal, of how to win political power for working people, remained. One conclusion which could be drawn from the events of 1839 was that without the cooperation of at least sections of the middle class working-class radicals lacked the strength needed to carry their demands. One of the most recurrent problems which Chartism's leadership had to face was that of formulating a coherent policy towards the series of proffered alliances with liberal sections of the middle class. At each stage of the movement's history, but particularly following the set-backs of 1839-40, 1842 and 1848, there were moves by middle-class political reformers — the Leeds Parliamentary Reform Association (1840-41), the Complete Suffrage Union (1841-43), the 'Little Charter' move and the National Parliamentary and Financial Reform Association (1848-50) — to forge an alliance with sections of the Chartist movement. The quest for a cross-class reform alliance forms a central theme in British political history through the 1860s to the agitation for the second Reform Bill. One of the most striking characteristics of the period of mass Chartist agitation, 1838-50, was the failure of these attempts at political class collaboration. However, while the mutually antagonistic forms of class consciousness forged in the pre-Chartist period provided a fundamental source of working-class radical unity, the practical and theoretical problems posed by successive middle-class cooperative overtures were still potentially divisive, a potential realised most fully in 1842-43.

The hulk which carried Frost and his comrades into exile had hardly set sail before middle-class reformers were considering the prospects of some form of alliance with the Chartists. In early February 1840, Joseph Hume wrote to Place:

> I want to know your opinion of the chance of the Chartists now acting more moderately if we were to put ourselves at their head to demand the

263

leading points of the Charter quietly, but by the strongest demonstration of numbers; whether, in fact, the working men would now join us in our demand for all, but in the understanding that we will be ready to take any part of our demand.[1]

Hume's emphasis on the need to proceed 'quietly', his readiness to compromise and assumption that any such alliance would be conducted with 'ourselves at their head' were indicative of the attitude of the middle-class radicals who held out the promise of a middle-class/working-class alliance. The following month, Roebuck wrote to his wife that he had met with the 'liberals' of Leeds who 'plainly said (being very moderate lads, mind), "We want a new *charter* without the name, which will unite the now conflicting opinions in the Liberal party." '[2] In April, Warburton wrote Place to enlist his support for a meeting called to consider suffrage reform and the repeal of the corn laws and which was intended to initiate a cross-class alliance. The Leeds manufacturers James Marshall and Hamer Stansfeld were the moving force behind this initiative which also involved the radical MPs Hume, O'Connell, Ellis and Molesworth. Place, who had so often played the role of broker between middle-class and working-class radicals, had also been in contact with Marshall and Stansfeld, but was sceptical about the chances of such an alliance.[3] However, the movement which was to lead to the formation of the Leeds Parliamentary Reform Association, and eventually to the Complete Suffrage movement, was already taking shape in the wake of Chartism's first defeat.

Central to O'Connor's status as the Chartist movement's most respected national leader was his intransigent class tone and class perspective. Above all, O'Connor stood for the necessity of the working-class radical movement to maintain its full independence and oppose all forms of middle-class reformism. The unity of the movement could be ensured only through an uncompromising stand for the full Charter. O'Connor clearly anticipated the moves of middle-class radicals over the coming months. In his parting address to the movement, he constantly returned to the theme of the prospects for a middle-class alliance and the dangerous threat of Whig-radicalism. He urged Chartists not to break ranks and succumb to overtures from sections of the Anti-Corn Law League or to join any agitation for 'suffrage extension'. 'Join them now, and they will laugh at you; stand out like men, and THEY MUST JOIN YOU for the Charter.' The repeal of the corn laws could never benefit the working class 'till they had the full benefits of representation, which could alone be granted

to them by the establishment of the Charter . . .' From prison he
called on the founding conference of the NCA to 'reprobate, de-
nounce, nay, FORBID any junction of the labouring order with any
other who does not live by labour, and whose benefit consists in
plundering labour . . .' In August, O'Connor proclaimed a political
alliance with the middle classes to be 'wholly and entirely impractical
. . . an invitation to sink the name of Radical and assume that of Whig',
and warned:

> that those starters from the garden of Whiggery, who thus step beyond
> the prescribed bounds of their party to entice us, are, of all others, the
> most dangerous and least to be relied upon; the most artful, cunning,
> deceitful, and dangerous party that we have to deal with.

He concluded with a condemnation of the 'London-join-the-middle-
class radicals' and the radical committees organised by Place and the
parliamentary radicals.[4]

The Leeds Parliamentary Reform Association was formed in May
1840, in response to the Commons' overwhelming refusal to consider
Villiers's motion for the repeal of the corn laws, and held its first
public meeting in late August.[5] The Leeds initiative, although locally
based, was taken in concert with the parliamentary radicals and was
understood to have national implications. The Leeds move to link
some form of suffrage extension to the agitation for corn-law repeal
was, however, merely the most impressive of a series of middle-class
overtures for a cross-class alliance in 1840.[6] It represented the most
significant attempt to forge a class alliance in the period previous to
the Complete Suffrage movement. Formally the LPRA was under
the control of a committee composed equally of middle-class and
working-class men. Real control, however, was in the hands of a small
group of extremely wealthy, large-scale manufacturers and merchants, most notably: James Marshall, owner of the world's largest
flax spinning factory, Hamer Stansfeld, Thomas Plint, Joshua Bower,
George Goodman. These men were prominent in municipal politics,
as town councillors, aldermen, former and future mayors and parliamentary representatives, and were the leaders of the Leeds free-
trade movement.[7] The LPRA was also backed by the middle-class
radical *Leeds Times*, which in the pre-Chartist period was distinguished for its support of working-class radicalism and factory reform,
and its editor, Samuel Smiles, who became the association's secretary.[8]

The LPRA was, however, by no means representative of unified
middle-class political opinion, but merely represented the position of

certain sections of Leeds middle-class reform opinion. Without necessarily accepting the view that the predominant political struggle within early Victorian cities took place within the urban middle class, the differences within this class were of importance. In most towns the suffrage-extension issue reflected significant intra-class and intra-party differences.[9] Thus the *Leeds Mercury,* under the control of Edward Baines and his son and among the most influential mouthpieces of provincial middle-class opinion, did not support the Leeds household-suffrage movement. While leaders of the LPRA argued that repeal of the corn laws could only be achieved through an extension of the suffrage, Baines was satisfied that free trade could be established without dangerously tampering with the terms of the 1832 reform settlement.[10] Richard Cobden and the Lancashire leadership of the ACLL tended to agree with Baines, the time was not right to initiate a campaign for suffrage extension or for a realignment of liberal forces within the Whig Party.[11] Recently attention has also been directed to differences within the LPRA itself, between large manufacturers such as Marshall and Stansfeld and members of Wakefield's 'uneasy' (or 'middling') class, represented most prominently by Smiles.[12]

While the question of the character and class composition of rank-and-file support for the LPRA remains problematic, it seems clear that the initiative failed to win widespread working-class support. And although O'Connor and the *Star* were the most outspoken opponents of the LPRA, no section of the Chartist movement lent support to the household-suffrage movement. Furthermore, if O'Connor, Hill and the Chartist movement at large failed to make any practical distinction between the motives and policy of the 'steam lords' of the LPRA and the essentially petty-bourgeois radicalism of Smiles and the *Leeds Times,* this was precisely for reasons noted by Dr A. Tyrrell. First, Smiles's 'expediency', the facility with which he moved from support for universal suffrage to household suffrage and then back to complete suffrage in pursuit of a middle-class/working-class alliance, was hardly calculated to inspire the trust of working-class radicals. Such vacillation underscored the ambiguous and increasingly marginal position of such lower-middle-class radicals in relation to the dominant class forces of early Victorian society.[13] Secondly, few working-class radicals shared either Smiles's reverence for Benthamite utilitarianism or his respect for philosophic radicals such as J. A. Roebuck. The previous two decades had witnessed an ideological and political rupture between popular radicalism and

Benthamite political economy.

In the columns of the *Star*, the LPRA — dubbed the 'Leeds Fox and Goose Club' — was exposed to detailed, scathing attack. Much was made of the differences between 'The Old Dog Fox', Baines, and the LPRA leaders.[14] The LPRA was characterised as representing merely 'a glimmer of the expiring flicker of Whiggery'. According to the *Star*, the middle-class reformers of the LPRA advanced from a position of weakness rather than strength, and were motivated by self-interest rather than principle.

> And so the wealthy, having failed in the Corn Law agitation, are now forced back upon the despised, the outlawed, the disfranchised portion of the community for support!

'Have the men of Leeds forgotten 1832?' asked the *Star* — 'No; nor never will.' As for the LPRA call for an inquiry into the condition of the working class, Hill advised Stansfeld: 'Examine how your wealth was acquired, and you will find the direct reason for the poor man's poverty.' The *Star* rejected the LPRA leaders' terms of social analysis which divided society into the 'industrious' middle and working classes on the one side and the landed aristocracy on the other, and which placed the burden of economic exploitation and political oppression solely upon the aristocracy. The motives of such middle-class reformers were transparent. O'Connor and the *Star* insisted that Chartists must not be drawn into any political alliance based on mere 'practical' reform. The unity, and therefore, the success of the movement was dependent on the strict adherence to the principle of universal suffrage.[15]

The open juncture betwen the LPRA and Daniel O'Connell served to intensify Chartist opposition to the Leeds move and confirm suspicions about the real motives of middle-class reformers seeking a cross-class alliance. According to the *Star*, the household-suffrage agitation was merely a means to an end: to destroy the Chartist party, divide English and Irish workers and bring O'Connell back into fashion within the English radical movement. In response to overtures from the LPRA, O'Connell, who had begun to lay the foundations of his last great popular agitation for Union repeal, proposed an alliance between Irish repealers and the English household-suffrage party. He accepted an invitation from the LPRA to attend a reform rally and dinner at Leeds scheduled for January 1841. The Leeds Chartist William Rider called on local Chartists to confront O'Connell: 'On the great day of gormandizing' they should compel 'the Old

Gentleman . . . to meet us working men face to face in open day'.[16]

Throughout 1839 and 1840, the Chartist movement had carried out a successful policy of intervention and disruption at middle-class meetings in favour of corn-law repeal. In early 1840, Harney recommended that Chartists extend this tactic to all middle-class public meetings:

> Do this — ring in the ears of the 'respectables' the cry of justice — let all your amendments be 'the Charter, the whole Charter, and nothing else than the Charter'; and show to the middle classes that if it must be a war of class against class — if they will tyrannize over you through the legislature — then, at least in public meetings, convince them that you too can play the despot.[17]

The reform meeting organised by the LPRA, at which O'Connell was to be the main speaker, presented an ideal occasion for Chartists to demonstrate their resolute opposition to middle-class leadership. The *Star* declared:

> The middle-classes feel themselves powerless, without the people . . . they again call the people to the rescue. They kindly offer to place themselves once more at your head, *and lead you!* . . .
> The middle classes will never again be permitted to take the lead in any great movements. The background is their place, and they must be made to know it and keep it.[18]

The Leeds reform festival was transformed into a symbolic test of class strength. The *Star* called on the northern Chartists to mount a mass counter-demonstration at Leeds in favour of universal suffrage, arguing that the Leeds move had to be dealt a death-blow to prevent the household-suffrage cry from spreading to other industrial towns.[19]

From prison O'Connor issued an appeal to the Yorkshire Chartists, asserting a personal claim upon their allegiance.

> Men of Huddersfield, Halifax, Bradford, and Dewsbury — men of the villages — you owe me a day! I have given you many a one. I am in the felon's cell on your behalf; my spirit will meet you on the 21st at Leeds; will you come and join it in the triumph of virtue over vice . . .[20]

The melodramatic tone, the personalisation of issues, the evocation of the image of the people's martyr were all indicative of a style of radical leadership. A master of the theatre of popular protest, O'Connor rarely failed to exploit the full potential of any pretext for agitation. He stressed the importance of political education through 'direct action', of constantly providing arenas for the demonstration of mass involvement; he understood the need to maintain and stimulate the tempo of agitation. O'Connor called on northern Chartists to send delegates to Leeds to represent them at the great reform confrontation, and recommended that Chartists not only mount a counter-demonstration but purchase tickets to the LPRA rally to be held inside Marshall's mill in order to frustrate completely the intention of middle-class reformers. The mobilisation of mass working-class opposition to middle-class reformers served not only to reinvigorate Chartist agitation, it also made it difficult for Chartist leaders to move, however tentatively, towards an accomodation with middle-class radicalism.

The Chartist response to the appeals of O'Connor, the *Star* and local militants like Rider was impressive. More than twenty-five local Chartist delegates, representing not only the Yorkshire and Lancashire districts but Birmingham, Glasgow, the North East and East Midlands, assembled in Leeds. Despite the cold and rain and the inconvenience of the scheduled time and day of the week, several thousand Chartists marched to Holbeck Moor for the 'Welcome to Dan' demonstration. The rhetoric of class, along with denunciations of O'Connell, was the order of the day. While the meeting, chaired by Joshua Hobson, passed a resolution expressing Chartist support for repeal of the Union, it also declared an unequivocal resolve never to join with O'Connell in any agitation. The possibility of violent confrontation between Chartists and O'Connellite Irish was averted principally because O'Connell failed to make an appearance at Leeds, having been delayed in crossing from Ireland.[21]

The LPRA rally at Marshall's mill, to which the Holbeck Moor contingent marched, also proceeded with relative order. This was because the LPRA and the parliamentary radicals had acceded to Chartist terms before the meeting, an implicit recognition of their defeat. When it became clear that Chartists had purchased several thousand of the cheaper (6d) tickets, the LPRA leaders agreed, on the evening before the rally, to allow an equal number of Chartist speakers on the platform and withdrew their household-suffrage resolution for an open-ended suffrage resolution to which both middle-class radicals and Chartists could address themselves. Hume, Sir George Strickland, Roebuck, Sharman Crawford, W. Williams (MP for Coventry) and Col. Thompson spoke for the middle-class radicals. Their views ranged from Williams and Strickland's support for household suffrage to Col. Thompson's declaration: 'He would not shrink from avowing himself a despised Chartist — he was a Chartist.' Moir,

Collins, O'Neill, Lowery, Deegan and John Mason addressed the meeting for the Chartists. In contrast to the Holbeck Moor meeting, their tone was moderate but firm. Mason called on the middle classes to join the Chartists; he disagreed with Hume, if necessary the working classes could obtain their rights without middle-class assistance. Lowery welcomed the opportunity for the working classes and middle classes to meet together:

> He appeared before the meeting as a working man and a Chartist . . . But though he was attached to his class, he had no enmity to any other. It was one of the proudest days of his life, to see the two classes, which had been supposed to be so much opposed to each other, met together to hear each other's wrongs, and to consult on the question of the suffrage.[22]

In effect, 21 January 1841 marked the end of the LPRA.[23] The retreat of the LPRA leadership and the virtual conversion of the Leeds reform festival into a Chartist event represented a decisive Chartist victory. Yet two further points stand out in relation to the development of Chartism over the next few years. First, the overt threat of physical intimidation towards O'Connell not only exacerbated tensions between Chartists and many Irish Catholics in the industrial North at a critical period, but contributed to the establishment of a pattern of violent confrontation.[24] Throughout the early 1840s, O'Connor and the NCA leadership continually emphasised Chartist support for the Irish demand for Union repeal, not only in an effort to attract Irish support to Chartism, but through a deeply held radical opposition to English rule in Ireland. However, many Irish workers, particularly in Manchester, followed O'Connell's leadership, opposed O'Connor and the Chartists and lent support, physical as well as moral, to the ACLL. A series of violent confrontations occurred in 1841 and 1842 at Manchester anti-corn-law meetings when O'Connellite Irish, organised into an Operative Anti-Corn Law Association, clashed with Chartists attempting to disrupt the proceedings of middle-class free traders. This open hostility culminated in March 1842, when O'Connellite Irish invaded a Manchester Chartist meeting to be addressed by O'Connor; the Chartists got the worst of the ensuing brawl.[25] It is difficult to gauge the extent of working-class Irish Catholic opposition to O'Connor and the Chartist movement. Certainly there were many Chartist leaders and activists of Irish descent, and English working-class radicals consistently took up the issue of Irish social and political rights. It would also be mistaken to generalise nationally from the somewhat extraordinary local events at

Manchester. It would appear, for instance, that O'Connor had more Irish support in Yorkshire than in Lancashire.[26] Still, the physical confrontations between Irish workers and Chartists does suggest a rift at the level of mass support; and while Irish opposition to the Chartists did not take the dramatic form that it did in Manchester, in other localities O'Connell's influence was enough to draw workers away from Chartist involvement.[27] The fragmentation within sections of the northern industrial working class, between Irish and English workers, was a source of Chartist weakness.[28]

Secondly, as Lowery's remarks at the Leeds reform rally reflect, despite the display of united opposition to middle-class leadership, a section of Chartism's leadership was at least amenable to the idea of reopening a dialogue with middle-class radicals. The drift towards acceptance of the need for a cross-class alliance was most pronounced among a section of the local leadership at Birmingham and London. As early as summer 1840, O'Neill, who had recently moved to Birmingham from Glasgow, stressed the need for middle-class support.

> In the influence of intelligence, numbers, and money lies your only hope. . . . But alone and unaided, you possess none of these sufficiently strong; you require a wider spread of political information to complete the first, and a junction with the middle classes to strengthen the other two.
>   Believe me I would be the last to recommend a junction, were I not conscious that it were highly advantageous, nay necessary, and more that it were possible, nay near at hand.[29]

At Leeds both Collins and O'Neill adopted a conciliatory tone. O'Neill presented an address to the LPRA from the recently formed Birmingham Christian Chartist Church stressing the mutual political and economic interests of manufacturers and workers. Following the Leeds meeting, Collins and O'Neill published two addresses, one to the working classes and another to the middle classes, welcoming the prospect of a cross-class alliance on the basis of the Charter.[30]

Few Chartist leaders, including O'Connor, categorically dismissed the possibility of circumstances developing under which Chartists might ally themselves with sections of the middle class. The question remained under what circumstances and upon what terms such an alliance was either possible or desirable, and what steps Chartists should take to promote such a juncture. M'Douall, speaking upon his release from prison in 1840, probably summed up the position of most Chartists; he maintained that if the middle class joined them then 'moral' force would be enough to carry the Charter.

> But he should be the last man in the world to ask the middle classes to join them, although if the middle classes wished to join them he would advise such a union, always taking care if they did . . . not to let them have any power in directing the movement. (Hear. hear.) They must look at the middle classes as men who would give them power in the day of battle, but not place confidence in them.[31]

The middle classes were to join them; the working classes were not to moderate their demands. Under no circumstances must the middle classes be allowed again to assume the leadership of the forces of popular radicalism. Chartism was based upon the deeply held belief of working-class radicals in the ability of the working class to transform society, to act independently of the other classes in society. Perhaps no theme was sounded more often in the pages of the Chartist press or from the Chartist platform than the need for working people to depend upon their own exertions alone in the struggle for democratic rights. George White told a Newcastle meeting in late 1840:

> For his part he had no expectation of ever receiving any assistance from the middle classes; the people would have to do their own work, and, they might depend on it, that they would never be helped to anything to which they did not help themselves. Although some men were endeavouring to get the middle classes to join the working classes in their struggle for liberty, he maintained that the working classes were powerful enough to obtain all they desired, provided they were willing to use the power they possessed.[32]

The point of difference between radicals such as White, M'Douall and O'Connor and those moving towards support for a middle-class alliance, such as Collins, O'Neill, Lovett, Vincent, Hetherington, was, at least in part, a difference in tone and emphasis, as well as tactics. O'Connor had no intention of courting a middle-class alliance, although he was willing to countenance the idea that if the working-class movement remained independent and well organised, that sections of the middle class might be forced to come over to the Chartist camp. The first priority was working-class unity. He resented radical leaders actively seeking a middle-class alliance, as it represented an implicit lack of confidence in the independent strength of the working class. Those Chartist leaders seeking a cross-class alliance were a distinct minority within the movement. Chartism was essentially a class movement and becoming more so in the 1840s. The struggle against the ACLL and against the ideas of political economy, as O'Connor stressed, had been particularly important in solidifying the forces of working-class radicalism; Chartist unity had been forged, given definition, in opposition to the efforts of middle-class reform.[33]

Between the demise of the LPRA and the overtures of the middle-class radicals of the Complete Suffrage movement in late 1841, O'Connor (as well as O'Brien) gave attention to the question of the 'middle classes' in the columns of the *Star*. 'No Union with the enemy; no surrender', was the motto O'Connor raised. Starting from the position that in the existing state of society the interests of capital and labour were fundamentally antagonistic and irreconcilable, he set out to prove 'the impossibility of any beneficial union being formed between those who live by their own labour, and those who live upon the profits of others' labour'.

> What is the '*casus belli*', the point in dispute? Is it not that the labourers, upon their own part, look for a better remuneration for their labour; while, upon the part of their employers, they look for a greater profit on that very labour? Nothing could be more clear than this, and nothing, therefore, can be more clear than that magic alone can affect the double object. . . .
> . . . Until the master is as much dependent upon the workman, for an augmentation of his capital, as the man is upon the master for employment in the pursuit, no union can be formed upon anything like equality.

O'Connor reminded Chartists that in 1838 he had divided society into two classes, ' "the rich oppressor and the poor oppressed", and as such I have ever since dealt with political society'.[34]

However O'Connor made a further distinction which was extremely important, between shopkeepers and manufacturers.

> In speaking of the middle classes, great and flagrant errors have been committed. The question has been argued as though the interests of all the middle classes were identical, whereas, the interests of shopkeepers and that of manufacturers are the very antipodes one to the other. The interest of the manufacturer is to have cheap labour; while the interest of the shopkeeper is to have dear labour. You must enlighten the shopkeepers and tradesmen of all denominations, and fight them against the real enemy — the steam Lords.[35]

Thus while there was no possibility of an alliance between the working class and 'the Steam Lords', the real exploiters of labour, there existed the possibility of a viable alliance with sections of the lower middle class — 'the industrious portion of the middling classes' — who shared a limited identity of economic interest with the working class.[36] The support which shopkeepers extended to working-class families during the 1842 general strike in several Lancashire towns lends some credibility to this view.[37] More important than any measure of shared economic interest, however, was the sharp political division which the 1832 Reform Act imposed upon English society. Throughout the Chartist period working-class radicals generally gained little support from members of the lower middle class, and the 'shopocrats' were often the object of Chartist denunciation for their complicity in the political oppression of the people.

> The vile shopocracy are the chief cause of the continued existence of the present cannibal state of things. They have the political power, and in one day could effect a complete change if they willed it. This they will not do; they look with a callous heart upon your suffering and give their support to the rulers who plunder and oppress you, and who, but for their support, could not exist for a day. War with the base profit-mongers! — War to the knife!![38]

Behind the militant tone of such Chartist denunciations lurked an ambivalence. The shopkeepers were the section of the middle class with whom working people had most daily contact and with whom they had most means of 'moral' persuasion. The widely employed Chartist tactic of exclusive dealing was designed to hit directly at shopkeepers, to expose their vulnerability and dependence upon the working class. There always seemed the possibility that significant numbers from the ranks of the 'shopocracy' might be forced into the Chartist camp, through either economic or political pressure.

Despite the class tone of much Chartist rhetoric, there remained an ambiguity about the Chartist attitude to the middle class at the level of theory; an ambiguity which derived from a tradition of artisan radicalism. I. J. Prothero has convincingly argued that even in the 1830s most working-class radicals still regarded the political divorce between the 'corrupt rulers' and the 'ruled' — the 'people' — as the main conflict in society, while discerning a shifting meaning of the term 'people' converging upon an identity with the working class by the 1840s. This ambiguity of language and the predominantly political perspective which most Chartist leaders adopted goes some way towards explaining how a radical like O'Brien, the most prominent proponent of what Patricia Hollis has termed the 'new' radical ideology of capitalist exploitation, could turn to support the proposal of a working-class/middle-class political alliance in 1842.[39]

In tone and emphasis there was very little difference between O'Brien and O'Connor in early 1841. Thus, in a series of letters to the

Star on the question of the middle classes, O'Brien declared the impossibility of an alliance with middle-class reformers; any such attempt was sheer 'moonshine', 'a cheat'. Were not England's prisons 'teaming . . . with the victims of middle-class legislation and a middle-class government?'

> No sane person would think of uniting for any purpose with known enemies, our proper business, as Chartists, is to combine together as one man, not *with* the middle class, but *against* them, in order to put an end to their usurpations.[40]

However, in response to a Chartist who questioned his categorical rejection of the prospects of an alliance with sympathetic representatives of the middle class, O'Brien demonstrated that in the last analysis his position was conceived essentially in political terms and was flexible.

> I should not be opposed to a union betwixt the middle and working classes, if I saw any likelihood of a *real* and *honest* union. But I see no such prospect; nor is there . . . any such intention on the part of the originators of this scheme [LPRA].[41]

But while it was obvious that the leaders of the Leeds household-suffrage movement had no 'intention' of forming 'a *real* and *honest* union', the issue was not so clear-cut with regard to middle-class leaders of the Complete Suffrage party who were willing to adopt the principles of the Charter, if not the name of Chartist. The overtures of the Complete Suffrage party, in early 1842, exposed the ambiguity of a Chartist position which depended upon an assessment of the 'sincerity' or motives of middle-class radicals.

The difference between O'Connor and many Chartist leaders sympathetic to the politics of class collaboration in late 1841 and 1842 was related to questions of practical politics and organisation rather than political theory. Above all, O'Connor sensed that an alliance with the Complete Suffrage Union's middle-class leadership might jeopardise the independence and national unity of working-class radicalism. Behind quibbles over the precise meaning of 'complete suffrage', his principal objection to the CSU was that:'They wish to make our movement auxiliary to their movement.' If middle-class radicals were sincere in their support for universal suffrage, they should join the NCA.[42] O'Connor remained suspicious of the motives of middle-class radicals, and for good reason. Behind the honourable intentions of Joseph Sturge, the CSU's major leader, he saw the interests of Richard Cobden, the ACLL and large-scale manufacturers.

'I am not sorry to see Sturge taking up this question', Cobden wrote in a revealing note to the Manchester ACLL leader, J. B. Smith, in December 1841. 'It will be something in our *rear* to frighten the aristocracy.' Cobden also saw the advantage of drawing working-class support away from O'Connor. 'At all hazards we must break the spell of Feargus and his hired retainers', he wrote Sturge around the same time.[43] O'Connor's opposition to the Complete Suffrage move-ment did not imply an abandonment of any hope of winning substan-tial middle-class support. However, O'Connor conceived of such a coming together of class forces not so much in terms of a formal organisational alliance, but rather in terms of a spontaneous move-ment of sections of the lower middle class into the Chartist ranks.[44]

No doubt both O'Connor and those who looked to the Complete Suffrage movement to bring together middle-class and working-class radicals overestimated the fluidity of class forces in the 1840s. To most members of the middle class the name 'Chartist' 'conjured up a terrible "raw head and bloody bones" '.[45] The Rev. Henry Solly, the Unitarian minister who supported the Complete Suffrage move, later wrote:

> it is necessary to recall the panic caused by the Chartist agitation . . . The widespread fears and deadly wrath excited, some years ago, by Fenian conspiracies, and at the present time by dynamiting Anarchists, are as nothing to the alarm and indignation caused by the movement among the working-classes, more than half-century since, for the People's Charter . . .

The Newport rising had had a profound impact upon the middle-class imagination. Solly related: 'it was not till the Newport insurrection . . . that I began to be infected with the prevalent horror and disgust attaching to the name of Chartist.'[46] It was hardly surprising that the middle-class supporters of the CSU rejected the label 'Chartist' and opposed the leadership of O'Connor whose name was associated, in the middle-class mind, with violent revolution.[47] Conversely, O'Con-nor never lost sight of the class nature of the Chartist movement and support for his leadership.

II The 1841 General Election

The general election of summer 1841, the first election since the emergence of the Chartist movement, marked the end of nearly a decade of almost uninterrupted Whig Government which had been ushered in by the reform agitation. The rapid and dramatic disintegration of Whig popularity was, of course, of great consequence to the development of British parliamentary politics. Since 1837, the Whigs' position had been weak in both Parliament and the country. For the Chartist movement and its leadership the election of 1841 posed difficult tactical problems concerning the course of action to be pursued by working-class radicals, generally without the vote and faced with two ruling-class parties. Closely related was the issue of cross-class political cooperation.

The policy of support for the Tories was attractive to many working-class radicals for several reasons. First, the Tories were the 'outs'. Secondly, working-class hatred for the Whigs was intense and widespread. To their early list of anti-working-class actions the government which had introduced the 'bastiles' and the rural police had added the transportation of Frost, Williams and Jones and the imprisonment of hundreds of Chartists. Thirdly, the opposition offered by some Tories to the new Poor Law and their support for further factory legislation — indicative of an opposition to the rise of industrial capitalism and the ascendancy of the industrial bourgeoisie — contrasted to the Malthusian doctrines of the Whigs and their middle-class, 'sham' radical supporters.[48] Finally, as the Chartist movement moved away from the more insurrectionary spirit of 1839 and towards the adoption of a strategy increasingly dependent upon legal, mass extra-parliamentary protest, the demonstration that the working class could influence the fortunes of Tory and Whig on election day, that they held the balance of political power, assumed a corresponding significance.

The argument that working-class radicals should support the Tories in retribution for the Whig betrayal of 1832 was not particularly novel by 1841; nor did it necessarily indicate any measure of support for the Tories.[49] W. E. Adams later commented: 'The whole of the governing classes — Whigs even more than Tories — were not only disliked, they were positively hated by the working population.'[50] The most prominent advocates of a pro-Tory policy during the early Chartist period were the Cobbettites who controlled the *Champion*, and who were concerned particularly with opposition to the new Poor Law, and the editors of the *Northern Liberator*. Both papers, for instance, supported the Tory candidate John Walter, owner of *The Times*, at the Southwark by-election in late 1839; and praised the Stockport Chartists' decision to back the local Tories at the municipal elections.[51] O'Connor and the *Star*, however, consistently opposed all such moves to lend any degree of support to Tory candidates. While not adverse to the prospect of the Tories turning out the Whigs, O'Connor urged Chartists to stand aloof from such a contest, in order not to be seen as condoning the policies of either party. The need was for the Chartist party to maintain its total independence and to demonstrate an unwavering commitment to principle.[52] In late 1840, the *Star* expressed apprehension 'lest our denunciations of Whiggism should administer any even the slightest comfort or hope to the Tories', and elaborated on the delicate tactical problem which Chartists faced:

> The difficulty in treating of these two factions arises from the fact, that their respective *merits* cannot be measured by any established rule, and we must, therefore, judge of them comparatively. The best notion we can give of the two parties is that difference made by Mr. O'Connor, when he said if the Whigs were the devils, the Tories were the devils in hell. The most difficult part of Chartist tactics will be to avoid Scylla without falling on Charybdis; to show positive hatred of, and maintain a stead opposition to Whiggery, without leaning one point towards Toryism; to avoid the several snares laid for them by 'liberal' Whigs and 'liberal' Tories and 'liberal' individuals and 'liberal' committees. If they confine their operations to organization and union, and their opposition to the party in power . . . no human ingenuity can much longer resist their just demands.[53]

The emphasis on electoral neutrality did not mean, however, that O'Connor regarded the next election as unimportant, nor did he envisage a passive Chartist role. On the contrary, from late 1839, he argued that the next general election would see the demise of the Whigs as a party and open the road to the Charter. As for the form of Chartist involvement at the next election, the National Convention and the founding conference of the NCA had both endorsed O'Brien's scheme. Chartists were to elect their own candidates at the hustings who would then be regarded as the 'real' representatives of the people.[54] In early 1841, with the impending prospect of an election, the *Star* reprinted O'Connor's 1839 recommendations for the formation of Chartist election clubs. The *Star* also reprinted one of O'Connor's favourite set-pieces, 'the auction and the sale', in which Lord John Russell and Sir Robert Peel bid against each other for the support of the independent forces of working-class radicalism which stand firm until offered universal suffrage.[55] As late as March 1841, the *Star* argued against Chartists willing to give support to John Walter on the grounds that he opposed the new Poor Law and helped to secure the return of the Dorchester labourers — 'This picking out of the best spots in the many-coated zebra, wont do . . .' — and reiterated its warning that on no account should Chartists lend support to Tories.[56]

Few historians of Chartism have noted the continuity in O'Connor and the *Star*'s opposition to any manifestation of pro-Tory sentiment within the Chartist ranks; most historians have chosen rather to interpret O'Connor's 'pro-Tory' policy at the 1841 election as confirmation of his latent 'tory-radicalism' or 'Cobbettism'. Furthermore, historians have failed to recognise the complexity of O'Connor's tactics, or his attempt to integrate what was basically a tactical issue into a more long-range, constitutional strategy for the obtainment of universal suffrage. The Chartist position at this election was not essentially 'pro-Tory', although much of the contemporary middle-class press understood it as such; nor was Chartist election policy imposed from above, but reflected in large measure rank-and-file Chartist opinion.

The formulation of national Chartist policy for the general election was greatly influenced by the success of the Nottingham Chartists at the local by-election of April 1841. The local Chartists decided to back John Walter, as an anti-Poor Law candidate, against the Whig free-trader, Sir George Larpent.[57] Opposition to the new Poor Law was a pressing local concern, with an enlarged workhouse under construction as a means towards abolishing all forms of outdoor relief. Under these conditions, the *Star* relaxed its line, bowing to the pragmatic dictates of election politics and the local initiative of working-class radicals. The *Star* emphasised, however, that Chartists should back Walter, 'not as Walter, but as an emblem of English hatred to starvation, transportation, incarceration, and everything that is base'. The *Star* explained:

> Now we look upon the question of the Poor Laws as next in importance to our charter; *not* that we expect any the slightest mitigation from the return of Mr. Walter, or from a whole Tory House. . . .
> If the Chartists had a man of their own, and if it was a general election, then their duty would be to stand by their own man; but here they must use their weight as the balance of power, and instead of being longer made tools of, they must now make a tool of Walter to beat the Whigs.[58]

The Nottingham election provided Chartists the opportunity to make their power felt at the polls, in one of England's most popular constituencies and strongest centres of Chartist support. National Chartist attention was focused on the Nottingham election.[59] The

Chartists who supported Walter did so under a principled understanding and with a high degree of discipline. Three hundred Chartist electors marched to the polls together before ten o'clock, in order to avoid charges of bribery, and voted for Walter. In a constituency reknown for corruption, impoverished stockingers forewent bribes in order to score an impressive political victory. The Chartist votes were the margin by which Walter won the election.[60] Working-class radicals had managed to break thirty-five years of Whig domination at Nottingham. However, as the *Nottingham Review* observed, the Whig defeat was a reflection of working-class hatred for the new Poor Law rather than support for the Tories.

> The feeling on the poor law was certainly most wonderful and seemed to pervade the breasts of all the lower classes. It is to the detestation entertained by the poor for that measure that Mr. Larpent owes his defeat and Mr. Walter his victory. It has not been on account of a liking for Tory politics.[61]

Working-class opposition to Toryism was demonstrated in 1842 when the local Chartists, along with O'Connor, supported Sturge against Walter.

The impact of the Nottingham victory nationally within the ranks of Chartism was profound. Speaking at Stockport, Jonathan Bairstow, NCA lecturer who had helped campaign at Nottingham, declared:

> Before the Nottingham Election, the Chartists were sneered at by all the hireling press in the country; but the conduct of the Chartists on that occasion had proved . . . the strength of the Chartists . . . more than anything the Chartists had done since the name of Chartism was heard.[62]

At nearby Leicester, local Chartists declared their resolve to return O'Connor at the next election.[63] However, the Nottingham election, while important, was the result of peculiar local circumstances. With the exception of a few other popular seats, like Leicester or Coventry, working-class radicals could not hope to exert the same measure of electoral influence as their Nottingham comrades. The role Chartists played at Nottingham, however, lent further credibility to the tactic of encouraging working-class support for Tory candidates in order to secure the defeat of Whiggery. Obviously, Chartists could anticipate only limited gains from any general election. O'Connor's concern was to provide the widest scope for working-class action, and to exploit to the full the potential for Chartist agitation and propaganda. During late May and June 1841, he outlined a programme of action which blended long and short-term perspectives for the advancement of working-class radicalism, and which combined gestures of symbolic protest with more pragmatic election tactics.

However, O'Connor's explicit abandonment of his former emphasis on strict Chartist neutrality followed the publication of the address of the National Petition Convention which declared:

> We are natural enemies of Whiggism and Toryism, but being unable to destroy both factions, we advise you to destroy the one faction by making a tool of the other.
> We advise you to upset the Ministerial candidates on every occasion, to doubt their professions, and disbelieve their husting promises.[64]

Rather than imposing a 'pro-Tory' strategy upon the national movement, O'Connor moved in conformity with the opinion of other Chartist leaders and local activists. Thus, in late May, O'Connor explained that while they were not in a position to establish Chartism, they did have the power to destroy the Whigs. To this end, he recommended Chartists 'in every instance where you have power, return Tories in preference to Whigs . . .'[65]

The election policy endorsed by O'Connor, the Petition Convention and the Chartist movement at large, was conceived as a tactical manoeuvre; the Tories were merely to be used as tools to crush the Whigs. O'Connor called upon Chartists to 'vote boldly against the devils, by voting for the devils in hell!' This policy did not preclude other forms of Chartist action or protest, nor was it necessarily incompatible with other electoral priorities. Thus, O'Connor called for the immediate formation of Chartist election associations; encouraged working-class exclusive dealing; offered to provide the property qualification for any Chartist returned at the poll; and placed particular importance upon the election of Chartist candidates at the hustings, recommending that those elected by show of hands assemble as a National Convention. Furthermore, O'Connor, as well as other Chartist leaders, suggested a range of criteria upon which Chartists could distinguish between the claims of non-Chartist candidates: did they support universal suffrage; how did they vote on the Chartist petition for the release of political prisoners; what was their position on the new Poor Law. Only when no other basis of selection could be found were Chartists to vote for Tories in preference to Whigs.[66] Wherever there was the chance to return a radical candidate, O'Connor urged Chartists to coalesce with either local Whigs or Tories. In reply to a request from Hull Chartists for advice on election tactics, he argued the need for practical compromise, including a coalition

with the local Whigs in order to ensure the return of the radical Col.
Thompson:

> But let me be plain . . . I say unite with the 'Devil' or with the 'Devil's
> Grandfather' to insure the Colonel's election. *Our object is to make the
> most of passing events*, that is to insure as goodly a number as possible in
> the House of Commons, who will constitute a real opposition and not a
> mere cog in the Whig wheel . . .[67]

From his earliest attempts to mobilise the forces of working-class
radicalism, O'Connor had stressed the potential for a radical party
within the Commons. One of his priorities at the 1841 election was
the return of as many radical representatives as possible; not necessarily Chartists, but men who were at least sympathetic to Chartist
political demands and who might form the nucleus of an anti-Whig,
radical parliamentary opposition. Such a group, holding the balance
of votes and backed by a mass popular movement outside Parliament,
might successfully exploit its position to push for fundamental socio-
political reform. Thus O'Connor urged Chartists to back radicals such
as Sharman Crawford at Rochdale, Col. Thompson's son at Tower
Hamlets, Fielden at Oldham and Roebuck at Bath. O'Connor's recommendation of support for Roebuck, a political economist and
supporter of the new Poor Law, is noteworthy. He explained that
while he opposed Roebuck as a political economist, there was more at
issue than merely the question of the new Poor Law. Thus, if Walter
were to run against Roebuck, he would advise Chartists to vote for
Roebuck, as 'the most likely to forward the cause of democracy';
whereas, in a contest between Walter and Hobhouse, a Whig minister, he would without hesitation support Walter — 'all the little good
being on Walter's side, I vote for the one fair spot, and against the
mass of putrid corruption'.[68] The support which O'Connor was willing
to extend to the Tories was, therefore, highly qualified, and the
election tactics which he advocated demanded an ability on the part
of working-class radicals to draw rather fine political distinctions.

Still, although he was unwilling to acknowledge it, O'Connor had
shifted his ground, and some Chartists, most notably O'Brien,
charged him with having forgotten his own strictures against the
editors of the *Champion* and *Northern Liberator*. The debate between O'Connor and O'Brien was conducted openly in the columns
of the *Star*; the tone was comradely, if occasionally sharp. Between
the lines there were, however, already signs that more serious personal and political differences stood between Chartism's two most
prominent national leaders. What is often missed is the substantial

measure of agreement which existed between the two men over tactics for the 1841 election.[69] O'Connor fully supported O'Brien's scheme for returning Chartists at the hustings. Similarly, both leaders felt the importance of trying to establish a Chartist presence inside the Commons, and to this end they were both willing to deal with either Whigs or Tories. Where the two leaders differed was over what course of action Chartists should pursue either when there was no Chartist candidate on the hustings or their candidate did not go to the poll. O'Brien maintained that the only principled political act was to abstain. O'Connor opposed abstentionism on practical grounds. He maintained that working men would vote whatever; and that being so, they must raise their hands in concert and cast their ballots upon a well-understood basis. His policy enabled working-class radicals to participate as fully as possible in the election proceedings, and to share, however marginally, in the defeat of the Whigs. O'Brien's position was politically purer; O'Connor's was the more practical. To O'Brien's charge that he now had embraced the Cobbettite position which he had formerly opposed, O'Connor replied that the difference between himself and the Cobbettites concerned 'the propriety of *supporting Tory principles* . . . and denouncing Whiggery, for the mere purpose of placing Toryism in the ascendant, upon the mere speculation of the repeal of the Poor Law Amendment Act'.[70] He recommended Chartists to support Tory candidates neither from political principle nor from any hope of direct amelioration of the social conditions of the working class.

Perhaps more significant than the tactical issue of Chartists voting Tory, was the importance which O'Connor placed upon the defeat of the Whigs in terms of the development of a non-revolutionary, constitutional strategy for carrying universal suffrage. O'Connor told Chartists: 'there are only two ways of effecting any great change; the one by physical revolution, the other by act of the legislature'. He maintained that the resort to physical revolution had been discredited, and stated his clear preference for socio-political change through constitutional agitation.[71] O'Connor continued to look to the model of 1832. He argued that the Whigs in opposition would be forced to mount once again a mass movement for popular reform in order to regain office, and that this time an united working-class movement would demand and achieve nothing short of universal suffrage. Thus he declared: 'I hold a Whig opposition to be indispensible to our cause.'

I contend for it that the hungry Whigs out of office in 1841, will do as the hungry Whigs out of office have ever done before; while the people in 1841, will take precious good care that the result shall not be the same . . .[72]

Rather than advancing a 'pro-Tory' strategy, therefore, O'Connor's perspective was peculiarly 'pro-Whig', in the sense that he relied upon a Whig initiative to open the door to reform. At the same time, however, he viewed 1841 as marking the culmination of the Whigs' protracted degeneration as a popular party, and looked to the prospects for a fundamental realignment of the forces of popular reform following their defeat. While O'Connor's assessment lacked sharp clarity, and, as O'Brien noted, was not free from inconsistencies and contradictions, his two positions on the possible development of English popular politics were not necessarily in contradiction, but were rather alternative propositions. The Whigs must either popularise themselves through reform, or face the disintegration of their party alliance. Nor was he alone in predicting the break-up of the Whig Party and the emergence of a more popularly based reform alliance; both O'Connell and Cobden, for instance, anticipated such a development. O'Connell wrote to Fitzpatrick, in May 1841:

> The fact, however, is that the Ministry as a Whig party cannot longer subsist; new political combinations must spring up. A new party must be formed, more radical than the Whigs, less radical than the Chartists. Out of office, the old tie between the Whig nobility as borough proprietors is broken for ever. To have the least chance of regaining office they must *popularise* themselves by adopting more popular measures.[73]

Through the break-up of the Whig Party and the realignment of reform forces, O'Connor anticipated that the Chartists might transform their strength outside Parliament into a small party within the Commons. This gradualist strategy was integrally related to his position on the issue of a middle-class/working-class reform union. He envisaged an enlargement of Chartism's social base through the coming together of the 'industrious classes' into 'one compact and united body'.

> I say *united*, and I say *all*; because tradesmen, shopkeepers, and all the intermediate parties between those who have raw property and those who convert that raw material into value by labour, must, of necessity, very soon discover that the people are the belly of the State, and that all other classes are but the members; and that the belly being starved, the members must perish.[74]

The realisation of this political conjunction — the break-up of the

Whigs, a regrouping of the forces of popular reform and an alliance of the 'industrious classes' — was to remain a central feature of O'Connor's strategy throughout the 1840s. The overtures of middle-class radicals in the early 1840s, along with the defeat of the Whigs, lent credibility to this perspective.

Generally Chartists accepted O'Connor's line for the 1841 general election, although there were splits within several local Chartist parties, including those at Nottingham and Leicester.[75] Chartist candidates stood at the hustings — M'Douall at Northampton, Vincent at Banbury, Sankey at Marylebone, Harney and Pitkeithley for the West Riding, Bairstow at Stockport, Leach and James Williams at Leeds, J. B. Hanson at Carlisle, John Duncan for Fife, Moir at Glasgow, and O'Brien's name was placed in nomination at Newcastle despite his being in prison. At Rochdale working-class radicals and middle-class reformers combined to return Sharman Crawford.[76] Throughout the industrial North the Whigs lost seats to the Tories, including the important West Riding.[77] Chartists claimed that the defeat of the Whigs demonstrated the power of a disfranchised but united working class. George White told the Birmingham Chartists: 'The Whigs and middle classes had now learned an important lesson, namely that they could not hold power without the assistance of the working classes.'[78] Radical middle-class opinion was no less impressed. The *Manchester and Salford Advertiser* wrote: 'It is evident that the people have, even by the present deceitful and fraudulent electoral system, an influence which enables them to turn the balance . . .' The liberal *Morning Chronicle* concluded that free trade could only be achieved now through an extension of the suffrage. In the *Nonconformist*, Edward Miall drew the same conclusion, noting the discipline and mass support exhibited by the Chartists at the hustings.[79] The Complete Suffrage initiative was closely linked to the Whigs' defeat and the strong Chartist showing at the election.

The 1840s witnessed no extension of the suffrage, no significant reform realignment, no lasting middle-class/working-class radical alliance. The 1841 election did not annihilate the Whig Party, although it marked an important moment in the transition from the Whig Party to the emergence of the Liberal Party. O'Connor was to be the only Chartist elected to Parliament, in 1847 for Nottingham. Along with others, O'Connor misjudged the prospects for constitutional change in the 1840s, underestimating the stability of the 1832 reform compromise and overestimating the fluidity of established party political alignments. 'The day of reckoning', as proclaimed in the *Star,* had not come. The apocalyptic tone of much Chartist rhetoric at the 1841 general election underscores, however, the strategic dilemma which working-class radicalism faced in the 1840s. Both the insurrectionary and constitutional routes to socio-political transformation were blocked by the consolidation of a powerful ruling-class alliance, willing to yield tactical concessions but not power. It was only in the 1860s, in the absence of a mass working-class movement concerned with the acquisition of state power, that the governing classes felt disposed to extend the suffrage to sections of the working class. It was under the banner of Gladstonian liberalism, not Chartism, that politically conscious working men were finally incorporated within the structure of nineteenth-century British parliamentary politics.

III The Crisis of 1842

On 26 August 1841, the 'People's Champion' was released from York Castle; on Monday, 30 August 1841, he was honoured with one of the most elaborate demonstrations of popular support in the history of English working-class radicalism. The full pageantry and splendour of the triumphal progress were evoked, harking back to the triumphal processions organised for radical leaders like Burdett and Hunt. 'My friends', O'Connor proclaimed, 'I appear before you to open the seventh session of Chartism in person.' The liberation of O'Connor provided an extraordinary occasion upon which to demonstrate Chartism's national unity; in his person were symbolised the class solidarity and steadfastness of Chartism, as well as the achievement of the movement in the face of government repression. Throughout the country local Chartists celebrated his release and return to active agitation not only as a tribute to the movement's most respected leader, but as a celebration of their own achievement and as a demonstration of local Chartist strength.[80] Following his release, O'Connor embarked upon the most sustained campaign of platform agitation of his life. His object was to unite the national movement, to recruit members to the NCA and to gather support for the second National Petition. Wherever he went he was greeted with mass demonstrations, triumphal processions and soirées. O'Connor's post-prison campaign represented an impressive reassertion of his commitment to the mass platform; however, the platform was now allied to the task of creating a permanent national Chartist organisation. Throughout his touring he reported on the recruits he had brought to the NCA ranks, which numbered in the thousands.[81] From autumn 1841 through spring 1842, O'Connor's presence gave impetus to Chartist agitation throughout England and Scotland, as the movement gathered momentum. By early 1842, Chartism had once more rallied its mass strength; organisationally, the movement was probably never in better shape. O'Connor stood at the zenith of his influence and popularity.

It was against the background of this tremendous resurgence in support that Chartism's strategic dilemma was again most clearly exposed. The Complete Suffrage movement raised once more the issue of the viability of an alliance with middle-class reformers; the 'general strike' of 1842 raised once more the prospect of breaking the bounds of constitutional protest in an effort to reclaim the birthright of an oppressed people.

(i) *Complete Suffrage*

The Complete Suffrage movement emerged from within the Anti-Corn Law League in autumn 1841, in the wake of the Whigs' election defeat. The Rev. Edward Miall, editor of the *Nonconformist*, and Joseph Sturge, wealthy Birmingham corn factor, Quaker, philanthropist, city alderman and anti-slavery campaigner, launched the Complete Suffrage initiative, aimed at reconciling the middle and labouring classes around a campaign for obtaining 'full, fair and free representation' of the people in Parliament.[82] The initiative quickly won support among prominent middle-class reformers such as Sharman Crawford, John Bright, George Thompson, Archibald Prentice, Lawrence Heyworth and sections of the provincial free-trade movement in England and Scotland, while it tended to lack the support of large-scale northern manufacturers. Sturge imbued the movement with the tone of a campaign of Christian conscience, a tone which attracted the support of a group of religious ministers drawn mostly from dissenting congregations. The movement reflected the sincere anxiety of sections of the middle class about the class tensions of the early 1840s; it also reflected the growing opinion that corn-law repeal was now contingent upon suffrage extension. However, Sturge failed to win the support of either the majority of the repeal movement or large sections of the middle class. In March 1842, he wrote to Place: 'I find so much prejudice amongst my own class that I feel somewhat discouraged at times . . .'[83]

What distinguished the Complete Suffrage initiative from earlier middle-class cooperative overtures was the acceptance of universal suffrage as the necessary demand around which to forge a cross-class alliance, with the result that a minority of Chartist leaders moved decisively towards embracing an alliance with middle-class reformers. The Chartists who signed the declaration circulated by the Complete Suffrage Association were mostly radicals who had already shown themselves sympathetic to such a reconciliation: Lovett, Hetherington, Neesom at London; O'Neill and Collins at Birmingham; Vincent, Philp, W. P. Roberts at Bath; James Williams at Sunderland; Lowery, now lecturing in Scotland.[84] None of these radicals felt that they were abandoning their Chartist principles; they believed Sturge to be well intentioned and his movement calculated to affect the desired goal of bringing together working-class and middle-class radicals.

O'Connor, the *Star* and the majority of Chartists were highly suspicious of the motives behind the Complete Suffrage movement; they were also suspicious of those Chartist leaders who lent their names to Sturge's declaration, most of whom had also been supporters of the 'New Move' in 1841. O'Connor dismissed the move as 'Complete Humbug', a plot to gain working-class support for corn-law repeal. If middle-class radicals were sincere in their desire to aid the working class in the struggle for political democracy, they should declare for the Charter and join the ranks of the Chartist movement. He thought it unlikely, however, that free-traders would come out in favour of Chartist demands:

> Collect the whole of the agitators for a repeal of the Corn Laws together, to-morrow, and offer them their measure upon the condition that they should grant yours, and they would rather see a duty of five pounds imposed on foreign corn than grant you the Charter, because it snaps the cord that binds labour to capital. Believe me, that machinery as now regulated is man's greatest enemy, and that the owners of that property will run you to revolution before they will give you any controlling power over it . . .

He advised working men to 'stand by YOUR CHARTER AND YOUR ORDER'.[85] As well as threatening the unity of the movement, O'Connor saw the moves of middle-class radicals as threatening the social critique, particularly the opposition to bourgeois political economy, which lay at the heart of the demand for the Charter. Significantly, the second National Petition included not only the demand for the six points of the Charter, but also the demand for the repeal of the Poor

Law Amendment Act. It was this inclusion, along with the demand for the repeal of the Act of Union with Ireland, which formed the basis of opposition to the Petition on the part of Lovett and the National Association and among sections of the Scottish movement.[86]

O'Connor's attitude to the CSU and the question of a cross-class alliance remained reasonably consistent throughout 1842. He was willing to express a personal respect for Sturge, supporting his candidature at the Nottingham parliamentary election as an universal-suffrage candidate, while opposing an alliance with the CSU.[87] The *Star* opposed the formation of the CSU in April 1842, on the grounds that two 'national' associations for universal suffrage could not co-exist: 'They must fritter away each others' strength; they can neither of them become 'National' without annihilating the other.' The rejection of the details of the Charter and the pre-existing Chartist association 'proves they [the CSU leaders] desire to effect not union but division among the people . . .' Chartists were advised to hold themselves aloof from the CSU, but not openly to oppose them as they had other middle-class reformers; if they called public meetings, Chartists should swell their numbers to ensure that the factions should not defeat the principle of universal suffrage.[88]

The attempt to impose an unified national response to the Complete Suffrage initiative exacerbated tensions between O'Connor and those Chartists sympathetic to Sturge. The principal charge against O'Connor and the *Star* was that of 'dictation'. At Bath Roberts declared that while they must be watchful of the middle classes, 'he would not be led by Feargus O'Connor nor the *Star*; he was not to be tyrannised over by a dictator . . .' To O'Connor's threat that he would come to Sunderland to move a vote of censure against him if he were to sign the Sturge declaration, James Williams replied that he had already signed the document. Lowery told O'Connorite critics that 'he had acted honestly and he would rather cut off his hand than retract his signature'.[89] Philp's enthusiastic welcome for the Complete Suffrage move drew particular criticism in the *Star*, as Philp was a member of the NCA Executive. Hill not only suggested that Philp had acted irresponsibly in his capacity as an Executive member, but called for his resignation in response to Chartist resolutions of censure. The other Executive members, chafing at what they considered to be an encroachment upon their independence and elected status, came to Philp's defence, although the Executive's position on the question of a cross-class alliance was essentially in line with that of the *Star*.[90] At the Chartist National Convention there was a general sense that the movement had suffered from 'denunciations', and that the *Star* had overstepped the bounds of democratic guidance.[91]

It proved difficult to contain the antagonisms aroused over the issue of cooperation with middle-class reformers, as the issue was one which went to the heart of the definition of Chartism. By 1842 O'Connor's leadership had become part of that definition. The Complete Suffrage movement was widely regarded as an attempt to supplant the leadership of O'Connor and the NCA. At the founding conference of the CSU held in Birmingham, Thomas Steele, O'Connell's deputy, distinguished between 'honest well meaning chartists, who really intended what they professed' and 'the Feargusites, who were quite a different class'. O'Brien, who attended as the delegate for Wooton-under-Edge, warned that such remarks would render the objects of the conference completely unattainable; he noted the suspicions which surrounded their proceedings, adding that 'he was not without his fears that he would be a little suspected by four millions of people, simply for sitting there'.[92] Although decidedly in the minority, the Chartist delegates were able to get the conference to endorse the six points of the Charter. What Lovett and his colleagues were unable to obtain was a commitment to the Charter itself. The name 'Chartist' was repugnant to middle-class delegates. Sturge explained:

> there was a great and almost universal alarm in the minds of the middle classes at the name 'chartist', on account of the improper and violent conduct of some who had borne this name; and few could conceive the difficulty he had amongst his own class to prevail upon them calmly and impartially to look at the subject . . . he was sorry that any had come pledged to the whole of the people's charter . . .

The Rev. Thomas Spencer objected: 'If I had wished to become a chartist, I could have done so at Bath . . . We are called together not to concede anything to one class . . . We have gone so far with our chartist friends that we ought not to be asked to go further.'[93] Middle-class radicals had no intention of becoming part of the Chartist movement. Implicit in the middle-class rejection of the name 'Chartist' was the suggestion that working-class radicals repudiate the tone and history, established leadership and organisation of Chartism.

O'Connor dismissed the CSU proceedings as 'a remuster of the rump of the Old Malthusian London Working Men's Association'. He came to Birmingham to rally the 'real' forces of Chartism, appealing in particular to the workers of the Black Country for support. He convened a rival Chartist conference which resolved that any man advocating less than the whole Charter, 'name and all', was 'an enemy of the working classes, and no longer belonging to the national movement'. As for the proposal for another, more representative Complete Suffrage conference, O'Connor assured Chartists that they would be properly represented; if elected, he pledged that he would move a resolution for the Charter, name and all, and opposed to the formation of any new national association, membership of the NCA to be considered 'the truest test of sincerity which can be given by those who approve of our principles'.[94] The final part of this resolution was directed as much at Chartist 'renegades' such as Vincent and O'Brien as middle-class radicals. Support for Sturge was closely linked to a rejection of the NCA. Thus O'Brien had told the CSU conference that he 'was most anxious to merge the chartist body in a national body. He was not satisfied with the present position of the chartist body . . .'[95] By spring 1842 Vincent was a paid, full-time lecturer for the CSU; only a few months earlier he had been encouraging Chartists to join the NCA. In May, he denounced O'Connor as a 'designing Demagogue'.[96] Philp lost his seat on the NCA Executive to Jonathan Bairstow, although he continued to recommend Chartists to join the NCA rather than the CSU.[97] By summer 1842 O'Brien's short-lived *British Statesman* had become a rallying point for anti-O'Connorite forces.

In a few localities, most notably Birmingham, Bath, Brighton and parts of Scotland, differences between O'Connor and leaders sympathetic to the CSU led to rifts within the Chartist ranks; in most localities, however, O'Connor and the *Star* retained the allegiance of working-class radicals.[98] George White no doubt reflected the sentiments of many Chartists in a letter to Cooper written from Birmingham:

> What disgusting and damnable nonsense, or villainy, or both it is for Vincent, Lovett, and others to keep bawling about the necessity of a union of the Middle and Working Classes, whereas the Middle Class are our most bitter and deadly enemies.[99]

There was widespread opposition to jeopardising the unity of the movement in the quest for an unlikely alliance with middle-class reformers. M'Douall argued that the movement's energies would be better directed towards winning the support of the trade unions.

> being a middle class man . . . he knew that the class would never muster five hundred in one meeting . . . The middle class man was fighting against his neighbour for profits, but the working classes were interested

in being united: he thought that they would never get the cordial co-operation of the classes . . . He looked much more to the trades than the middle classes. Once get out the trades and the middle classes must follow.[100]

M'Douall's position was given force by the events of August 1842.

While O'Connor remained opposed to an alliance with the CSU, by summer 1842 he was increasingly optimistic about the prospects of shopkeepers being driven into the ranks of Chartism through economic distress. For instance, at both Burnley and Nottingham there were signs that shopkeepers might support the Chartist cause. In an editorial entitled 'The Approaching End! The Squeaking of the Shopocracy', the *Star* declared:

> But Working People, the shopocracy *now* want UNION! They *feel* distress. They see ruin before them. Profits have failed. Trade is done up. Incomes are gone. Capital is being wasted. Savings are dwindling. One by one are the shopkeepers dropping into the Gazette and into the Insolvent List. They *now* want UNION! . . . Shall we 'Unite' for this? Yes! *as soon as ever the shopocracy are ready!* Notwithstanding their former conduct and treatment . . . notwithstanding that *they*, and THEY ALONE, have stood between us and justice . . . we will 'UNITE'! BUT THEY MUST BE READY! They must be up the mark! They must *know the cause*, and be *agreed* upon the REMEDY. . . . They must be prepared to help to obtain the CHARTER . . . Whenever the shopkeepers are *ready*, and will enter into proper terms and arrangements, WE WILL UNITE — but not before!
>
> Shopkeepers! What say you — Not ready? — Down with your noses to the grindstone! — You soon will be ready![101]

What O'Connor sought was not an alliance but rather the incorporation of a section of the middle class within the Chartist movement, a hegemonic relationship in which shopkeepers accepted the political programme, leadership and organisation of the working class. As he told a Chartist meeting at St Pancras: 'We will stand firm and united — We will listen to no coalition, no half measures. Mahomet must come to the mountain . . . We are the mountain — we are the people.'[102]

In the event, Chartism failed to incorporate any significant section of the middle class within its ranks. Predictably the prospects of the CSU also quickly collapsed. At the CSU conference convened in late December 1842, in the wake of the mass strikes of August and with the onset of government repression, the CSU council proposed its own 'People's Bill of Rights' as an alternative to the Charter; an attempt to disassociate middle-class radicalism from the 'anarchy and confusion' associated with the Chartist adherents of O'Connor. Lovett, isolated from both the main body of Chartists and his middle-class allies, now insisted upon a consideration of the People's Charter: 'it had borne the brunt of the present agitation, for five years, and in order to secure its enactments, vast numbers of their fellow country-men had suffered imprisonment and transportation'. It was precisely this history with which the middle-class radicals did not wish to be identified. In an extraordinary convergence of political positions Lovett moved and O'Connor seconded a motion in favour of the Charter which was carried by a large majority following an acrimonious debate; Sturge and his supporters withdrew.[103] In contrast to the earlier CSU conference to which delegates had been selected upon a very narrow basis, Chartists dominated the second Complete Suffrage conference. O'Connor and the *Star* had mobilised a campaign to return Chartists; Sturge's party had been defeated before the conference ever assembled. Sturge's own city of Birmingham was represented by six Chartists, including O'Connor. It was not that Chartists unfairly manipulated the return of delegates, although local election proceedings were often less than decorous; on the contrary, it was the CSU leaders, acting on Lovett's advice, who tried to 'pack' the conference by demanding that half the near four hundred delegates be chosen at separate meetings restricted to electors. Not surprisingly Chartists refused to submit to such arrangements. What was really reflected was the relative weakness of Sturge's party in the country. In most urban centres throughout England, Chartists had little difficulty in dominating open public meetings called to elect delegates.[104]

(ii) *The Strikes of Summer*

During the 1840s the Chartist movement resisted the overtures of middle-class reformers to enter into a formal alliance; few members of the middle class joined the Chartist movement. Chartism retained its class character and tone; the movement maintained its independence, its own leaders, institutions and programme. Herein lies the historical distinctiveness of Chartism. However, while rejecting a strategy of alliance with middle-class reformers, the movement remained constrained within the limitations of a strategy of constitutional agitation. By 1842 the strategy and rhetoric of constitutional protest no longer seemed pregnant with the ambiguities and potential legitimating force for further action which had prevailed in 1839.

The 1842 National Petition was a remarkable achievement, a testament to Chartism's enormous popularity; the movement collected over three million signatures, more than twice the number affixed to the 1839 Petition. However, the Convention sat only for three weeks; there was no discussion of 'ulterior' measures, no plans for a 'national holiday'. The question of what course of action was to follow the rejection of the Petition was left unasked.[105]

In 1842, the challenge to authority came much more directly from the resistance of working-class communities in the industrial districts of the North and Midlands to unemployment, high food prices, wage reductions, and, in the case of the miners, to truck payments and other forms of fraudulent remuneration. The depression of 1842 was perhaps the worst of the nineteenth century. By early August the textile workers of Lancashire and Cheshire and the coal and iron miners of Lanarkshire, Ayrshire and the Lothians had joined the Staffordshire colliers and iron workers on strike; by mid-August the West Riding and parts of the East Midlands and South Wales were also engulfed in strikes. The Home Secretary, Graham, believed the situation was more serious than that of 1839.[106] Although industrial in origin, the strikes quickly assumed wider political aims and in many districts an insurrectionary tone. At Stockport the workhouse was stormed; at Newton the police station demolished; at Preston a crowd attacked soldiers with stones and when the crowd refused to disperse after the reading of the Riot Act soldiers opened fire, killing four people. In the Dewsbury district turnouts strapped coarse grey blankets to their backs to sleep on during the anticipated march on London.[107] Throughout the industrial districts huge crowds of working people confronted troops. Frank Peel vividly recalled the scene as thousands of turnouts from the Bradford and Todmorden districts converged on Halifax, and how thousands of defiant women, 'poorly clad and not a few marching barefoot', refused to disperse upon the magistrates' order:

> When the Riot Act was read, and the insurgents were ordered to disperse to their home, a large crowd of these women, who stood in front of the magistrates and the military, loudly declared they had no homes, and dared them to kill them if they liked. They then struck up 'The Union Hymn' . . . Singing this stirring hymn they defiantly stood in their ranks as the special constables marched up, but their music did not save them, for the constables did not hesitate to strike them with their staves, and a 'melee' ensued which ended in the dispersion of the mob in considerable disorder.

The term 'general strike' fails to convey the texture of what happened in August 1842; the term is too modern. In many respects, the resistance of these weeks constituted the last major example of an older style of open popular politics based upon the support and participation of entire working-class communities.[108]

The events of summer 1842 took the national Chartist leadership by surprise; they had been preoccupied mainly with the question of an alliance with middle-class radicals and issues of organisation, including the formation of closer links with the trade-union movement. The confrontationalist, although not the class, tone of 1839 was largely absent. There was less violent rhetoric and few Chartist leaders who believed that Privilege would be overthrown in a matter of days.[109] During the summer 1839 many Chartist leaders had anticipated the sort of widespread violent clashes between working people and the forces of authority which occurred in 1842, although at the last moment they drew back from initiating this confrontation themselves. Had the conjunction of events been different, had summer 1839 seen the level of industrial conflict of 1842, the history of class conflict in Britain might have been quite different.

The call to transform the strikes of 1842 into a political stand for the Charter emanated from the localities, particularly from the mill towns of Lancashire. At the local level much of the leadership of the strike was Chartist; and although early on the demands remained economic, Chartists like George White did not hesitate to introduce the Charter at strike meetings. In Lancashire it was local Chartist leaders such as Richard Pilling, William Aitken, Sandy Challenger and Albert Woolfenden, all of Ashton, who linked the cry for a 'fair day's wage' to the demand for the Charter.[110] The direction of the trades delegates who met in Manchester was crucial, giving the overwhelming endorsement of the Lancashire trades to the proposal to extend the strike nationally and to remain out until the Charter became the law of the land.[111] The link between the Lancashire trades and the Chartist movement was neither new nor spontaneous, but reflected an established pattern of mutual support and overlapping leadership. The NCA Executive members M'Douall, Leach and Campbell had been actively campaigning for united action of trade unionists and Chartists, with considerable success.[112] It was no coincidence that M'Douall, whose leadership was closely linked to the Lancashire working-class movement, emerged as the most prominent Chartist advocate of a national strike for political rights.

The NCA conference which met at Manchester on the anniversary of Peterloo responded to the initiative of the trades delegates and local Chartists. The conference had originally been convened to discuss organisational matters. By a large majority the delegates approved the resolution M'Douall brought forward in the name of the NCA Executive to extend the strike for the Charter. There was, however, serious disagreement among the delegates over the prospects of the strike and the question of 'physical force'. Cooper, just off the train from the turbulent Potteries district, announced that he supported the NCA Executive's resolution 'because it meant fighting'.

> The spread of the strike would and must be followed by a general outbreak. The authorities of the land would try to quell it; but we must resist them. There was nothing now but a physical force struggle to be looked for. We must get the people out to fight; and they must be irresistible, if they were united.

While O'Connor sided with the majority of delegates in favouring an extension of the strike, he deprecated the use of violent language as well as any notion that the strike was to be the harbinger of revolution. The most forceful opposition to Cooper and M'Douall came from Hill, backed by Harney, the 'Marat' of 1839. Hill agreed that to extend the strike under the banner of Chartism meant fighting, but wondered who in their right minds would force an unarmed people into a confrontation with the military. He moved a resolution opposed to the call for a national strike for the Charter which won the support of only six delegates. The conference issued an address which stressed that the strike had been forced on the working class by the factory owners of the ACLL:

> This is not a voluntary 'holiday'. It is the forced 'strike' of ill-requited labour against the dominion of all-powerful capital. But as the tyrants have forced the alternative upon you, adopt it — and out of the oppressor's threat let freedom spring.

The address counselled 'against waging war against recognized authority'; 'the moral strength of an united people' was sufficient 'to overcome all the physical force that tyranny can summon to its aid'. The address reflected the hand of O'Connor.[113]

Little encouragement was given the political strike in the editorial columns of the *Star*. The paper maintained that the strikes were part of a conspiracy on the part of the 'great' employers of the League to force the government to concede corn-law repeal. This was in line with earlier predictions of O'Connor's. Working people must avoid being used to further the interests of Capital; Chartism must be kept distinct from the 'risings' and 'riotings'.[114] There was, however, a distinction between O'Connor and Hill's position on the issue. Unlike Hill, O'Connor did not oppose the call for a national strike for the Charter, although his support was perhaps never more than an accommodation to Chartist opinion in the country. He told Chartists:

> I would not have counselled; I would not have countenanced the present strike, had it been suggested as a means of carrying the Charter, and had the people been the originators of it; but as we have been assailed in our peaceful position, you have no alternative but to bow to, or to resist, the tyrant's will.

O'Connor defended the decision of the NCA conference: 'had the Chartist body abstained from taking any part in the recent proceedings of the masters, their conquered slaves would have attributed the failure to restore wages to Chartist apathy . . .' Hill, in contrast, regarded this decision as an act of irresponsible recklessness foisted on the movement 'by a few hot-headed and short-sighted men'; it was an invitation for the government to cram the prisons with honest working men. 'There was no element of nationality, and consequently, no element of success in it [the strike].' He condemned the NCA Executive for their efforts to continue the strike; they were relieving the ACLL of responsibility for the turnouts 'by making it the foster-child of Chartism'. M'Douall, for his part, argued that Chartists could not idly stand by and allow the ACLL and the masters to prevail unopposed. He conceded that 'revolution was not ripe as it was in France. The middle classes oppose us still, and the trades are not wholly with us. Either or both are necessary to the success of a revolution.' He agreed that the people were in no position to confront the military; but he supported the continuance of the strike 'chiefly because of my belief that some event may yet arise which we little dream of, which may run like wildfire through the nation and leave us victorious'. M'Douall's hope that the strike might spread to London once again underlines the importance of the geographic separation of the capital from the industrial districts and the tactical problems which this separation posed. Hill denounced M'Douall's address: '[it] breathes a wild strain of recklessness, most dangerous to the cause . . .'[115] Both Hill and O'Connor were clearly concerned that violent language and deeds might again expose the movement to large-scale government repression.

The strike for the Charter quickly faded; workers who remained out on strike by late August generally had reverted to wage demands.

Given the lack of centralised planning and coordination, the arrest of most of the trades and Chartist leaders, the confusion within the ranks of the strikers themselves over the objects of their action and the localised nature of the conflict, the failure to mobilise and sustain a national strike for the Charter is hardly surprising. Summer 1842 witnessed a massive eruption of class tensions, underpinned by widespread working-class aspirations for fundamental social and political change. The class lines were drawn with extraordinary sharpness. Furthermore, the Chartist movement achieved something which it had failed to achieve in 1839, the official support of large and significant sections of the trade-union movement. What was lacking was the extensive period of preparation which had characterised the 1839 challenge and the concentration of national attention upon the decisions of the Convention. The expectations which had prevailed in 1839, the sense that the country was on the brink of a decisive confrontation between the people and their corrupt rulers, had receded in the early 1840s; there was little talk of arming the people. Nor can we simply project the national potential for August 1842 by focusing on the most politicised centre, south-east Lancashire and north-east Cheshire. Finally, it is also important to recognise that the Chartist movement had decisively distanced itself from the sort of 'traditional' violence — such as the 'pulling down' of houses — which occurred in the Potteries. Where the strike was most political there tended to be less collective violence and destruction of property.[116]

In 1842 Chartism faced a dual crisis. On the one hand, the movement had to define its orientation towards middle-class radicalism, in particular to the CSU; on the other hand, the movement had to respond to the strikes of summer at a time when the Chartist leadership had retreated from the confrontationalism of 1839. In general terms, O'Connor's position reflected the strategic dilemma of the movement. He recognised no prospect for revolution; 1839 had shown the ineffectiveness of 'physical-force' tactics. At the same time, he refused to come to an accommodation with middle-class radicalism on anything but strictly Chartist terms, terms which middle-class politicians refused to concede. Strategically the movement had reached an impasse. As the strikes waned, O'Connor rather lamely redirected Chartist attention to the possibility of the Whigs being forced to bid for Chartist support in a campaign to oust the Tories from office; their terms would be 'thirty out-and-out Chartists in the House to give expression to the popular voice . . .'[117] O'Connor thus reaffirmed the essential constitutionalism, or even parliamentarianism, of his perspective.

The strikes of 1842 had important repercussions for the course of Chartism and the definition of class relations in the 1840s. Some Chartists, such as Philp, regarded the failure of the strikes as further indication of the necessity of an alliance with middle-class radicals. More generally, the level of class hostility and violence of August confirmed the social distance which separated the middle and working classes and rendered impossible the formalisation of a cross-class alliance.[118] However, the long-range effect of the strikes may have been somewhat different, contributing to a shift in the ruling-class response to the working-class movement. Thus John Foster has drawn particular attention to the impact of a process of 'liberalization' or ruling-class concession on the working-class movement, stressing that this was a conscious response 'integrally related to a preceding period of working-class consciousness'.[119] While almost certainly less conspiratorial and more fraught with internal contradictions than Foster has implied, by the early 1840s there is evidence, both national and local, of the beginnings of this process — a mellowing of tone and a more accommodative posture on the part of government and the propertied classes. Locally this initiative tended to be more cultural than directly political in emphasis, focusing on concerns such as education, temperance reform, leisure provision.[120] In terms of government social policy, there was a curbing of the aggressive thrust of the 1830s and a move towards a policy of conciliation — extended factory legislation, a relaxed Poor Law, measures to promote education and urban improvement. Without implying a 'crude correlation' between working-class insurgency and ruling-class concession, the fears of summer 1842 no doubt imparted an urgency to efforts aimed at attenuating the force of working-class radicalism and defusing opposition to industrial capitalism.[121] How significant the impact of these initiatives actually was upon working-class attitudes and the Chartist movement remains a more problematic question. It seems likely that the erosion of Chartism's mass presence in the mid-1840s more clearly reflected a shift of emphasis from within the working-class movement itself; a shift linked to the failure of Chartist strategy in 1839 and 1842, but also indicative of a gradual coming to terms with industrial capitalism.

In 1842 and 1843, the Tory Government also had recourse to more traditional means of dealing with working-class resistance. Once again the Chartist movement faced the arrest, trial, imprisonment and transportation of leaders and supporters. More than eleven hundred people were tried in connection with the strikes merely before the Special Commissions which sat at Stafford, Chester, Lancaster, Liverpool, York and Carlisle; seventy five protesters were transported.[122] However, although more protesters were convicted in 1842, the repression was probably less damaging to the Chartist cause than that of 1839; many of those convicted were not active in the Chartist movement, and fewer prominent national and local leaders suffered imprisonment. Still, the trial and imprisonment of Chartists again placed a great financial burden on the movement, particularly in hard-hit districts such as the Potteries, Black Country, Nottingham, Lancashire and Cheshire. Repression in North Staffordshire was particularly severe. In late August, John Richards, the grand old man of Chartism in the Potteries (and soon to be arrested himself), reported that 'a Tory reign of terror' had swept the district.[123] Judgement at Stafford was swift and decisive, no doubt due to the extensive destruction of property which had occurred in the district. Most notably, William Ellis, local Chartist leader and prominent figure in the Potters' Union, was convicted, probably unjustly, for demolishing a house during the riots at Hanley, and was sentenced to twenty-one-years transportation. Ellis's martyrdom became part of the collective memory of working-class radicalism; his name joined that of Frost, Williams and Jones in Chartist toasts and petitions.

O'Connor again stood trial, in March 1843 at Lancaster, for seditious conspiracy. He was charged in a 'monster indictment' along with delegates who had attended the NCA conference at Manchester and local leaders of the strike in Lancashire. The indictment included the NCA Executive members Leach, Campbell, Bairstow and M'Douall (who had escaped to France), Harney, Hill, Cooper, Doyle, Arran of Bradford, Arthur of Carlisle: fifty-nine in all. Graham had hoped to indict O'Connor and the Chartist delegates, as well as Ellis at Stafford, for high treason. The conspiracy charge was intended to tie O'Connor to the collective violence of August through association. Thus Pollock, the Attorney-General, who had been defence counsel for Frost, Williams and Jones in 1839, wrote to Graham:

> I propose to charge O'Connor as a general conspirator with the others, and not to proceed against him for Libel merely, or for acting as a Delegate, or taking part at the meeting of Delegates — I propose to try him in the same indictment with the worst of the defendants who headed mobs, made seditious speeches, and stopped mills and factories. I shall blend in one accusation the head and the hands — the bludgeon and the pen, and let the jury and the public see in one case the whole

crime, its commencement and its consequences.[124]

Pollock, Peel and Graham considered transferring the prosecution to Westminster for a trial at Bar before the full Court of the Queen's Bench. Not only would this have hastened the proceedings and involved the use of a Special Jury, but such a move would have provided a national stage for the trial of Chartism's leadership and the exposure of their 'formidable conspiracy'. This scheme was eventually abandoned because the proposal would almost certainly have been contested at Court, leading to further delay.[125]

Thus O'Connor and his comrades faced trial at Lancaster spring assizes. The trial lacked the sense of urgency which had prevailed at Stafford in the immediate wake of the strikes. Both judge and jury behaved with remarkable leniency. O'Connor and fourteen others were found guilty only on the fifth count, that of endeavouring to excite disaffection by unlawfully encouraging a stoppage of labour; sixteen were found guilty on the more serious fourth count as well, that of using threats and encouraging tumult to produce a stoppage of labour; twenty eight defendants were found not guilty.[126] Following the conviction, defence counsel sued for a writ of error on the grounds of incorrect wording of the indictment; none of the convicted were ever brought up for sentencing. O'Connor escaped imprisonment through delay, technicalities, the weakness of the case against him and finally, and perhaps most significantly, due to a tactical retreat by the Tory Government. However, this had not been the government's intention; on the contrary, O'Connor had been marked for prison.[127] Even so, the trial may have served the government's purpose in some measure: it again underscored the Chartist movement's vulnerability to government repression and served to remind leaders of the possible consequences of intemperate language and action. The movement also had to sustain the heavy cost of a large trial. Following the proceedings, Prince Albert wrote to Peel: 'I am sorry that Fergus escaped. Still the effect of the trial is satisfactory.'[128]

Finally, the internal dispute which raged between Hill and the NCA Executive also proved damaging to the Chartist movement. For some while Hill, backed privately by Cooper, White and Harney, had been moving towards a confrontation with the Executive. In part this was due to the ill-defined relationship of the *Star* to the NCA and its Executive; in part it was due to real concerns over the Executive's role.[129] The sharp differences over the issue of Chartist involvement in the strikes brought this antagonism to a head. Hill attacked the Executive, particularly M'Douall and Leach, for their leadership in

August and also pressed charges of misappropriation of NCA funds.
By late 1842 the attacks and counter-attacks which appeared weekly
in the *Star* had degenerated to the level of bitter personal recrimination.[130] While there was concern within the movement over the NCA
quarterly balance sheets and increasing doubts over the need to
maintain a full-time, paid Executive, there was also strong opposition
to the continuation of this controversy. Thus the North Lancashire
delegates called for a closing of the Chartist ranks; they were deeply
distressed over 'the very unpleasant differences which now exist at
headquarters . . . which threaten to impair, if not destroy, our moral
power and influence'.[131] O'Connor, who had remained aloof from the
dispute, belatedly intervened, disassociating himself from Hill's attacks and defending the character and conduct of M'Douall, Leach
and Bairstow.[132] However, the failure of the NCA to recruit large
numbers to its ranks after 1842 was due, at least in part, to the loss of
credibility which the Association and its Executive suffered at this
time. Taken in conjunction with the 'denunciations' over the CSU,
this conflict tended to confirm an image of a constantly quarrelling
leadership. The unity and high spirits which had prevailed upon the
liberation of the 'Lion of Freedom' had been undermined by the
events of 1842.

NOTES

1. British Library, Add. MSS 35151, fo. 208, Hume to Place, 9 Feb. 1840.
2. R. E. Leader, *Life and Letters of John Arthur Roebuck*, London 1897, p. 127.
3. British Library, Add. MSS 35151, fos. 249-52, Warburton to Place, 6 Apr. 1840; Place to Warburton, 7 Apr. 1840.
4. *NS*, 28 Mar. 1840, p. 5; 11 Apr., p. 4; 18 July, p. 1; 15 Aug., p. 1.
5. T. Mackay (ed.), *The Autobiography of Samuel Smiles*, London 1905, pp. 91-93; *Leeds Times*, 5 Sept. 1840, pp. 4, 6-7; *NS*, 5 Sept. 1840, p. 5.
6. L. Brown, 'The Chartists and the Anti-Corn Law League', in A. Briggs (ed.), *Chartist Studies*, London 1959, pp. 356-57; J. F. C. Harrison, 'Chartism in Leicester', ibid., p. 138; N. McCord, *The Anti-Corn Law League*, London 1958, p. 78; T. Tholfsen, 'The Chartist Crisis in Birmingham', *International Review of Social History*, 3, 1958, p. 474; *Northern Liberator*, 2 May 1840, p. 4; 23 May, p. 4.
7. *NS*, 12 Sept. 1840, p. 4; F. M. L. Thompson, 'Whigs and Liberals in the West Riding, 1830-1860', *English Historical Review*, 74, 1959, p. 227.
8. J. F. C. Harrison, 'Chartism in Leeds', *Chartist Studies*, pp. 83-84; A Tyrrell, 'Class Consciousness in Early Victorian Britain: Samuel Smiles, Leeds Politics, and the Self-Help Creed', *Journal of British Studies*, 9, 1970, pp. 106-09; D. Read, *Press and People, 1790-1850*, London 1961, pp. 93-94.
9. Cf. D. Fraser, *Urban Politics in Victorian England*, Leicester 1976, pp. 14, 115, 255.
10. *Leeds Mercury*, 21 Nov.-19 Dec. 1840; *Leeds Times*, 28 Nov. 1840-16 Jan. 1841;

D. Fraser, 'Edward Baines', in P. Hollis (ed.), *Pressure from Without in Early Victorian England*, London 1974, pp. 183-209, *passim*; id., 'The Fruits of Reform: Leeds Politics in the 1830s', *Northern History*, 7, 1972, pp. 89-111.

11. *Leeds Times*, 5 Dec. 1840, p. 4; *Autobiography of Smiles*, pp. 97-98.

12. Tyrrell, 'Class Consciousness', pp. 108-114. Tyrrell has picked up the major theme of R. S. Neale's provocative essay, 'Class and Class Consciousness in Early Nineteenth Century England: Three Classes or Five?', *Victorian Studies*, 12, 1968, reprinted in R. S. Neale, *Class and Ideology in the Nineteenth Century*, London 1972. Leaving aside Dahrendorf's ascription of authority structure as the key determinant of social class, and Neale's own extremely dubious divisions of class — the grouping of artisans with professionals rather than outworkers and factory workers represents an ahistorical, sociological abstraction which bears little relation to the development of class consciousness in the early nineteenth century — an artisan consciousness was the common denominator of working-class radicalism. Both Neale and Tyrrell demonstrate when they turn to historical examples the relative weakness and failure of the representatives of the 'middling class' when they tried to give their social philosophy political expression.

13. See Marx's comments on the petty bourgeoisie and its political representatives, *The Eighteenth Brumaire of Louis Bonaparte*, in *Karl Marx and Frederick Engels Selected Works*, one vol. ed., London 1968, pp. 121, 123. This is not, however, to deny the lower middle class a separate political identity or an influential role in radical politics in certain localities during the Chartist period. See G. Crossick's balanced discussion, 'La petite bourgeoisie britannique au XIXe siècle', *Le Mouvement Social*, no. 108, 1979, pp. 37-40.

14. *NS*, 28 Nov. 1840, p. 4; 12 Dec., pp. 4-5; 19 Dec., p. 4.

15. Ibid., 12 Sept. 1840, p. 4; 19 Sept., p. 4. The *Leeds Times*, 19 Sept. 1840, p. 4, welcomed the opposition of the *Star*.

16. *Leeds Times*, 24 Oct.-26 Dec. 1840; *NS*, 31 Oct. 1840-9 Jan. 1841, 12 Dec. 1840, p. 7 (Rider's appeal).

17. *Northern Liberator*, 21 Mar. 1840, p. 7. For instance, Chartists also interrupted anti-slavery and pacifist meetings.

18. *NS*, 19 Dec. 1840, p. 4.

19. Ibid., 16 Jan. 1841, p. 4. Following the Leeds initiative sections of the middle-class press began to assume a more moderate tone towards local Chartists. See, for instance, *Stockport Chronicle*, 1 Jan. 1841, p. 4; 5 Mar., p. 2; 2 Apr., p. 2.

20. *NS*, 16 Jan. 1841, p. 1.

21. Ibid., 23 Jan. 1841, pp. 1, 5; PRO, HO 45/41, fos. 3-5, Wemyss to Napier, 21 Jan. 1841.

22. *NS*, 23 Jan. 1841, pp. 1, 8; 30 Jan., p. 4; *Leeds Times*, 16 Jan. 1840, pp. 4, 8; 23 Jan., pp. 6-8; *Times*, 23 Jan. 1841, p. 5.

23. In autumn 1841, the LPRA again tried to rally support for a cross-class alliance. *NS*, 23 Oct. 1841, p. 8; 30 Oct., p. 4. Hume's attempt at a suffrage/free-trade alliance at London, based on the LPRA model, met with a similar lack of success.

24. See W. J. Fitzpatrick (ed.), *Correspondence of Daniel O'Connell*, London 1888, II, p. 256; *NS*, 17 Apr. 1841, pp. 4-5.

25. *NS*, 29 May-26 June 1841; 8 Jan. 1842, p. 2; 12 Mar., p. 1; *Manchester and Salford Advertiser*, 22 May-12 June 1841; 2 Oct., p. 2; *Manchester Guardian*, 9 Mar. 1842; *Stockport Chronicle*, 11 June 1841, p. 3; PRO, HO 45/46, fos. 22-23, Shaw to HO, 5 June 1841; J. H. Treble, 'O'Connor, O'Connell and the Attitudes of Irish Immigrants Towards Chartism in the North of England, 1838-48', in J. Butt and I. F. Clarke (eds.), *The Victorians and Social Protest*, Newton Abbot 1973, pp. 45-61; McCord, *Anti-Corn Law League*, pp. 99-103; also see J. M. Werley, 'The Irish in Manchester; 1832-49', *Irish Historical Studies*, 18, 1973, pp. 345-58.

26. The Barnsley Irish Catholic Chartists numbered over one hundred; relations between the Halifax Chartists and Irish repealers were friendly. *NS*, 18 Jan. 1840, p. 4;

19 June 1841, p. 1; 30 Oct., p. 7; 13 Jan. 1844. For an important reassessment of this entire question, see D. Thompson, 'Ireland and the Irish in English Radicalism, 1838-1847', forthcoming in D. Thompson and J. Epstein (eds.), *Studies in Working-Class Radicalism and Culture.*

27. See, for instance, reports of the relations between the Chartists and Irish repealers at Birmingham, *NS,* 31 July-18 Sept. 1841.

28. This is not, however, to suggest socio-political fragmentation on anything like the scale of the 1860s. Thus John Foster correctly interprets the Anglo-Irish hostilities of the later period as a significant index of the decline of working-class radical influence and class solidarity. See J. Foster, *Class Struggle and the Industrial Revolution,* London 1974, pp. 243-46.

29. *Northern Liberator,* 15 Aug. 1840, p. 3. A similar line was taken in the editorial columns of the *Southern Star,* 28 June 1840, p. 4; 4 July, p. 4.

30. *Leeds Times,* 23 Jan. 1841, p. 8; *NS,* 13 Feb. 1841, p. 5; 20 Feb., p. 1; compare the tone with that of the Birmingham NCA address, *NS,* 30 Jan. 1841, p. 1.

31. *Manchester and Salford Advertiser,* 22 Aug. 1840, p. 4; *NS,* 22 Aug. 1840, p. 7; also see P. M'Douall, *The Charter, What it Means! The Chartists, What They Want! Explained in an Address to the Middle Classes of Great Britain,* London 1845.

32. *Northern Liberator,* 5 Dec. 1840, p. 6.

33. O'Connor maintained: 'Until they met with the opposition of the Corn Law lecturers and others, they were never enabled to maintain so high and so flourishing a position . . .' *NS,* 23 Apr. 1842, p. 6.

34. *NS,* 6 Feb. 1841, p. 7.

35. Ibid., 15 May 1841, p. 1.

36. Ibid., 10 July 1841, p. 1; 4 Sept., p. 7; 13 Nov., p. 1; 18 June-23 July 1842; 13 Aug., p. 1.

37. For evidence of working-class overtures to shopkeepers and shopkeepers extending credit to strikers, see PRO, HO 45/269; HO 45/249C; F. C. Mather, 'The General Strike of 1842: A Study in Leadership, Organization and the Threat of Revolution during the Plug Plot Disturbances', in R. Quinault and J. Stevenson (eds.), *Popular Protest and Public Order,* London 1974, p. 133; T. Middleton, *History of Hyde and Its Neighborhood,* Hyde 1932, p. 119.

38. *Northern Liberator,* 21 Mar. 1840, p. 7 (Harney); also see the calls for exclusive dealing and denunciations of the 'ANTI-CHARTIST SHOPOCRATS', *Western Vindicator,* 29 June 1839, p. 1; 12 Oct., p. 3. Most Chartists would have found surprising T. J. Nossiter's assertion that 'The retailer constituted a much more credible threat to the established order than the working man . . .' 'Shopkeeper Radicalism in the 19th Century', in T. J. Nossiter, A. H. Hanson, S. Rokkan (eds.), *Imagination and Precision in the Social Sciences,* London 1972, p. 407.

39. I. J. Prothero, 'William Benbow and the Concept of the "General Strike" ', *Past and Present,* no. 63, 1974, 141-46; P. Hollis, *The Pauper Press: A Study in Working-Class Radicalism of the 1830s,* Oxford 1970, chs. 6 and 7; also see O'Brien's editorials in *PMG,* 25 Oct. 1834, p. 298; *British Statesman,* 9 July 1842.

40. *NS,* 27 Feb. 1841, p. 7; also see O'Brien's letters, ibid., 27 Mar.-17 Apr.; *McDouall's Chartist and Republican Journal,* 13 July 1841, pp. 141-42.

41. *NS,* 6 Mar. 1841, p. 7.

42. *NS,* 26 Mar. 1842, p. 7; 16 Apr., p. 4.

43. Manchester Public Library, Smith Papers, Cobden to Smith, 4 Dec. 1841; British Library, Add. MSS 50131, Cobden to Sturge, 27 Nov. 1841 — both references quoted in D. Read, *Cobden and Bright, A Victorian Partnership,* London 1967, p. 30.

44. *NS,* 2 July 1842, p. 4; 22 July, pp. 1, 7.

45. M. Fletcher, *Letters to the Inhabitants of Bury,* Bury 1852, letter 4, p. 8.

46. H. Solly, *These Eighty Years,* London 1893, I, pp. 344-45; also see Frances Trollope's preface to *Michael Armstrong,* London 1840.

47. *Nonconformist,* 13 Apr. 1842, pp. 234-44; H. Richard, *Memoirs of Joseph*

Sturge, London 1864, pp. 317-18; C. H. Elt and S. Allen, *Complete Suffrage and Feargus O'Connor*, London 1844, pp. 2-3; for denunciations of O'Connor in the middle-class press, see, for instance, *Anti-Bread Tax Circular*, 26 May 1841, p. 23; 30 Dec., p. 91.

48. For a breakdown of parliamentary groupings and voting on various social and political issues, see W. O. Aydelotte, 'Parties and Issues in Early Victorian Egland', *Journal of British Studies*, 5, 1966, pp. 95-114.

49. See, for instance, Lowery's speech, *NS*, 5 Oct. 1839, p. 1.

50. W. E. Adams, *Memoirs of a Social Atom*, London 1903, I, p. 237.

51. *Champion*, 3 Nov. 1839, p. 4; 1 Dec., p. 4; 15 Dec., p. 5; 23 Feb. 1840, p. 1; *Northern Liberator*, 22 June 1839, p. 3; 10 Aug., p. 4; 28 Sept., p. 4; 19 Oct., p. 4; 9 Nov., p. 4; 16 Nov., p. 4; 14 Nov. 1840, p. 4; 21 Nov., p. 4. The two papers merged in late April 1840.

52. *NS*, 20 Apr. 1839, p. 1.

53. Ibid., 10 Oct. 1840, p. 4.

54. Ibid., 31 Aug.-5 Oct. 1839; 28 Dec., p. 8; 1 Aug. 1840, p. 1.

55. Ibid., 27 Feb. 1841, p. 4; 6 Mar., p. 7; 12 Dec. 1840, p. 4.

56. Ibid., 20 Mar. 1841, p. 2.

57. *Nottingham Review*, 9-23 Apr. 1841; *Midland Counties Illuminator*, 24 Apr. 1841, pp. 41-42; *NS*, 17 Apr. 1841, p. 1; *Times*, 17 Apr. 1841, p. 4.

58. *NS*, 24 Apr. 1841, p. 4; *Midland Counties Illuminator*, 24 Apr.-15 May 1841, also gave full support.

59. The election brought forth support from a wide range of radical leadership. Vincent, Fielden, Oastler, R. J. Richardson all called on Chartists to return Walter, as did William Eagle, the radical candidate at Nottingham at the 1834 election. Pitkeithley, Bairstow and Crabtree travelled down from Yorkshire to campaign, as did Cooper, Markham and Swain from Leicester.

60. *Midland Counties Illuminator*, 1 May 1841, p. 46; *NS*, 24 Apr. 1841, p. 4; *Times*, 28 Apr. 1841, pp. 4-5.

61. *Nottingham Review*, 30 Apr. 1841, p. 3.

62. *NS*, 26 June 1841, p. 6.

63. *Midland Counties Illuminator*, 8, 15 May 1841, pp. 51, 54-55.

64. *NS*, 22 May 1841, p. 6; also 5 June, p. 1. This position had already been adopted in *McDouall's Chartist and Republican Journal*, 22 May 1841, p. 58; and was embraced even by the 'moderate' Chartist press, see *English Chartist Circular*, I, no. 26 (July 1841), p. 101.

65. *NS*, 29 May 1841, p. 7. In the previous two weeks, O'Connor had been moving tentatively to this position.

66. *NS*, 29 May-26 June 1841; *McDouall's Chartist and Republican Journal*, 12, 19 June 1841, pp. 81-82, 89-91.

67. *NS*, 29 May 1841, p. 8 (my emphasis in quotation).

68. Ibid., 26 June 1841, p. 4.

69. For the debate between O'Connor and O'Brien, *NS*, 12 June-10 July 1841; for another critique of O'Connor's election policy, see W. Thomason, *O'Connor and Democracy Inconsistent with Each Other*, Newcastle 1844, pp. 10-13.

70. *NS*, 26 June 1841, p. 7. It was precisely this distinction which stood between O'Connor and a radical leader like Matthew Fletcher.

71. *NS*, 10 July 1841, p. 1; also 31 July, pp. 4-5.

72. Ibid., 26 June 1841, p. 1.

73. *Correspondence of O'Connell*, II, p. 266, also see p. 274; for Cobden, see *Autobiography of Smiles*, pp. 97-98.

74. *NS*, 10 July 1841, p. 1. M'Douall had hoped that the Chartists might return twelve Chartists in 1841. *McDouall's Chartist and Republican Journal*, 19 June 1841, pp. 89-90. In 1846, both the NCA Executive and O'Connor again raised the prospect of returning a small Chartist party to Parliament. *NS*, 21 Feb. 1846, p. 1; 18 July, p. 1.

75. *Nottingham Review*, 11 June 1841, p. 3; *NS*, 7 Aug. 1841, p. 5; British Library, Add. MSS 27835, fos. 167-68, Seal to Place, 15 July 1841.

76. *NS*, 5 June-10 July 1841; *McDouall's Chartist and Republican Journal*, 10, 17 July 1841, pp. 111-12, 121-22; R. G. Gammage, *History of the Chartist Movement*, Newcastle 1894, p. 194; D. S. Gadian, 'Class Consciousness in Oldham and Other North-West Industrial Towns 1830-1850', *Historical Journal*, 21, 1978, pp. 170-71, for Rochdale.

77. For a general account of the results and significance of the 1841 election, see B. Kemp, 'The General Election of 1841', *History*, 37, 1952, pp. 146-57; N. Gash, *Politics in the Age of Peel*, London 1953, pp. xiii, 239; F. M. L. Thompson, 'Whigs and Liberals in the West Riding', p. 224.

78. *NS*, 31 July 1841, p. 2.

79. *Manchester and Salford Advertiser*, 24 July 1841, p. 2; *Morning Chronicle*, 16 July 1841, p. 3; *Nonconformist*, 6 Oct. 1841, pp. 441-42.

80. *NS*, 4 Sept. 1841, pp. 6-8, for a full description of the liberation. From mid-July the *Star* carried reports of local Chartist groups preparing for O'Connor's liberation and invitations for him to visit their locality.

81. See, for instance, *NS*, 4-25 Dec. 1841, for reports of his tour of Lancashire and the West Riding.

82. *Nonconformist*, 6 Oct.-17 Nov. 1841; E. Miall, *Reconciliation between the Middle and Labouring Classes*, Birmingham 1841, with preface by J. Sturge; Richard, *Memoirs of Sturge*, pp. 297-98, 301-05; S. Hobhouse, *Joseph Sturge; His Life and Work*, London 1919, ch. 6. No really adequate account of the Complete Suffrage movement exists, but see A. Wilson, 'The Suffrage Movement', in P. Hollis (ed.), *Pressure from Without*, pp. 83-93; also see T. R. Tholfsen, 'The Origins of the Birmingham Caucus', *Historical Journal*, 2, 1959, pp. 162-71.

83. British Library, Add. MSS 27810, fos. 128-29, Sturge to Place, 28 Mar. 1842. Hobhouse, *Sturge*, p. 73, claims that Complete Suffrage Unions had been formed in between fifty to sixty towns in Britain by March 1842.

84. *NS*, 19 Feb. 1842, p. 5; 12 Mar., pp. 4, 7; 26 Mar., p. 5; W. Lovett, *Life and Struggles of William Lovett*, Fitzroy ed., London 1967, p. 227; Tholfsen, 'Chartist Crisis in Birmingham', pp. 479-80; B. Harrison and P. Hollis, 'Chartism, Liberalism and the Life of Robert Lowery', *English Historical Review*, 82, 1967, pp. 509-10.

85. *NS*, 19 Feb. 1842, p. 1; also see 18 Dec. 1841, p. 1; 22 Jan. 1842, p. 4; 19 Feb., p. 8; 26 Feb., p. 4; 26 Mar., p. 1.

86. Ibid., 15 Jan.-26 Feb. 1842; British Library, Add. MSS 37774, National Association Minute Book, fos. 16, 22, 28; A. Wilson, *The Chartist Movement in Scotland*, Manchester 1970, pp. 170-72.

87. *NS*, 26 Mar. 1842, p. 7; 14 May, p. 4, O'Connor maintained: 'Sturge's movement and Sturge in Parliament are two very different things.' *Evening Star*, 23 Dec. 1842; T. Beggs, *History of the Election of the Borough of Nottingham, 1842*, Nottingham 1842.

88. *NS*, 16 Apr. 1842, p. 4; also see 23 Apr., p. 6, for O'Connor's speech at the National Convention.

89. Ibid., 12 Mar. 1842, p. 4; 26 Mar., p. 5; 2 Apr., p. 4; 9 Apr., p. 4; 23 Apr., p. 8.

90. Ibid., 12 Mar.-2 Apr. 1842; 21 May-11 June; R. K. Philp, *Vindication of His Political Conduct*, Bath 1842.

91. *NS*, 23 Apr.-14 May 1842.

92. *Report of the Proceedings of the Conference of Delegates of the Middle and Working Classes*, London 1842, pp. 11-12.

93. Ibid., pp. 55, 59. The Chartist delegates to the conference were: Lovett, Neesom, Charles Westerton, Collins, Vincent, Charles Clarke (Bath), O'Brien, Richardson, James Mills, Bernard M'Cartney (Liverpool), John Mitchell (Aberdeen), Joseph Brook and James Dewhurst (Bradford). Only delegates who had signed the Struge declaration were allowed to sit. Lovett eventually withdrew his resolution which specifically mandated the next CSU conference to consider the Charter.

94. *NS*, 19 Mar. 1842, p. 1; 2 Apr., p. 1; 9 Apr., pp. 1, 4; 21 May, p. 1.

95. *Proceedings of the Conference*, p. 64; *NS*, 16 Apr. 1842, p. 4; 7 May, p. 1; 14 May, p. 7, for the 'reconciliation' between O'Brien and O'Connor; J. B. O'Brien, *Vindication of His Conduct at the Late Birmingham Conference*, Birmingham 1842; also see *British Statesman*, 2 July 1842, p. 1; 5 Nov., pp. 1-2. The *National Association Gazette* (16 Apr. 1842, pp. 126-27) recommended Chartists to join the CSU, noting in particular O'Brien's support for the Complete Suffrage movement.

96. *NS*, 5 Mar. 1842, p. 5; *British Statesman*, 8 May 1842, p. 10; B. Harrison's entry for Vincent, in J. M. Bellamy and J. Saville (eds.), *Dictionary of Labour Biography*, London 1972, I, pp. 329-30. As late as December 1841, O'Connor had referred to Vincent as the 'Benjamin Franklin of Chartism'. *NS*, 24 Dec. 1841, p. 1.

97. *NS*, 4 June 1842, pp. 4-5; *British Statesman*, 25 June 1842, p. 1; 9 July, p. 1.

98. Tholfsen, 'Origins of the Birmingham Caucus', pp. 165-70; for Birmingham also see PRO, HO 45/261, fos. 13-28, *passim*; HO 65/10, fos. 123-31; R. B. Pugh, 'Chartism in Somerset and Wiltshire', *Chartist Studies*, pp. 202-11; T. M. Kemnitz, 'Chartism in Brighton', (Sussex Univ. D.Phil thesis, 1969), pp. 354-69; Wilson, *Chartist Movement in Scotland*, pp. 174-79.

99. PRO, TS 11/601, White to Cooper, 12 July 1842.

100. *NS*, 23 Apr. 1842, p. 8.

101. Ibid., 2 July 1842, p. 4; see 18, 25 June; 9-30 July; 13 Aug.

102. Ibid., 17 Sept. 1842, p. 2.

103. Ibid., 31 Dec. 1842, pp. 1, 4, 5; Richard, *Memoirs of Sturge*, pp. 315-18; Lovett, *Life and Struggles*, pp. 234-37; T. Cooper, *The Life of Thomas Cooper*, Leicester 1971, pp. 220-27; Wilson, 'The Suffrage Movement', pp. 89-91.

104. *NS*, 27 Aug. 1842, p. 4; 17 Sept., p. 4; 5 Nov., p. 4; 19 Nov.-24 Dec.; *Nonconformist*, 23 Nov. 1842; Lovett, *Life and Struggles*, pp. 229-34.

105. *NS*, 23 Apr.-14 May 1842.

106. C. S. Parker, *Sir Robert Peel from His Private Papers*, London 1889, II, p. 541. We are very much in need of a full-scale national study of the strikes. Although Mick Jenkins, *The General Strike of 1842*, London 1980, moves in this direction, it remains essentially a study of the strikes in the Manchester district. Also see Mather, 'The General Strike of 1842'; A. G. Rose, 'The Plug Riots of 1842 in Lancashire and Cheshire', *Transactions of the Lancashire and Cheshire Antiquarian Society*, 67, 1957, pp. 75-112; G. Rudé, *The Crowd in History, 1730-1848*, New York 1964, ch. 12; R. Challinor and B. Ripley, *The Miners' Association: A Trade Union in the Age of the Chartists*, London 1968, ch. 2; J. M. Golby, 'Public Order and Private Unrest: A Study of the 1842 Riots in Shropshire', *University of Birmingham Historical Journal*, 11, 1968, pp. 157-69.

107. *NS*, 20, 27 Aug. 1842; Gammage, *History of the Chartist Movement*, pp. 220-25; T. D. W. and N. Reid, 'The 1842 "Plug Plot" in Stockport', *International Review of Social History*, 25, 1980, pp. 55-79; F. Peel, *The Risings of the Luddites, Chartists and Plug-Drawers*, 4th ed., London 1968, p. 341.

108. Peel, *Risings*, pp. 333-34; D. Thompson, 'Women and Nineteenth-Century Radical Politics: A Lost Dimension', in J. Mitchell and A. Oakley (eds.), *The Rights and Wrongs of Women*, Harmondsworth 1976, p. 130.

109. Prothero, 'Benbow and the Concept of the "General Strike"', p. 171.

110. *NS*, 6 Aug. 1842, p. 8; 13 Aug., p. 1, for White; PRO, TS 11/602, White to Cooper, 27 July 1842; for Ashton Chartists, see PRO, PL 27/11.

111. *NS*, 20 Aug. 1842, pp. 3, 5; 27 Aug., pp. 1, 7; Jenkins, *General Strike*, ch. 6. Graham regarded the trades delegates as the 'Directing Body . . . the link between the Unions and the Chartists . . .' Cambridge Univ. Library, Graham MSS (microfilm), Graham to Warre, 15 Aug. 1842.

112. *NS*, 19 Mar., p. 5; 23 Apr., pp. 6, 8; 30 Apr., p. 8; 4 June, p. 1; 11 June, p. 1; 9 July, p. 6; 13 Aug., p. 1; Mather, 'The General Strike of 1842', pp. 124-31; Jenkins, *General Strike*, pp. 134-37; also see R. Sykes, 'Early Chartism and Trade Unionisn in

South-East Lancashire', forthcoming in *Studies in Working-Class Radicalism*.
113. *NS*, 20 Aug. 1842, p. 5; also 3 Sept., p. 1; 17 May 1845, p. 6; Cooper, *Life*, pp. 208-11; *The Trial of Feargus O'Connor and Fifty-Eight Others*, Manchester 1843, *passim*. The address published in the name of the NCA Executive, written by M'Douall, was more insurrectionary in tone than the conference address.
114. *NS*, 16 July 1842, p. 1; 13 Aug., pp. 4, 8; 20 Aug., pp. 4, 8; F. O'Connor, 'Causes of the Outbreak', in *Trial of O'Connor*, pp. 415-39. Both Peel and Graham felt that the League bore substantial responsibility for the strikes. See G. Kitson Clark, 'Hunger and Politics in 1842', *Journal of Modern History*, 25, 1953, pp. 366-70.
115. *NS*, 20 Aug. 1842, pp. 4, 8; 27 Aug., pp. 4-5; also P. M. M'Douall, *Letters to the Manchester Chartists, Letter 1*, London n. d. [1842?]. It is clear that it was Hill, not O'Connor as most historians seem to believe, who denounced M'Douall and also clashed with Campbell and Leach.
116. I owe this last observation to Robert Sykes. For a description of the Pottery riots, see 'An Old Potter' [Charles Shaw], *When I Was a Child*, n.p. 1903, ch. 18; also R. Fyson, 'Chartism and Class Conflict in the Potteries', forthcoming in *Studies in Working-Class Radicalism*.
117. *NS*, 27 Aug. 1842, pp. 4-5.
118. *Union Advocate*, 1 Nov. 1842, copy in British Library, Place Collection, Set 56 (Nov. 1842-Jan. 1843), for Philp; cf. *NS*, 13 Aug. 1842, p. 4.
119. Foster, *Class Struggle*, p. 3, and ch. 7; also his intro. to Jenkins, *General Strike*, pp. 16-18.
120. See, for instance, P. Bailey, *Leisure and Class in Victorian England*, London 1978, pp. 36, 45, 52-55; T. R. Tholfsen, *Working-Class Radicalism in Mid-Victorian England*, London 1976, ch. 4; R. Colls, ' "Oh Happy English Children!"; Coal, Class and Education in the North-East', *Past and Present*, no. 73, 1976, p. 76; R. D. Storch, 'The Problem of Working-Class Leisure. Some Roots of Middle-Class Moral Reform in the Industrial North: 1825-50', in A. P. Donajgrodzki (ed.), *Social Control in Nineteenth Century Britain*, London 1977, pp. 138-62.
121. P. Richards, 'R. A. Slaney, the Industrial Town, and Early Victorian Social Policy', *Social History*, 4, 1979, pp. 100-01; however, see J. T. Ward, *Sir James Graham*, London 1967, chs. 8 and 9, *passim*, for the limitations of this conciliatory attitude; also see R. Johnson, 'Educating the Educators: "Experts" and the State, 1833-39', in *Social Control*, particularly pp. 90-100; and G. Stedman Jones's important discussion in 'Rethinking Chartism', forthcoming in *Studies in Working-Class Radicalism*.
122. G. Rudé, *Protest and Punishment; The Story of the Social and Political Protesters Transported to Australia*, Oxford 1978, pp. 68-69, 131-34; L. Radzinowicz, *A History of English Criminal Law and its Administration*, London 1948-68, IV, p. 250.
123. PRO, HO 45/260, Richards to Hobson, 22 Aug. 1842.
124. Graham Papers, Pollock to Graham, 9 Oct. 1842, quoted in F.C. Mather, 'The Government and the Chartists', in *Chartist Studies*, pp. 391-92.
125. Mather, 'Government and the Chartists', p. 392.
126. *Trial of O'Connor*, for the entire proceedings.
127. Mather, 'Government and the Chartists', p. 393; Ward, *Graham*, p. 213; *Personal Remembrances of Sir Frederick Pollock*, London 1887, I, pp. 204-05. Also see the provocative interpretation of the government's handling of the trial offered by Jenkins and Foster, in *General Strike*, pp. 16-18, ch. 10. It is not clear, however, that the evidence sustains either this somewhat conspiratorial view of the trial proceedings, or the sweeping interpretation of the origins of working-class reformism. The evidence suggests that Pollock was much disappointed by the outcome of the trial, noting that the judge had 'totally lost sight of the great features of the case'. Nor is it obvious that O'Connor's attitude towards the trial signalled a new position with regard to his notions of legitimate agitation. As his actions of the previous summer demonstrated, O'Connor had already rejected the confrontationalism of 1839.

128. British Library, Add. MSS 40436, fo. 93, 10 Mar. 1843. I am indebted to Peter Barber for this reference. O'Connor claimed the trial cost him between £300 and £500.

129. *NS*, 21 May 1842, p. 4; 11 June, pp. 1, 4; 30 July, pp. 1, 4; 6 Aug., pp. 1, 4; 13 Aug., pp. 4, 7; 3 Dec., p. 6; 10 Dec., pp. 1, 4; PRO, TS 11/600, Campbell to Cooper, 15 July 1842; TS 11/601, Bairstow to Cooper, 5 July 1842; TS 11/602, White to Cooper, 27 July 1842.

130. *NS*, 12 Nov.-31 Dec. 1842; *British Statesman*, 10, 17 Dec. 1842.

131. *NS*, 10 Dec. 1842, p. 8; 24 Dec., p. 1, for Chartist opinion in London and Manchester. Few Chartists believed that Campbell's intentions had been dishonest.

132. *NS*, 7 Jan. 1843, p. 1; 4 Feb., p. 1; 19 Nov. 1842, p. 1, O'Connor defended M'Douall against attacks from O'Brien.

CONCLUSION

I Postscript to 1842

The year 1842 marked a watershed in the history of popular radicalism. Chartism's second great petition campaign again demonstrated the enormous power of the mass platform to mobilise popular support for radical demands; it also demonstrated the limitations of a tactic which left the movement disillusioned and divided once Parliament had rejected the unified appeal of the people. The defeat of the strikes of summer was perhaps the last occasion during the nineteenth century upon which large numbers of working people in England's industrial districts moved towards an insurrectionary confrontation with the forces of ruling-class authority. During the mid-1840s there was a shift registered in the working-class challenge to the ascendancy of industrial capitalism. The mass politics which had dominated the period 1838-1842 began to lose its hold within sections of the working class. With the onset of limited economic recovery, sections of skilled workers saw the prospect of achieving some measure of economic and social improvement, as well as the possibility of creating protective institutions within an increasingly stable socio-economic order. By the mid-1840s the working-class movement had also begun a process of separating into its constituent parts: temperance reform and educational improvement, trade unionism, cooperative retailing, factory reform. Chartists played key roles in all these various forms of working-class activity, but it became more difficult to sustain the highly integrated movement of the early 1840s. It must be stressed that this was but the beginning of a process of fragmentation and de-politicisation which was to become much more pronounced in the late 1840s and 1850s.[1] In 1847-48, Chartism once more rallied large numbers to its banner, although the movement never regained the organised strength it had possessed in 1842.

O'Connor continued to work to provide a Chartist initiative within the working-class movement. Chartists campaigned in favour of Ashley's factory bill; momentarily dropped differences with O'Connell to back his last great push for Union repeal; mounted opposition to the Militia Bill in 1846 around the slogan 'No Vote! No Musket!' and cooperated with trade unionists to form a National Anti-Militia

310

Association.[2] Following 1842 Chartists became even more closely involved with the trade-union movement. Chartists gave the lead to the opposition to the Master and Servant Bill in 1844; were crucial to the formation of the National Association of United Trades; rallied support for the great miners' strike of 1844. This involvement reflected the increased importance of trade unionism in the mid-1840s.[3] While Chartists provided leadership and the *Northern Star* offered an essential medium of communication, the Charter itself was often, perforce, dislodged from the centre of agitation. The *Star's* advice to the miners captures something of this changed relationship: 'We need not caution them to avoid politics in their present position, to keep the peace, and drive spies and informers from their ranks.'[4] The concern was to avoid sectarianism, to rally united working-class support; as usual O'Connor sensed the importance of not distancing the Chartist movement from the immediate struggles of working people. However the impression is inescapable, national Chartist leadership had become more difficult; there was often a note of exasperation in appeals for renewed Chartist agitation. Thus, in 1844, O'Connor commented: 'It has been asserted that poverty was the parent of Chartism. I admit it, no man could with truth deny it . . .' He complained: 'Seeing the vast array of wealth, of power, and of controul opposed to you, you appear to hold your very lives upon sufferance, and are satisfied to exist upon toleration.'[5] The *Star* railed against trade-union leaders who neglected to acknowledge Chartist cooperation in their struggles and against 'the aristocracy of labour' which held itself aloof from an united workers' movement through a misguided effort 'to uphold its poor privilege of superiority over its own order'.[6]

By the mid-1840s, there was also a shift in the terms of reference which shaped radical discourse. While the older radical critique based upon the fundamental political division between the Privileged and the People continued strong, the economic division between Capital and Labour became increasingly central to Chartist social and economic analysis. The large-scale owners of capital, particularly the factory owners, were now more frequently the main target of attack; although the terminology employed by O'Connor and other Chartists — 'the aristocracy of capital', 'the steam aristocracy' — suggests the need to appropriate a more traditional rhetoric, to dress the new enemy in the garb of the old. The ideological battle against bourgeois political economy, against free trade and free competition, intensified: a last stand before free-trade principles gained full hegemonic sway in the 1850s. O'Connor told Chartists: 'this [the free-trade movement] is the second struggle — the Reform Bill was the first — for the ascendancy of active capital over sluggish land'.[7] He constantly stressed the universal impact of the unregulated introduction of machinery upon Labour: 'As the great leveller, machinery makes no distinction between the aristocracy and democracy of trade, but all suffer from the devourer.'[8] Only the Charter could offer real security against the encroachments of rampant Capital. Furthermore, the system of unfettered competition not only worked to the detriment of the working class, but the increased concentration of capital into the hands of large capitalists had disastrous effects upon small masters and shopkeepers.[9] However, if the objective conditions for an alliance between working-class radicals and members of the lower middle class appeared theoretically promising, the coming together of the 'industrious classes' into an united political force remained an elusive goal. In the years following 1842, O'Connor and the *Star* offered a redirection for Chartism. The concentration on the 'labour question' — according to the *Star,* 'the one absorbing topic of the times' — the chiding of the 'labour aristocrats' and the denunciations of the great capitalists, the anticipated disaffection and radicalisation of the 'industrious portion of the middle classes', were all interrelated elements of this redirection.[10]

Chartism's strategic dilemma remained unresolved, as 1848 was to demonstrate. O'Connor continued to look to the possibility of returning Chartists to Parliament and to a realignment of popular political forces, particularly following the repeal of the corn laws. The 1847 general election was certainly no vindication of this outlook, although O'Connor's return and the move to contest his return gave impetus to the revival of national Chartist agitation. Despite the experiences of 1839 and 1842, there seemed little alternative to a national petition campaign to rouse the latent energy of Chartist protest. At the Manchester conference, convened in late 1845 to consider Chartist strategy, O'Connor observed: 'Petitioning was the only method on which they could make their principles generally known.' He predicted five million signatures for the next National Petition.[11] Significantly, however, it was the land plan which proved the major Chartist initiative between 1842 and 1848; it was the promise of a portion of the soil which captured the imagination and support of working-class radicals. The land plan combined the prospect of an immediate amelioration of the condition of the working class, through relieving the pressure on surplus labour, with a generalised artisan vision of an alternative political economy, one based upon independent production and small commodity exchange, limited ownership and competition. In many districts Chartist land-plan branches provided the base from which the Chartist movement revived in 1847-48.

II Perspectives

As well as offering a reevaluation of O'Connor's political leadership, this study has set-out to provide a framework for understanding the dynamics of national Chartist agitation during the movement's early years. It has been argued that, above all, Chartism's distinctiveness is to be found in its national character and its status as a class movement. A heightened sense of working-class political exclusion after 1832 combined with the progressive narrowing of the margins of artisan independence and control over the process of production gave sharp resonance to the Chartist rhetoric of class. Obviously, the intensity of class feeling varied between differing trades and within differing communities; however, this was less important than a prevailing sense of shared class interests and common class oppression. It was this which enabled Chartism to fuse disparate groups of working people into a formidable national movement for political democracy. The movement was held together, however, by more than the political demands embodied in the People's Charter. Behind the demand for universal suffrage, for working-class political power, there was a moral critique of the social values becoming dominant under industrial capitalism and a shared vision of an alternative economic and social order.[12] It was Chartism's social programme, rather than the purely political demand for the suffrage, which stood between working-class radicalism and middle-class radicalism.

As Chartism's most prominent national leader, O'Connor played a central role in maintaining the movement's national challenge. At least until 1848, he was able to unite the forces of Chartism behind his leadership. While sensitive 'to the necessity of preserving local power', O'Connor continually sought to convince Chartists 'of the indispensible necessity of upholding and strengthening the national movement, which may be termed the fly wheel by whose revolutions local machinery can be most effectually worked'.[13] O'Connor's popularity was based upon his unrivalled talents as an agitator, his brilliance as an orator, his indefatigable energy in the radical cause; but his standing within the ranks of Chartism was also founded upon the consistent and intelligent leadership which he had provided since the mid-1830s, his insistent class perspective and class tone, his emphasis upon the need to establish permanent organisations of independent working-class political struggle. He came to symbolise the independence of working-class radicalism. Certain aspects of his style of leadership, particularly its highly personalised character, may appear unattractive and may have proved detrimental to the cause which he so passionately espoused. However, his leadership style must be judged not against some modern model of revolutionary leadership, but within its own historical context. Nor should the paternalistic tone which he occasionally adopted obscure the essential democratic spirit which infused both his own and other Chartists' politics. O'Connor clearly understood the attraction of a leadership style which looked back to Hunt and forward to Ernest Jones. Yet among his achievements was the skill with which he interpreted established traditions of radical leadership within the changing context of the Chartist years. Thus the gentleman of the platform, the movement's great charismatic leader, attempted to channel the spontaneous energy of Chartist protest into support for national institutions capable of sustaining agitation over the long-term. While there remained tension between the need for effective national organisation and the desire of local militants to retain direct control over the movement, the establishment of the National Charter Association in the early 1840s marked an important break-through in terms of working-class political organisation. It must be stressed, that when looking at the NCA, the *Northern Star*, the National Convention or the organisation of local Chartism, it is not the dictatorial presence of O'Connor which proves striking, but rather the fierce commitment on the part of Chartism's leadership and support to the creation of democratic forms of organised resistance and struggle.

The tone of the Chartist movement was set by the mass demonstrations of 1838-39, by overwhelming displays of constitutional protest. The constitutionalism of these early years reflected the dominant tradition within English popular radicalism stretching back at least to the 1790s. While this constitutionalism imposed limitations upon the Chartist movement, constitutional reasoning and rhetoric also offered a potential for large-scale Chartist mobilisation and confrontation. In certain circumstances, which did not develop, the constitutionalism of the Chartist platform might have offered the sort of ideological underpinning, the legitimating force, necessary for full-scale insurrection. But while insurrection was certainly a possibility during the early Chartist years, revolution was not. The class forces ranged against the Chartist insurgents were too great for this. In the event, constitutionalism posed an intractable dilemma for the movement, leading to the abortive risings of 1839-40 and in the 1840s to a retreat from an earlier and more overt confrontationalism.

While the scale and intensity of antagonistic class feeling during the Chartist years were unparalleled, the ideological development of the movement was negligible. An agitator of extraordinary abilities, O'Connor was not an original theorist; neither were any of Chartism's major leaders. The ideology of Chartism was largely inherited, marking the culmination of a pre-Marxist democratic tradition of artisan radicalism. Chartism's distinction rests with its assertion of working-class political independence and with its emphasis on the role of state power in the exploitation of one class by another. The movement's failure to win working-class power had less to do with Chartism's ideological or theoretical limitations, as important as these may have been, than with the limitations imposed by the strength of opposing class forces. Yet while they failed in their ultimate goal, the dimensions of the historic task which Chartists set for themselves should not be forgotten. Nor should we forget the achievement: the National Convention, the possession of the most widely circulating working-class radical journal in Europe, the risings of 1839-40, the 'general' strike of 1842, the great Petitions, the Chartist schools, democratic chapels, cooperative stores, the poetry and the mass demonstrations. For over a decade working men and women sustained an impressive challenge to the force of emergent industrial capitalism. Under the banner of Chartism, they fought with a resilience perhaps best captured in O'Connor's words, 'and No Surrender'.

NOTES

1. See E. P. Thompson, 'The Peculiarities of the English', (first published in *Socialist Register*, 1965), in *The Poverty of Theory*, London 1978, p. 70; D. Thompson, 'Women in Nineteenth-Century Radical Politics: A Lost Dimension', in J. Mitchell and A. Oakley (eds.), *The Rights and Wrongs of Women*, Harmondsworth 1976, pp. 134-37. For this shift at a local level, see J. L. Baxter, 'The Origins of the Social War in South Yorkshire, c. 1750-1855', (Sheffield Univ. PhD thesis, 1976), pp. 494-542; F. J. Kaijage, 'Labouring Barnsley, 1816-1856: A Social and Economic History', (Warwick Univ. PhD thesis, 1975), pp. 522-28; C. A. N. Reid, 'The Chartist Movement in Stockport', (Hull Univ. MA thesis, 1974), ch. 5. Cf. A. E. Musson, 'Class Struggle and the Labour Aristocracy, 1830-60', *Social History*, 1, 1976, pp. 335-56, and see John Foster's reply, pp. 357-66.

2. *NS*, 25 May, 1844, p. 1 (ten-hours); 7 Oct.-2 Dec. 1843; 16 Mar. 1844, p. 1; 30 Mar., p. 1; 27 Apr., p. 8; 15 June-13 July (Ireland); 24 Jan.-14 Feb. 1846 (Militia Bill).

316   *Conclusion*

3. See. I. J. Prothero, 'London Chartism and the Trades', *Economic History Review*, 24, 1971, pp. 202-219; S. and B. Webb, *The History of Trade Unionism*, London 1920 ed., pp. 160-85, *passim*; R. Challinor and B. Ripley, *The Miners' Association: A Trade Union in the Age of the Chartists*, London 1968.

4. *NS*, 4 May 1844, p. 4.

5. Ibid., 27 July 1844, p. 1; also 3 Jan. 1846, p. 1.

6. Ibid., 24 Jan. 1846, p. 4; also see M. A. Shepherd, 'The Origins and Incidence of the Term "Labour Aristocracy"', *Bulletin of the Society for the Study of Labour History*, no. 37, 1978, pp. 51-67; J. L. Baxter, 'Chartist Notions of "Labour Aristocracy" in 1839', ibid., no. 40, 1980, pp. 13-16.

7. *NS*, 11 Nov. 1843, p. 1; also see ibid., 20 Jan. 1844, p. 4; 27 Jan., p. 1; 31 Aug., pp. 1, 4; 7 Mar. 1846, p. 7; 18 May, p. 5. For the continued influence of the 'old' analysis, see P. Hollis, *The Pauper Press: A Study in Working-Class Radicalism of the 1830s*, Oxford 1970, pp. 288-90.

8. *NS*, 24 Aug. 1844, p. 1. Also see J. Leach, *Stubborn Facts from the Factories by a Manchester Operative*, London 1844, for the advanced Chartist position.

9. *NS*, 16 Mar. 1844, p. 1; 4 May, p. 1.

10. This redirection became particularly important after the failure of the mass platform in 1848. See J. C. Belchem, 'Radicalism as a "Platform" Agitation in the Periods 1816-1821 and 1848-1851', (Sussex Univ. D. Phil thesis, 1974), pt. 2, particularly pp. 191-98, 262-68, 341-42, 471.

11. *NS*, 27 Dec. 1845, p. 1; also 3 Jan. 1846, p. 1.

12. See I. J. Prothero, *Artisans and Politics in Early Nineteenth-Century London: John Gast and His Times*, Folkestone 1979, p. 336; G. Stedman Jones, 'Class Struggle and the Industrial Revolution', *New Left Review*, no. 90, 1975, p. 58.

13. *NS*, 27 July 1844, p. 1.

Bibliographic Note

I have tried to indicate fully in the notes the sources and works upon which this study is based. Those readers wishing further bibliographic guidance should refer to J. F. C. Harrison and Dorothy Thompson, *Bibliography of the Chartist Movement*, Brighton 1978.

INDEX